AUSTRALIAN
CULTURAL HISTORY

Edited by

S. L. Goldberg and F. B. Smith

Research School of Social Sciences
Australian National University

Published in association with the
Australian Academy of the Humanities

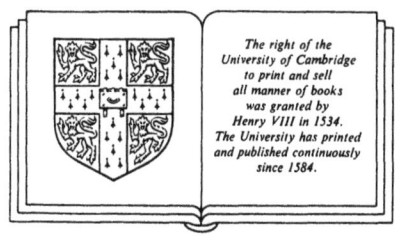

The right of the
University of Cambridge
to print and sell
all manner of books
was granted by
Henry VIII in 1534.
The University has printed
and published continuously
since 1584.

Cambridge University Press
Cambridge
New York   New Rochelle   Melbourne   Sydney

CAMBRIDGE UNIVERSITY PRESS
Cambridge, New York, Melbourne, Madrid, Cape Town,
Singapore, São Paulo, Delhi, Tokyo, Mexico City

Cambridge University Press
The Edinburgh Building, Cambridge CB2 8RU, UK

Published in the United States of America by Cambridge University Press, New York

www.cambridge.org
Information on this title: www.cambridge.org/9780521377584

First published 1988
Reprinted 1989
First paperback edition 1989
Re-issued 2011

A catalogue record for this publication is available from the British Library

National Library of Australia Cataloguing in Publication data
Australian cultural history
    Includes index
    1. Australia — Civilization.
    2. Australia — Social conditions.
    3. Australia — History.
    I. Goldberg, S.L. (Samuels Louis), 1926–
    II. Smith, F.B. (Francis Barrymore), 1932–
    III. Australian Academy of the Humanities.
994

ISBN 978-0-521-35651-0 Hardback
ISBN 978-0-521-37758-4 Paperback

CONTENTS

PREFACE

These essays constitute a modest introduction to Australian states of mind. The authors seek in their different ways to open up some of the serious but commonly unexamined ideas that Australians have projected about themselves, their communities, their nation, and have embodied in their institutions. Each writer has tried to resist the temptation to prescriptiveness, and also to that simplification allied to dismissive condescension that often mars discussions of these subjects, especially when the critic is possessed by Marxist or nationalist certainties.

Modest though they are, the essayists are also brave. Each has been persuaded to embark on a subject that crosses the academic boundaries of Australian History, Literary Studies and Sociology — at least as practitioners currently define them. Most of the authors have been bred to one of these familiar disciplines, but in these essays they have striven to look beyond such boundaries and to discern more general and more illuminating connections. There have been remarkably few attempts to do this kind of thing. Only Geoffrey Serle in his courageous survey of Australian painters, writers and musicians offers a general guide. There are four other enlightening introductions to Australian social norms, educational aspirations and scientific endeavour by W.K. Hancock, George Nadel, Michael Roe, K.S. Inglis and Ann Moyal.[1] But as yet there is no central text which could become the fulcrum of debate.

The papers in this selection originated at the annual seminars on the History of Culture in Australia begun in 1979 by the Australian Academy of the Humanities in association with the History of Ideas Unit in the Research School of Social Sciences at the Australian National University. Goldberg and Smith were entrusted with the job of organizing the seminars, which were to encourage the study of the activity of mind in Australia as expressed in philosophical, scientific, scholarly, religious, artistic and governmental pursuits. This book was conceived as a minor counter to the inevitable bombast of the Australian Bicentennial by providing a cool appraisal of some of the outcomes of 200 years of white occupation of the continent.

The appraisal is pluralist. Participants in the seminars regularly rejected bids to annex "culture" to a particular faction by defining it. They saw no case in theory and no compulsion on the evidence for making particular cultural manifestations peculiar to a class or for defining a class by its alleged "cultural" formation. In general, they endorsed John Rickard's analysis and saw no impassable divides between "high" (or "élitist") and "low" (or "popular" or "people's") music, drama, sport, television or opera, which all range, and have ranged, across the spectrum from avant garde or modernist to conservative forms and contents. Culture in Australia, the essayists tend to argue, is inclusive rather than exclusive. There have been and are minority "counter cultures", but these require mainstream forms against which to define themselves. The essayists are also chary of the organic metaphor "cultural maturity": the belief that somehow, at some particular time — which differs among the proponents of such notions — Australian writing, painting, ballet, music or scholarship became self-sustaining and distinctive. They see the story as a continuing process of local endeavour — see Robin Grove on ballet — interacting with wider international ideas and forms.

The essays appear disparate in their topics, but they converge on themes that regularly surfaced in the seminars through the decade. Whether in religion, or in education, or in expressing "patriotic" loyalties, Australians have evinced deep insecurities in their attitudes to the Imperial core and in their aspirations for themselves. The outcome has frequently been a complex mixture of assertiveness and defensiveness. Some of the results were highly self-congratulatory, (as in commentaries on Australian mateship, egalitarianism or military prowess) or hypercritical or corrosively inward-looking and ignorant of comparable societies — as in attitudes about race relations, political corruption or the misuse of the natural environment. The essays by Helen Bourke, Richard Selleck and John Hirst all seek, in their different ways, to reduce these deeply entrenched distortions. But these distortions helped to produce another effect as well: the expatriation of many talented Australians. Jim Davidson's study of Louise Hanson-Dyer suggests how the censorious know-nothingness of Australian suburbanites and farmers issued in the lack of both any large body of cultural "consumers" and a living critical milieu. These lacks drove many people abroad, to immerse themselves in esoteric forms of European or Asian culture, to bouts of nostalgia for their homeland, and sporadic misdirected sallies to Melbourne or Sydney to remedy Australian deficiencies. Expatriation in an English-speaking Empire came easily to Australians, as it did to South Africans and New Zealanders; but if many expatriates were restive third-raters, the cream comprised men and women whom Australia could neither sustain, nor lose without great cultural cost.

The "Anglo-Celts" of Australia did try in some ways to emulate the cultural activities of their home-nations — at least as these activities were represented to them by journalists, returned artists and academics, and Imperial visitors. Graeme Davison, John Rickard and Terry Smith show how Australians ventured on costly international exhibitions like those of Europe and North America, or indulged in grand opera, or patronized art that set Australian concerns in the tradition of British historical and genre painting. But in these fields, as in others, Australians — apart from a few brilliant individuals — clung to old cultural forms and gave them a conservative, mildly fresh content, rather than creating wholly anew. The exceptional individuals were men like William Farrer the wheat breeder; Lawrence Hargrave the aeronautical experimenter; John McGarvie Smith the bacteriologist and metallurgist; Joseph Furphy the novelist; A.G.M. Michel the mechanical engineer, and John Shaw Neilson the poet. These did make important original contributions to thought and work in Australia. But it is significant of the general cultural condition of Australia that each of them lacked the stimulus of able colleagues, public understanding and official support. The Australian clerisy was too scattered, too small, too unconfident, and too subservient to British precedent, to appreciate them, while the

Sydney and Melbourne "intellectuals" and governing circles were too populist, and too crudely acquisitive to support their work.

This great sextet were doing their work during the 1880s and 1890s when the three million or so working men and their wives and families, who formed the bulk of the newly settled immigrant population, were beginning to build their nation. Sydney, Melbourne, Brisbane, Adelaide and the provincial centres were developing into cumulated suburbias. Prosperity and technical innovations were making inter-colonial communications easier. But it was an unfortunate period of European and American history in which to find and form national beliefs. It was a time of powerful social Darwinism and chauvinist nationalism; faith in hierarchies of race ordained by nature, with British Australians at the top; anxieties about the inevitability of economic and social progress and the survival of the Empire; worries about health, as David Walker shows, sexual prowess and "race suicide" presaged by contraception, at which Australians were early adepts; uncertainties about the ethical and scriptural foundations of the Christianity that justified behavioural boundaries. All of these attitudes fermented in the emergent Commonwealth, and produced, as elsewhere, assertive anti-intellectual, censorious social norms. In Australia, moreover, these tendencies were exacerbated by the determination of its immigrant citizens to better themselves in an economy that was severely constrained by its weak capital base and dependence on a narrow range of unprocessed commodity exports to far-off markets over which Australians had no control. The immigrant society did achieve a modest comfort and a greater elbow room for its individual men and women, but the severe Australian environment precluded the growth of a large enough internal market to produce the huge fortunes and relative affluence of the United States. As Bill Rubinstein demonstrates, the outcome was a poverty of private patronage and the forced dependence of education and the arts on public taxation allocated by government.

The Australians persisted in dreams of bettering themselves socially. More avidly perhaps than in any other part of the Empire, they sought knighthoods, magistracies, invitations to Government House, presentations at Court, exclusive secondary schooling. By profession the society was egalitarian — certainly the absence of caste left it undifferentiated — but even to the present Australians struggled to make themselves genteel homeowners, and thereby made themselves, by their similar ambitions and attainments, remarkably homogeneous. During the century after the gold rushes they believed that country-living promised independence; yet the country regularly failed them. From the outset, Alan Gilbert and Don Aitkin suggest, most of them gathered uneasily in an archipelago of suburbias along the southeastern rim of the continent. They blamed their frustrated ambitions on land monopoly, the "money power", "Mr Fat", "middle men", bankers, trade unions, Roman Catholics and the Labor Party. Peter Spearritt shows how some of them sought proof of Providential differentiation and a luxurious refuge for their imaginations in the institution and the person of the monarch. Others found in vitalism and sport reassurance about their bodily prowess in a society that exalted male physical exhibitionism. This obsession took an influential atavistic, chauvinist turn in the productions of Norman Lindsay, P.R. Stephensen, M.H. Ellis and the Old Left historians and publicists, who together kept critical social analysis at bay in Australia.

Few Australians, Patrick O'Farrell asserts, resorted to deeply pious religion. The colonists carried their denominational allegiances with them from the British Isles, and these proved useful cohesive agencies in the new society, as David Hilliard implies of Anglicanism. Nevertheless, Australians, (unlike their American or South African counterparts) never tried to identify Providence or Divine grace with national or personal destinies. Religion in Australia underpinned a utilitarian ethical code, and it rarely was practised or seen as transcendental and redemptive.

The breach of promise in Australian life induced what some, including Dirk den Hartog, see as a closure of feeling. The convict past was veiled by common unspoken consent; the failure to establish a yeomanry was never analyzed; the destruction of Aboriginal society was collectively unrealized. In our chastened days of defeated millenarianism, changing national traditions and national vulnerability, these gaps in Australia's cultural history have assumed a new prominence. Playwrights and novelists, den Hartog argues, have exposed unexpressed hurts and sensed inadequacies, in their male characters especially — frustrations that have issued in a loud-mouthed inarticulateness. Indeed, these manifestations crop up in a great deal of the literature, history and everyday life of Australia. An assured cultural inheritance has yet to come — an attitude that justifies human existence in its particular world, and promotes its full expression. It might come more quickly if Australians could see — and own to seeing — a genuine glory in cultural achievements, whether in the arts, or the sciences, or scholarship, or public life, or in some other way that recreates the forms of civilized human life. So far our sense of glory has been devoted only to valour in war.

Notes

[1]   Geoffrey Serle, *The Creative Spirit in Australia A cultural history*, Melbourne, 1987. This is a revised edition of *From Deserts The Prophets Come*, Melbourne, 1973. W.K. Hancock *Australia*, London, 1930; *Country and Calling*, London, 1954. George Nadel, *Australia's Colonial Culture*, Melbourne, 1957. Michael Roe, *Quest For Authority In Eastern Australia 1835-1851*, Melbourne, 1965. K.S. Inglis, *The Australian Colonists*, Melbourne, 1974. Ann Moyal, *'a bright & savage land' Scientists in Colonial Australia*, Sydney, 1956.

The date at the end of each article indicates the year in which it appeared in *Australian Cultural History* The papers by Jim Davidson and Robin Grove first appeared in *Meanjin*.

Acknowledgements

The editors wish to thank the Australian Academy of the Humanities and the History of Ideas Unit in the Research School of Social Sciences at the Australian National University for their sustained interest and support. We also thank Mrs Frances Dixon for her invaluable practical help.

THE CULTURAL AMBIVALENCE OF AUSTRALIAN RELIGION

PATRICK O'FARRELL

In trying to appraise the importance or otherwise of religion in Australian history and society, at least two conflicting interpretations seem viable. Both have been and still are held by this author. What follows is an outline of some of the possible contending (and contentious?) arguments; they are neither rigorously pursued nor neatly resolved, but are presented rather as related *pensées* of varying validity or worth, the object being enquiry, not catechesis.

Until recently I held the view that Australia was best understood as a (the first) post-Christian society, in which religion was barely relevant culturally. Before setting out that line of thought in some detail, it might be useful to advert briefly to reasons for considering a contrary view to be pursued later.

The decisive stimulus for taking a more positive view of the importance of religion in Australia was my reading of the autobiography of B.A. Santamaria, *Against the Tide* (Melbourne, 1981). This chronicles his defeat, and that of the (largely Catholic) Movement, but the point of relevance to this discussion is how nearly this religiously inspired social movement came to victory in secularized Australia. This quite amazing closeness to political power, and the fact that failure at crucial points stemmed from division in *Catholic* ranks, must make us pause in concluding that Australian society is simply secular. It is not enough to say that *in fact* the Movement did not succeed, and to make social assumptions on that basis. Its remarkable degree of success, and the mode (and closeness) of its failure, call in question that allegedly secular nature of Australian society, at least at that time.

Two other recent books may be interpreted to support this questioning in a broader fashion. Robert Harbison in *Deliberate Regression: the disastrous history of Romantic individualism in thought and art, from Jean-Jacques Rousseau to twentieth-century fascism* (London, 1980) argues the case, as the title suggests, for the existence of the *deliberate* cultural contrivance of "man's oppression by God-substitutes of his own invention" — an argument which sees as both actively willed and destructive "the belief that salvation lies in unlearning". Harbison's stance highlights man's capacity to create (or undo) his cultural environment. Add to this the neutral information and analysis made available in Alan D. Gilbert's admirable *The Making of Post-Christian Britain: a history of the secularisation of modern society* (London, 1980), and the lesson may be drawn (by me) that despite the superficial appearances of inevitable and irreversible social process, secularization may be seen (like the Romantic movement) as a matter of choice and creation. Particularly given the fact that the sociological analysis of religion deals with its social context and not its essence, it is possible to view present society as merely in a new phase of its historically continuous religious-secular tension, in which the traditional form of the relationship is under challenge and change. Thus

it is possible to construe secularization as the illusion of the epoch,
which, like the Marxism to which the phrase was originally applied, is
real and prevalent but yet partial in application and false as a prophecy
of a new social order. This type of argument is strikingly pursued in H.
Daniel-Rops, *The Church in an Age of Revolution 1789 1870* (London,
1965) which stresses the remarkable contradictions in nineteenth-
century Europe between the two faces of a single society: between
aggressive irreligion and great sanctity. This contrast is often historically
obscure, since, for all that religious denial or apathy may be prominent
and powerful, religious affirmation may be quiet and deep — its witness
perhaps small and not in the public gaze, but rather in the mysteries of
the humble and the ignorant. Who can equal the luminous ignorance of
the Curé d'Ars?

These misgivings having been summarily aired, what of the argument
that, in the history and culture of Australia, religion has come close to
being self-contained and generally irrelevant?

The Australian week-end may be used as illustration. Saturday is
devoted to the substitute religions which dominate our culture —
shopping (materialism), sport (the T.A.B., football), and boozing
(laying in the grog for Saturday night). Religion proper is a Sunday
thing: on Sunday its irrelevance is tolerable as a curious spectacle for
those passing churches on their way to the beach.

From this may be deduced some basic cultural points. Religion is not
entirely culturally irrelevant, but its relevance is highly circumscribed.
It tends to be separate from mainstream culture, not integral; and its
adherents are regarded as either irrelevant to or at odds with the general
culture and its values. As such, religion is seen as a potentially and
sometimes actively divisive social force. Partly in consequence, and
partly for historic reasons, Australian culture appears to be basically
conditioned by an absence or weakness of religion. The religious or
church sub-culture that obviously exists is small and largely
self-contained, and its innovative impact on Australian society has been
negative — an absence producing a vacuum that has been filled by
substitutes more culturally powerful than the original: mateship,
unionism, egalitarianism, etc.

In contrast with Europe and America, the perceived image of religion
has been very negative: wowserish, divisive, reactionary. Perhaps this is
an index of how tradition itself has been viewed in Australia. Religion's
ethos from 1788 was strongly conservative, as distinct from the
radicalism evident in religious currents in the Reformation or the
seventeenth century. Or was it the kind and quality of clergymen?
Australia attracted many of Britain's clerical failures, the fools, the
second-rate, the well-meaning incompetents. The tight black suit and
rolled umbrella of the standard *Bulletin* caricature clergyman implies
his reputation for dismal spoil-sport pessimism in a land of informality,
warmth and optimism. The typical clergyman was seen as incongruous,
out of place.

This leads to the crucial matter of climate. The religion imported
into Australia was derived from the damp and gloomy British Isles. This
was expressed in similarly derivative architecture, and in general

elements of stance and style out of keeping with the Australian climate (Sydney's more than Melbourne's). The outward manifestations of a Mediterranean religion which corresponded with the climate were very different — colour, festivals noise and informality. The imported church architecture — narrow high windows, set pews, little space — suited Britain, but the churches of the Mediterranean tended to be open, cool and spacious. Particularly in the Australian outback, clerical black and other elements of British religious garb seemed formal and impractical to the point of being ridiculous. The whole external image of imported religion in Australia appeared as sombre, constricting, stifling in a land of colour, fun and freedom. Or simply, traditional religious expression was at odds with the set elements of the physical environment. It was also at odds with the cultural environment, in that the hierarchical disposition of much traditional religion did not appeal to developing egalitarian tastes.

But of course tradition also had its appeal: it was a source of attraction as well as a liability, though sometimes to different groups. The religion of the "old country" had the advantages of familiarity, and was thus comforting in a strange new land. It was also an index of respectability, of civilization, another dimension of the known and assumed patterns of social behaviour. And of course it was an adjunct to state and police power. But while these characteristics seemed merits to the governing orders, the lower orders saw them in reverse. Religion was seen as the preserve of the respectable, and a weapon of an authoritarian *status quo*. From this angle tradition in religion meant things inherently un-Australian — the Church of *England*. Only the internationalism of Roman Catholicism was proof against that particular form of cultural reaction.

I have argued elsewhere that "perhaps Australia can be best understood as the first genuinely post-Christian society, whose character was determined by the decline and disarray of religion and whose peculiarities reflect the juxtaposition of religion's assumed social irrelevance with the impact of the at times frenetic efforts of the denominations to assert themselves. Was Australia the first modern society without religious roots? There came here no truly religious people, save very few, and they founded here no indigenous religion. Elsewhere, however decayed, religion remained as part of the cultural heritage. Here it had to be built from nothing and on nothing. If the builders succeeded, in some part, in relating Australian man to his God, they failed — or largely failed — to relate him to his society or to his environment. Those crucial relationships were left to the play of other forces."[1]

Allied to this is the contention that "failing the development of the spiritual and the religious, such qualities as men possessed naturally within their humanity expanded to fill the gaps, the expansion necessarily thin and distorted to cover vast deserts of heart and mind. Seen thus, much of our history consists of the search for and creation of substitutes. Australia's dominant myths and legends, be they of bushman or bushranger, digger or trade unionist, blokes, mates and ockers, are all self-induced deceits and evasions, attempts to escape from or devise easy answers to fundamental questions about the human self, its identity and behaviour. These frauds have been enormously important in determining our self-image and have taken on their own reality."[2] So, goes the argument, Australia's pseudo-religious cultural innovations were generated as responses to the vacuum left by the absence or failure of religion.

This argument is persuasive, but not entirely so. To point up its flaws merely from the angle of religion: — Religion's negative social reverberations have been very strong in Australia — bigotry, prejudice, sectarianism. If religion were weak or socially irrelevant in Australia, how does one account for the continuing power of sectarianism? Certainly it could be argued that religious affiliation (as distinct from conviction or practice) became a convenient focus for social conflict or debate about the desirable nature of the Australian community: I have argued elsewhere, in relation to the Irish in Australian history, that religious issues (or at least nominal affiliations) embody differing concepts of Australian culture, notably the claims of pluralism against those of homogeneity.[3] But it is obvious at a glance that religious matters have also been at the centre of some of the (few) great debates in Australian history — in education and politics particularly; and arguments for the cultural irrelevance of religion fall foul of these objections.

Nevertheless, can it be suggested that the weight of Australian opinion — religionists' included — has sought to repress traditional religion as a socio-cultural force, and to keep it within the narrow confines of personal practice? A good example is the Australian Catholic school system. Seen from one angle, this is an enormous and powerful innovation in itself. Yet it has not sought to innovate, but has closely followed the educational lead of the state. Its cultural influence has been within Catholic confines.

This touches on another obvious question: why have there been no sects, no creative adaptive innovations in Australian religion? One answer might be that traditional religion offered scope enough for the religious impulse in Australia. That could be construed as flattering to the old denominations. Perhaps it is. But perhaps the authoritarian cast of traditional religion acted, with the apathy of the laity, to repress innovation. Besides, in matters of worship and liturgy, the derivative nature of religion was its strength. By those who practised it, religion was seen as the asserting of familiar links with God and civilization in the wilderness, as a traditional security against the new, and its uncertainty and threats. So the very lack of an Australian religious tradition was an initial advantage to religion in Australia. But, of course, this was a temporary gain. Eventually the lack of a native indigenous religious identity also came to mean lack of local innovation: no roots meant no local growth. Add to this the small size and the dispersal of the population, and it is no wonder that Australia continued to be a natural missionary frontier not only for the energies (or rejects) of powerful and dynamic forces in traditional religion but also for the recent imperialism of the sect movements of other countries — Seventh Day Adventists, the Church of Scientology, and so on.

Moreover, Australia had no imperative social need for indigenous sects. There was an absence of socio-religious issues that could be related to significant disadvantaged groups (e.g. Negroes) not catered for by existing religion. Aborigines were too few, nomadic and scattered; traditional church-structure was economically stratified already -- the Church of England at the top, Presbyterianism in the middle, Roman Catholicism at the bottom, internal energies tended to be channelled into sectarianism, not the manufacture of sects. Moreover the few innovative, creative minds in Australia tended to be non- or anti-religious. Because of the nature of the population, lack of education, and the anti-intellectual and authoritarian nature of much colonial religion (low-church Anglicanism, Irish Catholicism), the religious intelligentsia was small and conformist. To these explanations may perhaps be added the dominance of the physical environment and of the pioneering imperative over concerns of the spirit, to the diminution of the introspective genius. Not only the intellectual, but also the emotional (so obvious in some expressions of the religious impulse) was stifled in Australia. Indeed, any local or novel expression of any kind was suppressed: religious art, for instance, remained derivative or imported virtually until the 1960s. Certainly, various attempts were made to bring religion to bear on the social order, but these too were derivative — as the name and origins of the most recent indicate: the "Festival of Light". The Catholic Movement was also derivative, though to a lesser extent: its ambitions, to relate to the Australian political structure and situation, may be seen as a religiously inspired attempt at innovation which failed.

To sum up: what was/is the relationship of religion to Australian culture? The standard historical treatments suggest that the place of religion has been small, but not insignificant, neither vital nor irrelevant. This is too simple, too neat. The relationship has been complex and ambivalent, not to say contradictory, in which attitudes of apathy and tolerence co-exist with tension, unease, suspicion and guilt. So, surface tolerance of religion accompanies the bitter residues of sectarianism: "Catholics/Protestants may be all right, but they cannot be really trusted." An egalitarianism that repudiates the hierarchy of churches is lonely without their certainties. An Australian style of religion has neither evolved nor been built by churches that bear all the worst marks of migrants — insecurity, inability to communicate freely, inferiority complexes, caution to the point of being reactionary, pursuit of the second-rate. An uneasy tension exists between some sort of feeling of spiritual need, and the repulsion of the elements of foreignness or falsity in what is offered to satisfy it. The ordinary Australian dons a religious garb when necessary (for rites of passage) but with a sense of wearing someone else's suit — or rather, *a* suit when his natural wear is open neck shirt. (The matter is not one of *formality* but of feeling at home.) Even Australian atheists fail to take religion seriously; its existence is seen as a joke, rather than a challenge as it seems in other cultures.

Yet it is a simple fact that in Australia, as elsewhere, religion has had an important role in determining thought, values and behaviour.

Historians might grant it an initial civilizing, reformatory role, and later in the nineteenth century, a wowserish, repressive one; but the ongoing internal questioning within religious groups finds little expression in the wider culture. Why? Because of the division and hostility characteristic of the Australian scene. Cultural life is resistant to religion, religion suspicious of the wider culture — and both to a more intense degree than elsewhere.

Does this suggest that secularization — the growth of a religionless society, the decline of the idea of the sacred — is more greatly advanced in Australia? The question demands research which may find less an answer than better ways of formulating the question — and also highlight state and regional differences.[4] If it *were* to come up with an affirmative answer, an explanation may lie not only in Australia's peculiar origins, but in the crucial role of the state. The extent to which the functions and power of the state in Australia have come to take over, and displace, the social activities of religion has been little appreciated, especially outside religious confines. Reliance on the state has increased to the extent of significant erosion of former religious-orientated areas: in charity, hospitals, a whole gamut of social and psychological services and counselling work. The value systems inherent in this expansion are neutral (i.e. secular) as against the religious values formerly dominant. The flavour and ethos of such ubiquitous services have altered accordingly.

So much for this line of argument, that which focuses on the death or irrelevance of religion in Australia: daunting enough. But what of factors which explain this decline, suggest its temporary nature, or question its reality? The idea that Western society has indulged in *deliberate* regression, away from rationality and conscious individualism, and towards a depersonalized cult of the senses, is a useful and stimulating one, as it asserts, from a position outside the traditional Christian, a belief in choice and in the diminution of acceptance of conditioning, environmental or social. Thus secularization can be interpreted ultimately as a matter of choice, a contrivance, rather than an irreversible growth process natural to the times. And something that is created by option is similarly open to rejection. Indeed, the very history of Christianity offers this lesson. The triumph of secularization over Christianity is similar to that of Christianity over paganism; and as Christianity waned in public power, so will secularization. I have argued elsewhere that, in relation to Australia, the "secular" school system is to blame for the non-philosophical tenor of Australian society.[5] It is also responsible for the remarkable ignorance of religion — ignorance that has fortified and deepened the early ignorance and hostility prevalent in convict society, and strikingly evident in the convict notion that the devotees of religion were "scabs", traitors to genuine national traditions of behaviour.[6]

Can this be changed? — Or rather, is it a viable cultural generalization? No, it is only partly true. And yes, it can be changed. Religion can be created just as it can be destroyed. It was, historically, created in Australia, against an environment of apathy and hostility. It is being created now; the experience of the National Catholic Enquiry Centre shows that media advertising gets results. Advertising pays. It is also the case that the seeming decline of the churches is something of a historical constant. Religious indifference and decline were salient aspects of Australia around 1900, as a recent study demonstrates.[7] The Hanrahan syndrome (" 'We'll all be rooned', said Hanrahan!"[8]) is the usual religious response to the state of the sinful world. Indeed this should be so, in so far as the church is the assembly of the losers — which is what, in worldly terms, the church is supposed to be about. Yet, to borrow from Trotsky, a struggle goes on for the minds of the people, and in that struggle the front changes and fortunes ebb and flow.

So there are factors favouring religion, and against it. The nineteenth-century cult of science was followed by the twentieth-century cult of medicine (and of sociology, the problems of the individual being subsumed into the problems of society). But the taming of death meant that now life — old age, meaning, time — is the problem: longer life has merely extended the landscapes of fear. The cult of the state sprang from the conviction that the state had the power, and money, to resolve the problems of life. But the idea of the state as a social laboratory (an Irish-Australian view of it), producing effective solutions to social and individual problems, wanes with the eighties.

Is religion in any fit state to fill the gaps left by these fallen idols? Hardly. It lacks unity of purpose: witness the effect of a clear enemy on the church in Poland. It lacks clear convictions and objectives. Its intelligentsia tends to emotion and compromise. Its former secure stability is in question.

Basic questions about life's meaning and purpose will always be asked by relative few; the rest will follow. Santamaria's autobiography shows a religiously formulated answer almost operative in Australia in the 1950s. And this could happen again, not *in spite* of the cliché image of Australia as culturally a religionless desert, but precisely because of the validity of that stereotype — a mindless vacuum waiting to be filled, a soft indeterminate mixture waiting to be moulded.

This speculation involves an elitist view of social and cultural mechanics, and runs counter to some of the allegedly stable Australian characteristics — indifference, common sense, etc. The key question is, is secularization satisfactory? To religious zealots, never; to ordinary people, yes, in calm weather. But in rough? What when the props of seculardom — prosperity, owning one's own home, consumerism, free medical care, a beneficent state — are dropping away? The very industrialization and urbanization that have militated against religion could conspire to revive it as a cultural force. In the home of post-Christian seculardom, what is to be made of the quarter of a million primary votes polled by the Rev. Fred Nile of the Festival of Light in the N.S.W. Legislative Council elections of September 1981? The relationship between the secular and the religious elements and tendencies in Australian culture and society continues to be uncertain, complex, ambivalent. Or is it merely that the question of that relationship, being unpopular and foreign among the secularized intelligentsia, has remained neglected, unstudied? All the indicators are that religion or the lack of it — can tell a great deal about the history and nature of Australian culture.

1981

Notes

[1] Patrick O'Farrell, "Writing the General History of Australian Religion", *Journal of Religious History*, IX, 1976, 70.

[2] ibid.

[3] Patrick O'Farrell, "The Irish and Australian History", *Quadrant*, XXII, 1978, 17-21.

[4] For differences relating to Sydney and Melbourne, see Jill Roe, "A Tale of Religion in Two Cities", *Meanjin*, XL, 1981, 48-56.

[5] Patrick O'Farrell, "Historians and Religious Convictions", *Historical Studies*, XVII, 1977, 279-98.

[6] Allan M. Grocott, *Convicts Clergymen and Churches: Attitudes of convicts and ex-convicts towards the churches and clergy in New South Wales from 1788 to 1851*, Sydney, 1980, p. 11.

[7] Richard Broome, *Treasure in Earthen Vessels: Protestant Christianity in New South Wales Society 1900-1914*, St. Lucia, Qld., 1980, pp. 1-3.

[8] P.M. Farrell, O.P., "Becoming a Catholic: Is the Burden Tolerable?", *Australasian Catholic Record*, LVIII, 1981, 43. The reference is to a poem by "John O'Brien" in *Around the Boree Log*.

ANGLICANISM

DAVID HILLIARD

What are the images that are popularly associated with Australian Anglicanism? A gothic church with a graveyard and lych gate, the steeple peeping above the trees; a line of well-brushed choirboys entering a cathedral in procession; or a Bush Brother conducting Evensong from the Book of Common Prayer in a weatherboard church in the west of Queensland, the words of Cranmer competing with the blowflies while the sun beats down outside? Anglican culture in Australia is difficult to describe with precision, but three characteristics stand out. Until the 1980s the Church of England (as it was officially called until 1981) was the largest and most inclusive religious group in Australia. Throughout the nineteenth century, and until the 1920s, at least four in every ten Australians claimed nominal adherence to the Church of England, and in some places, such as the villages of southern Tasmania, it has always been the religion of more than half the population. Since the colonial period, however, the majority of self-declared Anglicans have not been closely attached to the church.[1] At the census, "C of E" was a convenient denominational label for those who had no specific religion, but who were neither Roman Catholics nor atheists. For the majority of "census Anglicans", their only connection with the church was that they used the rites of the Book of Common Prayer to mark the great occasions of life. In clerical circles these were colloquially referred to as "four wheelers", for they were first wheeled to the church in prams for their baptism, later in a car for marriage, and finally in a hearse for burial. Many others were linked emotionally to the Church of England, but rarely attended its services. They went to church on special occasions, such as Easter and Harvest Festival or, if they thought it their duty to make a public display of religion, "to show the flag". Growing up at Muswellbrook in the Hunter Valley in the 1930s, Donald Horne recalled that "most of those who took pride in their Anglicanism might attend church only on Anzac Day, the national day. To be Anglican was not necessarily to go to St Alban's. It was to see oneself among the ascendant."[2] It has always been hard to ascertain the size, at any particular time, of the inner core of Anglicans who had a strong sense of belonging to "the Church" and who attended weekly, but they existed in every community and in every class. This "remarkable capacity for ubiquity", Kenneth Henderson observed in 1948, was one of the strengths of the Church of England in Australia: "Wherever 20 or 30 are gathered together, two or three want the Church of England in the midst."[3]

Secondly, since the mid-nineteenth century Anglicanism in Australia has embraced a wide range of belief and practice. "Few things amuse intelligent Anglicans more than outsiders' puzzlement at their High-Low differences", wrote the journalist Patrick Tennison in 1965.[4] These divergences did not begin to emerge until the mid-nineteenth century, when the ideas of the Oxford Movement began to influence the

Australian church. From then on, as in England and elsewhere in the
Anglican world, the permissible limits of Anglican doctrine and
ceremonial expanded greatly. What was distinctive about the Anglicanism
that evolved in Australia was that "churchmanship" came to vary from
diocese to diocese. Each diocese developed its own style, traditions and
predominant theological outlook which proved remarkably resistant to
change. In England the Establishment had been "a force for compromise
and conciliation", which kept together within the national church all
parties and schools of thought, whereas in Australia, where the Church
of England was not established, "no such cohesive element existed".[5]
The variety was also a result of the strength of the diocesan unit in the
system of church government that became planted in Australia.[6] This
in turn was reinforced by the long and influential episcopates of many
Australian bishops. Almost every diocese has had at least one bishop
who ruled for two or three decades. Because he controlled the intake of
clergy, such a bishop left a strong personal imprint on the local church,
so that when the time came for electing a successor the traditions and
policies that he had initiated were almost invariably continued.

By the second quarter of the twentieth century these traditions were
very diverse. Everyone agreed that Anglicanism in Sydney was very
different from most of the rest of Australia. The diocese of Sydney was
strongly Protestant and evangelical in outlook, committed to
"Reformation principles" and strongly opposed to "high church"
doctrines and ritual practices. By the 1930s it had become dominated
by "out and out" conservative evangelicals, who were influenced by an
Irish tradition of militant Protestantism and by Brethren ideas of the
church as a "gathered community".[7] The piety of Sydney Anglicans
was fed by preaching, Bible study and prayer meetings. They were keen
on missionary outreach, both overseas and in outback Australia,
through the Church Missionary Society and the Bush Church Aid
Society, and they were prominent in non-denominational evangelical
organizations, such as the Scripture Union and the Inter-Varsity
Fellowship.[8] Some of them saw themselves as evangelicals first and
Anglicans second. At the other extreme of the Anglican spectrum was
Anglo-Catholicism, that had become well entrenched in the rural
dioceses of the outback, especially in Queensland. The most distinctive
institutions of Australian Anglo-Catholicism were the Bush
Brotherhoods, which were formed to minister to sparsely settled rural
areas. Bush Brotherhoods were companies of priests and laymen, who
promised to remain unmarried while they were members (usually for
a term of three years) and received only their keep and a small stipend.[9]
In Anglo-Catholic dioceses Anglicans were taught that it was their duty
to obey the teachings of the church and to attend Mass every Sunday,
and a well-furnished church was one that had six candles and a tabernacle
on the altar. In between was the tolerant comprehensiveness of the
diocese of Melbourne, in which both high churchmen and evangelicals
had parallel establishments and learned to live together, the somewhat
self-conscious "soundly Anglican" churchmanship of Adelaide,[10] and
low church Tasmania. For Australians, their experience of Anglicanism
could vary enormously, depending on where they encountered it.

Thirdly, Anglicanism in Australia retained much of the ethos of the established Church of England. It allowed more freedom of thought than any other major religious body, and within limits it was accommodating to its rebels and eccentrics. Until the 1950s the synods of capital city dioceses preferred to elect Englishmen as bishops — urbane men with Oxbridge degrees and upper-class accents. (The first Australian-born archbishop, Marcus Loane, was elected to the see of Sydney in 1966.) Anglicanism had a comfortable relationship with the established order. Although the Church of England had a quasi-established status in colonial society only until the 1830s, some of its legal privileges survived for another generation, and the idea that it was still in some sense a state church lingered on, at least in upper-class circles, until the mid-twentieth century.[11] Believing that they had some kind of pastoral responsibility for the whole community, Anglican clergy expected to take a lead in local affairs, and in many places they were accorded a slight precedence at official functions. From the late nineteenth century, many of them, especially low churchmen, were Freemasons. Often they were prominent in charitable work and in public organizations that encouraged popular education and healthy recreation. If an Anglican clergyman was a university graduate, he was expected to be a local centre of intellectual life — a man who could give a lecture on a literary or historical subject and who could discuss books with others. The wife of a parish clergyman was usually president of the local branch of the Mothers' Union, an Anglican women's organization brought to Australia in the 1890s which sought to uphold the "sanctity of marriage" and the ideals of Christian motherhood; it helped to shape the images of marriage and motherhood for Australian women.[12] Canon R.B.S. Hammond in Sydney and Father Gerard Kennedy Tucker in Melbourne became famous for the social welfare work they initiated.[13] Canon D.J. Garland of Queensland was largely responsible for devising the public ceremonies and rituals of Anzac Day: the march, the two-minutes silence, the wreath-laying at war memorials and the special church service.

From the 1840s, when Bishop Broughton in Sydney and Bishop Short in Adelaide unsuccessfully challenged the claims of Roman Catholic bishops to assume the title of a see within the British dominions, through to the religious euphoria that surrounded the Royal Visit of 1954, Anglicans proclaimed their connections with the Crown. This continuing relationship was demonstrated in many ways. Until 1962 the Australian church was not autonomous, but was tied legally in doctrine and worship to the Church of England at home, of which the monarch was the Supreme Governor. Every Sunday the services in Anglican churches, read from the 1662 Book of Common Prayer, included prayers for the sovereign and the royal family. At times of war and other national crises, church leaders and synods were quick to declare their unswerving loyalty to the Crown and the Empire.[14] In the capital cities there were personal as well as formal links between Bishop's Court and Government House, for usually the Anglican bishop or archbishop shared with the colonial or state governor a similar English upper-class background. Some governors were devout men who took a keen interest in church affairs, and a governor's wife was often state patron of the Mothers' Union. In the 1930s, for example, Archbishop Wand, who was appointed to the see of Brisbane from a fellowship of Oriel College, Oxford, found one of his few congenial companions in Sir Leslie Wilson, the Governor of Queensland. In this colonial city, Wand recalled, few people "could venture on any elaborate entertaining. Apart from Government House we were about the only people who had a couple of maids living in, and they would not want to be working late. The Governor and Lady Wilson showed themselves very good friends".[15]

For many Australian Anglicans, religion was about one's duty to support a noble and ancient English institution. Or if their background was Irish it was part of their loyalty to the Act of Union. To provide an authentic architectural setting for Anglican worship they preferred gothic — churches with towers or spires, modelled on the medieval parish churches of England. From the 1840s, Edmund Blacket and his disciples were enormously influential in forming for Australian Anglicans their idea of what a church *should* look like.[16] "The Church", it was often claimed, was the principal expression and upholder of the historic religious tradition of the English peoples, and it had helped to shape the character and beliefs of the English nation. Largely through its influence, so Archbishop Head of Melbourne told his diocesan synod in 1936, the British nation and the Empire had been kept "free, democratic and Christian".[17] The Church of England was not founded by Henry VIII, nor by Queen Elizabeth, as was claimed by Romanist apologists, but had an unbroken descent from the pre-Reformation English church, purified but not destroyed at the Reformation. The origins of "ecclesia Anglicana" lay in the free and independent church that had been planted in Britain in the second century, perhaps even at the time of the apostles. These ideas, of historic continuity and spiritual autonomy, were Tractarian in inspiration. By the mid-nineteenth century they were entering the thinking of Anglicans of all parties and schools of thought, though they were always more popular among high churchmen than among evangelicals, who looked to the Reformation rather than to the middle ages for inspiration. The sense of Anglican distinctiveness was further boosted by the expansion of the British Empire and the growth of imperial sentiment in the final decades of the century. Church and Empire went together. It seemed fitting that the country which ruled the greatest and most beneficent empire the world had ever seen should have its own ancient national church.

This English religious nationalism, and the concern to prove continuity with the pre-Reformation church, took many forms. From the 1870s and 1880s, the ancient British and Celtic saints were commemorated more widely. Anglican churches dedicated to St Alban, St Aidan, St Bede, St Columba, St Hilda or St Oswald began to appear alongside the traditional dedications to a saint of the New Testament or the Holy Trinity. Until the 1960s diocesan papers around the country occasionally ran series of articles on the "cathedrals of England" and the shrines and monasteries of the medieval English church.[18] Anglicans who fed on this literature became remarkably well informed about England's ancient ecclesiastical buildings and the architectural glories of each cathedral, though the vast majority of them were never able to visit England themselves. There was the popular custom of placing stones from medieval English cathedrals or ruined abbeys in the walls of Australian cathedrals and principal parish churches, as a sign of continuity and to symbolize "a great spiritual bond".[19] This demand, shared by Anglican churches elsewhere in the Empire, was fed by the deans of English cathedrals, who regularly despatched lumps of ancient stone to colonial dioceses as gifts. St John's Cathedral in Brisbane, for example, has stone from Canterbury Cathedral and the altar contains marble from Iona; Grafton Cathedral has stones from Bristol Cathedral and the Norman abbey of St Augustine, Canterbury; St Peter's Cathedral in Adelaide possesses stones from Canterbury Cathedral and Westminster Abbey. Almost every Australian cathedral, and many parish churches, have at least one such relic.

Since the late nineteenth century the cathedral has occupied an important position in Australian Anglican life, so that without a cathedral a diocese has seemed to lack a heart. In 1819 Governor Macquarie laid the foundation stone of a cathedral in Sydney, but the project was soon abandoned. He saw it as a great public building that was appropriate for a British colony, even without a bishop — and there was no Anglican bishop in New South Wales for another seventeen years. For Broughton and every other pioneer bishop of the mid-nineteenth century, their *cathedra* or episcopal chair was in a parish church. In England, meanwhile, the purpose of cathedrals was being widely discussed. Instead of being seen as large and dead monuments inherited from the past, they were portrayed by clerical reformers as dynamic centres of diocesan life: musical excellence, theological study, evangelism, a pulpit where leading preachers could address the great issues of the day, and a place of worship that held daily services and was open to all. These ideas on the cathedral as a religious centre for the whole community flowed through to Australia.[20] They had a strong influence on the cathedrals that were built in each colonial capital city in the late nineteenth and early twentieth centuries. The first of them was St Andrew's in Sydney, opened in 1868.[21] Two of the greatest English ecclesiastical architects of the nineteenth century were commissioned to design cathedrals in Australia: William Butterfield produced the original plans for St Peter's Cathedral in Adelaide and St Paul's Cathedral in Melbourne,[22] and John Loughborough Pearson designed St John's Cathedral in Brisbane, begun in 1901 and still incomplete. In a widely reported sermon preached in Adelaide in 1926, Canon R.P. Hewgill declared that the ideal cathedral should be a "people's church", "everybody's church", "free and open to all", whose services would attract people of every creed and no creed.[23] In Bishop Burgmann's vision for Canberra, St Mark's Library was to be the nucleus of a large religious centre, which was to be crowned by the Collegiate Church of St Mark. This would be "an Australian version of Westminster Abbey", a living symbol of the partnership between Church and State, which would "brood over the central and official part of our nation's Capital".[24]

From the late nineteenth century Anglican cathedrals filled several distinctive roles in Australian urban life. In the first place, because of their size and because of the church's direct links with England and the Crown, they were the usual places for the holding of special services on "great national days of sorrow or rejoicing": Queen Victoria's jubilees, coronations, the deaths of monarchs and national heroes, royal visits, victories in war, Empire Day, and the inauguration of the Commonwealth of Australia. For Anglican leaders, such occasions were a source of pride:

> Whatever hard words may be said by politicians about the refusal to admit anything like a State Church into the colonies, the fact remains that at national crises it is the Church which, with increasing power, is called upon to voice the spiritual instincts of the community.[25]

These state services in Anglican cathedrals combined a decently restrained and ordered worship of the divine with a demonstration of loyalty to the Crown, the Empire and English tradition. Their form became familiar and hardly changed over the years, until ecumenical services became more frequent in the 1970s. At the west door, to welcome the state governor and visiting dignitaries, there would be a cluster of senior clergy, wearing embroidered copes if they were high churchmen or black scarves, surplices and military decorations if they were low churchmen. There was the procession in strict order of ecclesiastical precedence, with bishop at the rear; the carrying of banners and flags into the cathedral, where they were received at the entrance of the sanctuary and placed close to, or laid upon, the altar; the order of service that was always an adaptation of Morning Prayer from the 1662 Book of Common Prayer; the formal official prayers; the carefully chosen choral music, the special lessons from the Old and New Testaments read by leading representatives of the participating bodies; the occasional sermon; the well-known hymns that everyone could sing, such as "Fight the good fight", or "O God, our help in ages past". And afterwards, for the bishop or the preacher, there was perhaps the pleasant prospect of luncheon at Government House. Cathedral clergy liked to think of their church as a shrine of the whole community, or at least the non-Roman Catholic section of it, and they encouraged the holding of annual services for youth, patriotic and professional bodies — such as the legal profession, the British Medical Association, the Royal Society of St George, the Boy Scouts and Girl Guides. There were close connections with the armed services, with church parades on great national days and ceremonies for the laying up of the colours of local regiments and battalions. In October some cathedrals, and churches close to a port, held a Trafalgar Day Mariners' Service, attended by representatives of shipping companies and sailing clubs. Now and again a progressive dean would attempt to hold special services for Industrial Sunday or Labour Day, but union leaders were not particularly interested and attendance was usually poor.

Anglican cathedrals were centres of music. For at least half a century their choirs played a major role in shaping the musical culture of Australian urban dwellers. In England the taste and standards of church music improved markedly in the second half of the nineteenth century, and the new ways were brought to the Australian colonies by pupils of the great English organists who took up posts in the new cathedrals. The Australian cathedrals did not seek originality in music, or in anything else, but sought to transplant the English cathedral tradition to the Antipodes: a choir of boys and men, daily choral services, dignified and beautiful worship. At St Paul's Cathedral, Melbourne, for example, the Chapter resolved in 1884 that the cathedral use should "conform as far as possible to what is understood as cathedral use in England".[26] More than sixty years later the Dean of Melbourne was proud to describe his cathedral as "a little bit of England in Australia": "Englishmen had designed the building and decorated it; the bells and the organ were English; the Prayer Book was the work of English scholarship".[27]

For at least fifty years the organists of Anglican cathedrals were leaders in the musical life of Australian cities. At a time when there were no permanent orchestras, a cathedral organist, if he had imagination and skill, could quickly assume a position of eminence in colonial music. Outside the cathedral he would teach and examine pupils, conduct choral societies, adjudicate musical competitions and provide music for civic occasions. At St Peter's Cathedral in Adelaide, J.M. Dunn, who was organist and choirmaster from 1891 until 1936, was conductor of the Adelaide Orpheus Society, and his successor, the Rev. H.P. Finnis, was conductor of the Bach Society.[28] In Melbourne there was Ernest Wood, organist of St Paul's Cathedral from 1889 to 1914.[29] He inaugurated regular organ recitals and conducted the first Melbourne performances of Bach's "St Matthew Passion" and Brahms' "Requiem". Stainer's oratorio "The Crucifixion" was performed for the first time on Good Friday 1893 and has been held annually ever since. His successor, Dr A.E. Floyd (1915-47), had been influenced by the reaction in English church music against the florid and emotional music of the Victorians. He introduced the cathedral choir to English music of the Tudor period, and in the 1920s began holding commemorative recitals to mark the centenaries and other jubilees of famous composers. These choral recitals drew big crowds. In 1916 four hundred people attended Evensong on a Wednesday afternoon to hear the first Australian performance of Orlando Gibbons' great anthem "Hosannah to the Son of David". In addition, Floyd brought music to a wider public through his lectures for the WEA, his reviews as a music critic and his radio session "The Music Lovers' Hour", which was broadcast every Sunday evening from 1948 for twenty-four years.[30]

The "cathedral tradition", personified by musicians such as Floyd, was regarded by many as the Anglican ideal. Until the 1960s Choral Evensong from a cathedral was broadcast every week by the ABC. The tradition, in a modified form, was passed on to Anglican parish churches in suburbs and provincial cities, often through men who had themselves been cathedral choristers and learnt music from one of the great organists. Anglican music was also encouraged by the Royal School of Church Music, founded in England in 1927 as the School of English Church Music and brought to Australia in 1933. The boys' choir was a distinctively Anglican institution. Through these choirs, thousands of boys, who turned out for a weekly choir practice after school and sang in two services each Sunday, learned to read music and picked up a smattering of theology and an appreciation of the language of the Prayer Book.

The role of Anglicanism in fostering musical culture was paralleled by its patronage of the crafts — stained glass, wood carving, embroidery and metal work. Anglican clergy and congregations commissioned altar crosses and candlesticks, processional crosses, communion vessels, bishop's croziers and pectoral crosses. Of the thirty-six commissions for stained glass windows given to the artist Napier Waller between 1929 and 1972, thirty were for Anglican parish churches or school chapels.[31] Church embroidery was a craft, and a social activity, that was much favoured by Anglican women of high church tastes. From the 1880s, when the movement began to redecorate church interiors in accordance with Tractarian ideas on "correct" Anglican worship, groups of women in Anglican congregations formed sanctuary guilds. Their members did the flowers, embroidered communion linen and altar frontals, and made tapestry kneelers decorated with ecclesiastical symbols. Elite groups of skilled embroiderers designed and made banners for church societies and copes and sets of eucharistic vestments for clergy. Anglican churches have also been closely associated with the English style of bell ringing, which was first brought to Australia in 1847. In the mid-1980s, of the thirty ringable peals in Australia, all but five are in Anglican churches or cathedrals, mainly in New South Wales and Victoria.[32]

The cathedral symbolized Anglican claims to religious leadership in the Australian community. Through their schools Anglicans aspired to a central role in the formation of national character.[33] Clergy who came to Australia from England brought the assumption that it was a sacred duty of the national church to instruct the young in its doctrines and that true religion should be a partner of useful learning. For the first fifty years of white settlement in Australia the Anglican monopoly of education was virtually unchallenged. Following the founding of a system of national schools in each colony, the abolition of state aid to religion, and the beginnings in the 1870s of state secular education, Anglicans gave up their parochial day schools. Not entirely: in every colony a vocal group of clergy continued to press for a chain of parochial schools, charging low fees, that would cater for the children of "Church" families. In general, however, Anglicans were happy enough to leave the work of primary education to the state and concentrated on secondary schools. It was in this area that the church left its mark. Archdeacon Broughton arrived in New South Wales in 1829 with clear ideas on the need for grammar schools that combined piety and sound learning. His object was to foster the growth of a class of landed gentry, men who would be equipped morally and intellectually to lead the young colony.[34]

With the English public schools as his model, Broughton in 1832 founded King's Schools at Parramatta and Sydney, but only the former survived. The other Anglican bishops of the early colonial period did the same, with the aim of creating the future leaders of the community. Launceston Church Grammar School, The Hutchins School in Hobart,

the Collegiate School of St Peter in Adelaide, Newcastle Church of
England Grammar School, Geelong Grammar School and Melbourne
Church of England Grammar School were all founded in the 1840s and
1850s.[35] The first Church of England secondary school for girls came
much later: Sydney Church of England Girls' Grammar School, 1895.
But Anglican influence in education extended more widely than this,
for there was a large group of private collegiate schools for boys and
girls that had personal rather than formal links with the Church of
England. Many of them were run by clergymen. In 1890, for example,
the Rev. Henry Plume, rector of Kurrajong in the Blue Mountains,
began taking a few pupils to prepare them for the matriculation
examinations. This small school, which started as part of his own
household, developed into Barker College.[36] In Melbourne, Emma
Bartlett Cook and two of her daughters founded Tintern Ladies'
College in 1877, as a school for the daughters of the well-to-do families
of Hawthorn. The Cooks were devout Anglicans and their school drew
many of its pupils from parishioners of the suburb's two Anglican
churches, Christ Church and St Columb's.[37] Most of those private
academies that survived were eventually incorporated in the system of
diocesan schools: for example, Barker, Tintern, Brighton Grammar,
Brisbane Church of England Grammar, Southport, Abbotsleigh,
Walford, Guildford Grammar. Several Anglican girls' schools, with a
distinctly high church atmosphere, were founded by religious orders.
In the 1890s English nuns of the Community of the Sisters of the
Church began schools in Adelaide, Melbourne, Perth, Hobart and
Sydney, and an Australian order, the Sisters of the Sacred Advent,
founded a group of schools in Queensland. In 1985 Anglican schools
were responsible for just over two out of every hundred school
enrolments, and four of every hundred at secondary schools. By
contrast, 20% of schoolchildren were enrolled in Roman Catholic
schools and a further 4% attended other non-government (mainly
Uniting Church) schools.[38]

What did Anglican schools have in common? In the first place they
were in practice largely independent of church control. Local dioceses
provided no financial support, school property in many cases was not
vested in diocesan trustees or synod, and few synods ever discussed
educational policy. Some schools were linked to the church through
synodal appointments to the college councils, in some the bishop was
chairman of the board of governors; others were Church of England
only by tradition or chaplaincy appointment. Because of this absence
of direction from the church, Anglican schools were very much what
their headmasters or headmistresses made them It was a system, as
Stuart Braga has observed in his history of Barker College, that
encouraged the "Jehovah-headmaster", who ruled the school with
benevolent omnipotence.[39] Secondly, there was a distinctive religious
ethos. Anglican secondary schools were always open to boys and girls
of all religious denominations whose parents could afford the fees:
there were no religious tests as a qualification for enrolment. In many
schools the religious teaching was "based on those points of belief on
which there is accordance through the greater portion of the Christian

Church".[40] Depending on the head and the chaplain, some schools placed more obvious emphasis on the doctrines and practices of the Church of England, though non-Anglicans were always exempted from religious instruction if they wished. At St Peter's College in Adelaide in the 1920s, for example, there was a daily service of Holy Communion in the school chapel — a custom that at the time was regarded as very high church — and the headmaster personally conducted daily prayers for the whole school. Preparation for confirmation involved twenty-four weekly classes, which included teaching on the practice of auricular confession, "with very happy results".[41]

In most Anglican schools there were some common features in the religious landscape. Chapel services were an integral part of school life: everyone was expected to participate in the public rituals of Christianity. Sir James Darling, one of the great Anglican headmasters, recalled that at Geelong Grammar compulsory chapel

> didn't do the boys any harm and it may occasionally have done them some good. It was a small price for them to pay for being at a church school, which was supposed to be a religious school. The wind of the Spirit bloweth where it listeth and surely is not less likely to blow in chapel[42]

And there was the chapel itself — in the older schools a prominent building, a peaceful and sacred place, with its lofty arched roof, stained glass windows, war memorials, heraldic shields, the atmosphere heavy with tradition. Services were dignified and liturgical: there was a school choir, anthems, psalms, observance of the liturgical seasons and major holy days such as Ascension Day and the feast of the school's patron saint, and the lusty singing of popular hymns. For most boys, at school and after, observed C.E.W. Bean, "the chapel symbolizes what the school stands for".[43] There was a strong emphasis in sermons and divinity lessons on the application of Christianity to everyday life. Christianity was a personal following of Jesus Christ, "the embodiment of ideal goodness". It meant good character, social responsibility, public service as a Christian vocation, respect for tradition, patriotism, obedience to the rules. Even if Christianity was not true, the Church of England was still an essential part of the social order, a guardian of national traditions and an upholder of morality. In his autobiography, the novelist Martin Boyd recalled his schooldays before the First World War at Trinity Grammar School, Kew, and the teachings of Canon George Merrick Long, its founding headmaster, who in 1911 became Bishop of Bathurst:

> To resist the brute, to protect the weak, to work for the general good, to face the truth, these things were instilled into us and illustrated by every lesson in history, Latin, Greek and English literature. It was unthinkable to show fear or to let down a friend.[44]

"Our boys' religion", Long once said, "must be that of the knight and not that of the monk".[45] In the early 1970s the council of Sydney Church of England Grammar School issued for the first time in its history a statement of the school's religious purpose, in which it spoke vaguely of "christian principles":

> The school expects that in their bearing and conduct, boys will manifestly live up to these concepts by being courteous to people of every kind at all

times. It is a matter of pride to all concerned with the administration of the school to believe that all boys leave the school with a clear concept of the obligations by a Christian gentleman.[46]

When the playwright Alexander Buzo recalled his schooldays at the Armidale School in the 1950s he had no strong recollection of its religious teaching. It was not, he said, an "overtly religious school. I think Anglicanism is a kind of 'Clayton's' religion anyway. The dogma of the faith was not forced into us."[47]

The extent to which these schools produced the large numbers of "strong, fearless, sane and reasonable Christian men" that their founders had dreamed of cannot easily be discovered. Anglicans of the upper classes were usually undemonstrative in their piety and only their closest friends may have been aware that they ever went to church. Bishops regularly complained about the small number of candidates for holy orders who came from church schools. But there was no doubt about their success in turning out leaders of the community. Headmasters and chaplains prided themselves on the successful men they had once influenced. Arthur Garnsey, who was chaplain of Melbourne Church of England Grammar School in the early 1900s, would often say to his wife in later years: "I'm proud to have prepared that man for confirmation." One of his former divinity pupils was Stanley Bruce, Prime Minister in the 1920s: "He took advantage of that contact to urge Bruce then to change some of his policies in international affairs."[48]

The Anglican urge to promote intellectual and moral leadership in Australia also led to the creation of residential university colleges — Church of England institutions affiliated to universities that had been founded on a secular and liberal basis. In every capital city except Brisbane, the Anglican college was the first to be affiliated with the university: St Paul's, Sydney (1854), Trinity, Melbourne (1872), St John's, Brisbane (1912), St Mark's, Adelaide (1925), St George's, Perth (1931), Christ College, Hobart (1933).[49] The only Anglican women's college was Janet Clarke Hall at the University of Melbourne, which began as a hostel of Trinity College in 1886.[50] The ideal was represented by the colleges of Oxford and Cambridge. Therefore the colonial colleges had a master or warden, tutors, high table, senior common room and as many of the traditional rituals of English collegiate life as could be transplanted. In Perth, Archbishop Riley personally drafted the plans for St George's College and ensured that the buildings, in Tudor gothic, were modelled on his own Cambridge college, Gonville and Caius. Like the secondary schools, the university colleges received no grants from diocesan funds, nor did they exclude non-Anglicans. Because they were small and independent they were shaped in many ways by their wardens. The office was a prestigious one. The college heads usually stayed in office for years and became personally identified with the institution: for example, Alexander Leeper, J.C.V. ("Jock") Behan and R.W.T. Cowan of Trinity College, Arthur Garnsey of St Paul's, Archibald Grenfell Price of St Mark's and J.H. ("Josh") Reynolds of St George's. The colleges had close links with the Anglican boys' schools of the state: young men bound for the professions passed naturally, with their school friends, from St Peter's College to St Mark's, or from Melbourne Grammar and Geelong to Trinity. In the 1920s, almost half the students admitted to Trinity came from Melbourne Grammar. The religious ethos of the colleges was urbane, open to intellectual currents of the day, with a strong sense of "the Church". Until the 1960s chapel attendance was compulsory, though in practice it was often evaded.

These colleges played an important role in the education of the political, business, professional and intellectual leaders of Australia in the twentieth century. In these institutions young men made lifelong friendships, picked up some literary and musical culture, absorbed a strong sense of what was or was not "done", and were encouraged to participate fully in university affairs. In its first ten years St Mark's College at the University of Adelaide had a total of 148 students and tutors, of whom eleven had graduated with first-class honours and eight had been awarded Rhodes Scholarships.[51] The history of Trinity College reads in places like a *Who's Who* of Australia, with long lists of judges, medical doctors, parliamentarians, senior public servants, captains of industry, headmasters and university professors who had lived at Trinity during their undergraduate years. Among them were Lord Casey and Lord Baillieu, Sir Edmund Herring, the historians Sir Keith Hancock, Manning Clark, Fred Alexander, Frank Crowley, A.G.L. Shaw, and J.R. Poynter, Professor Peter Karmel, Sir Roderick Carnegie, the Victorian conservative politicians Sir Rupert Hamer, Sir Arthur Rylah, and Peter Ross-Edwards, Ralph Gibson, chairman and historian of the Communist Party, and Peter Barbour, former head of ASIO. Many students from Janet Clarke Hall achieved leadership in medicine, education and the arts. Among them were eminent academics such as Dame Margaret Blackwood, Dame Ella Macknight and Dame Leonie Kramer, the folk-singer Glen Tomasetti and the novelist Helen Garner.

Until the 1960s the connection between Anglican education and eminence in public life was well established. Of those members of the federal parliament, prior to 1980, who were Anglicans, one half were educated at private schools. Geelong Grammar produced at least eighteen federal parliamentarians — second only to Scotch College, Melbourne — and Melbourne Grammar was not far behind.[52] In the 1950s the weekly paper *The Anglican* proudly announced every year the names of prominent Anglicans — usually men — who had been awarded imperial honours. In 1954, for example:

> Four of the eight Australians who received knighthoods in the New Year Honours List are practising Anglicans. Other Anglicans, active and nominal, are estimated to comprise more than three-quarters of the total number of Australians honoured in the list and to comprise nine out of ten of those honoured in England.[53]

Did the Anglican Church represent a distinctive force in Australian intellectual life? Bishops, senior clergy and prominent laymen were active in the early years of colonial universities.[54] Two leading figures in the foundation of the University of Western Australia, for example, were Sir John Winthrop Hackett, newspaper proprietor and registrar of the diocese of Perth, and his close friend (and fellow Freemason)

Archbishop Riley. After Hackett's death in 1916 he was succeeded as chancellor by Riley. It was not that the archbishop had much interest in scholarship for its own sake, but he was "an impressive figure before a public audience, both physically and vocally", and "always looked resplendent in university procession".[55] In the first half of the twentieth century there were among lay Anglicans some distinguished scholars — for example, William Bragg, Sir John Cleland, Sir Edgeworth David, Tasman Lovell, Sir Douglas Mawson, R.C. Mills and T.G.B. Osborn — but their work was not defined either by themselves or by others in terms of their religious affiliation. Often they kept their religious beliefs very private indeed. Individual Anglican clergymen achieved eminence in geology (W.B. Clarke), botany (William Woolls), anthropology (A.P. Elkin), linguistics (A. Capell), history (John McManners, G.V. Portus), psychology and the classics.[56] But the church was much less succesful in creating an educated leadership for itself. It produced only a handful of theological scholars with more than a local and transitory reputation. At first sight this is surprising, for the clergy who came to Australia in the nineteenth and early twentieth centuries from England and Ireland included a substantial number of graduates of one of the ancient universities. At the turn of the century, in dioceses such as Rockhampton, North Queensland and Adelaide that had a high proportion of English or Irish-educated clergy, about half of the clergy had university degrees. To ensure a well-educated indigenous ministry in the future, some bishops hoped to associate theological teaching with the new universities through the Church of England residential colleges. In Melbourne Bishop Moorhouse began a theological school at Trinity College in 1878 and persuaded some wealthy Anglicans to endow scholarships for theological students.[57] But it was theology on the cheap. Whereas the Presbyterian Church of Victoria spent two thousand pounds annually on the salaries of three theological professors at Ormond College, the Church of England spent only 160 pounds, on five part-time teachers. Because the universities excluded theology from their curriculums, the church had no incentive to develop the link.[58]

A very different model of theological education was to prevail within the Australian church. This was begun by Bishop Barker of Sydney, who in 1856 set up a small college at Liverpool, quite separate from the university, to train local candidates for the ministry.[59] As the demand grew for a locally-trained ministry, a second diocesan college was opened in Adelaide in 1882, and eight more were founded between 1890 and 1910, to train men for particular dioceses or colonies.[60] The reasons for this proliferation are easy to see: geographical isolation and a strong sense of regional identity, bishops who wanted to control the training of ordinands for their own diocese, and the desire to perpetuate a distinctive theological tradition. The only co-ordination was provided by the Australian College of Theology, founded by General Synod in 1891, which granted diplomas and certificates, but bishops were not obliged to accept its standards and could ordain anyone they wished. Until the 1960s Anglican theological colleges had many similarities. Most of them were small, with only a dozen or twenty students in residence. The proportion of university graduates was low: 10%

of the total in training in 1967.[61] They were poorly financed, and an American visitor in the early 1960s found their libraries "so tiny and obsolete that they made me weep".[62] They existed in isolation from other academic institutions. The task of the principal or warden was to instil into young men without much formal education a basic knowledge of theology and scripture, which would enable them to be ordained. Some of these theological teachers were men of intellectual ability and broad culture, but the need to teach half a dozen different subjects and the day to day work of running a small college was not an environment that fostered intellectual reflection or contributions to scholarship. In any case, most of them saw their role as teachers of a tradition, not as writers or researchers.

Only a handful of colleges rose above these constraints. In the interwar years, St John's College, first at Armidale then from 1926 at Morpeth, became an island of liberal scholarship. As warden, E.H. Burgmann gathered around him a group of scholarly clergymen and began a lively quarterly, the *Morpeth Review,* which covered a range of religious and social subjects.[63] His vice-warden, Roy Stuart Lee, later went to England, became vicar of the university church at Oxford and wrote some highly-regarded works on the relationship between religion and psychology.[64] Another member of the group was A.P. Elkin, who was just beginning his career as an anthropologist. From 1933 to 1938 he combined parish work at Morpeth with the chair of anthropology at the University of Sydney: he lectured at the university during the week from Monday to Thursday, and returned to Morpeth every weekend to conduct services.[65] But after Burgmann left Morpeth to become Bishop of Goulburn in 1934 the journal expired and the college reverted to being a narrowly ecclesiastical institution. After the Second World War Leon Morris of Ridley College, Melbourne, gained an international reputation as a New Testament scholar, but he stood almost alone.[66] Anglican culture in Australia encouraged intellectual activity in every area, except theology. The church looked to the Mother Church in England for its theological inspiration, just as it looked to England for its bishops, its architectural styles and its music.

The Anglican culture described in this essay was at its most self-confident between the 1880s and 1950s; since the 1960s it has crumbled rapidly, as new expressions of Anglicanism have emerged in Australia. Since the mid-1980s, when the Roman Catholic Church overtook it in size, the Anglican Church is no longer the largest religious body in the country. Its old assumption of automatic superiority has largely dissolved. Men of importance in the community no longer think it an advantage to give some of their free time to church affairs, and women have moved into positions of lay leadership. Since 1978 *An Australian Prayer Book* has been widely adopted, and the use of the Book of Common Prayer has become confined to a small number of proudly conservative congregations. In church music the "cathedral tradition" struggles to survive and rarely are cathedral organists eminent figures in a city's musical life, but at the local level there is more variety and experimentation with new styles. As the influence of religion in public life has declined, state services and church parades have become much less common and are not the great occasions of Anglican pageantry that they once were. In almost every city Anglican theological colleges have entered co-operative teaching arrangements with colleges of other denominations and academic standards have risen. The English gentleman bishop is a figure of the past. Australians and a few New Zealanders occupy all the major sees. Bishops no longer wear frock coat and gaiters as their formal dress, but almost every Bishop still signs his official signature with a cross and the title of his see: for example, +Keith Adelaide, +Barry Riverina and +John North Queensland. In Anglicanism, picturesque customs are hard to give up.

1988

Notes

For comments on an earlier version of this paper, I am grateful to Dr Brian Dickey, Dr Stuart Piggin and the Rev. Dirk van Dissel.

1   For church attendance rates in late nineteenth-century Australia, see Walter Phillips, "Religious Profession and Practice in New South Wales, 1850-1901: The Statistical Evidence", *Historical Studies*, XV, 1972, 385-94, and Hugh Jackson, "Churchgoing in Nineteenth-Century New Zealand", *New Zealand Journal of History*, XVII, 1983, 43-49.

2   Donald Horne, *The Education of Young Donald*, Sydney, 1967, p.23.

3   Kenneth Henderson, "Anglicanism in Australian Life", *Anglican Review*, No.4, 1948, p.31.

4   Patrick Tennison, "Is the C. of E. in a Mess?" *Bulletin*, 27 March 1965, p.22.

5   S.E.I. Judd, " 'Defenders of their Faith': Power and Party in the Anglican Diocese of Sydney, 1909-1938" (Ph.D. thesis, University of Sydney, 1984), p.30.

6   Ross Border, *Church and State in Australia, 1788-1872: A Constitutional Study of the Church of England in Australia*, London, 1962.

7   On Sydney Anglicanism, see Marcus L. Loane: *Hewn from the Rock: Origins and Traditions of the Church in Sydney*, Sydney, 1976, *Mark these Men: A brief account of some Evangelical clergy in the Diocese of Sydney who were associated with Archbishop Mowll*, Kambah, A.C.T., 1985, *Men to Remember*, Kambah, A.C.T., 1987, chs. 5-6; Judd, "Defenders of their Faith"; W.J. Lawton, "The Better Time to Be: The Kingdom of God and Social Reform. Anglicans and the Diocese of Sydney, 1885 to 1914" (Ph.D. thesis, University of New South Wales, 1985).

8   Keith Cole, *A History of the Church Missionary Society of Australia*, Parkville, Vic., 1971, John and Moyra Prince, *Tuned in to Change: A History of the Australian Scripture Union, 1880-1980*, Sydney, 1979; John and Moyra Prince, *Out of the Tower*, Homebush West, N.S.W., 1987.

9   R.A.F. Webb, *Brothers in the Sun: A History of the Bush Brotherhood Movement in the Outback of Australia*, Adelaide, 1978.

10   David Hilliard, *Godliness and Good Order: A History of the Anglican Church in South Australia*, Adelaide, 1986.

11   For example, Frances Margaret McGuire, *Bright Morning: The Story of an Australian Family before 1914*, Adelaide, 1975, pp.83-84.

12   Sabine Willis, "Homes are Divine Workshops", in Elizabeth Windschuttle (ed.), *Women, Class and History: Feminist Perspectives on Australia, 1788-1978* Melbourne, 1980, pp.173-91.

13   B.G. Judd, *He that Doeth: The Life Story of Archdeacon R.B.S. Hammond, O.B.E.*, London, 1951; John Handfield, *Friends and Brothers: A Life of Gerard Kennedy Tucker, Founder of the Brotherhood of St. Laurence and Community Aid Abroad*, Melbourne, 1980.

[14] For the First World War, see Michael McKernan, *Australian Churches at War: Attitudes and Activities of the Major Churches, 1914-1918*, Sydney and Canberra, 1980, ch 3; Hilliard, *Godliness and Good Order*, pp.83-87.

[15] J.W.C. Wand, *Changeful Page: The Autobiography of William Wand, formerly Bishop of London*, London, 1965, p.141.

[16] Peter Bennie, "Anglicanism in Australia", *Quadrant*, XVI, 1972, p.37; Joan Kerr, *Our Great Victorian Architect: Edmund Thomas Blacket (1817-1883)*, Sydney, 1983.

[17] Archbishop of Melbourne, *Charge to Synod*, 1936, p.10.

[18] For example, "How our Forefathers Built", *Church Chronicle*, Brisbane, January 1950-November 1952; "Famous Anglican Sees ', *The Anglican*, Sydney, 20 January 1966-24 August 1967.

[19] For example, *St. Arnaud Churchman*, March 1936, pp.11-12.

[20] 'The Value of a Cathedral System in a Colonial Diocese", in *The Official Report of the Church Congress held at Hobart on January 23rd, 24th, 25th, and 26th, 1894*, Hobart, 1894, pp.69-94.

[21] S.M. Johnstone, *The Book of St. Andrew's Cathedral, Sydney*, Sydney, 1968.

[22] Albert B. McPherson, "That Uncomfortable Genius: A study of the building of St Paul's Cathedral, Melbourne, and the role of its architect, William Butterfield, 1878-1884" (M.A. thesis, University of Melbourne, 1980).

[23] "The Ideal of a Cathedral", in A. Snell (ed.), *R.P. Hewgill, Priest, 1875-1960*, Richmond, S.A., 1979, pp.31-33.

[24] L.M. Murchison (comp.), "Bishop Burgmann and St. Mark's", *St. Mark's Review*, No.50, November 1967, pp.27-32.

[25] *Church News*, Adelaide, 15 February 1901.

[26] Paul Harvie, "The First Sixty Years of Music at St. Paul's Cathedral, Melbourne, c.1887-1947" (M.Mus. thesis, University of Melbourne, 1983), p.8.

[27] *Church of England Messenger*, Melbourne, 7 September 1951, p.282.

[28] *Register*, 16 November 1926; *Advertiser*, 4 March 1936; *Adelaide Church Guardian*, February 1961, p.9.

[29] Harvie, "The First Sixty Years of Music at St. Paul's Cathedral, Melbourne", ch. 3.

[30] For some reminiscences of Floyd, see Ralph Gibson, *My Years in the Communist Party*, Melbourne, 1966, pp.92-93, and Bruce Naylor, "Musical Melbourne Fifty Years Ago", *Victorian Organ Journal*, October 1986, pp.26-27.

[31] Nicholas Draffin, *The Art of M. Napier Waller*, Melbourne, 1978, p.12.

[32] John D. Keating, *Bells in Australia*, Carlton, Vic., 1979, pp.78-92.

[33] On Anglican schools, see Norman G. Curry, "Anglican Educational Enterprise", in John Cleverley (ed.), *Half a Million Children: Studies of Non-Government Education in Australia*, Melbourne, 1978, pp.47-76.

[34] G.P. Shaw, *Patriarch and Patriot: William Grant Broughton, 1788-1853, Colonial Statesman and Ecclesiastic*, Carlton, Vic., 1978, pp.28-32, 46-67; R.J. Burns, "The Colonial Background", in John Cleverley (ed.), *Half a Million Children*, pp.37-39.

[35] For the aims of their founders, see, for example, A. Grenfell Price, *The Collegiate School of St. Peter, 1847-1947*, Adelaide, 1947; Geoffrey Stephens, *The Hutchins School: Macquarie Street Years, 1846-1965*, Hobart, 1979.

[36] Stuart Braga, *Barker College: A History*, Sydney, 1978.

[37] Lyndsay Gardiner, *Tintern School and Anglican Girls' Education, 1877-1977*, East Ringwood, Vic., 1977.

[38] Australian Bureau of Statistics, National Schools Statistics Collection, Australia, 1985.

[39] Braga, *Barker College*, p.130.

[40] Curry, "Anglican Educational Enterprise", p.61.

[41] *Church Standard*, Sydney, 5 December 1930, p.31. See also P. StJ. Wilson (headmaster of Brighton Grammar School), *Precepts for Members of the Church of England: Six Studies*, Melbourne, 1943.

[42] J.R. Darling, *Richly Rewarding*, Melbourne, 1978, pp.146-47.

[43] C.E.W. Bean, *Hear, My Son: An Account of the Independent and Other Corporate Boys' Schools of Australia*, Sydney, 1950, p.116.

[44] Martin Boyd, *Day of my Delight: An Anglo-Australian Memoir*, Melbourne, 1965, p.27.

[45] Boyd, *Day of my Delight*, p.29.

[46] Geoffrey Sherington, *Shore: A History of Sydney Church of England Grammar School*, Sydney, 1983, p.223.

[47] Corrie Perkin, "Teachers with Class", *Good Weekend: The Age Magazine*, 6 February 1987, p.9.

[48] David Garnsey, *Arthur Garnsey: A Man for Truth and Freedom*, Sydney, 1985, pp.21-22.

[49] James Grant, *Perspective of a Century: A Volume for the Centenary of Trinity College, Melbourne 1872-1972*, Melbourne, 1972; A. Grenfell Price, *A History of St. Mark's College, University of Adelaide and the Foundation of the Residential College Movement*, Adelaide, 1967; Fred Alexander, *Campus at Crawley: A Narrative and Critical Appreciation of the First Fifty Years of the University of Western Australia*, Melbourne, 1963, pp.512-22.

[50] Lyndsay Gardiner, *Janet Clarke Hall, 1886-1986*, South Yarra, Vic., 1986.

[51] *Year Book of the Church of England in the Diocese of Adelaide*, 1935-36, pp.161-62.

[52] Joan Rydon, *A Federal Legislature: The Australian Commonwealth Parliament, 1901-1980*, Melbourne, 1986, pp.149-51.

[53] *The Anglican*, 8 January 1954.

[54] K. Rayner, "The History of the Church of England in Queensland" (Ph.D. thesis, University of Queensland, 1962), pp.342-43; Judith M. Brown, *Augustus Short, D.D.: Bishop of Adelaide*, Adelaide, 1974, ch. 23.

[55] Fred Alexander (ed.), *Four Bishops and their See: Perth, Western Australia, 1857-1957*, Nedlands, W.A., 1957, pp.86-87.

[56] Elena Grainger, *The Remarkable Reverend Clarke: The Life and Times of the Father of Australian Geology*, Melbourne, 1982; Lionel Gilbert, *William Woolls, 1814-1893: 'A Most Useful Colonist'*, Canberra, 1985; Tigger Wise, *The Self-Made Anthropologist: A Life of A.P. Elkin*, Sydney, 1985; G.V. Portus, *Happy Highways*, Melbourne, 1953.

[57] Grant, *Perspective of a Century*, pp.103-11.

[58] A.deQ. Robin, "Theology and Theological Training in Australia: An Outline Historical Survey", *Journal of the Royal Australian Historical Society*, LIV, 1968, 356-67.

[59] Marcus L. Loane, *A Centenary History of Moore Theological College*, Sydney, 1955.

[60] Church of England in Australia, General Synod, *Theological Education: Report of a Committee appointed by the General Synod of the Church of England in Australia*, 1969, pp.4-6.

[61] *Theological Education*, p.9.

[62] Howard A. Johnson, *Global Odyssey: An Episcopalian's Encounter with the Anglican Communion in Eighty Countries*, New York, 1963, p.267.

[63] Roy S. Lee, "Burgie at Morpeth", *St. Mark's Review*, No.50, November 1967, pp.1-6; H.M. Green, *A History of Australian Literature: Pure and Applied*, Vol.II, 1923-1950 (rev. ed., Sydney, 1985) pp.1333-34; Tim Rowse, *Australian Liberalism and National Character*, Malmesbury, Vic., 1978, pp.158-60.

[64] *Freud and Christianity* (1948); *Psychology and Worship* (1955); *Your Growing Child and Religion* (1963); *Principles of Pastoral Counselling* (1968); obituary in *Church Scene*, Melbourne, 1 May 1981.

[65] Wise, *The Self-Made Anthropologist*, ch. 10.

[66] Robert Banks (ed.), *Reconciliation and Hope: New Testament Essays on Atonement and Eschatology, presented to L.L. Morris on his 60th Birthday*, Exeter and Grand Rapids, 1974.

THE ROOTS OF ANTI-SUBURBANISM IN AUSTRALIA

ALAN GILBERT

When Governor Phillip drew up plans for the first European settlement in N.S.W. in 1790, he wrote to Lord Sydney at the Colonial Office in London proposing that the streets should

> be laid out in such a manner as to afford a free circulation of air; and when the houses are to be built, if it meets with your lordship's approbation, the land will be granted with a clause that will prevent more than one house being built on the allotment, which will be sixty feet in front and one hundred and fifty feet in depth . . .[1]

The Governor's good intentions came to nought amidst the cramped, haphazard rabbit-warren that was early Sydney; yet before a century had passed, the social values implicit in his plans, and even the spatial dimensions which he had suggested for residential allotments, had become part of the dreams and realities of a majority of Australian lives. When, in the first decade of the twentieth century, an American author, Frederick C. Howe, sought to illustrate his belief that in suburbanization, not urbanization, lay the best future for democratic societies, it was to Australia that he turned. "The great cities of Australia", he explained, "are spread out into the suburbs in a splendid way. For miles about are broad roads, with small houses, gardens, and an opportunity for touch with the freer, sweeter life which the country offers".[2]

The suburbanization of Sydney and Melbourne had begun by mid-century, and in the period after about 1870 a general expansion of suburban settlement had absorbed the bulk of a rapid and sustained growth of the colonial population. Melbourne, the largest of the Australian cities, grew from 268,000 to 473,000 in the 1880s alone, and 70% of the increase was suburban. On a smaller scale, Brisbane and Adelaide followed a similar pattern, while Perth waited until the fifteen years after 1895 for its initial suburban boom. In Sydney, the suburban element of the population grew from 38,949 in 1861, when it represented 40% of the metropolitan total, to 369,721 (77%) in 1901.[3]

The lure of the suburbs was a persistent social force in Australian society. There was an abundance of suitable land on the margins of the growing cities. Metropolitan transport-networks expanded rapidly after about 1875, with railway and cable-car systems fostering the commuter habits that the motor-car would reinforce after 1945. Combined with the relentless entrepreneurship of real-estate "land boomers" and the early appearance of building societies and mortgaging, these networks made possible the separation of inner-city centres of work from suburban centres of residence. A suburban, commuter life-style became a realistic aspiration in a society in which patterns of income distribution, while far from egalitarian, were considerably more equitable than those of Britain or Europe. Most of these factors were evident to R.E.N. Twopeny, an English journalist, when (after seven years in the colonies), he wrote *Town Life in*

Australia in 1883. As a visitor seeking to understand Melbourne, he was impressed by the fact that

> nearly everybody who can lives in the suburbs, and the excellence of the railway system enables them to extend much farther away from the city than in Adelaide or Sydney. It is strange that the Australian townsman should have inherited so thoroughly the English love of living as far as possible from the scene of his business and work during the day.[4]

Strange though it may have seemed to Twopeny, the lure of suburbia did indeed involve the persistence of values and traditions derived from England. There were strong anti-urban traditions in English culture, and the rapid urbanization of the industrial age had served only to sharpen ancient arcadian visions. To the genteel classes of England, the city had its seasons for duty, business or pleasure; the countryside, however, remained without question the natural habitat of the species. At another social level, puritanism, while often the faith of urban men, had always been deeply suspicious of urban culture. Had not John Bunyan portrayed "Vanity Fair" as a distracting place where few were able to keep "hearts and spirits in any good order"? To the shrewd yeoman mind of William Cobbett, London became the "all-devouring Wen" of the new industrial society; while to William Blake it was a place where all too evidently the "mind forg'd manacles" of the urban environment left marks of "weakness" and "woe" on every human face. Thus, long before sociologists gave us the term, the kinds of people who migrated to the Australian colonies were prone to see urbanization as a potentially alienating, de-humanizing force. As the historian J.A. Froude put it in the very same year that Twopeny was writing about Australian towns, a purely urban life-style threatened a people with "degeneracy".[5]

In the Australian context, attitudes such as these were reinforced by the mythology and symbolism of the "bush". C.E.W. Bean, reflecting on the character of the Australians who went to war in 1914-18, claimed that even city-bred Australians were at heart "bushmen" in their values, virtues and vices.[6] He was right, at least in the sense that, for many urban Australians, city living retained strong negative associations. In poetry resonating with the popular attitudes, Henry Lawson's "Faces in the Street", which first appeared in the *Bulletin* in 1888, pictured city folks as care-worn and pallid, weary, listless and sad. It was probably a conscious evocation of Blake's terrible vision of "Marks of weakness, marks of woe" on the faces of Londoners that made Lawson write:

> And cause have I to sorrow, in a land so young and fair,
> To see upon those faces stamped the marks of Want and Care;
> I look in vain for traces of the fresh and fair and sweet
> In sallow, sunken faces that are drifting through the street.

The city, so pictured, was a trap for the human spirit. But the "bush" — the relentless Australian wilderness — was a forbidding alternative. Few could survive there. "The poor of the city have friends in woe, no matter how much they lack", Lawson conceded in "Out Back"; "But only God and the swagman know how a poor man fares Out Back".

Thus the city was a practical necessity, the "bush" an idealized dream. This made the suburb a marvellous compromise. Lawson's "Faces in the Street" distinguished, interestingly enough, between the "city proper" and its "suburbs". For it was in the latter that urbanized Anglo-Saxons, in Britain and America as well as in the Australian colonies, realized the dream of bringing nature to town — nature tame and civilized, not red in tooth and claw. In "marvellous Melbourne", Graeme Davison has pointed out that even the working-class end of the real-estate market offered what one advertisement called "the health, pleasure and comfort of life in a cottage surrounded by its own garden . . . with all the advantages of country life". Most working-class families managed to obtain a small garden, and even the back streets of Collingwood in the 1880s "had potted ferns in the windows".[7] But almost everyone who could aspired to a detached house in a proper garden setting, with guaranteed seclusion, fresh air, open space, lawns and trees.

Yet the possibility of retaining rural associations and natural symbols was only part of the lure of the suburbs. The ownership of house and land enhanced a family's economic and social status. To quote words that have echoed *ad nauseam* through Australian suburbia for more than a century, it was a "good investment": the best opportunity most Australians would ever have of substantial capital gain. Socially, the ownership of real property was very important. Australian values owed much to an Anglo-Saxon culture in which, over the centuries, the distinction between freehold tenure and tenancy of land had persisted as a primary criterion of status. It still meant much to be a freeholder; and for the proud suburban home owner, the suburban dream realized meant independence, security, pride and self-respect — all ancient, evocative yeomen virtues.

It was also a dream inspired by generalized notions about the importance of private, domestic family life. The suburban home was vaunted as a retreat in which the commuting worker could isolate himself and his family from the pressures of the work-place and the city. Indeed, suburbia was from the beginning virtually synonymous with domesticity. Suburbs were places for families and children: for the men, the "breadwinners" returning daily, places to be husbands and fathers; for the women, places to concentrate on being wives and mothers. Suburbia was, *par excellence*, the great Australian habitat for the production, protection and socialization of children. Its characteristic images were those of proud and loving housewives maintaining the home for husbands and children; of "handymen" pottering around their homes at weekends, or frolicking with their children; of family evenings spent, as the anonymous author of *Australian Etiquette* put it in 1885, in "games, debates, wall pictures, songs, duets, suppressed mirth, and uncontrolled laughter".[8]

Imagery and reality often differ. My immediate goal has been to describe the lure of the suburban life-style, rather than to explore the realities of suburban life. The latter would require a considerable qualification of the former, not least because, like the personal histories of the people and families who compose them, suburbs are complex, varied, often contradictory social systems.

Yet there has been surprising *continuity* since the infancy of Australian suburbia in the 1850s in the attitudes, values and motives underlying suburbanization. Recent cultural trends — notably those associated with feminism and environmentalism — have modified some of the stereotypes, or at least altered the language and terms of their articulation. Housewives who aspire as strongly as ever to the traditional norms of motherhood and home management might now feel more defensive about these "suburban" roles. Under the same pressures, the once-sharp role-differences, which (in theory at least) left the paternal breadwinner mercifully isolated from the world of aprons, teatowels, clothes-lines and soiled nappies, have become more blurred. At the same time, there has been a marked improvement in the image of the inner-city environment, from which suburbanites once fled in horror. The lure of the inner suburbs and city centre, powerful in the last quarter of a century, has been in many ways an anti-suburban development. But none of these changes has altered two primary facts. First, that a substantial majority of Australians live in suburbs; and secondly, that the lure of the suburb, like the values and expectations associated with suburban life-styles, remains today recognizably the same as it was in colonial Sydney or "Marvellous Melbourne". Anti-suburbanism, however powerful, has had no easy victory. In the life of Australian suburbia it meets a tenacious social resistance, a deep-rooted cultural complacency.

To what extent there is anything unique about this suburban society (or its critics) remains problematical in the absence of detailed comparisons with North America, Britain, continental Europe and elsewhere, where suburbs also form an important part of the pattern of human settlement. But even superficial comparisons suggest that, while there is much in Australian suburbanism and anti-suburbanism that is common and derivative, there are also certain distinctive elements. For example, there seems to be much less emphasis on the social importance of home ownership in continental Europe than there is in Australia; and in the absence of prejudice against residential leasing, the ratio of leasehold to freehold is higher there. In suburban Sydney in the mid-1970s, over 80% of all private houses were owner-occupied, and in the words of an urban sociologist, "almost everyone who did not own their own house would wish to do so".[9] Compared to Europe, then, Australian suburbia has been deeply involved in both the attainment and the expression of economic security and social respectability.

North American suburbia may closely resemble Australian suburbia in the symbols and attitudes associated with suburban ownership, but in other respects neither the lure of the suburb nor the strength and character of anti-suburbanism seem to offer precise parallels. In America, as in Australia, the attractiveness of suburbia has owed much to a persistent anti-urban bias: to an idealized vision of rural life and, obversely, to a view of urbanization (in Thomas Jefferson's words) as "pestilential to the morals, the health, and the liberties of man".[10] But the American suburban dream seems to place a unique emphasis on the suburb as a homogeneous community. In a society distinguished by ethnic and cultural diversity, suburbs have been both welcomed and resented as havens of homogeneity, places where essentially like-minded residents can insulate themselves from at least some of the problems and tensions of the wider society. In *The Crack in the Picture Window*, published in 1956, John Keats fulminated against this aspect of American suburbia; but his attack would not have quite fitted the Australian situation, in which suburban homogeneity has never been so conscious and important a goal, except perhaps for some of the immigrant communities that settled in the inner suburbs of Melbourne and Sydney after World War II.

In Australia, when suburbia is criticized as an environment promoting "mindless conformism", what is implied is a general criticism, a questioning of values and attitudes shared *across* the entire suburban culture. In America, discussions of suburban conformism seem more often to refer to something communal and segmental: to the role of suburbanism in the reinforcement of differences *between* homogeneous neighbourhoods. In both the United States and Britain, moreover, the kind of generalized invective directed against suburbanism in Australia often seems to be reserved for more diffuse targets — for "provincialism" or "small town" culture. There is no direct Australian equivalent, for example, to the American metropolitan culture's contempt for "Main Street"; and it follows, perhaps, that anti-suburbanism, as a specific, systematic cultural critique, may be more powerful in Australian life than elsewhere. At present, however, all such comparisons must remain tentative. What is certain, if still too little explored, is the reality of Australian anti-suburbanism itself.

"It is hard to imagine how one can understand Australia", Donald Horne wrote in one of the most important passages in *The Lucky Country*, "unless one approaches sympathetically the life most Australians lead and the values they follow". But instead of doing this, he suggested, most Australian writers have seemed either "to caricature their fellow countrymen or idealize them for qualities which most of them do not possess". There is, he said, "no Australian Orwell, searching for the temper of the people, accepting it, and moving on from there".[11] Supposing Horne is right, it is clear that an "Australian Orwell" would have to do most of the searching and accepting in suburbia, where most Australians live; and without our Orwell, suburbia, more than any other Australian environment except perhaps the "bush" itself, has been caricatured. Indeed, Horne concluded, "suburbanism"

> one way or the other, is likely to be the target of practically all intellectuals. And since most Australians live in the suburbs of cities this means that intellectuals hate almost the whole community.[12]

This provocative passage raises the question of what we mean when we speak of "intellectuals" or an "intelligentsia". Not all intelligent people are intellectuals — that is, part of an intelligentsia. Nor, for that matter, are all intellectuals particularly intelligent. For what distinguishes an intelligentsia is not intelligence *per se*, but attitude; not knowledge so much as cultural orientation. Intellectuals are concerned with abstract and theoretical understandings of reality. They like to organize knowledge into cognitive systems. They are fascinated by the *meaning* and *significance* of things that other people accept in a practical, taken-for-granted way. Thus what Horne was saying in 1964 was that a negative view of suburban life and culture was something common to "practically all intellectuals" — common, that is, to practically all understandings of Australian social reality, part of practically all the cognitive systems through which different sections of the Australian intelligentsia make sense of their culture. Divided on almost everything else, the "left" and "right" of the intellectual spectrum agreed on this one thing at least. They hated suburbia. They despised it.

Consensus may be an economic good and a social panacea, but it has a degenerative effect on the quality of intellectual life. Unchallenged, ideas become clichés, values degenerate into prejudice, social theory is trivialized. The result is a virtual contradiction in terms — a "conventional wisdom" of the intelligentsia. Australian intellectuals have not reached a complete consensus about "suburbia": some observers have qualified their judgments in important ways; a few stand entirely aloof from conventional anti-suburbanism. Yet the fact remains that a generalized hostility has prevailed, and that a cliched antipathy still too often passes for genuine social analysis.

Why this should be so is no simple question, firstly because anti-suburbanism has many roots, and secondly because it is often expressed in highly emotive, pejorative terms that are not readily susceptible to logical analysis. It is therefore more as a matter of convenience than of confident conceptualization that I want to explore anti-suburban consciousness under five main headings:— anti-suburbanism and the decline of community, the metaphysics of anti-suburbanism, anti-suburbanism and the minority culture, anti-suburbanism and class, and anti-suburbanism and feminism.

1. *Anti-suburbanism and the Decline of Community*

Suburbanization is part of the larger process of urbanization. Without questioning the suburb's unique blending of urban and rural values, there can be no doubt that its matrix is emphatically urban. A suburb is part of a city, essentially and inextricably; and like the city proper, it is an object of the lingering opprobrium attaching to urban life even in long-established urban cultures. And because the city is an appropriate symbol of all those complex transformations — economic, social, cultural and demographic — that are sometimes encapsulated in the term "modernization", anti-suburbanism contains an unmistakable anti-modern animus.

Thus in one guise anti-suburbanism is part of an attack on modern urban-industrial society as a whole. This generalized hostility is a deep and ubiquitous factor in most forms of modern cultural pessimism.

Civilization, the argument runs, began rapidly to degenerate sometime in the later eighteenth century; and industrialization, as Lawrence puts it in *Women in Love*,

> was the first great step in undoing, the first great phase of chaos, the substitution of the mechanical principle for the organic, the destruction of the organic unity, and the subordination of every organic unit to the great mechanical purpose.13

Modern urban-industrial culture, owing its existence to the truimph of the "great mechanical purpose", could not but be impoverished, demeaning and inauthentic. This idea obsessed Lawrence, and his disenchantment identified him with one of the great traditions of nineteenth- and twentieth-century European culture. As Marcuse puts it in his arrestingly-titled *One-Dimensional Man*, the whole process of modernization, with the metropolis as its symbol, has been a process of "moronization . . . and the promotion of frustration".14

As well as this general overlap between anti-urbanism and anti-suburbanism, there are other attitudes involved in the latter. For, on most variants of the case, the suburb ends up getting a much *worse* press than the city proper. It becomes the epitome of all the worst characteristics of the city — a distillation of pure mediocrity, alienation and false consciousness — but without any of the redeeming features that a city has even within the anti-urban traditions of modern pessimism. Indeed, the city traditionally has been an ambiguous symbol in European culture: on the one hand evil, corrupt and de-humanizing, on the other a magnet for those seeking a better, richer, more exciting way of life. This ambiguity is important, for it explains the two contrary criticisms of suburbanism that stem from the perceived differences between city and suburb.

Suburbanism evolved as a compromise between the myths and realities of city life and the impracticalities of arcadian alternatives. Viewed positively, this compromise meant that the suburb was celebrated as an ideal mixture of the best elements of town and country. But like all compromises, it was also exposed to two distinct types of negative criticism. Indeed, it could be seen to have the *worst* of both worlds: sharing the tendency of urban living to destroy traditional forms of community, and at the same time destroying the freedoms of choice and association characteristic of authentic city life.

The crux of the hostile analysis is the suburb's tendency to isolate people in privatized family units, and isolate the units themselves in partial and tenuous communities of residence. Whereas in the city proper, a rich and complex diversity of partial communities and associations offers compensation for the modern "decline of community", in suburbia there is no such global culture, only isolated segments and tenuous associations based on the marginal significance of residence and domesticity. On such a view, suburbanism represents a trivialization of culture; it attracts metaphors like "one-dimensional", "flat", and "faceless".

2. *The Metaphysics of Anti-suburbanism*

Many Australian intellectuals have detected spiritual degeneration in the impact of the suburb on traditional values. The life of the suburb

not only destroyed community values without putting anything
worthwhile in their place, the criticism goes; far worse, it actually
legitimated and reinforced the resulting "nothingness", and made it
seem normal. The denizens of suburbia were not merely "lost souls",
they were so dead spiritually that they could be smugly complacent
about their condition.

However arrogant the presumption by one human being that the
consciousness of another is false, the notion of suburban culture as
false consciousness lies at the heart of Australian anti-suburbanism.
It inspired, for example, the spectacular attack that Louis Esson
made on the suburban life of early twentieth-century Australia. "The
suburban home must be destroyed", he wrote in 1912.

> It stands for all that is dull and cowardly and depressing in modern life. It
> endeavours to eliminate the element of danger in human affairs. But without
> dangers there can be no joy, no ecstasy, no spiritual adventures. The suburban
> home is a blasphemy. It denies life.[15]

Esson, with his wife, Hilda, was one of a group of Australian
intellectuals who lamented the direction that Australian culture
appeared to be taking in the twentieth century. They looked back to
the 1890s as a time when the development of a rural civilization —
socialist, pastoral and uniquely Australian — had seemed possible. But
the possibility had died, they believed, amidst the glib materialism and
stifling conformism of suburban life.[16]

Whether or not D.H. Lawrence was actually influenced by such views
we do not know. He certainly reinforced them when (after spending a
single weekend in Sydney in May 1922) he wrote the scathing opening
chapters of *Kangaroo*. "The *vacancy* of this freedom is almost
terrifying", he said of Australian suburbia,

> the openness and the freedom of this new chaos, this litter of bungalows and
> tin cans scattered for miles and miles, this Englishness all crumpled out into
> formlessness and chaos.[17]

After a single train journey through Sydney's southern suburbs to the
Illawarra, Lawrence sensed

> the absence of any inner meaning: and at the same time the great sense of
> vacant spaces. The sense of irresponsible freedom. The sense of do-as-you-
> please liberty. And all utterly uninteresting. What is more hopelessly
> uninteresting than accomplished liberty? Great swarming, teeming Sydney
> flowing out into these myriads of bungalows, like shallow waters spreading,
> undyked. And what then? Nothing. No inner life, no high command, no
> interest in anything, finally.[18]

Lawrence chose a metaphor of shallow waters spreading undyked, while
the novelist, George Johnston, in *My Brother Jack*, wrote of suburbia as
a desert.[19] But the melancholy vision was the same.

Anti-suburbanism is heir to the recurrent anathema that
Romanticism has pronounced for more than a quarter of a millenium
against the rationalism, meliorism and materialism of the modern world.
Suburbanites are criticized because they feel safe, and because their
lives are comfortable. Esson believed that suburbanism was "deplorably
immoral", because its tendency was "to eliminate the element of
danger in human affairs"; for Johnston, poor suburbanites were better

than wealthy ones because "they still grappled with an existence where audacities were possible, and even adventure".[20] To such observers, suburbanism seemed too pleasant, too trivial, too domestic, too smug, and far too insulated from the pain, poverty and powerlessness of "real" life. In its criticism of suburban culture, in short, the Australian intelligentsia behaves in an ancient, if precarious, tradition — that of a prophetic minority.

3. *Anti-suburbanism and Minority Culture*

The idea of the intellectual as modern prophet is best understood by scanning horizons far wider than those of Australian culture. I have in mind the kind of distinction that F.R. Leavis elaborated in *Mass Civilization and Minority Culture*, when he defined the intelligentsia, the "minority culture", and distinguished it from its surrounding "mass civilization", in the following terms:

> in any period it is on a very small minority that the discerning appreciation of art and literature depends: it is (apart from cases of the simple and familiar) only a few who are capable of unprompted, first-hand judgment. They are still a small minority, though a larger one, who are capable of endorsing such first-hand judgment by genuine personal response.[21]

With this minority culture, Leavis believed, rested "the implicit standards that order the finer living of an age, the sense that this is worth more than that, this rather than that is the direction in which to go, that the centre is here rather than there". Without such cultural leadership, he argued, "distinction of spirit is thwarted and incoherent".[22]

Leavis had many critics, but one aspect of his analysis that transcended much of the debate was his perception that minority cultures are peculiarly embattled in the environment of modern civilizations adept in the arts (and the technologies) of cultural counterfeiting. A minority culture is not just a sophisticated version of its wider culture; it is an alternative version. Mass civilization is not just inferior, it is actually an enemy of those "standards that order the finer living of an age".[23]

As Leavis would have been the first to insist, there is something distinctively modern and western about this view. In other cultural *milieux*, the *illuminati* and the masses have shared a common culture, only at different levels of sophistication. Medieval Christendom, for example, exhibited obvious cultural congruence between its minority and popular cultures. Again, the modern Maoist commitment to mandatory involvement between intellectuals and masses implies a belief that the role of the intelligentsia is not to shape values and standards or dictate cultural trends, but rather to serve the cultural goals and aspirations of the masses. In neither case is the cultural congruence always evident in the accompanying *social* reality, but that is not the point. For a sharp contrast remains between such cases, on the one hand, and the modern western tradition of a gap between intelligentsia and mass culture on the other.

This sense of threat — of genuine culture beseiged by the forces of a powerful yet contemptible mass civilization — has been caught up virtually from the beginning of the modern industrial age in the complex term "Philistine". Indeed, there is an arresting similarity between Clemens Brentano's definition of Philistinism in 1810 and the attack on Australian "suburban man" in a series on Australian culture in *Meanjin*, a left-liberal journal of social and literary criticism, in 1966-7. As Brentano put it, Philistines

> live solely commonplace existences. To them the means of survival seem the only end. They do everything in terms of their earthy lives, ... these are the sole terms they can conceive of. Philistines mix poetry into their lives as a necessity, only if they are accustomed to having it as a regular interruption .... Sunday ecstasy terminates in a deeper sleep than they usually enjoy. On Monday they can work better than ever. Their social life has to be conventional, just like everyone else's, and stylish; even their pleasures they manufacture the way they do everything — laboriously and formally.[24]

"Behold the man", Allan Ashbolt wrote in highly evocative language about the Australia of the 1960s:—

> on Sunday mornings in the suburbs, when the high-decibel drone of the motor-mower is calling the faithful to worship. A block of land, a brick veneer, and the motor-mower beside him in the wilderness — what more does he want to sustain him, except a Holden to polish, a beer with the boys, marital sex on Saturday nights, a few furtive adulteries, an occasional gamble on the horses or the lottery, the tribal ritual of football, the flickering in his loungeroom of cops and robbers, goodies and baddies, guys and dolls?[25]

For the *Meanjin* school, suburban man was a failure because his mass society — industrialized, affluent and consumer-orientated — was anti-intellectual, short-sighted, hedonistic and mediocre. Salvation, such as it was, lay in an escape from the artificial rationality of suburban existence, and in a rediscovery of the essentially natural rhythms of life, which an industrial civilization can obscure but never eliminate.

Ironically, however, the realities of suburban life were changing even while the *Meanjin* writers were taking aim at their rigid one-dimensional stereotypes. By the early 1970s, the environmentalist movement was influencing at least some "suburban" values. Bumper-stickers about saving seals and whales and fighting for wilderness areas, together with political slogans showing acute concern about nuclear technology, global poverty or the exploitation of women, now adorned the motor-cars; and the cars themselves were fuel-efficient and pollution-free, and still cleaned on Sunday mornings. Native plants and obsolete craft skills were re-discovered, and new kinds of suburban community groups were formed to enhance the quality of social life or to change it. All such departures from the complacent, artificial rationality of the suburban stereotypes have made suburbia a little less easy to caricature. Perhaps they raise the question of whether the stereotypes were ever very accurate. Moreover, they call into question the kind of distinction between minority culture and mass civilization on which so much anti-suburban thinking seems to have been based.

4. *Anti-suburbanism and Class*

Quite apart from the intellectual élitism of the minority culture, however, suburbia has been a target for intellectuals who adopt Marxist perspectives. Marxism has two basic quarrels with suburbanism, one cultural and the other social. Philosophically, Marx opposed bourgeois liberalism on the grounds that its understanding of the nature of freedom was false, and that its emphasis on conscious rationality was deluded. Individual freedom, Marx believed, operating in a social context, produced corporate tyrannies, just as individual rationality produced corporate irrationality. True freedom was possible only within the corporate constraints of a planned, ordered, socialist society; and a humane social rationality could be achieved only through the conscious control of economic forces. This was the most sophisticated possible justification of the charge that bourgeois liberalism was based on false consciousness. Suburban culture was inauthentic, according to the Marxist critique, because its sense of individual freedom was false, and because its ostensibly rational structures were instruments of alienation and tyranny.

The history of suburbia does provide telling examples of some of the dilemmas of individualism, a fact which gives Marxist anti-suburbanism a keen philosophical cutting-edge. The lure of the suburb was based on the self-interest of individuals and families. Those who chose it sought a freer, less regimented, more natural life-style. Or so it was in the beginning. As Lewis Mumford has written,

> While the suburb served only a favoured minority, it neither spoiled the countryside nor threatened the city. But now the drift to the outer ring has become a mass movement, it tends to destroy the value of both environments without producing anything but a dreary substitute, devoid of form and even more devoid of the original suburban values.[26]

Without sharing the implied approval of the original suburban values, Marx would have appreciated this example of individual freedom of choice based on conscious rationality producing an unlooked-for social irrationality.

It is at the level of social structure, however, that Marxists (and left-wing intellectuals in general) mount their most insistent attack on suburbia. In a witty and perceptive article, "Heaven and a Hills Hoist: Australian Critics on Suburbia", Tim Rowse noted in 1978 the significance of Sir Keith Hancock's insight, half a century earlier, that "there are no classes in Australia except in an economic sense".[27] Hancock had found an arresting way of saying that while the structural prerequistes of a class society existed in Australia, powerful cultural forces operated to stifle the development of genuine class consciousness. Rowse, for his part, was concerned to point out that "suburbia" was not, in the final analysis, separable from the realities of class exploitation. There are "profound connections", he argued, "between the exploitation of labour at work and in the home, a connection now being explored by Marxist feminists".[28]

Yet Rowse could not deny that, although the latent class divisions in Australian society might be strong, there has been an "undeniably strong tendency for these divisions to be obscured in the forms of life led outside the workplace". Suburbanism, the most pervasive of the forms of life led outside the Australian work-place, is thus seen as a cultural system opposed to class. If the life of inner-city working-class suburbs does not quite fit this implied opposition between "suburbia" and class, the individualistic, domestic, consumer-oriented, emulative values of workers who have moved their families into the housing estates and lower-priced suburbs of the outer dormitory areas of Australian cities does certainly seem to confirm it. That suburbanism means *embourgeoisement* is hard to deny. John Anderson, doyen of Sydney's radical intellectuals for a generation, gradually abandoned his original view of the working classes as somehow emancipated from the alienation of the mainstream bourgeois culture, and came to the view by the 1950s that "bourgeois values" had become "most rampant in the proletariat".[29] It was a perception that left-wing intellectuals shared, and it helps explain their anti-suburbanism.

But there is a twist to the story. Regrettably (in the eyes of such critics), there has been a nationalistic element in the obfuscation of class conflict. Since 1955, Barry Humphries has created a series of characters, including archetypal suburbanites like Edna Everage and Sandy Stone, and through them has been able to secure the attention of many sections of the intelligentsia. Humphries himself is no friend of what he calls "Australia's vast and unexplored suburban tundra",[30] but his characters, and Edna especially, have come to symbolize a certain indigenous Australianism that has made them widely endearing. In *Australian Liberalism and National Character*, Rowse has observed that "for many Australian intellectuals pride in Australian culture has always been a temptation to be resisted". But he also concedes ruefully that the temptation to take a "cockeyed pride" in Edna Everage has often proved irresistible.[31]

The reason is obvious. As Australian intellectuals painfully exorcized their inherited "colonial cringe", there was a powerful nationalistic urge to welcome almost any manifestation of a distinctively local character. But for those with left-wing ideological commitments, the discovery of "Australianness" in suburbia was unacceptable on openly political grounds. Rowse states explicit ideological objections to scholars who "use 'suburbia' as a defining image of Australian society". For by so doing, he explains, they "lend their support to this obscuring of class conflict".[32]

This is perilously like calling on intellectuals to pretend that something pernicious is not there, in the hope that, ignored, it might go away. But is it hard to imagine how anti-suburban strategies will ever make suburban Australians conscious of a class predicament they do not feel. On this point Hugh Stretton's *Capitalism, Socialism and the Environment*, one of the few scholarly works in Australia to portray suburbia in more or less positive terms, has wise words for what he calls the "hard" socialists who, seeing the masses "seduced" by capitalism, respond by "doubling their distrust of ownership". "It does not occur to them", says Stretton,

> that the house and garden and car turn people away from the party of equality chiefly because the party of equality officially despises the house and garden and car, and the life they allow.[33]

Stretton himself accepts the attitudes and values of suburban culture on their own terms. Privatization, material comforts, and segmental cultural attachments and social commitments, might blunt the sense of horizontal social solidarities and vertical social antagonisms that lead to class-consciousness; but this does not make them undesirable in themselves. Of much-maligned Australian suburbanites, Stretton concludes simply:

> Most of them do not wish to divide most of their time between cocktail parties and avant-garde theatre; to have to choose between watching television in a landless apartment and socializing in strictly public places. They want a much more complicated pattern of diverse activities, private and familial and social and public, including a great many active, productive, creative activities. They also know ... that their outgoing social lives will be better in proportion as their home resources are individual and good, *not* standardized and poor.[34]

5. *Anti-suburbanism and Feminism*

The notion that suburban culture is anti-feminist parallels the idea that it is anti-class. The suburban ideal involves a separation of the arena of domestic life from the arena of work and business; but while most men participate in both, many women suburbanites are ascribed a relatively segmental form of social existence. Their work in the domestic sphere can be regarded as unpaid (although trends in divorce settlements complicate this aspect of the analysis); there is certainly a good deal in the argument that suburban housewives form a great, hidden, oppressed labour-force, unprotected by unionization, unrequited by the satisfactions arising from formal criteria of skill and competence, and bereft of vital rights of job-portability and economic independence. When the housewife does get a job in the formal economy, she is still too often a "working mother", and her income a "second income", Her essential roles as wife and mother prescribe for her a home-oriented life-style, and this sets her apart both from her husband and from unmarried females, each of whom, in their own way, seems to enjoy social variety.

For feminists, the equivalent of that false consciousness that obscures class realities is the view that women are the beneficiaries of suburbia, not the victims. The debate is not about the centrality of domesticity in suburban culture; it is about different ways of understanding the reality. Suspicions about domesticity easily spill over into a generalized anti-suburbanism. Indeed, anti-suburbanism has some of its deepest roots in a modern Romantic literature associating domesticity with philistinism. Mumford, expanding on the idea that "the suburb serves as an asylum for the preservation of illusion", wrote:

> Here domesticity could flourish, forgetful of the exploitation on which so much of it was based. Here individuality could prosper, oblivious of the pervasive regimentation below. This was not merely a child-centred environment: it was based on a childish view of the world, in which reality was sacrificed to the pleasure principle.[35]

Mumford's sociological insights left room for the concept of exploitation, but other critics sometimes see only the domesticity itself.

The domestic character of the suburban environment — with its connotations of animal-like procreation, its stifling effects on individuality — became a specific object of contempt. Domesticity was itself an enemy, and so too were women and children, for in them "normality" was enshrined, with all its mediocre values and concerns. As Samuel Beckett's character, Murphy, put it, women "can't love for five minutes without wanting it abolished in brats and house bloody wifery".[36] In this way, the "normality" of home and family, generational interaction, and all the accompanying economic realities of bourgeois society, could be seen, in Kierkegaard's words, as the "modern tyranny".[37] It was an analysis with which, strangely, feminists and anti-feminists might both agree, and alike condemn suburbia as the environment where the tyranny was most entrenched.

Objectively, both the idea of woman as beneficiary and the idea of woman as victim recognize that suburban society tends to define the social and cultural horizons of women (and children) more completely than it does those of men. This has been true even since middle-class women began to enter the work-force in greater numbers. But what does it signify? There is simply too much testimony, and not only from feminists, describing the suburban housewife as "bored", "depressed', "frustrated" or "alienated", for the criticism to be ignored. But there is counter-evidence as well. What little research has been done does not neatly endorse the stereotypes. For example, when in 1981 Sydney University's Community Research Centre conducted a large-scale social survey of the Baulkham Hills Shire in Sydney's western suburbs, it found that, in general,

> the wives preferred their suburban roles as full-time mothers. Few were anxious to return to the workforce despite the fact that a high proportion of them had tertiary qualifications.[38]

How typical these women were we simply do not know in the absence of further research, and how to interpret the views they expressed raises problems of theory as well as matters of fact. But their apparent contentment is a reminder that Stretton's controversial conclusions cannot be ignored. "You do not have to be a mindless conformist to choose suburban life", he wrote in 1976.

> Most of the best poets and painters and inventors and protesters choose it too. It reconciles access to work and city with private, adaptable, self-expressive living space at home. Plenty of adults love that living space, and sub-divide it ingeniously. For children it really has no rivals.[39]

For an Australian scholar these were brave, fighting words, inviting fresh efforts to distinguish the myths of suburbanism from the realities of suburban life.

Imagery and reality often diverge very widely. Any attempt to describe suburbia, rather than simply to explore the lure of the suburban lifestyle, would no doubt entail considerable qualification to all the stereotypes. A social geography of suburbia, for example, would reveal, at any period of Australian suburban history, marked variations in lifestyle, settlement patterns, affluence, and architecture. Socio-economic imperatives, notably pressures on working-class wives to join the work-force, have meant that the stereotypes of domesticity have never been more than approximately valid. The recreational customs of Australian men have frequently transformed the homecoming of the "breadwinner" into something less than the celebration of domestic bliss. With the passing of a pioneer generation, a new suburb filled with young adults and children becomes a place where the older residents, now grandparents and pensioners, live alongside a second generation of new young home-makers. The second-generation suburb thus inherits the problems of homogeneity lost.

For this reason, in trying to account for anti-suburbanism it is worth considering the possibility that a good deal of ignorance is involved. Confronted with apparently irreconcilable stereotypes of smug complacency on the one hand, and chronic depression on the other, there is reason to question the empirical basis of the judgments. And when Ronald Conway, in *The Land of the Long Weekend* (1978), pictured Australian suburbs as "dotted" with "nervy housewives" and "crowded with flatulent, faceless men who know even less about themselves than about the women they married", he surely begged the question of whether lack of awareness might work both ways.[40]

For recognizing faces in crowds can be dependent on closeness to the crowd; "facelessness" can be a misnomer for poor observation. There is interesting recent evidence suggesting that Australian life is richer, more varied, more critical, more "cultured" — in the conventional sense — than the stereotypes of Australian society would suggest. A survey commissioned by the Australian Council of the Arts discovered, in a typical cross-section of the population (most of them, therefore, suburbanites), good reasons to modify the conventional picture of a smug, privatized, dull, domestic suburbia. The importance of home, family and domestic privacy was indeed confirmed, and the five most popular leisure activities were listening to the radio or music at home, reading books and magazines, sight-seeing and picnicking, gardening and do-it-yourself home-improvements. At the same time, however, more than 50% of the sample expressed an interest in the visual arts, notably traditional Australian paintings, crafts, photography, and prints and drawings; more than 40% claimed to be interested in music; two people in every three expressed an interest in the performing arts; and the 29.7% who valued involvement in competitive sports only just out-numbered those going to classical music and serious plays and theatre.[41] Did many of the respondents to the survey lie? and if so, why did they tell these lies? The tribe still awaits its anthropologist as well as its Orwell; and in the meantime, it is plausible to suppose that anti-suburbanism is based partly on ignorance or misconception. Barry Humphries' "vast suburban tundra" is indeed largely unexplored.

1985

Notes

1 *Historical Records of New South Wales*, I, Part 2 Phillip, 1783-1792, Sydney, 1892, 147-8.

2 F.C. Howe, *The City, the Hope of Democracy*, New York, 1905, p.35.

[3] A. Birch and D.S. Macmillan (eds.), *The Sydney Scene, 1788-1960*, Melbourne, 1962, p.166; G. Davison, *The Rise and Fall of Marvellous Melbourne*, Melbourne, 1979, pp.11-14; M. Neutze, *Urban Development in Australia*, Sydney, 1977, pp.20-46; C.T. Stannage, *The People of Perth*, Perth, 1979, pp.240-43.

[4] R.E.N. Twopeny, *Town Life in Australia*, London, 1883 (reprinted, Melbourne, 1973), p.26.

[5] J.A. Froude, *Oceana*, London, 1886; quoted by A. Briggs, *Victorian Cities*, Harmondsworth, 1968, p.59.

[6] C.E.W. Bean, *The Official History of Australia in the War of 1914-1918*, I, Sydney, 1936, p.43.

[7] *The Rise and Fall of Marvellous Melbourne*, p.140.

[8] Quoted by Davison, ibid., p.139.

[9] T. Brennan, "Urban Communities", in A.F. Davies and S. Encel (eds.), *Australian Society*, Melbourne, 1965, p.304.

[10] M.S. Marsh and S. Kaplan, "The Lure of the Suburbs", in P.C. Dolce (ed.), *Suburbia: The American Dream and Dilemma*, New York, 1976, p.38.

[11] D. Horne, *The Lucky Country*, Penguin ed., 1964, p.25.

[12] ibid.

[13] D.H. Lawrence, *Women in Love*, London, 1954, p.223.

[14] H. Marcuse, *One-Dimensional Man*, London, 1968, p.234.

[15] Louis Esson, *The Time in not yet Ripe* (ed. by P. Parsons), Sydney, 1973, p.73. See also, D. Walker, *Dream and Disillusion*, Canberra, 1976, pp.24-30.

[16] For a fuller analysis, see Walker, ibid., pp.1-10.

[17] D.H. Lawrence, *Kangaroo*, Harmondsworth, 1950, pp.32-3.

[18] ibid., p.33.

[19] G. Johnston, *My Brother Jack*, London, 1964, p.259.

[20] ibid., p.258.

[21] F.R. Leavis, *Mass Civilization and Minority Culture*, London, 1930, pp.3-4.

[22] ibid., p.5.

[23] ibid.

[24] C. Brentano, *The Eternal Philistine* (1810); quoted by H.H. Hugo (ed.), *The Romantic Reader*, Harmondsworth, 1977, pp.475-77.

[25] "Godzone" Series, *Meanjin*, XVV, 1966, 373.

[26] L. Mumford, *The City in History*, New York, 1961, p.506.

[27] T. Rowse, "Heaven and a Hills Hoist: Australian Critics on Suburbia", *Meanjin*, XXXVII, 1978, 12.

[28] ibid.

[29] *Australian Highway*, September 1958, 75; quoted by J. Docker, *Australian Cultural Elites*, Sydney, 1974, p.139.

[30] *An Evening's Intercourse with the Widely-liked Barry Humphries*, Pan Enterprises Programme, Her Majesty's Theatre, Melbourne, 1981.

[31] Rowse, "Heaven and a Hills Hoist", loc. cit., 8.

[32] ibid., 4, 5, 12.

[33] H. Stretton, *Capitalism, Socialism and the Environment*, Cambridge, 1976, p.202.

[34] H. Stretton, *Ideas for Australian Cities*, North Adelaide, 1970, p.39.

[35] Mumford, *The City in History*, p.494.

36 For an exposition of Kierkegaard's view see R. Currie, *Genius*, London, 1974, pp.88-115.

37 Quoted by Currie, ibid., p.175.

38 *Sydney Morning Herald*, 27 May, 1981; see *Sun-Herald*, 16 September, 1984, for recent conflicting evidence.

39 Stretton, *Ideas for Australian Cities*, pp.20-21.

40 R. Conway, *Land of the Long Weekend*, Melbourne, 1978, p.88.

41 Australian Council of the Arts, *Australians' Attitudes to the Arts*, Sydney, 1981, *passim*.

"COUNTRYMINDEDNESS" – THE SPREAD OF AN IDEA

DON AITKIN

This is a reflective essay, rather than the discussion of findings based on recent research. My own work on rural politics began in the late 1950s and ended ten years later.[1] In the 1970s research in political science shifted into new areas, and the exploration of Australian political institutions, particularly the political parties and their environment, rather declined. It was not that all the important work had been done – we still do not have a good book on the A.L.P., for example – but that areas like public policy, somewhat neglected in the past, attracted more attention. And there are not many Australian political scientists, and not all of them by any means are fascinated by Australian politics.

One of the questions which was not answered in the 1970s, though it arose from the findings of the research of the 1960s, was how the Country Party came to play such a major part in Australian politics after 1920, even though it was the smallest of the three major parties. From 1919, it shared in power for 43 of the next 64 years; when out of office it conserved its strength and maintained its coherence; it had a profound effect upon the direction of economic policy, especially after 1949; and in time its major rivals found themselves incorporating essential parts of its platform and policy, in order to have credence in the countryside.

The Country Party was above all an "ideological" party, a fact not recognized for fifty years, partly because virtually all commentators on politics were from the city, and for them country people almost by definition were unsophisticated. The political party of country people, therefore, was portrayed as a simple, sectional grouping selfishly pursuing the economic aims of a small minority of Australians and devoid of higher motives or greater interest. Part of the cause lay also in the fact that Australian politics generally were seen as rather grubby, all about economics, and inferior in intellectual meaning to the titanic struggles between sets of ideas that were presumed to go on somewhere else. For those who felt this way even the A.L.P. was hardly ideological in character, while the Liberal Party was outside serious consideration.

These days, the cultural cringe embodied in that kind of outlook has largely disappeared, and more attention has been given to the ideological complexity of the parties, even the despised Liberals. But there remains a certain indifference to, even condescension towards, the Country Party, or National Party as it is now styled. This exists among citizens at large, just as among critics and commentators. The party is described as "not really a party" or just the "rural rump of the Liberals"; it is commonly criticized as "too powerful" or "too greedy for power".[2] But hardly anyone outside the party talks about what it stands for. And that is something of a puzzle, because what it stands for is clear enough, and has been clear for well over half a century.

The word that came to describe its view of the world was "countrymindedness". The origins of that word are not certain, but my guess is either that Earle Page heard it and popularized it, or that it was coined by one of the Country Party's editor-journalists, perhaps E.C. Sommerlad or V.C. Thompson. In either case, the word came to be popular in the late 1920s or early 1930s. It was much more than just a tribal chant, for, to make the point again, the Country Party was more than just a tribe (though it profited from a tribal feeling) and much more than just an economic pressure-group. It had developed an ideology of its own.

I take an ideology to be a system of values and ideas that among other things presents a more or less extensive picture of the good society, and of the policies and programmes necessary to achieve it; distinguishes goodies from baddies; accounts for the historical experience of a group; and appears as "truth" to that group while being at least plausible to outsiders. Ideologies, unlike philosophies, obtain their force very much from social experience; they cannot be proved wrong, partly because they are sufficiently elastic to accommodate awkward facts.

The concentration on the group is important.[3] There has been a good deal of debate among political scientists about the utility of a term like "political culture" because it is too much of a black box, like "hegemony".[4] But some of that criticism is muted if the political culture, or ideology, is firmly connected to a specific group. Farmers and graziers form an easily identified and relatively firmly bounded group, while "country people" can be defined in various ways and form another larger group. Both partook of "countrymindedness".

The elements of the ideology are not hard to establish. They had a number of origins, and a powerful emotional engine was available to drive the whole ideology, which was one reason why it achieved the importance it did. In its high period, roughly 1925-1960, the elements were these:

(i)   Australia depends on its primary producers for its high standard of living, for only those who produce a physical good add to a country's wealth.

(ii)   Therefore all Australians, from city and country alike, should in their own interest support policies aimed at improving the position of the primary industries.

(iii) Farming and grazing, and rural pursuits generally, are virtuous, ennobling and co-operative; they bring out the best in people.

(iv)   In contrast, city life is competitive and nasty, as well as parasitical.

(v)   The characteristic Australian is a countryman, and the core elements of national character come from the struggles of country people to tame their environment and make it productive. City people are much the same the world over.

(vi)   For all these reasons, and others like defence, people should be encouraged to settle in the country, not in the city.

(vii) But power resides in the city, where politics is trapped in a sterile debate about classes. There has to be a separate political party for country people to articulate the true voice of the nation.

In short, "countrymindedness" was Physiocratic, populist and decentralist, but it was not at all silly or implausible. Not only that, it was able, like the Labor Party's own rival ideology, to borrow something from the emerging Australian legend. Farmers and country people generally saw themselves as practical, innovative, self-reliant, and "Australian" rather than "British".[5] The remainder of this essay sets out an argument about where "countrymindedness" came from, why it was so pervasive, and why it has recently waned.

Origins

To search for the origins of an ideology is to search for a group. It is easy to say that white Australia began as 100% urban and has remained strikingly urban since. But in fact it was not until the mid-twentieth century that urban and suburban life became the dominant or typical form of Australian residence. Before the gold rushes of the 1850s, the great majority of settlers and convicts were in country areas; and even at the end of the nineteenth century only a little more than one third of the people of N.S.W. lived in Sydney, though Melbourne was approaching the 50% mark with respect to the population of Victoria. Until the 1860s, most rural occupation was pastoral, but the rapid increase of population in the 1850s brought an increased demand for food as well as the opportunity to settle more people on the land. (It is worth remembering that by this stage the Australian colonies had been involved in directed immigraton for some thirty years.)

From 1860 to 1890, there was an economic boom of familiar proportions, and it was founded on rural growth. The American Civil War led to an increased demand for wool, European industrialization produced an increased demand for wheat, and in the later years technological improvements allowed the export of meat and dairy products. There was also a developmental public-works boom, with railways, ports, roads, bridges and telegraphs changing the face and the society of the colonies. One major effect of all this was the creation and the stabilization of a large rural population. It was stabilized because by 1890 virtually all the inland agricultural land had been taken up. After 1890, rural growth occurred only in small degree — in some dairying areas, as a result of irrigation schemes, and to accommodate returned soldiers.

The great boom, growing even headier in the 1880s, produced very high expectations that were based on extraordinary prices: £1,000 an acre was paid for urban land in country towns in the late 1870s. The bust that followed in 1890-1 and ushered in the depression of the 1890s was disastrous everywhere; but when the depression was over, and growth began again, it did not take place to any great extent in country areas. As we have seen, the depression had coincided with a natural end to growth, for good reason. Not only that, the railway octopus had brought harm as well as good to the countryside, by killing local industries that could not compete against cheaper goods brought up the line from the city or from overseas.

We know now that Australia was not going to support a closely settled yeomanry and a pattern of small, close towns and cities on the American model. Our climate and soil will not sustain such a population at Australian standards of living. But that was not so clear in 1890 — indeed, it would have seemed a heresy had anyone spoken such a message. Yet some of the signs were available: country people were complaining as early as 1870 about the loss of their sons and daughters to the big city.

Again, we know now that the large families generated in the second half of the nineteenth century because of rapidly declining infant mortality were not containable within the countryside, because the farms were not divisible, there was no new land to take up, and the industries of the towns had been destroyed by railway-borne competition. But it did not seem so obvious to country people then. The failure of their areas to expand in population and wealth, after more than a generation of steady growth and high expectation, was most upsetting, and country people looked for an explanation of their predicament in their political economy — as many others before them and since have done.

The Group's Self-identification

The establishment of railways and the telegraph created a colony-wide polity out of what had been simply a scattered population. In similar fashion, it made working people aware of their common interests and common problems, and country people aware of theirs. Railways and telegraphs assisted in the development of a country newspaper network.

Country people were aided in coming together politically by the fact that they did not compete, or competed in only a marginal way. Almost all the wool and much of the wheat was sold overseas, and there was not much product variation. So there was a natural community of interest without the suspicion induced by competition. And there were common enemies (powerful and oligopolistic wheat-buyers, and governments who controlled land rents and taxes as well as railway freight charges) and common anxieties like drought or flood.

In the 1880s and 1890s, across all the colonies, farmers and graziers began to set up what we would now call "interest groups" to represent to governments the economic concerns of their members. Before very long, and for good reason, these groups were putting forward "political" views, and articulating a "country versus city" perspective. In 1891, the first parliamentary Labor Party was formed in N.S.W., which indicated that a colony-wide outlook now existed among voters. In 1893, the first parliamentary "Country Party" was established. It was not as successful as the Labor Party, and did not last for long, because its members found that there were too many issues on which their point of view was not relevant.

In the new century, the organized farmers and graziers became more powerful and more representative, and grew less happy with the political order. Federation had pushed the issue of free trade and protection up to the national level, where protection had a decisive victory. Farmers' costs rose at a time when increasing international competition in the foods and fibres that Australia produced lowered the level of prices. Although the phrase had yet to be voiced, farmers and graziers found themselves caught in a "cost-price squeeze". They were not cheered by the establishment of the arbitration system, which they saw as a device for protecting the wages of city people at the expense of those who lived in the country.

The Great War curtailed the export trade, and afterwards Australia discovered that some of its traditional markets had gone: the war had enhanced European agriculture, and encouraged the development of substitutes like margarine. Postwar recovery in Australia occurred much faster in the cities than in the countryside.

From 1890 to 1920, the self-perception by country people that they were different, and had different interests, and were vulnerable, grew steadily. Finally, their organizational leaders decided that the time had come for them to go political. This happened soon after the war, though in Western Australia it occurred a few years earlier. In most cases the intervention in electoral politics was instantly successful, and a share in government followed not long after. From the early 1920s, the Country Party has been a major and successful political force.

The party's ideology, advanced rather diffidently at first, became more and more confident, until it had the status of a "settled policy". Even the A.L.P., overwhelmingly an urban party after the establishment of the Country Party, found it necessary to put on a rural face and draw attention to its rural clothes. This state of affairs continued until 1972 in Federal politics, when Whitlam and the Labor Party won office on a policy which paid scant attention to rural concerns and without winning more than a few rural seats.

The Success of the Ideology

Two very different human processes underlie the success of the Country Party's ideology: the transmission of information and values from parents to children, and the movement of population.

The first requires little comment. Children tend to acquire the social and political values of their parents as naturally as they learn to speak or to recognize which piece of cutlery is used for which dish. Of course, not everything is learned in that way, and children reject, consciously and unconsciously, some of the influences that come from their parents. Yet it is that transmission which is basic to the continuation of human societies in recognizable form; it is basic, to give a pointed example, to the way in which children coming of age in the mid-1980s decide that they "are" Labor, Liberal or National, almost a century after those political labels first began to acquire their meaning.

Once the idea of "countrymindedness" was established in the countryside, say from 1890 on, it was inevitable that the idea would be passed on. It was a very satisfying ideology anyway, and one which reinforced local pride and feeling. It was one for which other sustaining institutions were in process of development, such as country versus city sporting contests, "Country Week" in tennis and other sports, the Country Women's Association, the country radio-network of the A.B.C. and its "Country Hour", country abattoirs (or "country killing centres", as they are known in the trade), country wool-auction centres, and so on.

Not only that, the "metropolitan primacy" of four of the six states and the pattern of settlement in Queensland meant that the contrast was always between "Sydney and the bush". A country person instinctively compared the metropolis to his or her town or village or farming area, always with a mixture of envy and anger. Those contrasts still exist, even if they have been muted by affluence.

Yet the Country Party was only one of three parties able to win seats in the country, and the urban proportion of the Australian population grew at almost every census until the 1970s. How did the ideology come to have such an effect in the cities?

The answer lies in the movement of population after 1850. In the second half of the nineteenth century, there was a large immigration into Australia, which was repeated after the second world war. It seems that in both periods the immigrants have preferred life in the cities. Moreover, it is likely that many of the nineteenth-century immigrants had a somewhat Arcadian view of cities and of Australia. Both Graeme Davison and Coral Lansbury have pointed to the anti-city, pro-country views of immigrants who nevertheless preferred to live in Sydney and Melbourne.[6] It was, after all, London which was the archetypal city, and they were a long way from that. The reception of "countrymindedness" was more favourable than it might have been, then, partly because a substantial proportion of city-dwellers came from overseas and knew little about the bush (even Henry Lawson made only one trip into the countryside as a grown man). It is curious, to say no more, that the great popularizers of the bush were urban writers.

Immigrants were important, but the surplus rural population was even more so. From about 1870 on, a steady flow of country people made their lives in the cities. They were the sons and daughters of farmers, rural workers and country townspeople, who could not find work, or sought education, or were restless. The drift to the city has continued for a century, and shows no sign of ending, even if it has been balanced recently by a flow in the opposite direction.

The drift meant that the "country cousin" was a real, rather than a mythic figure. John Barrett found that 55% of an admittedly small Melbourne sample in 1972 had either grown up on a farm or in a country town or had some comparable tie.[7] My own national survey of 1967 showed an even more powerful phenomenon: movement in both directions. About a third of those born in the country had left for the cities, while about a sixth of those born in the cities had gone to the country. The 1967 metropolitan electorates contained 19% country-born, the rural electorates 17% city-born.[8] If we can assume that these proportions were not greatly different over the preceding 80 years, we have a major contribution to a plausible hypothesis about the dominance of "countrymindedness" as an Australian ideology.

And finally, we ought not to ignore its elements of common sense. Generations were taught that Australia rode to prosperity on the sheep's back. For the first 70 years of this century at least, country themes and figures were woven into the image that the outside world had of Australia; and it was not very dissimilar to the image that Australians had of themselves. "Countrymindedness" may have been ignored as an ideology simply because it was taken so much for granted.

Decline

The ideology is dominant no longer, as will be evident to anyone who has lived through the last thirty years. From about the time of the departure from politics of the last great country leader, Sir John McEwen, in 1971, "countrymindedness" lost ground. There is of course no sharp line in these matters. But the post-war expansion of Australian population and affluence carried with it the causes of the decline.

First, the large post-war immigration consisted of people who flocked to the cities but had no Arcadian view of the country. Second, from the 1960s, the cost-price squeeze and the widening horizons of country people meant that the family farm, the economic unit that had underpinned the ideology, went into a decline: thousands of farmers left the land, and thousands of farmers' sons chose other occupations for themselves. Third, affluence and the technological changes that came with it reduced the real and psychological distance between country and city. Television, better roads and cars, and frequent air-services have tended to incorporate the countryside into the national culture and political system.

In 1972, the contribution of primary production to Australian export earnings fell below 50% for the first time; for most of this century it had been around 90%. The exploitation of mineral resources had, apparently permanently, changed one of the bases of Australia's political economy. In that same 1972, Labor for the first time won office without a substantial addition of country seats. In 1976, the relative decline of the country could be seen to have slowed to a halt, and 1981 brought the first census in which the rate of growth of the country population was faster than the city rate. Between 1975 and 1983 the Country Party changed its name to "National Party", the timing differing from State to State; in some areas there was an intermediate change to "National Country Party". The new party is not yet different in personnel or in programme, but it no longer emphasizes "countrymindedness". There is a constituency, but it is too small to rely on if the party is to survive.

In my judgment "countrymindedness" is finished as an ideology, even though its institutional and administrative arrangements will continue indefinitely. The group has lost its cohesion, and it has also lost its relative size, while the city populations contain a declining proportion of those with rural backgrounds. The proportion of those who were born in the cities of parents who themselves were born in the cities is increasing. Like other aspects of Australia's history the ideology may have a future as part of the romantic past, but it has ceased to have power in the practical present. Yet it did have a great run.

1985

Notes

[1] I was not one of the originators of the study of rural politics in Australia, since Ulrich Ellis, Henry Mayer, Joan Rydon, Don Rawson and especially Bruce Graham, from whom I learned a great deal, were all before me. Most of my work in this field is either summed up or referred to in *The Colonel: A Political Biography of Sir Michael Bruxner*, Canberra, 1969; and *The Country Party in New South Wales: A Study of Organisation and Survival*, Canberra, 1972.

[2] See my *Stability and Change in Australian Politics*, Canberra, 2nd edition, 1982, pp.65-7.

[3] Here I have been much influenced by social anthropologists like Mary Douglas: see, for example, *Essays in the Sociology of Perception*, London, 1982.

[4] For a statement of what Australian political culture might include see Colin A. Hughes, "Political Culture", in Henry Mayer and Helen Nelson, (eds.), *Australian Politics — A Third Reader*, Melbourne, 1973. For a trenchant criticism of the utility of the concept, see Tim Rowse, "Political Culture: A Concept and its Ideologues", in Graeme Duncan (ed.), *Critical Essays in Australian Politics*, Port Melbourne,1978.

[5] This is probably too simple. There were farmers who saw themselves as "Australian" pure and simple; there were some who saw themselves as "British" and "Australian" at once and saw no contradiction; there were some who saw themselves as "British" first and "Australian" second; there were others for whom Britain was always "home". After the first world war, I should think, the first group was much the largest.

[6] Graeme Davison, "Sydney and the Bush: an Urban Context for the Australian Legend", *Historical Studies*, XVIII, 1978, 191-209; Coral Lansbury, *Arcady in Australia: the Evocation of Australia in Nineteenth-Century English Literature*, Melbourne, 1970.

[7] John Barrett, "Melbourne and the Bush: Russel Ward's Thesis and a La Trobe Survey", *Meanjin*, XXXI, 1972, 462-70.

[8] *Stability and Change*, pp.190-2.

EGALITARIANISM

JOHN HIRST

"Egalitarianism — see under myths": so runs the index entry in a standard sociological text on Australian society, and it illustrates a stock way of handling this vexed question.[1] One can understand the despair behind this approach — why won't the populace who believes this is an egalitarian society read the books on social stratification and class formation? To this there may be an obvious answer. While historians are also interested in the development of myth, for them egalitarianism has a more substantial existence. The desire for equality in social, political and economic realms has been a major force in our history, with results that are quite palpable.

One of the difficulties of the term is the variety both of the equalities which have been sought and the standards by which they have been measured. This even applies to historians or sociologists studying egalitarianism in Australia, who have not always made their own positions clear enough or taken care to separate them from those of the people they are studying. Some egalitarians, for example, seek equality of opportunity: they regard unequal outcomes in wealth and social prestige as acceptable so long as all have an equal chance of obtaining them. To egalitarians of another sort such outcomes are unacceptable: they wish to see equal material outcomes, or at least no gross differences in material rewards between various occupations. There have been egalitarians of these two sorts both in our history and among the observers of our society. Those who deride the view that Australia is an egalitarian society point to the undoubted existence of class structures and status hierarchies. On the other hand, Australians who claim their society is egalitarian may believe that opportunity is open to all or be pleased that people of different status address each other as equals and that everyone has the vote. This introduces two other kinds of equality: that of manners, and that of political rights. The failure to distinguish between various forms of egalitarianism has not only produced confusion; it has precluded discussion of the relationship between them, now and in the past. I don't intend to offer here anything like a full account of egalitarianism in our history. The paper gives some impressions derived from my study of nineteenth-century New South Wales society, and it bears mainly on equality of opportunity, of political rights, and of manners. Much of the paper is concerned with some of the inequalities that developed when equality of opportunity was the ideal.[2]

I

Egalitarianism, in the sense of opportunity for all regardless of birth, has rightly been considered as something which the great bulk of the free migrants of the mid-nineteenth century wanted to see enshrined in the new country. Any attempt to recreate here a closed system of privilege was fiercely resisted. Nominated members of Legislative Councils were anathema to a generation brought up on the battles against Old Corruption. Wentworth's attempt to found a colonial aristocracy for his constitution was laughed out of court. The terms on which squatters held their land were seen as an attempt to restrict land ownership to a few hands, and (worse) to re-establish a feudal order of lords and serfs. The squatters were relentlessly pursued and politically crushed. The land, the prime resource of colonial society, was thrown open to all.

There is a widespread view, to which serious historians have given support,[3] that the migrants were also egalitarian in another sense: having escaped an old world society, they are said to have been opposed to the creation here of a society of deference, ranks and titles. On this view, the history of the egalitarianism of manners would begin at this point. On the face of it, there are grounds for doubting this. The old society which denied migrants their opportunities would also have ingrained in them its own signs of success. In so far as the motive for migration is the desire for social advancement, a society of migrants will not forget the old marks of social pre-eminence.

Political democracy was not part of the old world, and its establishment in New South Wales in the 1850s might be thought to signal an acceptance of the intrinsic worth of every man which would also have affected manners. Clearly, democracy does imply the equal worth of every man, or it may be justified in such terms, but this was not the bearing it had in New South Wales at its foundation. The introduction of political democracy was not accompanied by the establishment of a democratic ideology. There were many reasons for this, not the least of them being that the word "democracy" itself was still suspect. It had not altogether lost its associations with direct popular rule and republicanism. The Liberals could not afford to be seen as un-British in their constitutional plans, for the British constitution was still widely revered. When Wentworth had declared that he wanted a British and not a Yankee constitution, the Liberals accepted this, and argued that their plan for two elected houses was a better embodiment of the principles of the British constitution than his own, given the colony's different social composition. In this they were fortunate to have the authority of leading British statesmen, who declared that there was no longer any necessity for colonial constitutions to be closely modelled on the British. The time was past when a departure from a nominated upper house in a colonial constitution was taken as threatening to the House of Lords at home. There were also in the 1850s respectable British precedents for widening the franchise. Chartism, which had been a handicap to the cause of colonial democracy, was finally defeated in 1848. Middle class reform groups then reappeared with more limited programmes, and the cause had been taken up in the House of Commons by no less a figure than Lord John Russell, the hero of the first Reform Bill, who had now renounced his earlier view that that measure was final. These movements in British opinion were relied on heavily by the Liberals and were crucial to their success.

Such a strategy precluded the emergence of a democratic ideology that would have implied too thorough a denunciation of British society, from which the colonial constitution still had to be able to derive its authority and to which colonial society still gave its loyalty. There is a striking contrast between the fierceness with which the privileges of nominated Legislative Councillors and pastoral lessees were attacked and the gingerly approach to manhood suffrage. Indeed, the very form in which the franchise was extended indicates the limited commitment to democracy: the old property qualifications for the vote were re-tained and the manhood qualification was merely added to them.

The introduction of political democracy can best be seen as a measure adopted by those who were close to success in order to strengthen their hands for the final battle against the squatters. The supporters of manhood suffrage were warned that they would eventually become victims of the forces they were prepared to unleash. These warnings were ignored; some say because there was less reason in Australia to fear the multitude.[4] Perhaps so; but the impatience and recklessness of the aspiring migrant must also be considered. He had no care or respect for society until he had attained what he considered his proper place. This was the migrant's dilemma: would he in his destructive phase be so successful that there would be no basis finally upon which to claim the distinction he craved?

What would be the basis for distinction in colonial society was a central concern of a very perceptive lecture given in Melbourne by Archibald Michie in 1859. Michie was a Liberal, a supporter of man-hood suffrage and a defender of the Eureka rebels. He gave his lecture the rather cumbersome but pertinent title, "Colonists: Socially and in their Relations with the Mother Country".[5] It begins by welcoming those aspects of colonial society which distinguish it from England: here everyone — gentle and simple, educated or ignorant — works for his living. There is no disdain for manual labour, and no pathetic attempts by the genteel poor to keep up appearances. "The revolution set in when gentlemen began to dress sheep for the scab. The revolution surely is complete when a French marquis is driving a dray in Collingwood and the son of an English peer is in the police, and ex-fellows of colleges are in the deep sinkings of Ballarat." But these changes in fortunes and in old certainties have not established — and, Michie insists, never can establish — entire social equality. Like-minded people will want to associate with each other; and what is seen and criticized as exclusiveness is frequently no more than that. Further-more, men will continue to want to be distinguished from their fellows by titles and other marks of honour. In democratic America men grasp at any title they can lay claim to and are constantly be-captaining each other. This is a natural human vanity — and a beneficial one; for would it not be "disastrous for society —nay, could society even exist? — if we were in the mass utterly indifferent to the good or ill opinions of our fellow citizens". For Michie, the colonists were merely Britons overseas, and they should be eligible for all the titles available to the inhabitants of the United Kingdom — a surprising view for a colonial Liberal to voice while the battle against privilege still raged. Michie went so far as to put in a good word for Wentworth's peerage scheme. A peerage should perhaps only be conferred in rare cases, but the principle for which Wentworth contended was correct: a colonist held a degraded rank as a British citizen if he were deprived of the opportunity of gaining British honours.

The *Sydney Morning Herald* was delighted by Michie's lecture. Fighting a losing battle against the New South Wales Liberals, it was pleased to take up and strengthen Michie's views. The affected contempt for titles of honour, it claimed, was hypocrisy: "Social distinction is everywhere desired, and nowhere more than in democratic countries, where the passion for rising in the world is stimulated by the possibility of it."[6] Was the *Herald's* view of its enemies correct? Were the distinctions of the old society still sought in the new democracy?

II

The social distinction most readily available to the aspiring colonist was that of becoming a gentleman. Gentlemen had a distinctive dress — frockcoat, top hat, kid gloves — and received public recognition from other gentlemen.[7] Policemen were instructed to salute them.[8] In letters addressed to them and in any formal listing of names they were given the title "Esquire". Working-people addressed them as "Sir".[9]

The history of the gentleman in Australia has suffered much from the aristocratic bent of his historians. Paul de Serville in his study of Port Phillip gentlemen is much concerned with gentle birth and good family. Geoffrey Bolton associates the colonial gentleman with the ownership of broad acres.[10] By traditional English standards, these are the correct criteria to adopt; but in the colonies, gentlemen did not have to meet them. In the 1850s in New South Wales the men claiming to be gentlemen and recognized as such were squatters, landowners, merchants, bankers, professional men, chief clerks and those of independent means.[11] This rather lax conception is reflected in Burke's *Colonial Gentry* published in the 1890s — a work that both Bolton and de Serville find puzzling. De Serville takes it to task for belying its title.

> The genealogies are exiguous, often covering no more than three generations although attempts are made at times to graft new branches onto old trees. The heraldic aspects are even less impressive. An English critic pointed out that at least a third of the entrants were technically not gentlemen, lacking coats of arms. . . . Nor could the 563 odd entrants be said to compose a gentry in the accepted sense of the term, since many were not landed, much less members of historical or ancient families of the untitled nobilites.[12]

Bolton is a little more prepared to see standards relaxed but was it not, he asks, "generous to include W.O. Hodgkinson, a Micawber-like journalist and mining speculator who happened to be Minister for Mines in Queensland in 1891 and had neither wealth, permanent position, nor ancestry beyond a father who was a Mr Hodgkinson of Birmingham?"[13] No, it was not generous. He was certainly a gentleman

— as was Mr Micawber of course, once he was in Australia and had become a sheepfarmer.

The widening of the ranks of the gentleman in the colony was made possible because in England there was a long standing ambiguity about the term, pressure for widening of the ranks, and uncertainty about where the line of exclusion fell. Gentlemen were of good family and held land, but they also had to possess the gentlemanly virtues – they were scrupulously honest and considerate. A man who lacked these virtues could be described as "no real gentleman" even though he had land and an ancient lineage. But if this were so, could the practice of the gentlemanly virtues entitle one to the status of gentleman even without land and lineage? It was at this point that those without the traditional claims could exert pressure. Not that gentlemen had ever formed a closed order; old families had married new wealth, and after one or two generations, new wealth was old enough. Undoubtedly, it was now much easier, in the nineteenth century, to become a gentleman, or to seem to become one; but the uncertainty about the term was still only at the edges of a group that could be recognized clearly enough by the old criteria.[14]

In Australia the balance changed. The core of true gentlemen was small and not self-sustaining; the claimants at the edges numerous. There were enough true gentlemen to retain the rank's traditional prestige, but too few, owning too few resources, for the traditional criteria to maintain a commanding influence. Everyone in the colonies – including those with the best claims to be gentlemen – was closely involved in money-making. This was traditionally forbidden to the English gentleman, who could invest his fortune to advantage but was essentially a man of leisure, not preoccupied with money matters. If trade in sheep and cattle, or speculation in squatting runs, was allowable, on what grounds could merchants be excluded from the gentlemanly ranks? Both the Australian Club in Sydney and the Melbourne Club – the institutions of the gentlemanly élite – had merchants among their founding members.[15] No doubt these were men who came closest to the gentlemanly ideal in character and education, but their acceptance into the Clubs meant that the traditional prejudice against trade could not be used to deny gentlemanly status to other merchants. All merchants became gentlemen, even if they were not all accepted into the Clubs. The rule against trade took on a new form in Australia: it was used to draw the line below merchants and so to exclude shop-keepers. Wholesale trade was allowable to a gentleman; retail trade was not.

The groups which became gentlemen in Australia were making (or were soon to make) claims to that status in England, but there, these claims could be resisted or made to look doubtful. In Australia, they could not, with the paradoxical result that there was ultimately less uncertainty about who was a gentleman in Australia than in England. In Australia, the criteria of good family (which was particularly limiting) and land ownership disappeared; "gentleman" became the status of anyone holding a certain position in the occupational hierarchy or possessing independent means. Membership of a traditional English rank thus became available to the successful migrant of whatever background.

But one uncertainty remained. The new-made colonial gentlemen knew they were doubtful gentlemen by traditional English standards, which were overlooked in the colonies but not forgotten. The colonial gentlemen set about to meet them as best they could. By old-world standards many of these attempts were pathetic. Paul de Serville laughed at family-trees that went back only three generations; what would he think of vague references to "good yeoman stock"? Or of the ex-convict pastoralist claiming that his ancestors must have been people of some consequence because of the quality of their tombstones in the village churchyard? The gentlemen in Australian cities — merchants, bankers, company directors, professional men — frequently sought a country "estate": 10 acres, sometimes more, sometimes less, beyond the city proper where they built their mansions and villas. They worked in the city but lived in what might just be called country. The grand town house did not flourish in Australian cities, because town wealth immediately claimed gentlemanly status and tended to move out of town. In Adelaide, a country life for city gentlemen was most happily accomplished: the Adelaide Hunt Club met at the gentlemen's mansions and followed the trail over their estates and the neighbouring farms, all within sight of the city itself.

The widening of the ranks of gentlemen in the colonies was a fairly rapid but traumatic process. Gentlemen who had, or thought they had, good traditional claims to gentlemanly status regarded themselves as superior to the would-be gentlemen; but would-be gentlemen with the summit of their ambition in sight were not disposed to accept a subordinate place. They subjected any claims to superior status to remorseless analysis: How had so-and-so made his money? What was the real reason for his coming to the colony? Who were his wife's people? Such was the staple of day-to-day gossip, and often of public feuding. Men with new wealth, doubtfully acquired, could sometimes claim superior origins to those with old. Being an old family carried some status in New South Wales, but the old families were particularly vulnerable because some of the founders were of doubtful origin and all had made their money in ungentlemanly ways. Challengers could not meet the traditional criteria, but they used them to denigrate occupiers. Just because the new men could not be excluded, the contentions for place and precedence were fearsome. In small societies, where so many were parvenus and the traditional standards were being set aside, there could be no agreed basis for the ranking of gentlemen. The result was the bitter personal feuding and the litigiousness we find in early Sydney and Melbourne — and in other colonial societies where status became problematic.[16]

In England, a gentleman needed no title to have an unequivocal claim to his status. In the colony, as the traditional tests were being set aside, titles, official recognition and official position became more significant. If you could occupy an official position traditionally held by an English gentleman, then your claim to be a gentleman was more secure or precedence could be claimed over other gentlemen. In England, some men who had no other claims became gentlemen by this route — most notably, military officers. But though all officers were accepted as gentlemen, they were always eyed narrowly: there were regiments and regiments, and officers could well be rootless men, adventurers and jilters. As one officer was well pleased to find, no such suspicion attached to officers in New South Wales.[17] A captain or a lieutenant — the title itself — was something solid and certain when other old-world claims were doubtful and contentious. In this uncertainty begins the amazing career of the Australian doctor whose title meant little in England but worked wonders here.

To be received at Government House became an important acknowledgement of gentlemanly status. Government House was not a court at the apex of society. Having begun as a place where all the colony's officers and gentlemen gathered, all who became gentlemen expected to be received there. At levees, they all could go. A levee at St James's was a gathering of the kingdom's élite, who in the 1850s and 60s still wore court dress to the Palace; at Government House in Sydney, it was a gathering of the colony's gentlemen, who wore gentlemen's evening dress. Governors differed in policy about whom they invited to dinners and balls, but because invitations to Government House held such significance, the tendency was to liberality. Certainly, invitations were not left unquestioningly to the Governor's discretion. Lady Denison, whose husband was successively Governor of Van Diemen's Land and New South Wales in the 1850s, records the difficulties they had with invitations. After invitations had gone out for a ball, every day brought a number of protest letters to the A.D.C. asking whether his Excellency had heard anything prejudicial to the writer's character or whether it was considered their situation disqualified them from the honour of an invitation. Some, more indignant, wrote direct to the Governor. So vital to status was official recognition that the clerks in the Ordnance Office threatened to write home to the Board of Ordnance to complain at the indignity of being overlooked.[18]

The House of Commons was a gathering of gentlemen, and those few members who might not have been true gentlemen enjoyed the title. Before responsible government in New South Wales, the Legislative Council was similarly composed overwhelmingly of those whose gentlemanly status was already secure. After responsible government and with the introduction of manhood suffrage, men of lower status entered the parliament: small traders and dealers, shopkeepers, publicans and country newspaper proprietors. These men and all their colleagues took the title of gentleman. The securing of this status was one of the attractions of becoming an M.P. A good many Members who voted for manhood suffrage were still getting used to the feel of a top hat.

III

In England the Justice of the Peace was the epitome of the country gentleman, serving his monarch and dispensing justice to his inferiors. In New South Wales the Justices, as in England, constituted the Courts of Petty Sessions and took a large part in local administration. But the position became valued for its social prestige. In England the title of J.P. could add some lustre to a gentleman's name; in New South Wales it was the best endorsement of gentlemanly status and local pre-eminence. A place in the Commission of the Peace was therefore much coveted, and colonial success-stories did not end merely with riches, but with the hero on the magisterial bench. This, for example, was the clearest way that Dickens could signal Mr Micawber's success; indeed, the position was so especially valued by colonists just because its message was so clear not just to local eyes but to relatives and friends at home. Every aspiring emigrant was conscious of the audience he had left behind.

With responsible government the right of appointing Justices of the Peace passed from the Governor to the Ministry of the day, and the seal of gentlemanly status became one of the spoils of popular politics. Places in the Commission of the Peace were used to secure support in the House and to reward constituents — just as with roads and bridges, but with the advantage to Government that they cost nothing. The first premier, Donaldson, a Conservative, asked all Members to submit suggestions for additions to the magistracy. This resulted in 177 new appointments.[19] The Liberals who quickly supplanted the Conservatives were more prodigal. In his five years of office to 1863, Cowper, the Liberal premier, made some 800 new appointments.[20] At one time he reported he had 200 applications on his desk.[21] There was no attempt at a careful scrutiny of these candidates. When there were complaints that new magistrates could not write or make themselves understood, Cowper blandly replied that all appointments were recommended by someone. He was a master of the patronage business. He always spoke as if magistrates were appointed in order to better supply the bench of the local courts. Certainly, there were regular complaints that court business had to be postponed because magistrates did not appear. But since a position in the magistracy was sought chiefly for its social prestige, and not because men wanted to spend one day every week on the bench, appointing more magistrates did not necessarily improve attendance at the courts. The "need" for more magistrates was thus never ending.

In the country, the new Liberal appointments to the bench included store-keepers and other town business-people. These men were local leaders of the Liberal cause, but even by colonial standards had doubtful claims to be gentlemen. The existing country magistrates, chiefly landed men, were now being forced to accept them as equals. Cowper boasted that in making his appointments he broke with the usual practice of asking local magistrates whether new appointments were acceptable to them.[22] In many cases they clearly were not, and Cowper provoked the old order into a counter-revolution. Magistrates declared that they would not sit with the new men and at Goulburn and Mudgee magistrates resigned *en masse*.[23] They focused their objections on one particular appointment, declaring that the new man was unfit by social position and antecedents for the bench and was transparently being rewarded for political services. The townspeople of Goulburn and Mudgee enthusiastically supported the new appointments, and were angry that the local gentry should attempt to keep in their hands an honour which the Liberal government in Sydney was opening to them.

In the colony at large, the grounds of objection taken by the resigning magistrates — social position and antecedents — were widely condemned. But the old magistrates won these battles, though not the war. It was true, as the Goulburn magistrates alleged, that the new appointment there, the editor of the local paper, had been dismissed in his youth from the Public Service for offering to bribe his supervisor. The government could not ignore this objection, and it was for this reason, and not because he had once run a pub on the Yass road, that his commission was withdrawn. At Mudgee the new appointment, a store-keeper, had once briefly served as a police constable under the supervision of the magisterial bench of which he had now been made a member. This was the particular circumstance used by the old magistrates to support their general case against appointments of this sort. The government ignored their protest, and the newcomer would have remained on the bench had he not over-played his hand. In answering the objections made to him, he proclaimed his own gentility — his father was an Irish gentleman of "independent but not very large means", and many near relatives were peers of the realm — and attacked the antecedents of the local magistrates at their weakest point. Mr W.R. Blackman was now a land-holder, but his parents had kept a public house at Mudgee. The store-keeper magistrate declared they had been suspected of sly-grogging and that the mother of the J.P., still living, was a drunk. When threatened with legal action for libel, he publicly apologized and lost his place on the bench.

"Social position", which the protesting country magistrates made a test for the bench, was rejected by the Liberals. Cowper said the tests were character and intelligence.[24] A Select Committee that had examined the question in 1858 had opted for character and education but a requirement for formal education the premier thought too restrictive.[25] Among what survived of the Conservatives in the Legislative Assembly there was sympathy for the resigning magistrates, but given the constraints of popular politics they could not talk of "social position" with impunity. James Martin, the Conservative leader in the House, and the *Sydney Morning Herald* accepted the tests of character and education, and criticized many of Cowper's appointments for failing to meet them.[26] Under the protection of parliamentary privilege, Martin could detail his objections to new appointments. He declared that Chapman, a Sydney paper-hanger, was unfitted for the bench, but although the social slur in this reference to occupation was clear enough, Martin insisted that his objection concerned the paper-hanger's fitness and not his social position: the education a paper-hanger might receive suited him for mechanical pursuits, but not for dispensing justice. But such a test was no more acceptable than social position. Chapman's virtues were self-evident. As one of his many parliamentary defenders said, he was upright, honest and had raised himself by his own industry.[27] And what could be said against a country-town worthy, also queried by Martin, who was as well known as the town itself "for he has grown with its growth and strengthened with its strength"?[28] Education, as Cowper said, was too narrow a test. Instead, stress was laid on the virtues of shrewdness, knowledge of the world and sound common sense. A too close attention to the character and abilities actually needed to perform duties on the bench could not be allowed. Something other than a career open to talent was being contended for: a title had to be open to self-made wealth.

"Character and intelligence" rather than social position served their turn in opening the ranks of the magistracy, but they had their dangers. Strictly applied, they meant that anyone — no matter what his wealth, class or status — could be a magistrate. The ambiguity in the position of the magistrate — was he a man of a certain social rank or a man with certain abilities and qualities of character? — was similar to that surrounding a gentlman. If the virtues a gentleman should possess were made the sole defining characteristics of gentlemanly status, then gentlemen would cease to occupy a pre-eminent place in the social and economic hierarchy. Cowper's government had to face this implication of their policy when it was revealed that they had made a working-man, a lowly employee at a sheep station, into a magistrate.[29] The government was seriously embarrassed by this. No record could be found of who had made the recommendation. The government's final defence was that the appointment had been a mistake. Some Liberal supporters suggested that their enemies had smuggled the name in to discredit the government. A few bold Liberals made a show of defending a working-class appointment to preserve the integrity of the "character and intelligence" principle. But working-men were by general consent not eligible for the honour. A limit had finally been reached.

James Martin became premier in 1863, and his government undertook a revision of the magisterial lists. Its declared aims were to exclude those unfit by education, means or character; all members but one of a family in the same neighbourhood; people in active business (this would exclude shop-keepers) unless no one else was available; and those who rarely or never attended the bench. There were by now 1,250 Justices of the Peace, and Martin reduced these to 628.[30] It was generally conceded that a culling of the lists was necessary if only to exclude the dead and the departed, but a purge of these dimensions shook the social foundations. After the first howls of rage came demonstrations that the government had not been true to its own principles, and claims that it had been as much influenced by political allegiance as its predecessors. The gross inconsistencies, which even a cursory examination of the list reveals, suggests that this must have been so. The furore over the exclusions was such that Martin had to reinstate 26 of the excluded. His tampering with the Commission was partly responsible for his defeat in Parliament as soon as the House reassembled and at the election which followed. Cowper returned to power and 98 more of the purged were reinstated within twelve months.[31]

IV

How far could the democratizing of social distinction proceed? The distinctions became more defensible as access to them was widened, but would the new men so lower the tone that respect would vanish? My impression is that in the 1860s and 1870s the positions of gentleman, certainly, and of magistrate, more doubtfully, retained their prestige. With parliamentarians the case was different. There was a rapid collapse in respect for them. This was not solely a response to the widening of the social positions from which parliamentarians came, extreme though that was. A criminal record excluded a man from the magistracy but not from a seat in the House. What sealed the parliamentarians' fate was that in their deliberations they outraged the gentlemanly ideal. The House was frequently in uproar; insults and imputations were freely hurled; there was none of the restraint and good manners which should characterize the gentleman. The accounts of colonial history which describe this as the age of the bourgeoisie are a poor guide to the government and politics of the period. First, because the parliamentary benches were not filled by the solid bourgeois. As Chris Connolly concludes it is truer to say of the new Assemblies, as one Conservative did at the time, that they were made up in large part by "publicans — expiree convicts — journeymen mechanics — Wesleyan lay preachers".[32] The great merchants who had helped the Liberal movement early soon deserted to the Conservative side. Connolly described the Assembly as "middling class". Secondly, the Assembly in its deliberations did not display the sobriety which one associates with the bourgeoisie. They failed as gentlemen, which was what they claimed to be; they could not even meet the tests of decency and respectability. But to the dismay of the respectable, the larrikin members were regularly returned by their constituencies. If the "Age of the Bourgeoisie" is a poor guide to the politics of this period, the "hegemony of the mercantile bourgeoisie" is worse. The wide popular franchise gave parliament a distinctly unrespectable odour.

   Just as the respect for parliament and public life was falling, new honours became open to leading public men. An honour from the Queen was immune from the dangers which might lower the value of colonial distinctions. It came from the fount of honour herself, and it associated its local recipients with the venerable orders of the mother country. The award of imperial honours remained a prerogative of the Colonial Office.[33] It received recommendations from Governors but even these were not always acted on. Governors were lobbied by ministers, individual aspirants and their friends. In the 1860s the Australian colonies were the most clamorous for honours of all the self-governing colonies, and received the most. Since I haven't examined the situation in other colonies, I cannot be sure of the reasons for this, but I suspect that imperial honours were sought more avidly in the Australian colonies because political power had passed from the hands of the social élite. Before responsible government, a place in the Legislative Council marked a man as one of the élite. With manhood suffrage and the coming of the "middling class" to the Assembly, a place in the House, even a leading place in the House, no longer had this cachet, especially as there was a clear tendency for old wealth to shun and despise the parliament — to which in any case it had difficulty in gaining access. But what did old wealth matter, if the new political leaders could answer its taunts with royal honours?

During the 1860s the Colonial Office deliberated on how it could accommodate the growing demand for honours, chiefly from Australia. There were too few vacancies in the Order of the Bath. If the existing orders were expanded to take in the Australians, would they lose status in English eyes? If a special order were established for the colonies would Australians be prepared to accept it? Finally in 1868 the Order of St Michael and St George, which had been inherited by Britain with the Ionian Islands and which had been used to reward services in the Mediterranean, was expanded into a general colonial order. It had the advantage of a grand name and a lineage. It was to reward services for the colonies as well as in them. The first appointments to the new order included the distinguished Colonial Secretaries Lord Derby, Lord John Russell and Earl Grey. With these baits, the order was successfully launched and gratefully received in Australia.

The New South Wales Liberals took a prominent part in pressing for honours. The cabinet, meeting as the Executive Council, passed resolutions recommending particular people for honours, to the dismay of the Colonial Office which was not prepared to allow colonies to be self-governing on this issue. A continuing concern of the Liberal government was to secure an honour for its premier, Cowper. His Conservative predecessors had been honoured, even though their hold on office had been so brief; and the Liberals saw no incongruity in seeking a similar mark of royal favour for the man who had introduced manhood suffrage and swamped the Upper House.

I trust that I have said enough to show that liberal democrats, the victors of the battles against old world privilege, wished still to retain social distinctions which were marked by titles, special modes of address and of dress. Against this must be set the many features of late colonial society which shadow forth a different world, closer to our own, with less deference and more egalitarian manners. There was the independence of working-men, arising from high wages and labour shortage; the disrespect of the Irish for English pretension; the "egalitarianism tempered by the checks of respectability" that characterized the wide membership of friendly societies and mutual improvement groups; the wide support for common schooling in the new state schools.[34] There is some evidence — I wish I had more — that the only acceptable terms for social mixing were those of equality, with the result, as de Tocqueville noted in America, that cross-class socializing declined.[35] Yet for all these signs, commentators insisted on the Britishness of the colonial social order, especially in New South Wales, even while noting some aspects of life that we now take as constituent parts of our egalitarianism. Trollope referred to the maintenance of the British mode of thinking on "social position", a view not disturbed by close observation of those archetypal egalitarians, the nomad pastoral-workers whose attitude to their superiors he described as "civil".[36] Froude, who visited Australia in 1886, detected no reluctance to respect men of high rank, and declared "There is room in Australia for all orders and degrees of men", though

admittedly he did not move very far from the Government Houses and
the people he met there.[37] Twopeny observed more widely. He records
the independence of servants, and the prickliness of tradesmen if they
thought they were going to be patronized, and yet he writes confidently
of the gentlemanly order and of polite society, and takes a favourable
view of the future of the Australian aristocracy after four generations.[38]
Australia's fascination for overseas observers was its newness and its
democracy, and yet their message is that neither characteristic had had
a transforming effect on social relations. Trollope specifically drew the
comparison with the United States where

> all institutions of the country tend to the creation of a level, to that which
> men call equality, — which cannot be obtained, because men's natural gifts
> are dissimilar, but to which a nearer approach is made in America than
> has ever been effected in Europe. In Australia, no doubt and especially
> in Victoria, there is a leaning in the same direction; but it is still so slightly
> in advance of that which prevails among ourselves as to justify an observer
> in saying that the colonies are rather a repetition of England than an imitation
> of America.[39]

V

Colonial society wore a double aspect. It was a new society and by its
own standards an egalitarian one, in that opportunity was open to all
regardless of old world tests of rank and birth. But so long as success
dressed itself in traditional garb, colonial society could also look, or
be made to look, like the old world reincarnated. This was its
vulnerability. From the 1880s, a new radicalism and socialism reached
the colony from the mother culture. A democratic society committed
to equality of opportunity and the absence of old world distinctions
— like the United States — might have been largely impervious to these
forces. New South Wales with only a half-hearted commitment to
democracy, and nurturing old world distinctions, was not. Herein lies
one answer to the question which Geoffrey Bolton has asked: why did
Australia, with a social structure like the United States, acquire British
class institutions?[40] It was from this time also that the egalitarianisms
with which we are familiar were firmly established. I will briefly refer
to three of the new egalitarian forces: the Labor Party, the *Bulletin*,
and the literature of Lawson and Paterson.

Those who want to highlight the tameness of the early Labor Party
draw attention to the number of items in its first programmes concerned
with democratic reform: the abolition of plural voting, which the
retention of the old property qualifications had allowed; the relaxation
of resident qualifications to give votes to nomadic workers; the reform
of the Upper House; the introduction of the referendum.[41] Those who
want to explain Labor's success should note the great advantage it
acquired by being the first party in a democracy to be thoroughly
committed to democratic principles. It had everything to gain by
democracy becoming more complete; and its moral claim to represent
the people was greatly enhanced by advocating principles that could
not readily be denied. The party could use the principle of political

equality to assert the worth of the working-man and to claim attention for his needs. But the working-men the party sent in to parliament were always suspected of being likely to betray the cause; and for this reason, if no other, they did not put on the garb of gentlemen. Unlike some earlier members of low status, they were noted for their sobriety and attention to their duties. Previously men had used parliament to advance their own status; the effect of Labor in parliament was to dignify the working-class.

The final catch-all point of Labor's first platform read: "Any measure that will secure the wage-earner a fair and equitable return for his or her labour". "Fair and equitable": here begins the egalitarianism which Hancock traced in the pages of his *Australia*. The success of the Labor Party with that formulation derived in part from its ability to make it a democratic cause. The egalitarianism of equality of opportunity had, as we have seen, made little claim on political democracy; democracy was first fully exploited by an egalitarianism of distributive justice.

The *Bulletin* of J.F. Archibald exercised an immense influence, and yet it did not persuade Australians to renounce imperial titles or break the ties with Britain, two causes for which it campaigned relentlessly. What it conveyed more ·persuasively was a style: cheeky, irreverent, opposed to all humbug and pretence, delighting to find the hypocrite in the advocate of any cause it did not support. These attitudes are rightly taken to be widespread in Australia, and they form one of the cornerstones of the egalitarianism of manners. So integral are they to the Australian ethos that it is tempting to think that they must have been well entrenched long before the first *Bulletin* rolled off the press in 1880. Archibald himself did not think so. The natural tendency of Australians as British colonists was to toadyism and flunkeyism. He deplored the fact that while Australia was rightly expected to adopt ways and means best suited to itself for its "commerce and money-grubbing", it slavishly followed England in "politics, social relationships, and religion".[42]

Our understanding of Archibald has been greatly enhanced by Sylvia Lawson's biography, *The Archibald Paradox*, which presents him as a cosmopolitan nationalist. Archibald wanted Australia to sever its connection with the rottenness of aristocratic England, yet it was the English republican and radical movement which inspired and encouraged his republicanism. In the mid-eighties Archibald visited England, and sent back articles to the *Bulletin* on the caste, monoply, and privilege that disfigured the society which Australians called "home". In London, he had his vision of what the future held: the Liberals as a reform party were finished; it was the party of idleness, privilege and great wealth, of that "gilded bauble" the crown and of the Whig nobles with broad acres stolen from the people. A social revolution was imminent. The Labor Leagues were rallying and had plans to send working-men into the Commons. Soon there would be over 200 of them and they would wear cheap tweed suits or, better still, affront that perfumed Assembly with a grimy Crimean shirt. These men would speak for the toiling masses, the millions who lived in one room. Australians should follow this lead. The two representatives of Labor in the New South Wales Assembly were a disgrace: they had put on top hats and frock-coats, which are as "offensive ... marks of what the world calls social superiority as are stars and garters and Windsor uniforms".[43]

Archibald knew something of both sides of the coming revolution in the metropolis, and he used the standards of both in the *Bulletin* to show how pathetically provincial New South Wales was. He told the "aspiring vulgarians" who scrambled after honours and Government-House invitations what the old world thought of them. A travelling Lord, after being feted by these people in Australia, returns to his London club and says, "A very good kind of people, you know; awfully vulgar and coarse, but anxious to please".[44] But what made Australia's hankering after old-world titles and distinctions even more pathetic was that the old world itself had seen through them. The social revolution would sweep them away. Australians, to universal laughter, would be running after the "gewgaws of titles" while the rest of the world was discarding them.[45] Archibald, the man from the provinces, who knew himself the disdain for the colonial, and feared the world's laughter for his country, saw the way to make the province into a metropolis. Australia could seize its chance and become the leading democracy of the new order. Without entrenched interests and ancient wrongs, it could quickly sweep away monopoly, caste and privilege. Then the rest of the world, still struggling with these evils, would turn to Australia for inspiration and instruction.[46] To prepare Australia for this role, everything sacred had to be profaned. What we take to be typically Australian attitudes in Archibald's *Bulletin* were the responses of a cosmopolitan intellectual to a provincial culture.

The *Bulletin* made its impact through cartoons as much as text. One of its standard cartoon figures became the fat man, the bloated capitalist, dressed in top hat and frock-coat. During the coal-miners' strike of 1888, Capital as a portly gentleman first appeared in a tug-of-war with a working-man. The working-man says: "Hello! Who's the joker in the white gaiters and shiny beaver? I've never seen him down in a mine".[47] The gentleman's garb signifies fastidiousness and remoteness from the realities of toil. Many wearing this dress in Australia were self-made men who had indeed known hard toil, but that is not how they dressed themselves to appear. They wore the clothes of an English gentleman for whom it was a point of honour not to work and never to have worked. But although this dress gave a false message about background, as indeed many of its wearers wished, it was a very good guide to Labor's enemies. The cartoonists of the *Bulletin*, and later in the Labor press did not have to dress Capital up for ridicule; they found it already dressed fit to kill. There could be no doubt as to who would win in the image stakes between the soft hat and the bell-topper, and between sleeves rolled up and frock-coat. Gentleman's dress was now held up as a badge of shame. This was the cartoonists' contribution to an egalitarianism of manners.

The irony is that English gentlemen in the 1880s were abandoning the frock-coat and the top hat for ordinary street wear. Australian gentlemen were reluctant to follow this shift in fashion. Governors and their staffs, fresh from home, tried in vain to woo them from it by wearing tweeds and bowler hats, a style much less domineering than the old and more suitable to the climate.[48] Men's fashion, writes one of its historians, tends to harden into a uniform, unlike women's which is always changing.[49] Australian gentlemen might have clung to their uniform because it had assumed a greater significance in defining the gentlemanly order since the old world tests did not apply. It was this uniform that many had struggled for the right to wear. However, from the 1890s tweeds and lounge-suits did become more common. Is it too fanciful to suggest that the cartoonists had succeeded where the Governors had failed? But the cartoonists were not happy with the change. Up until World War I they still dressed Capital in top hat and frock-coat even though the real capitalist was becoming inconspicuous.

The nationalist writers of the 80s and 90s, nurtured by the *Bulletin*, must be understood as operating in the same radical milieu as Archibald. This is a point insisted on by Graeme Davison and Richard White in recent times.[50] Both have argued that Russel Ward's treatment of the writers in *The Australian Legend* is inadequate because he is too prone to regard the literature as a conduit, carrying the values and attitudes of the nomad bush-workers to a wider audience, and because he underplays the creative power of the writers themselves. Graeme Davison insists that instead of studying the bush-men as they were, a perplexing matter in itself, "we do better to begin, as we would any other exercise in the history of ideas, with the collective experience and ideas of the poets and story-writers themselves".[51] I accept all that Davison and White say in this regard. The creative writers were chiefly urban men, influenced by the social and political reform movements of their day; they reacted to an urban environment with an idealized version of country life, giving an Australian celebration of the common man which was then a vogue in European society generally. But none of this excuses us from looking at the literature itself, and considering what constraints and opportunities faced the writers whose scene was pastoral Australia. The writers who were "inventing Australia" did not work on a tabula rasa.

Tabus were broken in pastoral life which were upheld everywhere else in Australia. Gentlemen worked with their hands; they worked alongside their men; and in pioneering days at least wore the same clothes as their men. An age-old inequality disappeared as employees took to horses and met their masters eye to eye. Pastoral properties were not managed from homestead offices. Whoever was in control had to ride as well as the stockmen and boundary riders he employed, to move around the property, to assist on occasion in the real work as well as supervise it. A pioneer squatter might eventually leave the work to a manager, and keep more to his homestead or retire to the city; some proprietors were absentees who had never left the city; but always there were gentlemen squatters directly involved in the dirty work of the pastoral industry. The term "bush-man" was first applied to those who possessed the bush skills, whether they were owners or workers.[52]

The literature of Paterson and Lawson is described by Russel Ward as portraying the bush workers as egalitarian collectivists combining to outdo the wealthy squatters. Had the bush workers really been depicted in this way, the literature could not, in a capitalist society, have gained the acceptance and influence Ward claims for it. Certainly, when unions are mentioned – they are by no means a common theme – they are treated favourably, and good bush-men support them. But squatters are not portrayed unsympathetically. They are respected as pioneers, and judged on an individual basis. The mateship between workers is generally personal and limited in scope; a man is loyal to his mate or mates, which is not quite the same as loyalty to the working class. The social dichotomies are not chiefly between employers and employees, but between bush and city, and between Australians and the English. The dominant impression of the bush-workers is of their unassertive self-confidence. They are completely at home in their environment, suffering no enduring indignities on account of their status as employees. They become romantic figures in a way no peasant or yeoman farmer could, because of the roving nature of their work. In most industries so to dignify and celebrate the life and skills of the worker would imply some devaluation of the owner and employer – as parasites, exploiters or simply effete. The cult of the peasant and manual worker in Europe had this subversive edge. But in the pastoral industry, as the literature takes no pains to hide and as everyone knew, the employing class possessed bush skills as well and had furthermore the aura of hard-working pioneers.[53] Thus the unique character of the pastoral industry, where employers and employees at the extremes of the status hierarchy toiled in the same enterprise, allowed for a most potent yet unthreatening message to be conveyed about the worth of working-class figures. The literature is democratic in its implications, and not socialist; the status order is subverted, but not the economic.[54] The more noble and romantic the bush-man became, the more he confounded the socialist account of the plight of the working-man under capitalism. The literature could thus be accepted into the schools and the homes of the middle class. Its acceptance has grown with time, and becoming as it were the Holy Writ of the Australian nation, it must be rated as one of the most powerful forces sustaining the view that Jack is as good as his master, a view that sustains in turn the egalitarianism of manners. Jacks have often enough thought themselves as good as their masters, even if only silently; what has been rare is for their masters to agree with them. We have to find in Australia the reasons why, to use Craig McGregor's words, the wealthy "feel under some pressure to be accepted by ordinary working Australians rather than the other way round".[55]

The egalitarianism of manners is generally acknowledged to be one egalitarianism that does really exist in modern Australia. To give an adequate account of its history would require a much closer attention to the details of social life than I have been able to give. My impression is that it made its greatest advances, not in the 1850s, but in the 1880s and 1890s. Certainly, it was then that it first had firm ideological support, in the general sense that the worth of working people was being proclaimed and the pretensions of others were being derided, and issued in specific injunctions. Lawson's verse is well known:

> They tramp in mateship side by side —
> The Protestant and Roman,
> They call no biped lord or sir,
> And touch their hat to no man.[56]

These lines would have had no point if these marks of deference had disappeared 30 or more years earlier.

The egalitarianism of manners is regarded as a trifling thing by those who want to see complete equality of opportunity or equality in the distribution of material goods. I don't think it should be undervalued. Despite the growth of the social sciences, most people still spend little time filling out questionnaires on status systems. They do spend a lot of time meeting other people. If those encounters do not induce the heart-ache and corroding anger that can be the other side of deference, then egalitarians of all sorts should rejoice.

1986

Notes

[1]   A.F. Davies and S. Encel (eds.), *Australian Society: a Sociological Introduction*, Melbourne, 1965.

[2]   Detailed documentation for the general judgments and assessments offered below will be provided in my forthcoming study of New South Wales society and politics in the 1850s and 1860s.

[3]   W.K. Hancock, *Australia*, Brisbane, 1964, p.45; G. Serle, *The Golden Age*, Melbourne, 1963, pp.92, 269.

[4]   C.N. Connolly, "The Middling-Class Victory in New South Wales, 1853-62: a Critique of the Bourgeois-Pastoralist Dichotomy", *Historical Studies*, XIX, 1981, puts the case that the liberals were less fearful of democracy because property-ownership was, allegedly, more widespread (p.374).

[5]   Published with this title, St Kilda, 1859, see esp. pp.6-8, 13-14, 17.

[6]   *Sydney Morning Herald (S.M.H.)*, 4 January 1860.

[7]   M. Fletcher, *Costume in Australia 1788-1901*, Melbourne, 1984, *passim*.

[8]   Police and Hackney Carriage Regulations, *N.S.W. V. and P.*, 1859-60. vol. 2, pp.13, 24.

[9]   G.L. Buxton, *The Riverina*, Melbourne, 1967, p.146; H.W. Haygarth, *Recollections of Bush Life in Australia*, London, 1848, pp.30, 90; T. Major, *Leaves from a Squatter's Note Book*, London, 1900, pp.12, 15; G.C. Munday, *Our Antipodes*, London, 1852, vol. 3, pp.20, 77, 123; Annie M. Baxter, *A Lady in Australia*, Melbourne, 1873, pp.6, 47, 50, 53.

[10]   *Port Phillip Gentlemen and Good Society in Melbourne before the Gold Rushes*, Melbourne, 1980. "The Idea of a Colonial Gentry", *Historical Studies*, XIII, 1968, 307-28.

[11]   See, for example, W.S. Jevons, Social Survey of Sydney, *S.M.H.*, 9 November 1929.

[12]   op. cit., p.23

[13]   op. cit., p.324

[14]   H. Nicholson, *Good Behaviour, being a Study of Certain Types of Activity*, London, 1955; S. Raven, *The English Gentleman: an Essay on Attitudes*, London,

1961; S.R. Letwin, "The Idea of Gentlemen", *Encounter*, LVII, Nov. 1981, 8-19; P. Mason, *The English Gentlemen: The Rise and Fall of an Ideal*, London, 1982.

[15]   Australian Club, Minute Book 1838-1845, Mitchell Library, MSS 1836/3; de Serville, op. cit., p.65.

[16]   Paul de Serville, op. cit., records these processes in Melbourne. His theme however, is the decline of the "real" gentlemen. The evidence presented in the book can equally well be used to show the emergence of a new, broader order of colonial gentlemen.

[17]   Munday, op. cit., vol. 1, p.375.

[18]   Sir W. Denison, *Varieties of Vice-Regal Life*, London, 1870, Vol. 1, pp.43-4, 336.

[19]   Select Committee on the state of the magistracy, *N.S.W. V & P*, 1858, vol. 2, Evidence pp.79-85.

[20]   A. Powell, *Patrician Democrat: The Political Life of Charles Cowper 1843-1870*, Melbourne, 1977, p.132.

[21]   *S.M.H.*, 20 August 1862.

[22]   *S.M.H.*, 19 August 1863.

[23]   See Mr W.R. Riley, Appointment and Removal from Bench, *V & P*, 1859-60, vol. 2; Mr Myles Marke Lyons, ibid., 1860, 1861-2, vol. 1.

[24]   *S.M.H.*, 30 September 1863.

[25]   Select Committee on the state of the magistracy, *V & P*, 1858, vol. 2. Report, p.9.

[26]   *S.M.H.*, 29 November 1859.

[27]   Chapman's case was referred to by several speakers during the long debate on Martin's censure motion in August 1863, see esp. *S.M.H.*, 19, 22, 28 August 1863.

[28]   *Illawarra Mercury*, 16 August 1864.

[29]   *S.M.H.*, 29 November, 17, 20 December 1859.

[30]   *S.M.H.*, 27, 28 July 1864.

[31]   For the successful censure of Martin, *S.M.H.*, 19 October – 3 November 1864. The reinstatements are reported in the *Government Gazette*.

[32]   Connolly, op. cit., p.379.

[33]   What follows is based on Colonial Office, Original Correspondence, Honours; Minutes and Memoranda, 1858-1868, 1874-1882, 1883-1887, C.O. 448/1A, 1B, 2. For comparative figures showing demand and awards for all colonies see in particular, 448/1A, ff. 100-106, 116-117; 448/1B, ff. 523-536.

[34]   The phrase is Nancy Renfree's, "Migrants and cultural transference: English Friendly Societies in a Victorian Goldfield town", Ph.D. thesis La Trobe University 1983, p.297. See also my "Keeping Colonial History Colonial: the Hartz Thesis Revisited", *Historical Studies*, XXI, 1984, 85-104; see esp. 96-101.

[35]   M. Gilmore, *Old Days: Old Ways: A Book of Recollections*, Sydney, 1963, pp.26-7; *The Letters of Rachel Henning*, ed. David Adams, Sydney, 1963, p.267. A. de Tocqueville, *Democracy in America*, vol. 2, Book Three, chapter XIII.

[36]   *Australia and New Zealand*, London, 1873, vol. 2, pp.252-4, vol. 1, p.312.

[37]   J.A. Froude, *Oceania*, London, 1886, p.109.

[38]   R. Twopeny, *Town Life in Australia*, London, 1883, pp.49-62, 92-3, 95-6, 104-7.

[39]   op. cit., vol. 2, pp.253-4.

[40]   G. Bolton, "How we Got to Here", p.38 in T. van Dugteren (ed.), *Rural Australia: the Other Nation*, Sydney, 1978.

[41] The first platform of the N.S.W. party is printed in B. Nairn, *Civilising Capitalism: The Labor Movement in New South Wales 1870-1900*, Canberra, 1973 pp.44-5.

[42] *Bulletin*, 19 November 1887.

[43] ibid., 14 March 1885. The *Bulletin* was very conscious of inequality in dress — the wowser's code was "collar and cuffs morality" (17 September 1887); "It is always a fustian coat that is taken off at the whipping post, never a coat of broadcloth" (23 April 1887).

[44] ibid., 10 June 1882, 19 December 1887.

[45] ibid., 1, 15 August, 21 November 1885, 2 January 1886.

[46] ibid., 19 November 1887.

[47] ibid., 1 September 1888.

[48] Twopeny, op. cit., pp.79-80; E. Kinglake, *The Australian at Home*, London, 1891, pp.6-7. Fletcher, op. cit., p.187 draws the wrong conclusion when she claims that Governor Carrington's wearing of tweed suit and bowler hat shows that these were perfectly acceptable to the upper class.

[49] J. Laver, *Taste and Fashion: From the French Revolution to the Present Day*, London, 1937, p.17.

[50] G. Davison, "Sydney and the Bush: an Urban Context for the Australian Legend", *Historical Studies*, XVIII, 1978, 191-209; R. White, *Inventing Australia*, Sydney, 1981, chapters 5, 6.

[51] Davison, op. cit., p.192.

[52] [A Bushman] John Sidney, *A Voice from the Far Interior of Australia*, London, 1847, followed this usage. G. Davison used Sidney's work in his "Alexander Harris and the Australian Legend", *Melbourne Historical Journal*, II, 1962, 55-8, to point out that graziers did not live apart from the men in the interior, contrary to Harris's view on which Russel Ward relied heavily.

[53] See my "The Pioneer Legend", *Historical Studies*, XVIII, 1978, 316-37.

[54] A.A. Phillips in *The Australian Tradition*, Melbourne, 1958, chapter 3, is a much better guide to the literature than Russel Ward.

[55] Quoted by H.G. Oxley in *Mateship in Local Organisation: a Study of Egalitarianism, Stratification, Leadership* . . . , St Lucia, 1974, p.27, which I have found the wisest book on these subjects. Oxley gently chides McGregor for claiming that *all* the wealthy feel this; "many wealthy men" would be more accurate — "the Australian Legend does not have women in it, and they probably did not feel the same pressures" (p.222).

[56] Quoted in R. Ward, *The Australian Legend*, Melbourne, 1958, p.228.

STATE EDUCATION AND CULTURE

R.J.W. SELLECK

One day, late in the nineteenth century, Sherlock Holmes and Dr Watson were travelling by train from Portsmouth to London. After they had passed through Clapham Junction, Holmes remarked: "It is a very cheering thing to come into London by any of these lines which run high and allow you to look down upon the houses like this." "I thought he was joking", Watson commented, "for the view was sordid enough." But Holmes soon explained himself:

> "Look at those big, isolated clumps of buildings rising up above the slates, like brick islands in a lead-coloured sea."
> "The Board schools."
> "Lighthouses, my boy! Beacons of the future! Capsules, with hundreds of bright little seeds in each, out of which will spring the wiser, better England of the future."[1]

In the cities of the Antipodes, the Australian equivalent of the Board schools, the state schools, had also made an architectural impact: they were strong, sometimes elegant, occasionally massive, buildings. And it was thought that these schools, like their English counterparts, would help to make a wiser and better country. "The great object", the journalist and public servant W.A. Duncan had told an audience in Brisbane in 1850, "is to educate the rising generation, and to enable them and their posterity to assume their position among the enlightened nations of the earth." At almost the same time George William Rusden, who in two years had ridden ten thousand miles in order to persuade colonists to start schools, stressed the need to offer youth "a very high degree of enlightenment" — it would lay "a firm foundation" for a life of "mental action, of virtue, wisdom, reflection, and ingenuity".[2]

In early nineteenth-century Britain such sentiments were regarded with suspicion because of the fear that schooling might make the working-man refractory or give him ideas above his station. Advocates of education in the colonies, though they knew of this fear, did not have much of a problem in dispelling it. Their fights, and they were long and acrimonious, were about the control and the nature of schooling. A.G. Austin, G.M. Dow, Ronald Fogarty, J.S. Gregory, Denis Grundy and others have shown how throughout the nineteenth century Australians struggled to decide what form of religious instruction should be given in the schools supported by the state and how much state aid should be given to schools controlled by churches.[3] In the end, and in different ways, the colonies came to the conclusion that, by and large, there should be no religious instruction in state schools and no state aid for church schools. During the struggle towards this conclusion there were many declarations about the importance of education, but the struggle itself, which lasted for a century, provided the most impressive evidence of the value which some colonists placed on education. If the beleaguered governors, clergy, press and politicians had felt no pressure to provide schools, they could have put aside the troublesome education problem and given their undivided attention to squatting on the land or searching for gold or furthering their personal and political designs. Instead, like punchdrunk boxers they kept circling each other, knowing that the fight had to be brought to an end but unable to deliver a knockout blow. In most colonies it took until the 1870s and 1880s before the blow was landed, and large numbers of city schools went to join the thousands of small wooden schools scattered around the countryside.

The impressive facades of the city state schools were striking additions to the urban environment. In Victoria in 1874 a parliamentarian remarked that there were "many very worthy persons who only woke up to the real significance of the Education Act ... when they found handsome buildings erected to which they could send their children to school".[4] In suburbs such as Collingwood, or in parts of Richmond or West Melbourne, the new schools started straight out of the bare earth — confident, minatory presences brooding over the workers' dwellings which surrounded them. Had he seen them, Sherlock Holmes would have been impressed. Yet if he had entered the schools he would have been struck by less generous sights: unlined walls, long cold rooms, rows of backless desks, bad ventilation, poor lighting and, at the rear of the rooms, the rows of hooks for hats and coats which symbolized an obsession with order, economy and efficiency. There was not much evidence of "a very high degree of enlightenment", and the hundreds of "bright little seeds" struggled to survive. The "sweetness and light", which for that school inspector Matthew Arnold were the accompaniment of culture, would not have overwhelmed Sherlock Holmes's senses.

I have been asked to provide some historical perspective on the relationship between state education and culture. I have taken "culture" to mean "high culture" — called by Raymond Williams "the general state of intellectual development, in a society as a whole" and encompassing not only the arts and humanities, but also mathematics and the sciences, including the social sciences. This is not a very precise usage of a word which, as Lesley Johnson's recent *The Cultural Critics* confirms, is notoriously slippery. But it is a common and a workable usage, and it has often been employed in discussion. In this paper "state education" means the school — elementary and secondary — which governments established in the late nineteenth and early twentieth centuries. The paper concentrates mainly on Victoria for, though I believe that its central argument is applicable to all states, that application would require modifications and explanations which cannot be made in the time available.[5]

To approach the problem I should like to look briefly at what the nineteenth-century state school taught, the methods it used, its values, rituals, customs and manner of organization — its "culture", to use that word as an anthropologist or sociologist might. The school's rituals, for example, suggest a stress on order, obedience and respect for authority: there are the meticulous marking of rolls daily at the appointed times; the practice of working in unison and in response to instructions — even when threading needles; the fussy straightening at the end of the day of the long rows of backless desks in the large high-ceilinged rooms; the formal manner of address to teachers; maxims laboriously copied on slates or in copybooks; the meticulous curls of the handwriting; the timetable's precise division of the day; the ubiquitous cane.

The manner in which the school was organized also gives an insight into its hopes. In each of a city school's large rooms there might be eighty or a hundred children, perhaps divided into three groups, which were sometimes separated from each other by a curtain. The one teacher was assisted by one or two pupil-teachers so that there could be three different lessons proceeding simultaneously. When no curtains divided the groups (which was the usual state of affairs), each child, the teacher, and each pupil-teacher could see and hear everyone else in the room. One observer remarked that "the whole system of instruction is carried on amid a Babel of confounding voices, where each must bawl louder than his neighbour in order to be heard".[6] Plainly this was not a method of organization designed to induct students into a complex body of knowledge. It did not assume a subtle intellectual interchange or a sensitive study of nuances of meaning; it prevented a close relationship between teacher and pupils or, for that matter, between the pupils themselves. The classroom in a state school could hardly be confused with a tutor's room at an Oxford college, where a student's paper might receive the tutor's undivided attention.

The curriculum offered by state schools reflected their ungenerous system of organization. For the last quarter of the nineteenth century it was restricted to reading, writing, arithmetic, grammar and geography; sometimes singing and military drill were added, and girls were taught needlework. Reading was usually confined to the reading-book, which was read aloud, often in imitation of an example given by the teacher. Writing meant penmanship, obsessively taught; composition received little emphasis, though considerable value was placed on spelling. Arithmetic was mostly devoted to performing calculations in which the obtaining of the correct answer, whether or not the method of obtaining it was understood, became the teacher's main concern. Geography required the rote learning of lists: places, populations and products, rivers and capital cities. Grammar involved much mechanical parsing and analysis, frequently practised on the best literature. "It is with a certain degree of modesty that I issue to the public this little work", wrote a state-school teacher in 1880 in his preface to *Milton Parsed*; he had chosen "the more difficult words" from the first three books of *Paradise Lost.*[7] When history was taught in Victorian state schools (it was not introduced until 1886 because of the fear that it would feed the religious disputes), children learned by heart about peoples, dates, and events which embodied a Whiggish and imperialistic view of the world.[8]

The narrowness of the state-school curriculum was made more conspicuous by what it did not offer. State-school children were not introduced to literature, except through the extracts in the class readers; they were not taught mathematics or, if the desultory "object lessons" are excluded, science; art was not part of their experience, nor was music (though "singing" was attempted), nor were the "classics", which were still very important in secondary schooling. Instead, as the contemporary usage made clear, state schools provided an elementary education: they introduced children to the "elements" of learning. The vocabulary contains and displays the metaphor, for knowledge had been broken into pieces, reduced to its elements, and, as was happening in Victoria's protected factories, those elements were then combined to make up a suitable product. When, in the secondary schools (which had developed independently of the state schools) English literature, the classics or Euclid was studied, a meaningful and complete entity was offered to students — a play, a theorem, a book of Virgil. However badly taught, however obscured by a dreary pedagogue, an original intellectual creation was brought into the classroom — and there was always a chance that Virgil or Homer might work his magic despite the teacher. In the elementary school students were not brought into direct contact with great minds. Instead, they were given the elements of learning, brought up on pedagogic artifacts especially constructed by middle-men and having little meaning or use, or life, outside the school.

As if to emphasize the industrial analogy, the Education Department, without much sense of disappointment, took over from the Board of Education that preceded it a method of paying its teachers based on the belief that they were lazy but could be made to work harder by a financial bribe: a substantial part of a teacher's salary was made dependent on the results obtained by pupils at examinations set by inspectors. The University's W.E. Hearn, a prominent advocate of payment by results, remarked:

> When each teacher had been paid . . . for the number of his children that have passed, the whole transaction is completed. The State has got the article that it wanted, at the price that it chose to fix, and of the quality ascertained by its own officers. With the mode of production of that article, with the management of the school, or with the other subjects taught or omitted to be taught there, it has no concern. It wants primary instruction of a certain kind, and it has got it.

Teachers knew that, whatever the Education Department had got, it was not an accurate measure of their efforts to educate the state's children. But the mechanical and industrial analogy encouraged the deceptive search for results, and together with the teachers' minds the curriculum narrowed, until only those subjects which were examined for "results" were considered worth teaching.[9]

The manner in which state school teachers were prepared for their task narrowed elementary education still further. The word "schoolmaster" with its connotations of authority and independence gave way in Departmental usage to the humbler term "schoolteacher". And to be a state-school teacher meant to be a defectively educated member of society's lower orders: *not* to have received a secondary education was almost a prerequisite for being a teacher. At the age of fourteen or fifteen, after completing an elementary education, the aspiring teacher became a "pupil-teacher" — that is, entered into a form of apprenticeship, for four years, with an experienced teacher. During school hours the pupil-teacher taught or helped to teach; out of school hours the "master" gave some instruction in educational theory and practice and in the "advanced" academic education which substituted for secondary education. As the master had received his training in the same way, intellectual stimulation was slight and professional conservatism was rendered endemic — the only model of behaviour put before a student was that of the overworked and undertrained master teacher whose horizons had been limited by payment by results. The handful of teachers taken out of this sytem went not to the University, the guardian of the "high culture", but to a teachers' college — called (significantly) "the training institution". "If you want to keep teachers in a comparatively low position in the social scale, establish an institution where you board, feed, and educate a number of young men and women for a year or two at the public expense", a contemporary remarked.[10] That was what the Education Department did.

These teachers and the schools they conducted were constantly watched to ensure that they walked the narrow path of social and cultural propriety. State schools and the Common schools which preceded them were permitted to offer for a fee, and out of school hours, some "extra subjects" which included the "secondary school" subjects — French, algebra, Euclid, the classics. These subjects were not very popular, but both the state and the Common schools were made to feel uneasy about offering them. There was a fear that through them the poor might be educated above their station or, a frequent and heartfelt accusation, that they might enable people who could afford to pay for an education to get it at a cut price. In 1869 a Common schoolmaster in Sale, in trouble because he offered extra subjects, wrote to the Board: "If you think that my arrangements are contrary to the spirit of the school act, or likely to injure the Common school and will kindly inform me so, *I will abandon it*." He remarked that Common schools "were viewed with prejudice as being only for the poor, and settlers around confided their children's education to tutors or governesses".[11] Many in authority shared this prejudice, and accordingly the framers of the 1872 Act resisted attempts to have free instruction extended beyond the elementary subjects. As J.W Stephen, who introduced the Act, remarked: "The Government did not wish to interfere with the higher class of education, either in the public schools or in the well-conducted private schools — it would be unjust as well as impolitic to do so." Therefore the extra subjects were to be offered under "a sort of self-support by the moderate system of fees which they proposed should be paid for them".[12]

But if the schools were not to get ideas above their station, they were also to be prevented from falling too low. The committee of the Common school at Sandridge (Port Melbourne) had to be forced to admit "barefooted children" — they were thought to "lower the tone and standing of the school before the public, and thereby impair its usefulness in the cause of public education".[13] A little later, the children who inhabited the lanes at the top of the city (Little Bourke or Little Lonsdale streets) — "gutter children", "street Arabs" or "larrikins" — "the neglected or uncontrolled children of vicious or over-indulgent parents", as C.H. Pearson described them[14] — were to be excluded from state schools. In introducing the 1872 Bill, Stephen said that a system of night schools or ragged schools would be provided in case these children lowered the tone of state schools or corrupted those who were more respectable. Speaking on the Bill, a parliamentarian remarked that Members had no doubt seen,

> as I have seen, on a morning, jogging away to school, nice tidy little children, with clean shoes and stockings, and nicely-brushed hair, respectable in their parentage, respectful in their behaviour, and decent in their conversation.

But no doubt they have also seen

> loitering about the gutters, girls whose feet were altogether unacquainted with shoes or stockings, whose hands and faces had no practical knowledge whatever of soap or scrubbing-brush, whose hair never felt a comb, whose nakedness was covered by a parcel of rags, and whose mouth was never opened except to utter ribaldry. Now are we to be told in a free country — why freedom is a farce under such circumstances — that, because these children happen to live in the neighbourhood of the same State school, they are to be sent to sit cheek-by-jowl with each other? What people are going to tolerate that kind of thing?[15]

The nineteenth-century Victorians were not the people, for those who founded the state system were more concerned with stability than with social mobility; their purpose was as much moral and political as it was intellectual.

The first state schools had their own culture which was appropriate for their task of "public instruction" — to borrow the terms of the Minister's title. The schools were to help the children who attended them to fit more comfortably into that station in life to which it had pleased God to appoint them — though it had been decided that the community would be the better if the children were taught nothing about God while they were in the school. The state school's rituals, its furnishings, its methods of organization, the manner in which its teachers were trained and paid, what it taught and what it chose not to teach: all made it clear that the school offered its pupils a substitute for the high culture and not an introduction to it. Both in its rationale and its working the school found inspiration in the industrial process. It was staffed by poorly trained men and women assisted by younger, less-skilled and more lowly-paid apprentices, who laboured under conditions which stressed economy and a mechanical efficiency and which worked against any subtle personal or intellectual relationships. In this there was a bitter irony: while the high culture about which Matthew Arnold wrote was not part of the state school child's expectations or educational experience, the industrial processes, whose devastating effects Arnold hoped to combat through culture, provided a model which helped the state school to deny the high culture to its students — or its "products", as Professor Hearn might have said.

II

At the beginning of the twentieth century, after a royal commission led by Theodore Fink, the state school and the Department itself began to change. The change owed something to local quarrels and the ambitions of Victorian politicians, to important visitors (such as the Webbs) who came, saw and criticized, and to educational laymen such as Alfred Deakin and Theodore Fink. But credit must also be given to a group of Departmental bureaucrats who fought a strenuous battle to improve state education.

One of these was Frederick John Gladman who arrived in Melbourne in 1877 to become principal of the Training Institution carrying a letter from Matthew Arnold who had known him since his pupil-teacher days. Arnold spoke of Gladman's "high cultivation" and wished him success "for the Colony's sake quite as much as for your own".[16] To the very small group of students who attended the Training Institution Gladman brought that "high cultivation", and his students returned to the schools deeply marked by his influence. Before he died prematurely in 1884 he had subjected state education to severe criticism and had trained a cadre of intense and ambitious young men.

Gladman trainees such as Frank Tate, who became Victoria's first Director of Education and Charles Long, who edited the *School Paper*, joined a small group of inspectors, college lecturers and teachers who, even through the bitter Depression of the 1890s, worked to abolish payment by results, to improve the system of teacher training, and to liberalize the methods of instruction and enrich the curriculum of the state school. In 1902 the Victorian Education Department introduced a new course of study in which reading and writing developed into something closer to what is now called "English", composition and poetry gained importance, elementary science appeared (often in the guise of nature study), and art in the primitive form of drawing, cardboard modelling, paperwork and brushwork came into favour. In arithmetic, emphasis was placed on reasoning rather than rote learning, history was given greater prominence, geography was to be taught in a practical way which gave its concepts some meaning, some music and some gymnastics (even if in the form of physical exercises for military drill) were recommended.[17]

The change cannot be attributed simply to educationists, for it reflected the powerful forces which in the 1890s and early 1900s were altering Australian society. The New Education, as the reform movement was called, must be viewed in relation to efforts to regulate conditions in factories, to establish wages-boards, to reduce or remove sweated labour, to begin to redistribute wealth through land and income taxes, and to introduce old-age pensions. Like these reforms the New Education owed much to overseas examples, especially British, or European and American as mediated by the British. It drew on German idealism, Rousseau's naturalism, the belief that education could be made a science, and various and conflicting convictions of Fabians, social imperialists and advocates of moral education. This paper does not analyze the incompatible aims and warring philosophies and visions of life with which the New Education was riven.[18] It concentrates on the fact that, whatever the movement's origins and inconsistencies, it was concerned with providing an introduction to culture, not a substitute for it: literature, art, music, science, history (albeit in uncertain and primitive guises and at a level designed to be suitable to young pupils) were offered to state school children.

This was not done by mistake. Frank Tate, one of the leading figures in these reforms, constantly and publicly insisted that teachers should not be weary, mechanical result-seekers but should be able "easily to take rank among cultured men". The state school, he insisted, should be

> sowing seeds of fuller, broader, gentler life, and be fostering them; should aim at turning children on the road towards becoming cultured men with beautiful manners and noble instincts, men who are capable of sound thought, and who are imbued with high ideal of life and life's work.

He denounced payment by results and claimed that the use of pupil-teachers, that "army of raw, ill-informed, untrained boys and girls", was the antithesis of his ideal of the "high-minded, enthusiastic, cultured teacher".

> The Department may condemn your body to "Tinpot Gully North", but it cannot keep your mind there. ... Be off to the forest of Arden, and there fleet the time carelessly with Rosalind, Orlando, Touchstone, and other ideal personages, more real than living man. There are trains starting for these excursions every second — trains of thought, I mean, and the Bradshaw guides to them are your volumes of good literature.[19]

Our more astringent and sceptical age may permit itself a superior smile at such fervour, but it ought to realize that early in the twentieth century the state school had embarked on a dramatic venture: the introduction of the culture, which had been the possession of the few, to everyone. School architecture reflected this more generous vision. From this period came the first example of a Victorian state school with stained glass windows, an art form which can only be appreciated from *inside* the school[20] — by the pupils and not by passers-by like Sherlock Holmes or the property owners who had been satisfied by the imposing facades of the first state schools.

The reformers met opposition from teachers who found their expertise stretched in unaccustomed ways, from parents who grumbled about paying for the materials needed for some of the new subjects, and from other quarters. Here is a correspondent to the *Argus* in 1903:

> I maintain that the efficiency of the schools is not as high as formerly, and that good, wholesome subjects, like reading, spelling, arithmetic, grammar, and geography, are not as thoroughly taught as they were, or as they should be, in consequence of so much time being taken up with such stuff as brushwork, clay-modelling, paper-folding, wood-carving, nature study (so-called), drawing, singing and music, science (sic), and so on ad infinitum.

Another grumbled. "If a lot of this nonsense were done away with, and plain common-sense reading, writing, and arithmetic taught, there would not be so many dunces. — Yours, &c., DISGUSTED PARENT." The attack was so constant that in 1906 the Education Department hired the Exhibition Building to show off the work of the state schools. As the Minister of the time said, the exhibition was an attempt to prove that "the statement made in some quarters that the children were not being grounded in the 'three R's was baseless". The "utilitarian knowledge" was being inculcated, but "the artistic, musical, and physical development of the child and the cultivation of the reasoning faculty claimed, and justly so, a large share of attention".[21]

The exhibition was much acclaimed, but shortly before the Great War, in the 1920s and again in the 1930s, when state-school course of study was further liberalized, the criticism continued. It continues today. The serious problems in literacy and numeracy faced by the community at the moment are not increased or rendered less worrying by admitting that, since the beginning of this century, there have been wailings in the educational corridors about the neglect of the three Rs in favour of "fads" or "frills". We may even gain a sense of proportion if we recognize that those who contrast today's fragile standards with the solidity of the 1930s seem unaware that the 1930s were once contrasted unfavourably with the golden days at the beginning of the century — when the state schools were being attacked because they were neglecting "good, wholesome subjects, like reading, writing, arithmetic, grammar, and geography". The defence of educational standards may sometimes cloak a fear of the state school's efforts to improve access to the high culture. This fear has commonly found expression in the assertion of a false dichotomy between the basic subjects and the cultural studies, so that a broadening of the curriculum can be said to reduce the attention given to the basic subjects and thus lead to a decline in standards. Before joining the company of those who complain about the neglect of the basic subjects, we might remember that they are singing an old song, and we might look closely at the singers. Included among them will be some who are protesting because the state school has shaken itself free from its preoccupation with the "elements" of learning and has taken the high culture for its province.

III

The late nineteenth-century Victorian educational scene contained more than the state elementary schools. There were Roman Catholic schools (mostly elementary in nature), hundreds of private institutions ranging from small schools offering elementary and sometimes a more advanced education to large schools supported by corporate bodies or the churches, and — at the top of the educational ladder, at least as far as prestige was concerned — the Public Schools, which in the harsh atmosphere of the Antipodes tried to fashion themselves after their English exemplars. A wide variety of curricula were offered by these schools: advanced elementary studies, the genteel "accomplishments" provided in girls' schools, courses designed to prepare for a business career and an academic (we should now say "secondary") curriculum. The schools that offered the secondary curriculum included both boys' and girls' schools, and Public, private and Roman Catholic schools. Their activities were dominated by the University's matriculation examination. Throughout the nineteenth century the classics and mathematics, the basis of the older view of a humane culture, battled for precedence with modern and utilitarian studies such as English literature, history, science and modern languages, in a struggle to decide which version of the high culture would be offered by the secondary schools. At all times there were serious gaps in their curriculum, at least as judged from the point of view of the high culture. Music and the arts were never strongly represented, and even after the modern subjects had won the day the position of science was uncertain. But for all their deficiencies, these secondary schools were the institutions that introduced Australians to the high culture.[22]

The cavernous gap between them and the state schools was crossed by a narrow and rickety bridge of scholarships, which enabled a few (a very few) state-school pupils to begin a secondary education. Elementary and secondary schooling were not two stages in a child's educational experience, they were two different kinds of education aimed at two different groups of pupils. They incorporated different educational cultures which reflected major differences in the social structure. Those who left the elementary school went immediately to work (if they were able to find it), and to work in the less rewarding of society's occupations. The secondary schools, especially the Public Schools, assumed that their students would be "occupying places in the world of politics — at the Bar, or the Pulpit, or for the medical profession".[23]

At the turn of the century, just as the effort to transform the elementary school was gathering momentum, some Victorians launched a challenge to the educational and social assumptions that supported the arrangements for secondary education. If the cultural foundations being laid in the elementary school were to be built on, the state would have to establish its own secondary schools. The private schools (which for the purposes of this paper will be taken to include the Public Schools) strongly opposed the establishment of state high schools, as also did Parliament, which was dominated by country Members and almost obsessively concerned with economy, the churches, did not wish secular education to be extended, and conservative groups in the community, who feared yet another extension to the state socialism which they bitterly resented. "Where will it all end?" asked the *Argus*; might we not soon have "state butchering, farming, banking, insurance, marriage regulating, &c?"[24] In such an atmosphere the private secondary schools were likely to be a powerful lobby.

In a bitter exchange brought about by plans to open the first high school in 1905, W.H. Fitchett from the Methodist Ladies' College argued that the state should stay out of "the general business of education" for its intrusion was "a form of socialism". Just as the private schools were emerging from the horrors of the 1890s Depression, they were faced with threatening competition, and Fitchett claimed that "vested interests to the extent of three-quarters of a million sterling were affected by the proposal". S.G. McLaren, headmaster of Presbyterian Ladies' College, remarked that girls from the state schools came to his school "rough and uncouth and they got polished and refined because they were able to mix with girls of the better classes whose parents were able to pay fees of twenty to eighty guineas". The beleaguered private schools took the view that secondary education, and the introduction to the high culture which went with it, was the right of anyone who could afford to pay for it, while the poor had to earn it by being clever and, in any case, had to be rubbed and polished until they were smooth enough to take their place in polite society.[25]

The first attempts to establish state secondary education foundered amid the shoals of such opposition and Tate, who was leading the forces who wished to establish them, expressed regret that his efforts had met resistance "not only from vested interests, but from those who might be expected to lead the people towards the light", the churches. He claimed that the University and the technical schools were "the upper stories of our educational edifice" but could be reached by almost none of the children from the state's primary schools: education's secondary story was "locked against the mass of the people, and can be entered only by private stairways for which a heavy toll is charged. Our few scholarships are like so many ropes hung out for expert climbers only. We need the broad, open stairway accessible to all." In explicit and deliberate contrast to his opponents, Tate argued that equal educational opportunities should be offered to all. "In a truly democratic state", he wrote,

> every one without exception has the chance, and knows he has the chance, to secure the prizes which our community life makes available. One aid to the removal of the bitter sense of injustice felt by so many to-day is to provide fully the means for self-development, and then sweep away any obstacles which prevent talent and character from making themselves felt.

The prizes being fought over were more tangible than access to the high culture, but they included that.[26]

It has since become clear that equality of opportunity is an illusory goal, though the belief in it has not entirely died — W.F. Connell lists it prominently in his influential discussion of Australian education's myths.[27] It is frequently contrasted with equality of educational outcome, which refers to a supposed equality of achievement at the end of the educational process. Even if equality of opportunity is limited to equality at the beginning of the educative process — that is, to an equal opportunity to benefit from schooling — it cannot be attained. Social, economic, cultural, class and family influences ensure that, on entry to schooling, there is no equality of opportunity. To persist in the belief in equality of opportunity is to ignore what the experience of the last eighty years has to teach.

However, it is partly because the founders of state secondary education in this and other countries held to this belief that we are now in a position to discard it. We have been able to see that the secondary schools they established in the search for equality have not been able to produce it. Yet to criticize them for undertaking the search would be to fail in historical imagination. Faced by educational arrangements that placed a high value on cultural studies, then denied them to most students, the founders of state secondary education sought a more generous alternative. Many of their contemporaries attacked them as radical and irresponsible social engineers, and as late as 1948 it was argued in England that "the ideal of a uniform system such that no one capable of receiving higher education could fail to get it, leads imperceptibly to the education of too many people, and consequently to the lowering of standards to whatever this swollen number of candidates is able to reach."[28] When T.S. Eliot wrote this, he could have known (had he wished to acquire the knowledge) that state education had not provided a uniform system.

But in the first two decades of the twentieth century, the Education Department of Victoria, believing that equality of opportunity was possible and desirable, fought successfully to establish secondary schools. In 1900 there were no state secondary schools; by 1914 there were 25 high schools and 22 higher elementary schools. At one time or another in the first years of their existence state secondary schools were called continuation schools, higher elementary schools, high schools, and agricultural high schools. The names reflected compromises and an attempt to be a less direct challenge to the private schools than they actually were. But the directness of the challenge becomes clear once their curriculum is studied. They offered four courses: academic, industrial, agricultural, and commercial. From the beginning, the demand for the academic course was overwhelming. In 1914 there were 4,251 enrolments in English, 4,013 in history, 1,711 in physics, and even in Latin there were 1,253; there were 291 in agriculture, and 200 in commercial subjects. Those who sent their children to the high schools wanted access to the high culture and, of course, to the socio-economic advantages it brought.[29]

This is the more remarkable because the Melbourne Continuation School, the first state high school, was established by a Director, Frank Tate, who had never attended or taught at a secondary school though he had a master's degree from the University of Melbourne. Its headmaster like the Director had come through the pupil-teacher system and had never been to a secondary school. Most of its staff came from a similar background — they had gained their university qualifications by studying privately and part-time. Thus in their first years at the school, they struggled to free themselves from the culture of the elementary school and to master a system of education of which they had no direct experience. They took as their model (it was the only available model) the enemy, the private secondary school. They adopted its methods and system of organization, its "frills" (prefects, school songs, uniforms, mottoes) and its curriculum. The application of each teacher who endeavoured to obtain an appointment at the new Melbourne Continuation School survives; across some, which were quite respectable, is scrawled in thick red crayon, "n.s.s. — not sufficient scholarship". Tate carried the same belief to the country when he insisted, sometimes to the astonishment of farmers, that the headmasters of agricultural high schools were to be no less academically respectable than the headmasters of city high schools. Their task was essentially the same: the giving of a secondary education, or the induction of children into an Antipodean version of Europe's high culture.[30]

However, despite the value placed on the high culture, the establishment of state high schools cannot be attributed to a disinterested desire for learning. As they moved into the twentieth century Australians realized that, if they were to hold their own in the increasingly bitter industrial and commercial struggle, secondary education would have to be more readily available. And, like other educational leaders of the time, Tate made little progress until he based his arguments on an appeal to national industrial prosperity. In 1908, in a report on a visit he had made to Europe and America, he wrote:

> If we can have the question discussed from the view-point of national well-being and apart from political and class prejudices, if we can, for the present, set aside for special treatment such confusing issues as the vested interests for private schools, and the extent to which the State should control school administration, I am certain that fair-minded men will come to the general conclusions set out in this report.

The establishment of state high schools was the report's most significant conclusion. For Australia to survive in the industrial and economic struggles it needed an educated workforce. "The history of the past thirty years", he said (also in 1908), when arguing that "school-power" was "an imperial necessity",

> yields ample evidence that command of markets is to be won by the nation that brings knowledge and training to bear upon the operations of producing and marketing commodities which the world wants, and that it is impossible nowadays to dissociate industrial progress and true education; attainment.[31]

Tate did not abandon his hope that state high schools would introduce children to the richness of their cultural heritage, and he used the *Church of England Messenger* to ask angrily, "Why should the Church ... advocate technical training for the masses and oppose a more liberal culture for them?"[32] But he came to realize that the community had more utilitarian purposes in mind and that he would achieve little unless he gave expression to them. So, quite deliberately, he linked state secondary education with technical education. Victoria was dotted with technical schools, then semi-tertiary institutions which had grown from schools of mining or industrial arts. As students entered these institutions at the age of seventeen or eighteen (or older), the technical schools were without structural connection to the elementary school whose pupils left at the age of fourteen or younger. If technical education (and, through it, an educated workforce) were to develop properly, the gap between the technical and the elementary school had to be filled. The high school, Tate claimed, could do it.

Donald Clark, the Chief Inspector of Technical Schools, at first accepted this view, but he quickly realized that the high-school students were not coming to the technical schools. If they undertook further education they went to the University, the Teachers' College or other institutions which prepared them for the professions of which they hoped to become members. To solve his problem and to give the community the technical skills it sought, Donald Clark established junior technical schools to which children went after their elementary education and from which they were to go to the (senior) technical schools. He made his intention clear: the technical schools did not have "a common objective like State Secondary schools, but they are in reality vocational training centers for an ever-increasing and ever-varying number of industries".[33]

The pressure for junior technical schools found the defenders of the high schools in an ambiguous position. They believed in the value of humane studies pursued for their own sake; some of them also believed in "the genuine cultural value of strictly technical education properly carried out" and hoped (time was to prove, vainly) that the junior technical school might embody this belief.[34] In any case, if they had supported Tate's position, they were trapped. Having justified high schools on the grounds that they would further industrial development by assisting technical education, they could not easily oppose the establishment of junior technical schools when it was shown that the high school had failed to assist technical education. Victorian education, at a moment of triumph, began an eerie reversion to nineteenth-century practices: the educational administrators who established state high schools to make the high culture more widely available, immediately started junior technical schools to provide an alternative to that culture.

Clark meant them to provide that alternative. Their course of study was to be different from the academic curriculum of the high schools. The teachers of the technical subjects, Clark insisted, were to be men "who have gained the technical experience under actual workshop conditions".[35] He looked with some anxiety towards "the well-trained academic scholar" who derived "internal satisfaction from his knowledge of classical and modern literature and from his mathematics". Such knowledge, Clark insisted, was "self-contained and bookish, and the community does not benefit".[36] He made his position absolutely clear when, in 1912, he said:

> The terms "broad", "liberal", "cultured", and other high sounding and soul satisfying phrases were often used to justify the wholly academic form of education. ... If we are to possess a successful system of Technical education we must see that academic specialization does not turn farmers from the plough, the workman from the lathe, or transform the born mechanic into a bad schoolmaster.[37]

At the time the state established junior technical schools, the expression "elementary education" was giving way to "primary education". The change in terminology promised an educational revolution: "primary" implied "secondary"; where "secondary" had been a *type* of education it was becoming a *stage* through which all children were to go. The promise was a rich one and one which only the state was willing to make. As the twentieth century progressed the promise was fulfilled — all children were given a secondary education of some kind. But what was offered in the name of a *secondary* education was changed. Instead of the high culture (and the occupations for which it was a preparation) many children were offered a substitute.

IV

F.R. Leavis has remarked that "only a minority is capable of advanced intellectual culture. ... It is disastrous to let a country's educational arrangements be determined, or even be affected, by the assumption that a high intellectual standard can be attained by more than a small minority."[38]

Certainly the *creation* of advanced intellectual culture is, almost by definition, the work of a very small minority, though it cannot be assumed that they are respectable members of the middle class — some (Kepler, for example) have been scholarship boys from brutal and impoverished families, while another spent demeaning years in Salzburg writing noble music for an ungrateful archbishop. The sharing in that culture, the re-creation of it, has been the privilege of a larger (but still small) minority, for the high culture is much more a part of middle-class experience than of working-class experience. Thus when middle-class children encounter the high culture at school they are meeting something with which the life-style, and especially perhaps the language, of the home have made them familiar. The working-class child is often meeting a stranger.

Leavis, Eliot and their colleagues have given such sociological observations the status of value-judgments. To make culture widely available, they believe, is to debase it. They can often be found claiming that there has been a lowering of standards in literature or art or political debate or journalism, which they attribute in part to the "democratization" of culture. Ironically, the democratization of the high culture is at times equally feared by more radical social critics. In the late 1920s, for example, the Victorian Education department was poised to abolish the junior technical school and to bring all the state's children into the high school. The technical educators within the Department were able to thwart the proposal partly because they were helped by the Labor Party and the union movement. For them, the academic curriculum was too evidently middle class to obtain sympathy. True descendants of Donald Clark, they rejected a chance to make the high culture available to all children for fear that it might seduce the working man.[39] Now, some fifty years and several educational revolutions later, the high culture is still the preserve of the minority. Despite the reform of state primary education and the establishment of high schools, state education has not provided that "broad, open stairway accessible to all". The decision of which the junior technical school is both product and symbol still deeply affects Australian cultural life. For however rich the educational experiences offered in this school, it has found great difficulty in shaking itself free from the intentions of its founding fathers — the provision of an alternative to the high culture.

To return to Matthew Arnold and Conan Doyle, and the hope that schooling might flood society with sweetness and light. State education, despite the establishment of secondary schools and the reform of primary education at the turn of the century, has not been able to realize that hope, and in part has worked to prevent its realization. Precisely because of these disappointments, there is much to fear in those who under the guise of reviving intellectual standards or of organizing a "back to basics" movement, proclaim the culturally impoverished nineteenth-century elementary school as an exemplar. The modern state may not have produced the "very high degree of enlightenment" of which Rusden spoke; in many cases it may be little more than a lonely lighthouse blinking on a cold and hostile world. But for many children it is the only source of light, and it has guided some, who would otherwise never have arrived, to culture's exciting harbour.

1981

Notes

[1] Arthur Conan Doyle, "The Naval Treaty", in *The Memoirs of Sherlock Holmes*, Penguin ed., Harmondsworth, 1952, p.215. My attention was drawn to this by its use in W.H.G. Armytage, *Four Hundred Years of English Education*, Cambridge, 1965, p.147.

[2] W.A. Duncan, *National Education*, Brisbane, 1850, p.23; G.W. Rusden, "National Education", *Argus*, Melbourne, 1853, p.218.

[3] A.G. Austin, *Australian Education 1788-1900*, 34rd ed., Melbourne, 1972; G.M. Dow, *George Higinbotham: Church and State*, Melbourne, 1964; Ronald Fogarty, *Catholic Education in Australia 1806-1950*, Melbourne, 1959; J.S. Gregory, *Church and State*, Melbourne, 1973; Denis Grundy, *"Secular, Compulsory and Free"*, Melbourne, 1972.

[4] Quoted in Lawrence Burchell, *Victorian Schools*, Melbourne, 1980 pp.110-11.

[5] Raymond Williams, *Culture and Society 1780-1950*, Penguin ed., London, 1968, p.16; Lesley Johnson, *The Cultural Critics from Matthew Arnold to Raymond Williams*, London, 1979.

[6] J.B.A., *Young Victoria: a contribution in aid of national instruction*, Melbourne, 1871, pp.15-6.

[7] J.J. Burston, *Milton Parsed*, Melbourne, 1880, p.v.

[8] A.R. Trethewey, "Social and educational influences on the definition of a subject: history in Victoria, 1850-1954", in P.W. Musgrave, (ed.), *Contemporary Studies in the Curriculum*, Sydney, 1974, pp.95-9.

[9] W.E. Hearn, *Payment by Results in Primary Education*, Melbourne, 1872, p.9.

[10] J.B.A. (see note 6), p.31.

[11] 69/18153 in Education Department of Victoria, Special Case File (SCF) 227, PRO (Vic.).

[12] *VPD 1872*, p.1883.

[13] SCF 325.

[14] Charles H. Pearson, *Report on the State of Public Education in Victoria* (Government Printer), Melbourne, 1878, p.9.

[15] *VPD 1872*, pp.1352, 1545.

[16] R.J.W. Selleck, "F.J. Gladman — trainer of teachers", in C. Turney (ed.), *Pioneers of Australian Education*, Sydney, 1972, p.78.

[17] *Education Gazette*, September 1902, p.47. The new course of study, with discussions of it, was printed in vols 2 (1902) and 3 (1903) of *Education Gazette*.

[18] For an attempt at this, see R.J.W. Selleck, *The New Education 1870-1914*, London & Melbourne, 1968.

[19] Frank Tate, "The training of teachers" *Australasian Schoolmaster*, June 1895, p.220 and *Literature as a Study for the Teacher*, Melbourne, 1893, pp.31-2.

[20] An observation made by Lawrence Burchell in a 1981 tour of historic schools, organized by Australian and New Zealand History of Education Society.

[21] *Argus*, 16 September 1904, p.7, and 11 July 1904, p.6; C.R. Long (ed.), *Record and Review of the State Schools Exhibition* (Government Printer), Melbourne, 1908, p.19.

[22] For the curriculum of the nineteenth-century secondary school, see E.L. French, "The humanities in secondary education", in A. Grenfell Price, (ed.), *The Humanities in Australia*, Sydney, 1959, pp.34-55.

[23] Sir James McCulloch in 1878, quoted in Larry Jagan, "Education and social structure: a study of secondary and university education in Victoria 1858-80" (M.Ed. thesis, Monash University, 1979), p.216.

24 *Argus*, 2 April 1907, p.7.

25 *Argus*, 7 December 1904, p.9 (Fitchett); Education Department of Victoria, General Correspondence 04/12918, PRO Vic. (McLaren).

26 Frank Tate, *Continued Education* (Government Printer), Melbourne, 1920, pp.11, 3; and *Preliminary Report of the Director of Education upon Observations made during an Official Visit to Europe and America* (Government Printer), Melbourne, 1908, p.11.

27 W.F. Connell, "Myths and traditions in Australian education", *Australian Journal of Education*, XIV, 1970, 253.

28 T.S. Eliot, *Notes Toward the Definition of Culture*, London, 1962, p.101.

29 For the figures, *Report of the Minister of Public Instruction 1914-15*, pp.64-5.

30 The many applications for this position are contained in earlier parts of Victorian Education Department, General Correspondence 1905, PRO (Vic.). The Comment on the agricultural high schools is in Victorian Education Department, High Schools General Correspondence 09/13462.

31 Tate, *Preliminary Report*, p.4; Frank Tate, *"School-Power"* – *an imperial Necessity* (Imperial Federation League of Australia), Melbourne, 1908, p.1.

32 *Church of England Messenger*, 29 October 1909, p.763.

33 *Report of the Minister of Public Instruction 1917-18*, p.19.

34 *Proceedings of the First Educational Congress* (Government Printer), Melbourne, 1912, p.48.

35 *Report of the Minister of Public Instruction 1913-14*, p.86.

36 *Report of the Minister of Public Instruction 1911-12*, p.130.

37 *Proceedings of the First Educational Congress* p.63.

38 F.R. Leavis, *Mass Civilisation and Minority Culture*, Cambridge, 1930.

39 B.K. Hyams and B. Bessant, *Schools for the People?*, Melbourne, 1972, pp.122-8.

INTELLECTUALS FOR EXPORT: AUSTRALIA IN THE 1920s

HELEN BOURKE

In *From Deserts the Prophets Come*, Geoffrey Serle reflects on the range of artistic and intellectual talent that has been temporarily or permanently lost to Australia. To a long list of expatriate writers he adds these:

> England had a notable minority of Australian vice-chancellors, professors, scientists, law-lords, Harley St. specialists, actors and singers and other musicians. About one-third of Australian Rhodes Scholars did not return home; the better part of one thousand Australian university graduates worked in Britain. For many of them Australia could not provide: scientists, like Florey, Cairns or Oliphant, or a historian like Hancock, lacking research facilities; a prehistorian like V. Gordon Childe or a philologist like H.W. Bailey; singers like Melba and innumerable other musicians; dancers like Robert Helpmann.[1]

To Britain we should add the United States and Canada as a destination for many of what A.A. Phillips in another context called our "venturesome minds", and to the creative artists, physical scientists, philosophers and historians we should add those social scientists who made their careers elsewhere: Clarence Hunter Northcott, Meredith Atkinson, H. Duncan Hall, Herbert Heaton, Stanley Porteous, Thomas Griffith Taylor, Persia Campbell, A. Radcliffe Brown, Elton Mayo. Some like Atkinson, Heaton and Radcliffe Brown were not native Australians but they invested substantial years of their lives here — the significant point is that they did not stay. Why could Australia, as Serle puts it, "not provide" for the creative and productive flowering of such talent?

As a contribution to the discussion of culture and the "tall poppy" I want to offer as case studies Herbert Heaton, economic historian and economist, Thomas Griffith Taylor, geographer, and George Elton Mayo, psychologist and industrial sociologist. These three abandoned Australia for North America in the 1920s and pursued distinguished careers there. None of them went as a young man. Heaton was already an expatriate, coming from England to Australia at the age of twenty-four, in 1914, but he was on his arrival full of enthusiasm for the potential of his work in his adopted country. Taylor and Mayo were both born in 1880 and had already spent over half their lives in Australia, being in their forties when they set out for America. Through these stories I want to focus on, if not to untangle, the mixture of factors producing a chosen exile or departure in this period from the War to the Depression. The stories raise large questions about the Australia that Heaton, Taylor and Mayo left. In these three cases the circumstances of their going cannot be separated from the nature and newness of the fields they professed, and from the relation of those fields to Australian society. The application of new "scientific" methods to social problems which these scholars advocated was not, in their view, a cloistered academic activity. By their very nature the social sciences required an extra-mural dimension, an engagement in the education of society at large, and a recognition of the importance of their kind of expertise in public policy and planning. The issues they addressed, therefore, and the responses they evoked, go some way towards illuminating the cultural and intellectual conditions in Australia which they believed had failed them in the 1920s.

*

Herbert Heaton was one of the leading figures in what was by then the second generation of professional economic historians in Britain and America. After his departure from Australia he was elected in 1926 to the Inaugural Council of the Economic History Society and became professor of economic history at the University of Minnesota in 1927, a position he held until 1958. After many years of teaching and writing, his eminence was recognized in his elevation to the presidency of the Economic History Association from 1948 to 1950. His *Economic History of Europe,* written in 1936, was for long the standard text, but he is less well-known as one of the first professional scholars of the economic history of Australia. His articles on the Basic Wage Principle and on Land Taxation in Australia appeared in the early 1920s in the *Economic Journal, Economica,* and Harvard's *Quarterly Journal of Economics.* His *Modern European History with special reference to Australia,* written in 1921 and revised in 1925, predated Shann and Hancock in many of its observations about the economic and social order of Australia. But for the circumstances related here he would have been the foundation professor of economics at the University of Adelaide. Instead, he left Australia in 1925 for a chair of economics and political science at Queen's University in Ontario, before moving soon after to Minnesota.

Heaton came to Australia in mid-1914, recommended by Sir William Ashley, under whom he had been teaching at the University of Birmingham, and by Albert Mansbridge, the founder of the Workers' Educational Association, to initiate the work of the W.E.A. in Australia. He was to fill the post of Director of Tutorial Classes at the University of Tasmania. The Tutorial Class movement was a new pedagogical venture, jointly conducted by the University and the W.E.A. and funded by the State government, concerned with the serious education of the worker.[2] Because of its specified clientele, it concentrated less upon the literature, culture and popular history that had been the usual stuff of the traditional extension lecture and offered instead the new social sciences. Following the programme developed in England for the Oxford Extension Movement by W.E.A. activists like R.H. Tawney, Henry Clay and Alfred Zimmern, Heaton and his colleagues in Australia introduced the worker to economics, industrial history, sociology and international politics. The essential task of this work, then, was to engage extra-mural students in the study and understanding of their contemporary society. This meant lectures on the growth of trade unionism, the development of socialist thought, ideas about worker participation, the origins of Bolshevism and the Russian revolution, industrial legislation and the welfare state, the nature of the Great War and the hopes of the Peace. Few of these topics figured in the curricula of Australian universities in 1920 where there was little study of the contemporary and the modern.

Heaton threw himself vigorously into this work, first in Tasmania and then in Adelaide where he transferred to begin the Tutorial Classes at the University of Adelaide in 1917. In both places his lectures stirred controversy and that degree of personal vilification that seemed to accompany public debate in this period. The first problems arose over his remarks on the Great War. In 1915 he explained to a Northern Tasmanian audience the origins of the conflict, pointing out the economic factors, and he went on to discuss the vexed question of how to end the War. He canvassed what were familiar left liberal ideas in England and America, suggesting that negotiation for peace ought to be preferred as policy to decisive victory.[3] The loud censure that this provoked reverberated in the press, in the University Council and in the Parliament. The *Hobart Mercury* had never taken to the W.E.A. idea. It was sure that the workers needed the "bread of a higher spiritual culture" rather than the "stones" of trade union history and it was quick to demand a parliamentary inquiry, and Heaton's dismissal, should he be proven "disloyal".[4] In an issue which carried lurid German atrocity stories, the *Bulletin* implied that this "imported person" was in sympathy with the "Apostles of Kultur who ravished Belgium".[5] A Tasmanian M.P. declaimed that the people of Tasmania were not sending their sons to the Dardanelles to fight for a draw. In the end the University and W.E.A. supporters like L.F. Giblin stood by Heaton, but after an inquiry he was warned to abstain from expressing personal opinion reflecting upon national policy.

In Adelaide, Heaton continued to address what he saw as the crucial issues of the day — the War and the peace settlements, Bolshevism, the League of Nations, the problems of post-war reconstruction and industry. He became increasingly critical of the state of public discussion on vital matters in Australia, charging that Australia was committed to policies by Australian statesmen who were doped by the Tory London press, and that back in Australia the complexity of issues was never appreciated because of the conservative bias of the overseas cables which supplied Australian newspapers. Challenged on the sources which informed him, Heaton replied that the *Nation,* the *New Republic,* the *New Statesman* and the *Cambridge Magazine* were among the journals he consulted to supplement his reading of the *Advertiser.* Australia as a nation, he declared, had few opinions.[6] We had never formulated any war aims of our own and now in the matter of the Peace,

> this allegedly advanced democracy of ours has sent out no word of hope of a better world, has barked at the heels of those who visualised a new and better international order, and has subscribed to doctrines worthy of a Machiavelli and a Metternich.[7]

This was an attack on Hughes's role at Versailles. Australia, Heaton argued, was neither ready nor able to handle any mandated territory or native peoples since her record on her own soil in these areas was not a pretty one. In March 1920, controversy again greeted his exposition of J.M. Keynes's *Economic Consequences of the Peace* which protested the punitive economic clauses of the treaty with Germany. However, in the public mind, the morality and urgency of a harsh Peace was firmly fixed and Heaton was again accused of being pro-German.[8] Just as he had always resisted the extremes of anti-German hysteria, so he approached the question of Bolshevism with the same academic caution. His lectures to the public surveyed the history of Tsarist Russia, explored the spectrum of socialist ideas and attempted a distinction between revolutionary theory and the excesses of the Bolsheviks. Such coverage was not appreciated by the masters of industry in Adelaide, faced as they were after the war with chronic industrial unrest which seemed to them to ripple out from the tidal wave of Bolshevism.

What bearing did this ferment have on Heaton's professional career? Heaton's job was an especially exposed one making him more vulnerable than most to public criticism and pressure. Apart from his extra-mural work, his appointment within the University was to develop the teaching of economics, and this particular subject was under the continual scrutiny and partial control of the commercial interests of Adelaide. The subject of commerce was surprisingly well-founded in Adelaide. Indeed, after Heaton's earlier employer, the University of Birmingham, this was the first university in the Empire to introduce commercial training for young business apprentices. In 1902 a certificate course had been established; this was upgraded in 1912 to a diploma but the University's refusal to develop it further into a degree course was a direct result of the business community's distrust of Heaton. The Board of Commercial Studies which presided over Heaton's university teaching was controlled by the representatives of the Chambers of Commerce and Manufactures in whose interests and with whose support the courses had been set up. The teaching of commercial subjects was what these bodies wanted; the study of economics was dangerously theoretical and disturbed them. In a public address in 1922, J.W. McGregor, President of the Chamber of Manufactures, voiced their view:

> The University, in its teaching of Economics, had, in the opinion of Manufactures, become, to a large extent, engaged in propaganda work and had been used as a lever by people holding socialist views.[9]

Similar teachings, he warned, had led Russia into her present condition.

As it happened, the field of economics had expanded and flourished under Heaton's guidance. When he came to Adelaide it was little more than a single course in the array of subjects taught by William Mitchell (one of Heaton's first observations had been that Australian professors occupied not chairs but sofas) but during Heaton's nine years there had been a steady growth in numbers and a diversity of courses which made it logical for Adelaide to follow the example of Sydney, Tasmania, Melbourne and Queensland in the establishment of a degree and a chair. The situation came to a head in mid-1925. Following a year's leave in England and Canada lecturing on Australia, Heaton received the offer of a prestigious chair from Queen's University and he used it as an opportunity to clarify his position in Adelaide. Would economics be upgraded and could he expect advancement? The University Council met hastily but on the advice of the Board of Commercial Studies, on which the outside members voted against Heaton, the Council replied that neither an honours school nor a degree was possible unless there was a professor at the head of the school.[10] As the Labour paper, the *South Australian Worker,* remarked, if Heaton had stayed in Adelaide until Doomsday he would not have been given the chair.[11] Heaton's academic reputation was beyond doubt both abroad and in Australia among his peers such as R.F. Irvine, D.B. Copland and L.F. Giblin, all of whom lamented his fate in Adelaide, but as the President of the South Australian Labor Party, deploring the University's action, concluded in the Parliament, Heaton's ability

> like that of many a good man in South Australia had not been recognised and he has gone to another country as so many have gone to other states.[12]

Heaton was by no means an extremist radical thinker — he called himself a "Lloyd George liberal" and may, like Tawney and other liberal intellectuals, have joined the British Labour Party in 1918 had he stayed in Britain. He did not receive the monolithic support of labour groups in Australia, being attacked by the socialist left and the promotors of the Labour Colleges as a tool of the capitalists who tried to dull the consciousness of the workers with bourgeois learning. But he did believe, and preach, that economics was concerned with welfare, with the distribution of wealth, and that economic policies must consider social consequences. He was not a technical economist and, unlike Copland, did not find business men congenial. Nor did he promise the positivist certainties of the new economic science which allayed the suspicions of commercial leaders. After 1925, William Mitchell battled with Heaton's opponents to persuade them of the need for a chair in economics in the face of their fears of subversive doctrine and, in 1929, L.G. Melville, a conservative actuary, was finally appointed to the position.

*

As Heaton sailed from Adelaide, Thomas Griffith Taylor, associate professor of geography at the University of Sydney, wrote to him requesting a copy of one of Heaton's articles. He also inquired whether Heaton had ever been in "hot water" for saying unpatriotic things. Heaton's reply was outspoken:

> My chief offence has been that I trod on the stupid golden corns of Adelaide's elderly plutocrats, and the sequel would make a good appendix to an Australian edition of Upton Sinclair's *Goose-Step.*[13]

Acknowledging the benefits of Taylor's work on Australia, Heaton asked whether Taylor had ever considered a move to North America where, unlike in his own land, his work was highly regarded. He had already mentioned Taylor's name to the University of Toronto which was planning to establish a department of geography. Taylor warmly responded:

> Our paths have been somewhat alike as regards public non-appreciation! However, my colleagues stand by my views and the "many-headed" will learn to agree with us — after we are dead.[14]

Three years later, in 1928, Griffith Taylor did leave Sydney to take up a chair at the University of Chicago. Seven years on from there he did become the foundation professor of geography at the University of Toronto where he stayed twenty years until his retirement. Taylor's career in Australia, and his departure, provide suggestive parallels with those of Heaton.

Griffith Taylor came to Australia at the age of thirteen in 1893. At the turn of the century he studied science at Sydney University, specializing in geology under Edgeworth David. After further study at Cambridge he was invited to join Scott's Antarctic expedition and, on his return to Sydney, he worked for the Commonwealth Weather Service doing research into meteorology and continuing his study of glacial topography. In 1916, his geological work in the Antarctic earned him a Doctor of Science from Sydney University and he enjoyed his share of the limelight that surrounded the survivors of Scott's journey to the Pole. It was in the Weather Service that he began to develop his life-long interest in the relation between climatic conditions and the expansion of human settlement. He assisted Edgeworth David in the survey of the site for Canberra and was a founding member of the C.S.I.R. and the Australian National Research Council. By 1920, he was the author of several books and his work was attracting considerable interest from leading American geographers such as Isaiah Bowman and Ellsworth Huntington.

In 1921, Taylor was appointed to the first full-time post in geography in Australia, that of associate-professor at the University of Sydney. Like Heaton at Adelaide, he sought unsuccessfully during his tenure to have his position upgraded. With a skeleton staff he built up a flourishing department while his own work continued to provoke international attention, particularly with the publication of his controversial study, *Environment and Race,* in 1927. He was awarded the Livingstone Centenary Medal of the American Geographical Society in 1923, and at various times during his subsequent career he was President of the British, American, and Canadian Associations of Geographers. By his death in 1963, the list of his publications was a long one, spanning sixty years of vigorous research and writing.[15]

Taylor's work and theories were certainly the subject of debate among geographers in the 1920s but it was not the struggle on the academic page that consumed his energy so much as what he self-consciously styled his "struggle to educate Australia". Like Heaton he took on the determined role of publicist, arguing that the nation's policy-makers and planners must understand the proper scientific basis for their projections and their use of the public money. The questions to which he urged the application of sound geographical principles were vital to Australia — the extension of human settlement and the future composition of the race, in all, the development and peopling of Australia. Taylor believed that in temperature, rainfall and soil, Nature had laid down a design for human settlement and he declared it the geographer's task to interpret this programme.[16] Interpreting Nature's plan for the future of Australia led him into a head-on collision with the so-called "boosters" of the day, those, including W.M. Hughes, who spoke of a land of two hundred million people, of yeoman holdings across the country — "cabbages in the heart of Australia" — and those who were busy with ambitious migration schemes to attract desirable settlers from England and Europe. Taylor relentlessly punctured this balloon, stating repeatedly in the academic forum and the popular press that a great part of central Australia was desert, comparable on his criteria to the Sahara. Accordingly, he asserted that the future population would be limited. 44% of Australia he labelled "arid"; of that, half was dismissed as "almost useless" and the rest might support pastoral stock in good years. His projection was for twenty million people settled in the east and the south and engaged in agriculture and manufactures. The future millions of Australia would live precisely where they lived in 1925 and the wise statesman, Taylor wrote, was one who would mould his policy "in harmony with the varying environment for which it is his privilege to legislate".[17] In particular, he meant that no money should be wasted trying to develop the north and the tropical sparselands, a view that ran counter to the interests of pastoralists and politicians from those parts. The projected North-South railway, from Adelaide to Darwin, was one of his special targets; he argued, instead, for a route to Darwin through the more economically viable areas of northern Queensland.

Taylor's designation of desert areas was quite specifically not based on the observations of travellers and explorers. He countered popular report with more calculable measures of rainfall, temperature and soils. The result was outrage. The West Australian government banned his geography text-book as a libel upon the state's potential and he was accused of being "unpatriotic" for publishing opinions and maps which could deter future migrants.[18] A typical letter to the *Sydney Morning Herald* catches the flavour of the controversy:

> All good Australians will most regret that a professor of the Sydney University has published a map which may be seen in other countries of the world, showing a huge area in Australia as "almost useless".[19]

There were further attacks in predictable places. The *Bulletin* and *Smith's Weekly* charged him with the sin of pessimism — he was a "Doctor Dismal", a "modern Jeremiah", a gainsayer of the future of a great nation. The *Bulletin* insisted that the north of Australia had assets calculated to arouse the envy of poor but fecund and ambitious neighbours yet Taylor had called the Northern Territory a "gigantic white elephant".[20] Visitors and explorers were enlisted in the debate. One eminent Arctic explorer, Vilhjamur Stefansson, according to the *Sydney Morning Herald*, had been unable, in his travels in 1924, to locate the "alleged desert" in Australia. This led the member for the Northern Territory to ask in the Parliament whether Taylor would now desist from his "perpetual slander" of the inland.[21]

The issue of the peopling of Australia in this period was not only about where future populations would settle but about which races should compose the population. Various migration schemes were preoccupying State governments and, in 1926, the Federal government established a Development and Migration Commission. It was not just

a question of White Australia but of which European migrants were to
be preferred. Following the United States Immigration Act of 1924
which imposed restrictive quotas in response to the increasing numbers
of South-Eastern European migrants, there was a clamour for similar
measures in Australia. Some practical steps were being taken to control
the numbers from Italy, Greece and the Balkans and there was little
resistance to the idea that supposedly inferior races should be excluded
from Australia's white democracy.[22] Taylor's contribution to the
debate, however, was to muddy the categories and confuse the
certainties about which races were the inferior ones. The theories he
advanced concerning the evolution, classification and migration of races
were partly derived from an existing and controversial body of
ethnological and anthropological thought, and partly his own
speculation.[23] He suggested that classification by skin and colour had
long been abandoned and that race and nationality — or colour and
continent — were no longer simple equations:

> Immigration problems concern the statesman of today considerably but
> they are not conversant with the major principles of ethnology and so
> confuse nation and race — the British and the German are taken to be Nordic
> and conclusions are drawn that this is more valuable than Mediterranean
> man.[24]

Such conclusions, Taylor insisted, were not trustworthy. In a highly
complicated and debatable thesis, relying on measure by the cephalic
index and on his own theory of climate zones and race migration,
Taylor advanced the proposition that there were primitive folk on all
continents, that there were ethnic allies to the British among the
aborigines of other countries, and that, on his criteria, "we are
confronted with a growing belief that the Chinese and perhaps the
Japanese are our superiors".[25] Thus he could view with equanimity
the prospect of mixed races in the tropical north and the employment
there of coloured labour. He did not believe in racial purity and scorned
the glorification of the Nordic race. The reaction to this was quite
vicious: the press invented terms like "counsel for the Yellow Streak"
and added lampooning cartoons. Under the headline, "To Smear
Australia Yellow", the *Sydney Sun* assured its readers:

> The Australian is in practically every sense a thoroughbred. Physically, and in
> native intellect, in all racial qualities that matter, he is as far above the average
> Mongol as "Gloaming" is above a rabbiter's hack. A more repugnant
> prospect than that pictured by the Sydney scientist it would be difficult to
> conceive . . . . Meanwhile Professor Taylor will have added to the circle of his
> admirers in the Commonwealth's Chinatowns.[26]

In his autobiography, Taylor's decision to leave Australia is dealt
with briefly and in institutional terms:

> Dissatisfied with conditions in my department at Sydney (lack of staff
> accommodation, and equipment, not to mention the matter of salaries), and
> seeing little prospect of improvement, I was to accept in July the invitation
> of the University of Chicago to become Professor of Geography there.[27]

His letter of resignation from the University of Sydney referred
to his lack of preferment but also to his desire to find a position where
his work was more appreciated.[28] The recurring complaint of "public

non-appreciation" is, in his recollected experiences, a dominant strain in his memory of Australia. For Heaton and Taylor, however, lack of public appreciation had not meant lack of public interest. They were never ignored and, although they met with some opposition from within their universities, they were to an extent consoled by the respect of overseas fellows and the few colleagues in their fields at home. A third exported intellectual, Elton Mayo, had almost none of these things. His case is a manifestation of a different malaise of the intellectual in these years in Australia — isolation and the lack of opportunity to develop. Yet, in the long run and in other climes, he became one of the "tallest poppies" Australia has produced, in terms of his impact on the definition of an intellectual and professional field.

*

Mayo is recognized as one of the seminal figures in the development of social theory and applied social science in the twentieth century because of both his empirical research at the Western Electric Company in Chicago — the so-called Hawthorne experiments — and because of his major books, *The Human Problems of an Industrial Civilisation*, written in 1933, and *The Social Problems of an Industrial Civilisation*, published in 1949. His work has been subjected to much scrutiny and criticism since the Hawthorne experiments but it was, nevertheless, the body of data and theory which set the framework for subsequent debate in this area. The opportunity for testing his ideas was given to Mayo in America but the foundations of his social thought were almost fully articulated by the time he left Australia in 1922.[29]

Even to this point Mayo's career had had some false starts. Born into a prominent Adelaide family in 1880, he had twice attempted medical studies, in Adelaide and in Edinburgh, and then abandoned this for some years of living in London, reading, writing occasional articles, and teaching at the Working Men's College. On his return home in 1904 he went into a partnership in an Adelaide printing-firm but he soon left it to resume his university studies, this time in philosophy and psychology under William Mitchell at the University of Adelaide. In 1911 he was appointed to the first lectureship in mental and moral philosophy at the new University of Queensland. Unlike Heaton and Taylor, he gained fairly rapid promotion to the foundation chair of philosophy in 1919.

Mayo's interest in political philosophy and his reading of Freud and the French psychologist, Pierre Janet, combined with his experience in medicine and in worker education to lead him into new directions, into the field of industrial psychology. His personal acquaintance with social anthropologists, Malinowski, Pitt-Rivers and Radcliffe Brown, drew his attention to the operation and place of human groups and to the function of work in human society. He moved also into the practice of clinical psychology in Brisbane during the War and was one of the pioneers in the treatment of shell-shock patients. Drawing on all this theory and practice, he began to formulate an analogy between the chronic industrial unrest in Australia and the mental neurosis caused by war. He argued that the individual's morale — or mental health —

was determined by the degree to which he understood the social purpose of his work, felt that it was "socially necessary" and was able to look beyond his task to the larger society. In his long essay, *Democracy and Freedom,* published in 1919, he wrote that when work signified "intelligent collaboration in the achievement of social purpose" then industrial unrest would cease to exist.[30] Such a collaboration was, he believed, available to those simpler societies studied by the anthropologists but the identity between the social code and the individual's motive had been lost in the disintegrating effects of industrialization.

As a psychologist, Mayo adopted Janet's theories of the sub-rational, of behaviour originating in what he called the "mental hinterland". It was in these reaches of the mind that work dissatisfaction lit up "the hidden fires of mental uncontrol". Following this proposition, industrial unrest was seen as a form of neurosis, the damages of which could be repaired by psychological techniques allied to the insights of social anthropology. Political and legislative solutions, such as higher wages or systems of arbitration, did not, in Mayo's logic, attend to the deeper causes of social disorder. In fact, revolutionary theory was consigned to the status of fantasy construction: what else, he asked, is Socialism but "an endeavour to regain a lost sense of significance in the scheme of things?"[31] Thus the key to social harmony, as Mayo saw it, lay in research of a psychological and sociological kind, not in politics or economics. Yet, in Australia, as he pointed out in 1919, there was no co-ordinated attempt to develop such inquiry:

> Beyond the shores of Australia, the world-storm rages with increasing intensity; our will to internal cohesion is constantly disturbed by social disorder and a class-hatred that is fast becoming stereotyped. Yet we alone, of all the civilised nations, give no serious consideration to the deeper social causes of disorder.[32]

Mayo addressed this message to many bodies and journal readers in the post-war years but, although knowledge of clinical psychology was increasing among medical men, there was no scope or support for the sort of field-work which Mayo wanted, investigating and classifying industrial problems at the factory level. Feeling increasingly frustrated, and also encumbered by his university duties, he simply threw up his job to make yet another start elsewhere. He set off for England via the United States, leaving his family in Australia until he could support them. On the West Coast of America he arranged a private lecture-tour to promote his ideas. Here his talks and articles attracted immediate interest, securing him a Rockefeller grant at the Wharton School of Finance at the University of Pennsylvania. He conducted research there into the reasons for high labour turnover at a textile mill near Philadelphia; his experiments were credited with reducing turnover and increasing output. This work brought him also to the attention of the Harvard School of Business Administration to which he was invited in 1926 and where he became professor of industrial research until 1947. It was there that he joined, and shaped, the experiments being conducted at the Hawthorne plant of Western Electric; the results of these investigations became synonymous with his name. The successful manipulation of small work groups at the Hawthorne plant appeared to vindicate Mayo's idea that if work could be perceived by the workers as a social function rather than as a source of personal frustration then spontaneous human co-operation — and improved industrial output — would result.[33] Such a theory was particularly congenial to Mayo's new American context because it both challenged and dissolved the concept of class consciousness and supplanted it with a principle of social integration.

Mayo became a major figure at Harvard and a major figure in the development of social theory. What was to him, in Brisbane, a bleak future was transformed into a career which in its trajectory would have been beyond Mayo's dreaming before he left Australia. The question of the possibilities of career, of diversity of choice and opportunity, is often a decisive factor in the choice of expatriation. The career of another social scientist, Persia Campbell, is further illustration of what was available elsewhere. She was already unusual in Australia when as a young woman graduate of the University of Sydney in 1918 she left to study under Graham Wallas at the London School of Economics. Like Taylor, she engaged with the problems of race and labour: her book *Chinese Coolie Emigration* was published in 1923 and the following year she went to Bryn Mawr College to extend her study to American immigration problems. Returning to Australia, she worked from 1926 to 1930 as a research economist with the N.S.W. Industrial Commission and taught W.E.A. classes in economics. One of the first recipients of a Rockefeller grant, she studied American agricultural policy at Harvard, publishing a book on this in 1933. Her expatriation was no doubt secured by her marriage to an American at this time but the range of her subsequent career is still of interest here. In the 1930s she became involved in consumer advocacy and took a Ph.D. at Columbia on the subject of consumer representation in government. Her thesis on the New Deal was published in 1940 and, then a widow, she joined the economics faculty of Queens College, New York, where she remained until her retirement as Emeritus Professor in 1965.

From her academic base, Campbell was able to work as a grass-roots organizer of the consumer movement from its beginnings to its full development as a national body. She worked to promote consumer education among low-income groups, wrote many pamphlets and articles, and was active in radio and television broadcasts. In 1954, she became the first consumer counsel to advise the government of New York on consumer legislation. In 1962, she was appointed by Kennedy to the President's Council of Economic Advisers and was retained by Lyndon Johnson. Her mission was not confined to the United States, extending to participation in international conferences on women in the Pacific and Asia. She became the representative of the International Organisation of Consumers Unions at the United Nations as a member of the board of directors of Consumers Union which published *Consumer Reports*.[34] What Persia Campbell might have done had she returned to Australia is, of course, unknown, but in 1932 it would have been difficult for a woman economist to have launched a career which would so combine academic, public and participatory, and governmental roles. This, as in Mayo's case, is not so much a question of tolerating the "tall poppy" as of providing a theatre for ability — the soil to nourish such talent.

*

What wider inferences concerning the conditions for intellectual work may be drawn, then, from these stories of expatriation? There is undoubtedly the matter of personality. Both Heaton and Taylor were energetic combatants in controversy, provocative in style and sometimes mischievous in their wit. They, and Mayo, were convinced of their own rightness, perhaps of their superior sophistication, and their visions were never bounded by Australia. They yearned for success, for appreciation, and in Mayo's case for a fulfilment which had as yet eluded him. The desire to make a contribution and to find an audience has always propelled people from the periphery to the centre and from the provincial to the metropolitan. But, personalities aside, the conditions for intellectual work in Australia in these years were difficult. There were complaints of the endemic burdens of university work, poor funding, growing student numbers and understaffed departments. Opportunity for research and for preferment was narrow and tardy. Not the least of the limitations were the related tyrannies of distance and intellectual isolation. Taylor spoke of the impossibility of creating what he called a "geographical atmosphere" in which to work when his was the only full-time post in an Australian university — he wrote to Heaton, "I should like to be nearer the centre of things".[35] At Chicago alone there were four chairs in geography so that the reinforcement he sought was both more available and more possible in America. Much of the isolation felt by these figures was due to the newness of the fields they professed: the social sciences had only the shallowest roots in Australia at the end of the War. The neglect of Mayo's ideas stemmed from this. The field towards which his theory was heading did not exist in Australia, except for some primitive welfare measures in a few industries. Lateral and eclectic thinking which fused political philosophy with barely established disciplines like sociology, anthropology and social psychology, was destined to fall on infertile ground.

At a still broader level we may be alerted by these stories to the relationship between the university and the community in this period. It was at once too close and too remote. The funding of the universities was from state government Bills and parliamentary members sat upon the university governing bodies. The opinion of the legislature was important, making the universities sensitive to criticism that might result in questions in the House or the alienation of members of the business community who might supply supplementary funds for new developments. In small, provincial cities like Adelaide and Hobart, the style and message of a well-known speaker from the university commanded a deal of public attention; the public lecture was as yet unchallenged by radio or moving pictures and received a full report in the newspapers. On the other hand, the very rationale of universities themselves had not bitten deeply into Australian public life. There was little faith in research. Despite occasional philanthropic bequests, there was no investment of private or public money in social inquiry or in research institutes like, for example, the Brookings Institute or the Social Museum at Harvard. There were no Australian equivalents to the Rockefeller or the Russell Sage Foundation to fund and encourage the collection and analysis of social data. Without such private philanthropies, the social sciences in the United States would never have enjoyed their spectacular take-off in the 1920s. There was in Australia a developing organization of the physical sciences by the end of the War as evidenced by the C.S.I.R. and the Australian National Research Council but the recognition of social science expertise in assisting national planning was much slower to eventuate. These expatriates urged the relevance of "scientific" social knowledge to the solution of social and national problems, but at the same time they rejected the narrow utilitarian acceptance of their fields that governments and public preferred. The expatriates were disconcerted by the profound suspicion of theory which was a salient part of the anti-intellectualism that had repelled them.

Mayo, Taylor and Heaton were all engaged in outsider occupations in traditional universities. The issues they addressed involved them in criticism of their contemporary society at a time when university curricula paid little attention to the modern. Outside the university, the role of such intellectuals was even more unrecognized. As P.D. Phillips wrote in 1928 in the introduction to a series of essays entitled *The Peopling of Australia,* there was

a crying need in the Australian community for a development of that class vaguely but sufficiently described as "publicists" which does so much to clarify and assist social discussion in the older countries of the world.[36]

But those who set out to fill such a role — to make and inform opinion in Australia — courted the dangers of public reaction and of journalistic comment which was far more inclined to polarize issues than to refine their complexities. Challenging the components of the national psyche, White Australia, Australia Unlimited, the Standard of Living, the Imperial Tie or the Bolshevik menace, was a hazardous business in the public arena. Heterodoxy — like the "tall poppy" perhaps — needs more complex and differentiated societies in which to thrive.

1984

Notes

[1] Geoffrey Serle, *From Deserts the Prophets Come,* Melbourne, 1978, p.127.

[2] See A. Mansbridge, *An Adventure in Working-Class Education, Being the Story of the Workers' Educational Association 1903-1915,* London, 1920.

[3] *Mercury,* 25 August 1915.

[4] ibid., editorials, 17 April 1915 and 10 September 1915.

[5] *Bulletin,* 16 September 1915.

[6] *Advertiser,* 23 June 1919.

[7] H. Heaton, "Australia and the League of Nations", *Australian Highway,* Vol I, no.3, 1919, 10-11.

[8] *Register*, 16 and 17 March 1920.

[9] *Advertiser*, 28 November 1922.

[10] *Minutes of the Board of Commercial Studies*, University of Adelaide, 29 May 1925.

[11] *South Australian Worker*, 26 June 1925.

[12] F.W. Birrell, *South Australian Parliamentary Debates*, 6 August 1925, p.335.

[13] Heaton to Griffith Taylor, 14 September 1925, Griffith Taylor Papers, MS 1003/9, National Library of Australia.

[14] Taylor to Heaton, 26 October 1925. Griffith Taylor Papers, op. cit.

[15] See G. Taylor, *Journeyman Taylor. The Education of a Scientist*, London, 1958. A bibliography of Taylor's writings is contained in J.K. Rose, "Griffith Taylor 1880-1963", *Annals of the Association of American Geographers*, LIV, 1964, 624-9.

[16] G. Taylor, "Geography and Australian National Problems", Presidential Address to Section E, Australasian Association for the Advancement of Science, Wellington 1923, XVI, 4343-441.

[17] Taylor to *Sydney Morning Herald*, 7 March 1925. Taylor's Presidential Address to A.A.A.S. 1923, op. cit., gives an extended discussion of his views. See also Taylor, "The Frontiers of Settlement in Australia", *Geographical Review*, XVI, 1926, 1-25.

[18] See Ian Douglas, "Frontiers of Settlement in Australia — Fifty Years On", *Australian Geographer*, XIII, 1977, 298-9.

[19] A. Middleton to *Sydney Morning Herald*, 6 June 1924.

[20] Presidential Address to A.A.A.S. 1923, op. cit., 484 and *Journeyman Taylor*, p.171.

[21] See J.M. Powell, "Taylor, Stefansson and the Arid Centre. An historic encounter of 'Environmentalism' and 'Possibilism' ", *Journal of the Royal Australian Historical Society*, LXVI, 1980, 163-83.

[22] A.H. Charteris, "Australian Immigration Policy" in P.D. Phillips and G.L. Wood (eds.), *The Peopling of Australia*, Melbourne, 1928, pp.72-107.

[23] For the full statement of Taylor's theory see G. Taylor, *Environment and Race; a study of evolution, migration, settlement and status of the races of man*, London, 1927.

[24] Taylor, "Race and Nation in Europe", *Australasian Journal of Psychology and Philosophy*, IV, 1926, 4. See also Presidential Address to A.A.A.S. 1923, op. cit., 476-82.

[25] ibid., 476.

[26] *Journeyman Taylor*, p.178.

[27] ibid., p.205. For another discussion of this episode see J. Powell, "Griffith Taylor Emigrates from Australia", *Geographical Bulletin*, X, 1978, 5-13.

[28] Taylor to Vice-Chancellor, University of Sydney, 30 July 1928, Griffith Taylor Papers, op. cit., N.L.A.

[29] Mayo's ideas are discussed more fully in H. Bourke, "Industrial Unrest as Social Pathology: The Australian Writings of Elton Mayo", *Historical Studies*, XX, 1982, 217-33.

[30] E. Mayo, *Democracy and Freedom*, Melbourne, 1919, p.60.

[31] Mayo, "The Will of the People", *Industrial Australian and Mining Standard*, 26 January 1922, p.160. For an elaboration of these ideas see Mayo's five articles published in "The Sociological Department" of *I.A. & M.S.* during January and February 1922.

MEN OF WEALTH

W.D. RUBINSTEIN

Wealth, I fully realize, is a dirty word at discussions of culture, and I touch this subject only with some trepidation. You will recall, of course, George Bernard Shaw's famous remark to Sam Goldwyn, the Hollywood producer: "The difference between us, Mr Goldwyn, is that you're only interested in art and I'm only interested in money". It will become clear as I go on, I hope, that I am only interested in art. Vulgar or not, in one respect wealth is a surprisingly good test-case for the subject of Australian tall poppies and their putative demise, for the chief and explicit concern of one side in Australian politics, since 1890 at least, has been the cutting down of rich tall poppies. Certainly, any discussion of the subject must address the attitude of Australian Labour and Australian Socialism to the rich.

However, let me begin by spelling out some of the major persistent historical traits in Australian wealth-holding and in the wealth élite, for I want to ask if the reason for the persistence of these traits has been the character of the rich themselves or certain wider, and more basic characteristics of Australia's place in the world. The answer that suggests itself to that question also suggests, I think, the reason for some persistent traits in Australian culture and national character apparently far removed from those of the economic élite.

This is not the place to present a barrage of quantitative statistics on the rich in Australia, and conclusions on this subject have already been published in several places.[1] Nevertheless, I must summarize some of those conclusions briefly for the sake of the argument to be suggested here. I have systematically studied the wealthy in Australian history from the probate records in all of the states between 1817, when the N.S.W. records begin in a usable form, and 1939, and have — thus far in my research — systematically investigated the lives and careers of the fifty top wealth-leavers per five-year period (e.g., 1880-4, 1885-9, 1890-4) in N.S.W. and Victoria. I have thus studied the lives and careers of many hundreds if not thousands of such wealthy persons from whatever biographical material exists. But as well as that, I have examined the lives and careers of the wealthiest persons in Britain, according to much the same criteria, since the early nineteenth century;[2] and it is from this international perspective that I chiefly wish to discuss my conclusions about the nature and evolution of wealth-holding in Australia and about the wealthy class in Australia — conclusions that, in so far as my data permits any, are very similar for all of the states.

The most significant conclusions about wealth and the wealthy in Australia until World War II and possibly beyond are three. The first is the demonstrably low level of fortunes achieved by Australia's wealthiest persons compared to those in other developed societies, especially America but also Britain and Europe.[3] The second is the broad similarity of the occupational fields in which Australian fortunes were made, with pastoralism and commerce, especially the woollen export trade and related areas, predominating at least until the inter-war period. The third is the broad similarity of the social and ethnic backgrounds of Australia's wealthy men: Scots Presbyterians and English Anglicans disproportionately — strangely enough, groups from the *non-*industrialized areas of Britain — provided the great bulk of the Australian wealthy down to World War I at least, while Irish Catholics (as we might expect) and Protestant dissenters (more surprisingly) were under-represented.

Each of these topics is a broad one, and each would obviously require a lengthy essay to treat in a considered way; my discussion here can only be of the briefest nature. As to the first, the comparatively low level of wealth enjoyed by Australia's rich, this is clearly shown in the following graphs.[4] They record the peak and tenth-highest fortune left in each five-year period in America, Britain, and N.S.W., and the peak, tenth, and twentieth-highest fortunes left in N.S.W. and Victoria.[5]

A glance at these tables — which are arranged by a logarithmic scale — reveals a clear-cut conclusion. Compared with American or even British levels of wealth-holding, Australian peak fortunes, even in N.S.W. and Victoria, were extremely low. Being very rich (and hence, presumably, economically powerful) meant something quite different in America, Britain, and Australia.[6] Until World War II, there was a gap of between four and twenty times between the *peak* levels of wealth in America and Britain, and of between three and ten times between Britain and the two largest Australian states. These differences first appear early in the history of each society and persist without much change to the last year of the study. In the United States, even before the Civil War, the fortunes of the greatest capitalists, such as Astor and Vanderbilt, were certainly already far larger than Britain's peak business fortunes, despite Britain's status as the "workshop of the world". The very wealthiest American multi-millionaires of the post-Civil War "Gilded Age", such as Rockefeller, Mellon, Ford, and Carnegie, were immeasurably wealthier than any individuals in history. In contrast — and in contrast to other parts of the white Empire like South Africa and Canada — Australia's top fortunes were extremely meagre. Australia produced fewer than thirty bona-fide sterling millionaires in the period between 1788 and 1939, and only a single person — the Sydney retailer Samuel Hordern — who left more than £3 million.

Possibly the first reaction many people will have to this conclusion is that it is not surprising — who would expect otherwise? Although, as we shall see, there are good and cogent economic reasons that partly explain the performance of Australia's economic élite, the very expectation that Australian élites would not be comparable to others elsewhere is part of a pattern of expectations — the psychological demeaning of Australia's international standing — which, though notoriously widespread, is without any real rational basis. Why *should* Australia's economic élite have been significantly less successful than their equivalents elsewhere? Because Australia is a new country? — But so in the United States. Because it lacks major natural resources? —

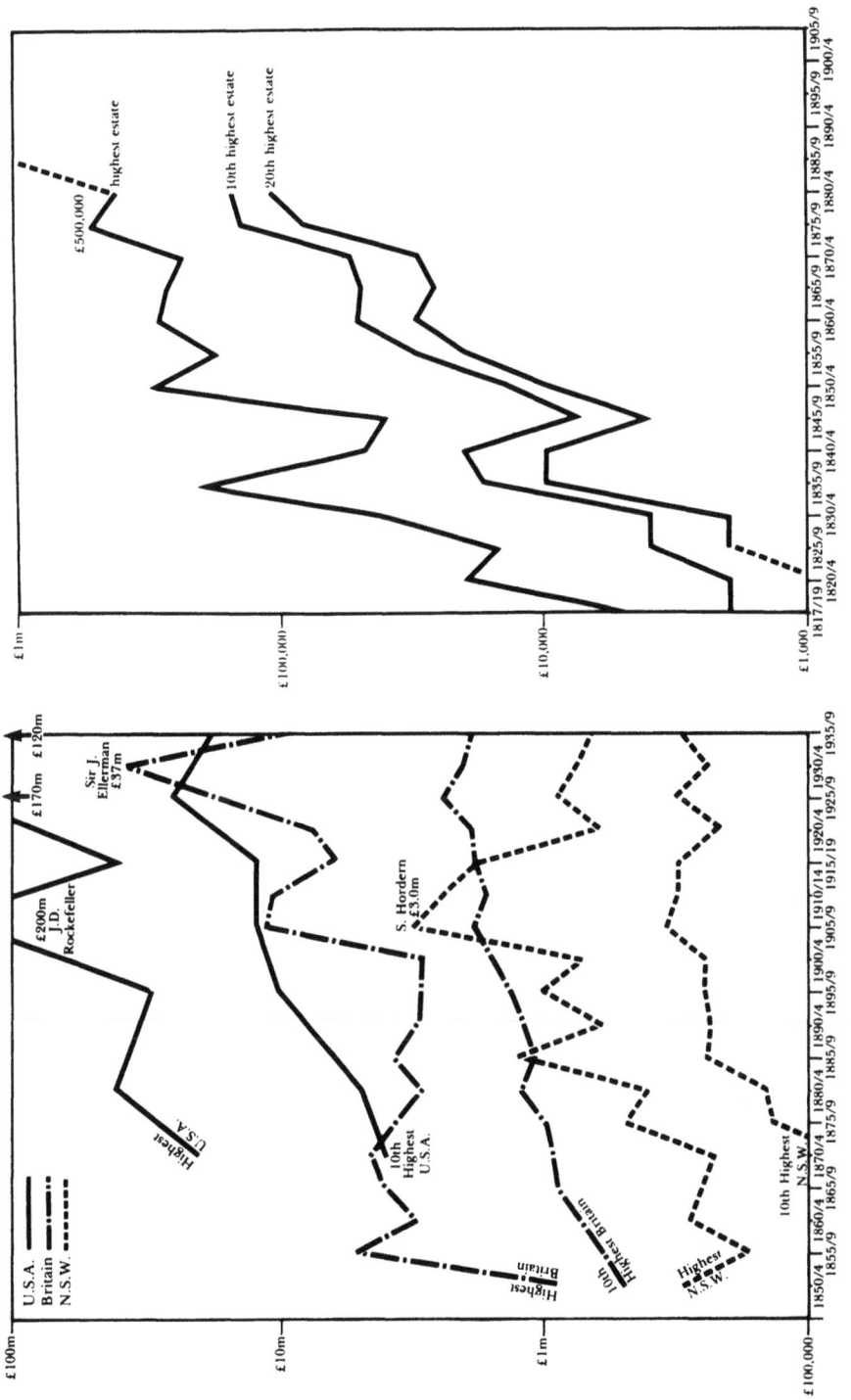

Table 2: New South Wales 1817/19—1880/84

Table 1: Peak Fortunes, United States, Great Britain,
and New South Wales, 1850/4—1935/9

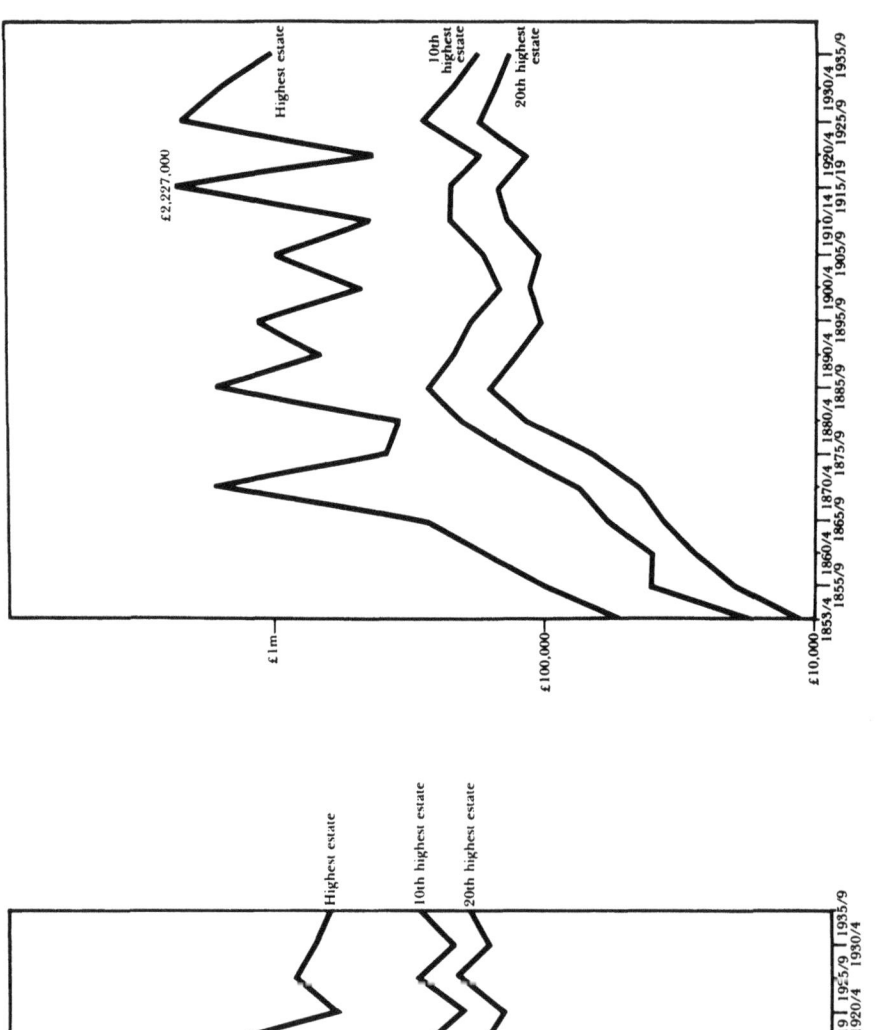

Table 4: Victoria 1853/4–1935/9

Table 3: New South Wales 1885/9–1935/9

But many if not most wealthy men in other countries earned their fortunes in other ways than the exploitation of resources. Because it is an unpopulated country lacking a large market? — But it was part of an empire, a giant economic unit, on which the sun never set. Because of legal constraints on the accumulation of wealth or on capitalist economic activities? To be sure, railways were state-owned and internal tariff barriers existed until 1901; but can these really explain such a phenomenal difference?[7]

One factor many would point to in explaining this difference is the quality of Australia's entrepreneurs. It could quite well be that Australia's very small population threw up, simply on a random basis, far fewer highly talented businessmen — talented at being businessmen, that is — than Britain or America. And certainly, Australia's prevalent national ideology did not encourage entrepreneurship in the same manner and with the same insistence as Horatio Alger's America or even Samuel Smiles's Britain. Yet no one who has studied the careers of Australia's leading entrepreneurs in detail can fail, I think, to be impressed by their quality — in particular, by the willingness of many to try a new line of endeavour and to expand their areas of enterprise into new fields where there was often pre-existing stiff competition and where they had little apparent expertise. It is worth looking very briefly at a number of such careers, all of men who appear among the top wealth-leavers in Victoria and N.S.W.

Robert Towns (1794-1873) was apprenticed to a colliery vessel in North Shields, rose from mate to master and then shipowner, and settled in Sydney in 1843. After working as a mercantile agent for Robert Brooks & Co., he traded in sandalwood in the South Pacific and had ten whalers. He next turned to pastoralism, and by 1867 had 42 runs covering an estimated 2,000 square miles in the Kennedy district of Queensland alone, plus 154 runs covering 1,600 square miles in Queensland and N.S.W. Townsville is named for him. Turning his activities to finance, he served as a director of the Bank of N.S.W. for eleven years and as its President for three. He was President of the Sydney Chamber of Commerce, and director of many companies. He found the time to serve as Member of the Legislative Council in N.S.W. for fifteen years. Despite his lowly origins, he married William Charles Wentworth's half-sister. William Moffitt (1802-74) was apprenticed as a bookbinder in Liverpool, sentenced to seven years' transportation for stealing tea, and was assigned to the Engineers' Department upon arriving in Sydney in 1827. Within a few years, he set up as a book-binder, stationer, engraver, and copperplate-printer. Prospering, he served as director of the Australian Joint Stock Bank, and acquired Sydney freehold properties, mortgages, debentures, and bank shares. He published pioneering almanacs and local directories, and executed the first banknotes for the New Zealand Bank. Nathaniel Levi (1830-1908), a Jewish migrant from Liverpool, worked as a clothier, arrived at the goldfields as an autioneer, and joined a wine, spirit and general merchants firm. He became interested in coalfields and sugar beets, of all things; he opened a distillery at Footscray; and he began a newspaper, the Melbourne *Daily News,* which lasted for two months.

For many years he held the sole lease for all advertising on the Victorian
Railways. He erected the Liverpool Buildings in central Melbourne,
served as the first Jew in the Victorian Parliament, and was one of the
founders of the Melbourne Chamber of Manufactures, as well as its
President. David Mitchell (1829-1916), the son of a tenant farmer in
Forfarshire, was apprenticed to a mason and arrived in Melbourne in
1852 to work as a mason. His first house was a shanty on a lot in
Richmond. He began the next year as an independent building
contractor, won the tender for the masonry work on St Patrick's
Cathedral, began a lime and cement foundry, and later opened a plaster
factory. He had cheese, butter, bacon, ham and soap factories at Cave
Hill, and a dairy with Victoria's "first mechanical milking device". He
acquired pastoral stations in the Upper Murray and the Western
District, and owned vineyards and wineries. Principally a building
contractor, he gave Melbourne the Menzies Hotel, the Scots Church,
the Masonic Hall, the Presbyterian Ladies' College, and the Exhibition
Buildings. To the world he gave his daughter, Dame Nellie Melba.[8] In
their enterprise, drive and business success, these figures, and many
others, could quite plainly stand comparison with their colleagues in
Victorian England and "Gilded Age" America. Yet their pecuniary
rewards, when set beside a Rockefeller or even an Overstone or a
Baring, were extraordinarily meagre. Towns left £74,000, Moffitt
£230,000, Levi £54,000, and Mitchell £290,962. Obviously, they
became wealthy men; but they were poor by any international
standard.

The level of these Australian fortunes was low compared to the very
wealthiest Australians, however — men who apparently lacked the
same wide-ranging business talent as those just described, and
concentrated instead on one particular line of business. Samuel Hordern,
for instance, who left over £3 million, was chiefly if not entirely a
retail merchant. So was Sidney Myer. Sir Samuel Wilson was chiefly
if not entirely a pastoralist. William John Turner Clarke, in comparative
terms possibly the richest-ever Australian when he died in 1872,
was chiefly a pastoralist. Paradoxically, men who were extraordinarily
good or lucky at one type of entrepreneurial activity often wound up
much richer than wide-ranging business tycoons. Yet this is not so
surprising if we consider the second of the general points made above,
that Australian fortunes were disproportionately earned in a number
of characteristic areas. In N.S.W., for instance, pastoralism and
commerce were the chief occupational fields of the majority of top
wealth holders in virtually every cohort group in my study, and I am
sure this is true a fortiori of the other states until the inter-war period
at least. There was in Australia, as there is in every country, a
typology characteristic of its wealth structure and economic élite — a
pattern that delimits, defines and constrains the type of entrepreneur
who will ultimately be most successful. These typologies limit both the
amount of wealth and economic control that successful entrepreneurs
can acquire of exercise, and the fields or areas in which economic
success can be achieved. Although entrepreneurs occasionally "beat
the system", to do so requires individuals of almost superhuman abilities,

possibly from outside the normal socio-cultural groups likely to produce most successful entrepreneurs.[9]

In a recent article on "Entrepreneurial Effort and Entrepreneurial Success", I have discussed this phenomenon in an international context, and I argue that place of origin is more important than ability.[10] I think that the same might apply to place of entrepreneurial success too. The evident inability of Australian entrepreneurs to amass wealth on a scale comparable to those in other advanced societies, seems to me primarily the effect of limitations inherent in Australia's place in the world economic-system at least until 1939. How and why this was so is obviously a complex and contentious issue, and it would be inappropriate to discuss it here; but the most salient point is that the ability of Australia's entrepreneurs had little or nothing to do with their over-all degree of economic success. Men like Sir Edward Knox, the founded of C.S.R. who left £124,000 in 1901; or James Rutherford, manager of Cobb and Co., who left £212,000 in 1911; or A.R. Lysaght, the steel-maker who left £126,000 in 1920, would certainly have been multi-millionaires had they been American entrepreneurs — and possibly the founders of companies that might be household names around the world and of dynasties the social equal of European aristocracies. Instead, they possessed only a local fame and little influence not merely beyond Australia but beyond their state or town.

What this suggests, I think, is that much of Australia's *apparent* propensity to cut down tall poppies is illusory, and due entirely or almost entirely to the fact that seemingly tall poppies are actually short ones. There are qualifications and complexities that should be added to that sweeping statement, of course, but broadly speaking — and speaking here exclusively of wealth and entrepreneurial success — I know of remarkably little evidence to support the contention that Australians do cut down tall wealthy poppies. The mechanisms by which many other industrial societies since the 1890s have deliberately attempted to equalize wealth and income, from death duties to capital-gains taxes, have been present in Australia only in a limited or ineffective form, or not at all. Yet despite the absence of such equalizing legislation, most studies of Australian income and wealth distribution have noted the comparatively equal distribution of income and wealth in Australia.[11] To be sure, Australia (like many other Western societies) developed and has maintained a populist rhetoric of tycoon-bashing, finance- and capital-bashing, and radical egalitarianism (almost invariably combined with White Australian racism). This arose at about the same time as the Australian Labor Party became a major political force aorund 1890.[12] Yet one may wonder what concrete results the continuing rhetoric of Australian populism and radical egalitarianism ever produced. The most notable political event to occur in the heyday of populistic rhetoric, Australian federation, enshrined a Constitution that made European-style socialism near-impossible of achievement; and this Constitution was, after all, enacted by popular electoral majorities of those who bothered to vote in all of the states. The most significant economic enactment of this era, the Harvester Judgment, could well be seen as part of the historic Australian compromise wherein working-class wages were set at historically high rates in exchange for high tariff walls and a White Australia, Empire-linked overseas policy; in any case, the Harvester Judgment was made against H.V. McKay, the millionaire agricultural-machinery maker whose anti-unionist policies were quite extreme by the standards of Australian businessmen.[13] Although the populist and radically egalitarian rhetoric of the Australian labour movement was (and perhaps still is) a potent force, it accomplished remarkably little by the standards of nearly any other Western society.

It is also a question whether the rhetorical denunciations of business life and capitalism extended to any personal animosity towards the businessmen themselves. During the period to World War I it is striking how many of Australia's wealthiest men were elected to state parliaments, just as Britain's millionaires were at this period and just as the American Senate was known at the time as the "millionaires' club". Just to take one example of this from a slightly earlier era, the great pastoralist William John Turner Clarke — "Big" Clarke, who died in 1872, leaving nearly £2 million — was throughout his career possibly the most attacked and reviled business figure of his day. When he first stood as a candidate for the Victorian Legislative Council in 1856, *Argus* stated:

> As far as we can learn Mr. Clarke possesses nothing whatever to recommend him, except a monstrous pile of wealth and a certain kind of intelligence that might once have been cultivated to some good end, but which has for many years been entirely confined to the one absorbing occupation of money-making until it has become quite unfit for all other uses . . . . Everyone has heard of his enormous gains — no one has heard of his doing or attempting to do any good with them . . . . We cannot for a moment suppose from what we hear of Mr. Clarke that he cares a straw for the colony, except in as much as the colony contains Mr. Clarke's property.[14]

Clarke was, needless to say, triumphantly elected and returned throughout his career. At the 1862 election he received three times as many votes as his opponent; his biographer notes that

> a quite remarkable feature of the voting was the overwhelming support accorded Clarke in the country districts and particularly, in the areas where he was a large landowner. His popularity with his neighbours, as revealed by the poll was quite extraordinary . . . . [Clarke] had become a legend in his lifetime. People expected him to be mean and they joked about his miserly habits. They also expected him to enlarge his holdings and in some curious way they respected him for his financial achievements . . . . Members of the Hobart or Melbourne establishment were happy "to drop his name" as an acquaintance but it was to the man in the street that he most appealed. They could identify with his struggles, his ambitions his mode of life.[15]

All the historical evidence known to me points to this being the prevalent Australian attitude to businessmen until the time of World War I or later: a thinly-veiled admiration for those truly successful entrepreneurs, shown in such ways as easy election to Parliament, and co-existent with a populist rhetoric of egalitarianism. Although these two co-existing attitudes may seem incompatible and certainly paradoxical, that is surely only a superficial view of the matter. Plainly, the prevalent Australian rhetoric of populist egalitarianism was the product of what sociologists term "relative deprivation" — the perception that one's peers are more advantaged than oneself, and that one is penalized or victimized unfairly – a sense of Australian inferiority when compared to Britain, to Europe, or even to America. That tacit comparison with America is especially important and particularly galling. For while Australia and America were seemingly sister democracies, twin daughters of Britannia, it was America which rose between 1860 and 1910 from frontier obscurity to the status of world super-power, economically the strongest country in the world by the early part of the twentieth century, while Australia languished as a small, remote, beleaguered white island, still a synonym around the world for remoteness. Given this pervasive sense of relative deprivation, it is not surprising that the few genuinely world-class products of Australia (whether in the economic sphere or any other) should be admired, boosted, and championed by these self-same Australian radical egalitarians – indeed, touted with a bravado and bombast, characteristic of the age, that bespoke only vulgarity and inner doubts. The absence of a strong and, by international standards, dominant Australian economic élite probably contributed to the force and significance of Australian populism and the ambiguity of its platform and demands. A reading of the *Bulletin* and similar journals shows that while the City of London and international finance capitalists were regularly denounced, few Australian entrepreneurs were singled out for similar odium. Although the laws of libel plainly were a factor here, it is no less true that the odium of populists was directed overseas, not at Australian targets.

I would like, more controversially, to extend some of these observations to other spheres of Australian life where I believe there is an unexpectedly strong parallel to the economic sphere. We have found that there were natural limitations, flowing from Australia's peripheral or semi-peripheral role in the world economic system,[16] which defined and constrained Australia's native economic élite, both limiting the size of their fortunes and their economic significance, and ensuring that only in certain economic areas – predominantly pastoralism and commerce – were substantial fortunes to be made at all, regardless of the quality or ability of the entrepreneur. It seems to me that a similar process has been at work in other areas of Australian life, including cultural life: Australia's peripheral or semi-peripheral situation has worked automatically to make the products of Australian cultural and intellectual life ignored or denigrated among the centres of Western cultural and intellectual life in European and, in this century, in North America. The point is that this process has been at work regardless of the intrinsic merits of these Australian cultural artefacts. This process has served, of course, to reinforce Australia's populism, its sense of relative deprivation, its natural inferiority complex, its long-standing "culture cringe". With some notable (and rare) exceptions, prior to the very recent past Australian cultural products have been generally ignored, and certainly regarded as exotic and remote rather than important or significant or central, simply because they were made in Australia. If I could add a personal note here, I grew up and was educated on the east coast of the United States, and without having

a really keen or central interest in the subject, studied literature at high
school and university. Yet in all the years I did so I never once
encountered an Australian writer, and I do not believe I ever heard of
Marcus Clarke, Henry Handel Richardson, Henry Lawson, A.D. Hope
or whomever one wishes to name. I am sure my experience was
altogether typical. Possibly in the last ten years the popularity of
Patrick White and of Australian cinema has changed this; I will return
to this possibility later on. But I am equally certain that much the same
is true of every cultural field, though music, which is truly international,
may be a partial exception because of people like Dame Nellie Melba
and Percy Grainger.

Much the same experience was once America's, and it might be
useful to contrast the two. Until the very end of the nineteenth century,
Europe invariably considered America a land of barbarians and refused
to grant any centrality to its cultural products. The two cases are not
exactly parallel, of course, for America had already produced, before
its rise to world leadership, figures like Poe and Emerson who were
influential in Europe, and had also given democracy to the world. But
over-all, the attitude of Europeans to America was one of amused
contempt until the late nineteenth century. What changed this was the
rise of America to world economic and political leadership and, after
1918 and more especially 1945, to world centrality. The increasing
centrality of the United States as it were retroactively legitimated its
cultural products, and a significance was discovered in figures such as
Melville, Whitman, Henry Adams, and Charles Ives, which had hitherto
been unperceived. America, of course, really did become central after
1918. New York did become the world's cultural capital; America's
universities carried out most of the world's significant research; more
Nobel Prizes went to Americans than any other nationality; and so on.
With Australia, many people still believe that the relative disregard of
its cultural products is actually well-deserved, rather like the
psychiatrist who told his patient, "Now I know why you have an
inferiority complex: you're inferior"; and not even the greatest admirer
of Australia could contend that it really is a second, undiscovered
America. Nevertheless, I wonder if Australians known and admired
only locally would not be considered internationally significant if
they had lived and worked elsewhere. It is not hard to imagine a
flourishing Ph.D. industry about Henry Handel Richardson had she
been a compatriot of Edith Wharton's and Edna St Vincent Millay's.

Part of the reason why Australian cultural artefacts are "objectively"
less significant than those elsewhere is the third of the points I made
earlier: the ethnic and socio-cultural groups that mostly settled the
continent. Australia notably lacked the two groups that contributed so
disproportionately to American and European culture: the small
Protestant sects like the Congregationalists, Quakers, and Unitarians,
and those from a cosmopolitan European cultural background, either
those socialized in the "official" culture — French Catholics or German
Lutherans — or, more notably, those marginal to European culture like
the Jews. The relative absence of these groups, in the context of a
society whose own élite, along with its value-system, was marked by

weakness, by an inferiority complex and by a colonial identity in every sense, probably imposed limits on the richness and significance of Australian cultural artefacts up to 1945. This mediocrity was reinforced by factors *sui generis* to Australia. One was its peculiar university system, traditionally marked by the importation of young Oxbridge or Scottish professors of considerable promise but little output, to enjoy lifetime tenure remote from the centres of research, without resources and in a climate of cultural conventionality. There was also the myopic Babbitry of, for example, the trustees of the Felton Bequest;[17] censorship; anti-Oriental paranoia, and not least, the long and under-noticed record of the "ratbags" who were so much a part of the Australian cultural and popular scene from the 1860s or 1870s to the 1930s (or later). These included eccentrics like Edward Cole the book-seller; political cranks and theorists of every description from Social Creditors to international socialists; sexual experimentalists like William Chidley; unconventional artists like Norman Lindsay; and many others. Every English-speaking country possessed a similar element, of course, especially America of the (roughly) 1875-1925 period; but every other country also possessed, or at least had access to, a high culture of genuine distinction — a culture comprising not only art, music and literature, but a growing scientific and technological community that increasingly formulated the common image of the world and received increasingly large amounts of public spending. In Australia, apart from the small and isolated university sector, the cranks and eccentrics seem to have comprised whatever cultural life there was; and most of them worked outside the artistic realm altogether or produced little or nothing of any great value. They were certainly not the equivalent of the experimental modernists of Vienna, Paris, or Bloomsbury, or even of the eccentrics of, say, contemporary New England, men like Wallace Stevens or Charles Ives who turned out, fifty years later, to have anticipated modern culture. With a handful of exceptions — and possibly some who await rediscovery or reassessment — the Australians' record is notably arid.

Finally, the very fact of Australian remoteness meant that if talented Australians were to be noticed, they had to leave to seek their fortunes in the wider world. The list of notable Australian cultural figures who lived and worked for substantial portions of their careers in England or elsewhere from — Melba and Richardson to Patrick White — is arguably longer than for any comparable nation. This again meant that little of note was produced in Australia itself. There were few fields, from science and medicine to painting and music, in which a really talented Australian could stay at home and remain abreast of his peers, at least until the 1960s. Hence the many peculiar odysseys of Australian cultural figures — like Percy Grainger, for example, champion of "Nordic" racism, who lived and died (in 1961) in New York, of all places.

When all these factors are considered, the question whether Australians do cut down their tall poppies assumes a different aspect, I think. As far as Australia's economic élite is concerned, my view is that external and largely ineluctable circumstances limited, and delimited, the nature of its peak performances, despite the talent or ability of its entrepreneurs. I would also argue that something quite similar has been true in the cultural realm. There were simply few tall poppies to cut down. However, the question still remains, whether Australians did cut down such tall poppies as there were. One the whole — and, again, the parallel with the economic sphere is clear — I would say no. Indeed, when a truly talented Australian did appear, the typical Australian attitude was one of naïve adulation: Melba is perhaps the best example of this. Such an attitude is entirely consistent with the nationalistic drum-banging of relative deprivation. Australian attitudes towards, say, sex or left-wing politics and their advocates may have been extreme but were not basically inconsistent with those at the time in England or America. The real question here is whether there has even been a case of a talent of obvious international stature who chose to remain and work in Australia but who, remaining here, was harassed and brow-beaten to the point where he could not continue in his field. It is difficult to think of any such case, though it is hard to reckon here with the many talented Australians who voluntarily lived abroad. Nevertheless, if such cases did exist, I doubt if a list of them would be as long as many people imagine.

Since 1945, and certainly since 1960, the basic situation of Australia as a remote, semi-peripheral, minor nation has increasingly changed, and I am quite certain that what I have been describing in its past is no longer true. As a stable, pleasant, prosperous, democratic preserve, Australia appears increasingly to offer more satisfactory living conditions than the centres of the northern hemisphere, and it has become more cosmopolitan, pluralistic, and diverse. Much of its old relative deprivation has gone — though certainly not all — or been transformed. Much, probably most, of its pervasive racism has gone as well. The transformation of the A.L.P. from a chauvinistic, racist party of populism into a party of permissiveness and the "green" left is especially striking. Australia now exports its culture and cultural values, and is highly regarded for these around the world. Yet, strangely enough, an Australia that has been transformed in this way is perhaps more likely to cut down its tall poppies than the Australia of old. An ideology of genuine egalitarianism, of genuine freedom from the culture-cringe, and of genuine attempts, often politically inspired, to be free of Britain and America, may present more difficulties to the would-be national leader in some cultural sphere than the old Australia did. Moreover, the ease of international travel and communications may well make expatriation more common rather than less.

I would, therefore, regard the transformation of Australia over the last forty years as a mixed blessing for anyone who genuinely values independence and high achievement in the arts or sciences. High achievement in the arts or sciences has usually occurred in periods of general national good will and well-being — as in Elizabethan England — or in periods marked by the precise opposite, by a revolt of original thought and creativity against a formalistic official culture: *fin-de-siècle* Vienna or the American expatriates in 1920s Europe are obvious examples. A relatively tolerant, enlightened and prosperous Australia, where patriotism is devalued and national achievments rare is likely, I suspect, to have too anodyne a culture to produce much of lasting value. There is also the inexorable march of consciousness and sensibility from what might be termed the literate to the numerate, a change that Australia, largely lacking the scientific resources and dedication of America, Western Europe or Japan, is ill-placed to share. Australia will doubtless go on awarding more and more Australian knighthoods to its Sidney Nolans, Joan Sutherlands, and Patrick Whites, but it might well produce fewer and fewer of them.

1984

Notes

[1] Most notably Rubinstein, W.D., "Wealth in Australia", *Quadrant,* June 1980; "The Top Wealth-holders of New South Wales, 1817-1939", *Aust. Econ. Hist. Rev.,* XX, 1980, 136-52 and "Elites in Australian History", in Robert Manne, ed., *The New Conservatism in Australia,* Melbourne, 1982.

[2] On Britain, see Rubinstein, *Men of Property: The Very Wealthy in Britain since the Industrial Revolution,* London, 1981.

[3] On this subject, see also Rubinstein, "Entrepreneurial Effort and Entrepreneurial Success: Peak Wealth-holding in Three Societies", *Business History,* XXV, 1983, 11-29.

[4] These are taken directly from my essay in Robert Manne's collection, op. cit.

[5] The American data was compiled by Professor Frederic Jaher (University of Illinois), the British and Australian data by me. It should clearly be noted that Australian wealth-holders who returned to Britain and left substantial wealth there (like Sir Samuel Wilson or the Salting family) are included in the *Australian* figures, not the British.

[6] Such European figures as we have are similar to those for Britain. The peak fortunes in France and Germany just before 1914 are very similar to those in Britain at the time, far below America's peaks and far above those in Australia. See *Business History,* XXV, 1983, loc. cit.

[7] A number of qualifications should be noted here. Of course, Australia's population was only a tiny fraction of America's. In 1850 Australia's total population (excluding Aboriginals) was 405,356; in 1890, 3,151,355; and in 1920, 5,411,297. In contrast, the population of the United States in these three years was 23,191,876; 62,447,714; and 105,710,620. But Australia was part of a world-wide Empire, and small size in itself does not invariably imply dependence. It should also go without saying that Australia and America are *similar* in many respects; in fact, few countries are more similar in a host of cultural, information, and value-oriented ways.

[8] The information on these figures comes from their notices in the *Australian Dictionary of Biography.* The information on Levi is supplemented by the manuscript autobiography, "Sketches from the Career of a Representative Citizen, the Hon. Nathaniel Levi, J.P., ex M.L.C.", LaTrobe Library, State Library of Victoria.

[9] In Rubinstein, "Entrepreneurial Effort . . ." loc. cit., pp. 24-6, I discuss the case of Sir John Ellerman, possibly the only British entrepreneur whose career constitutes such a successful and anomalous *tour de force.*

[10] ibid., p. 21.

[11] See Leonard Broom, F. Lancaster Jones and Jerzy Zubrzycki, *Opportunity and Attainment in Australia,* Canberra, 1976, pp. 47-50 and Rubinstein, "The Distribution of Personal Wealth in Victoria, 1860-1974", *Aust. Econ. Hist. Rev.,* XIX, 1979, 26-41.

[12] The subject of Australian populism remains scandalously ill-explored by historians. Humprey McQueen's *New Britannia* is still the most suggestive study. See also Baiba Berzins, "Douglas Credit and the A.L.P." in Robert Cooksey, etc., "The Great Depression in Australia", *Labour History*, 17, 1970, 148-60.

[13] There is a similar ambiguity, of course, in Australia's great radical moment at Eureka. The Stockaders were, after all, in revolt for the right to become instant millionaires on the goldfields, not for a radical programme of reform.

[14] *Argus*, 18 August 1856, cited in Michael Clarke, *"Big" Clarke*, Melbourne, 1980, pp. 149-50.

[15] Clarke, ibid., pp. 204-5.

[16] The terminology here is Wallerstein's. I employ it because it is useful, and this does not imply anything about my endorsement of Wallerstein's system. Similarly, although this paper might appear to be an exercise in "dependency theory", I would be extremely wary of endorsing this perspective without qualification. Some "dependent" countries — like colonial America — prove remarkably independent. *Sui generis* cultural factors, unlinked to economic dependency, often exist and prove more important than these linkages.

[17] For the remarkable record of lost opportunities in the purchase of available European art for Melbourne, see Leonard B. Cox, *The National Gallery of Victoria 1961-1968: A Search for a Collection*, Melbourne, n.d.

MODERN NERVES, NERVOUS MODERNS:
NOTES ON MALE NEURASTHENIA

DAVID WALKER

In the editorial notes which introduced the first number of *Vision* in May 1923, there were bold pronouncements about what the magazine stood for. It was certainly to be a new magazine; like all new magazines it was to be fresher and more challenging than its competitors. It would display an unmistakable intellectual vitality; there would be a willingness to tackle big ideas in a big way. Though this was to be a new kind of magazine for Australia, the editors made it obvious that they did not want to be called modern. By 1923 they had formed a very clear idea of what being modern in the art world entailed: "physical tiredness, jaded nerves and a complex superficiality are the stigmata of Modernism." To be modern would be to both accept and reflect the exhaustion that seemed so evident in post-war Europe. It seemed to follow that Europeans were much more exhausted as a people than Australians. A new magazine, one that responded to Australian conditions, could hardly afford to be modern in this enervated fashion. The *Vision* group insisted that they would "vindicate the youthfulness of Australia, not by being modern, but by being alive".[1]

Energy, vitality, youthfulness and Australia were all high on *Vision's* list of priorities and closely bound together. There was a large claim being made here that Australians were a much more highly energized people than the unfortunate Europeans. If Australians were a people of superior energies, as was often claimed, it seemed to follow that vitality would become the hallmark of Australian cultural statements. More than that, readers of *Vision* were assured that this magazine was the work of Australian artists, a group notable for their energetic, manifestly robust presence. The Australian artist in full possession of youthful energies was depicted as quite a different being from the tired European. The Australian artist had become a person physiologically incapable of experiencing or understanding what *Vision* took to be the modernists' major theme: the nuances of exhaustion. If Australians were a different people, and the *Vision* writers believed they were, it was because they were physiologically superior to their European contemporaries. They were more vital.

Vision saw it as part of its mission to celebrate and enlarge the sphere of bodily energies. *Vision* wanted to attract subscribers with active minds who shared their belief that vitality was the foundation of great art. If culture in Australia was conducted along such lines, there seemed little doubt that it would enhance the body and its energies, rather than produce "the jaded nerves" of the physiologically modern. *Vision* combined a complex identification with health, youth and vitality, with the explicit conviction that modernism was a sure sign of a culture in collapse. Accordingly, one might expect that the ability to respond to the high achievements of European culture, the greatness of the old masters, would be more keenly developed among Australians than among modern Europeans. Vital old Europe would live again in the new Australia. Australia would be the last great European nation, the final repository of European culture, and the only surviving remnant of a living Europeanism in which racial pride was the key element. *Vision* was part of a much broader and diversely expressed racial pride movement. This was one of the visions behind *Vision*, that Australia would become the sort of society in which the greatest Europeans would have felt at home and in which the old masters would consort happily with Australian artists. Though there are different ways of representing the concerns of this magazine, it is clear that contrasting statements about energy and exhaustion were pervasive.

It ought to be noted here that Norman Lindsay, a frequent contributor to *Vision* and student of vitality, was wary of attempts to explain "Creative Effort" and "Mind" as expressions of race or nationality. Lindsay insisted, nevertheless, on his own rather rarefied physiology of the mind. Mind was "substance plus force held together by a geometrical pattern". He invited those who were curious about this substance of mind to make a careful analysis of "electro-dynamics" and the "energy of the light electron" from which it would become "apparent" that the substance of mind was governed by "the universal law under which all atomic force becomes matter". Quite so. When Mind encountered the beauty and rhythmic perfection of great art "its substance must become vitalized; its atomic compactness redoubled". It was the task of creative effort to vitalize the substance of mind.[2]

Appeals to the superior vitality of the Australian artist were not confined to *Vision*. The *Age*, which would later dismiss *Vision* as a crude Sydney attempt at culture, took modern art as the theme for an editorial in April 1920 — prominent notice for a topic often discussed in its pages. When the editorialist contrasted modern European art with its Australian counterpart, he found mere "soul squirmings" among the Europeans; it was weak, trivial stuff when compared with an Australian art that was manifestly "young and healthy and going its own virile way with little time to waste on introspection". Again, we find the notion that since Australian art was grounded in a different physiological experience, it could not help but express its superior vitality. At this level, vitality was not something the Australian artist set out to acquire; it was not something learnt, but an endowment. Moreover, on this question, *Vision* and the *Age* both seemed convinced that vitality was essentially a male endowment. The artist in Australia was characteristically a young male of superior energies. For the *Age*, art was almost a branch of athletics.[3]

Similar affirmations can be found among writers close to the Victorian Socialist Party. Frederick Sinclaire (former editor of the *Socialist* and from 1915 editor of *Fellowship*, a journal that attracted a number of key Melbourne intellectuals) drew a sharp distinction between the vital, energetic and robust Australia he identified with the unexpectedly large anti-conscription cause, and the exhausted culture of Imperial Britain clamouring, so it seemed, for yet more young men to fight and die. Again, Sinclaire seemed convinced that what he believed to be the real Australia was as conspicuously energetic as the Imperial culture was exhausted. This was clearly a different argument from any to be found in the pages of *Vision*, but there is nevertheless a similar conviction that a peculiar vitality was one of the native endowments of the Australian.[4]

Vance Palmer, who knew Sinclaire and wrote for his magazine, also saw close links between physical vitality and literary production. He left his readers in no doubt that robustness and vigour were among the special qualities of Australian literature. Again underlining the special male quality of this observation itself was Palmer's 1923 statement that Australian literature had largely been confined to a male readership. To have women take over this readership, he suggested, would bring a superfluity of tears and a hothouse atmosphere. He feared the creation of a tearful, neurasthenic, emotionally-enfeebled community. The suspicion that male energies were becoming exhausted in a weepy and womanized world is plain enough in Palmer's writing for us to conclude that he too saw male energies as a physiological barrier against the inroads of neurasthenic modernism.[5] In passing, we can note how closely Palmer's concerns echoed those of Basil Ransome in *The Bostonians*: "the masculine tone is passing out of the world; it's a feminine, a nervous, hysterical, chattering, canting age".

Palmer's defence of masculine energies did not convince P.R. Stephensen, who dismissed Palmer's work as weakly imitative of current European literary fashions. Stephensen believed that there had been a "decline of physiological standards in the Australian community"; it was this physiological decline that explained what in 1941 Stephensen termed Australia's "mental decadence". Stephensen clearly wanted nothing to do with psychiatry, and he labelled its University practitioners "Mumbo-Jumboists, practising modern witch-doctory"; he saw them as yet another demonstration of the madness of modernism. Stephensen believed that the cure Australia needed was not mental, but physical. This psychological decline entailed mental havoc and Stephensen listed twenty-six symptoms.[6]

The twenty-six symptoms form a strange assembly, not least for the enormous significance Stephensen was prepared to discover in what might seem trivial failings. To move from "inattention" as a symptom of mental decadence, to the "extinction" of the Australian community "within a relatively short period of historic time", is to take a giant step, but one in keeping with a physiological tradition in which a wrong action or a bad habit could lead to ruin. Included were such conditions as "listlessness", which headed Stephensen's list and which was a close relative of neurasthenia; but other forms of mental failure were failure of creative power, deficiency in imagination, inability to convince, and incapacity to recognize decadence. Other conditions pointed more directly towards a failure of the nervous system: instinctive shiftiness, incapacity to look straight, and incapacity to walk straight. Though he struggled to keep the possibility of an Australian culture alive, Stephensen often doubted if modern Australians possessed "the vitalistic impulse from which a new Nation is engendered".[7] Above all, Stephensen declared himself convinced that the modern Australian was physiologically inferior to the Australian of the late nineteenth century, a criticism which he applied to men and women, though he blamed the men more, believing that it was their responsibility to preserve the integrity of the culture. As Stephensen saw it, the generation of culture was an essentially male pursuit; it was only in diseased times that women and Jews took control in the way Stephensen imagined they were doing.[8]

While Stephensen wrote of how invigorating Australian literature ought to be, Australians consumed tonics as never before in the continuing belief that to be modern was to be exhausted. Stephensen was fond of claiming that Australian literature had vitalizing and strengthening properties, and was much more vigorous than its modern English counterpart. One of his techniques was to draw up an Australian eleven who were to be pitted against the best the British could offer. In this manner, a literary contest was given explicitly physical overtones. It was impossible to imagine batsman T.S. Eliot withstanding fast bowler Xavier Herbert. Even our women were more manly than their men. This appeal to physical prowess as the foundation of a healthy literature suggested that the purpose of literature was to encourage and display the vital energies of the people, a troubled aspiration at a time when Stephensen believed that national energies had never been at a lower ebb.

If we turn our attention from the literary to the medical sphere, some striking parallels emerge. While the *Vision* group planned their new magazine and called for scripts, the *Medical Journal of Australia* published an article in 1923 on the diagnosis and treatment of neuroses. The author emphasized that neurasthenia was a particularly common modern complaint, and despite the Freudian gloss of the article, he offered a familiar physiological explanation: "the condition is brought about when the daily expenditure of nervous energy is greater than the daily income ...". In the same number of the journal an American company advertized its new system of Organotherapy as a successful cure for neurasthenia. The advertisement warned that "the storm and stress of modern civilization exhaust the reserve force of the organism" just as the Great War had done.[10]

It might appear from the evidence to date that the relationship between modernity and exhaustion was a product of the years of the Great War. There can be no doubt that the war was considered a peculiar drain on nervous energies; but theories of modern exhaustion pre-dated the war by many years. Nor was the suggestion that physiology and culture were closely linked at all new. In 1896, A.G. Stephens remarked that "literature was based on physiological principles". He made the claim in an essay on the Brontes in which he argued that the literary genius which ran so strongly through the family was the product of diseased nerves.[11]

There is a striking, though very different, demonstration of the role of the body in Stephens' account of a visit to Archibald, his old *Bulletin* editor. Archibald was in Callan Park asylum after being certified insane at the instigation of the *Bulletin's* business manager. It was a nasty episode and Archibald was convinced that he had been wrongly incarcerated. Stephens entered the asylum at 6.00 p.m. just as "several bands of lunatics" were going to their dormitories for the night. Archibald was not in the main building itself, but in a large cottage some distance away. When Stephens entered, Archibald introduced a Hansard typist as his wife: "Did you ever see a finer girl than that?" Archibald now fell into an extravagant monologue on his publishing plans, at the end of which he told Stephens that he felt terribly strong: "Just feel that muscle". Stephens did so, and while he considered the muscle "hard enough" he recognized that the poor fellow was only "skin and bone". Stephens later commented that Archibald was very conscious of his personal strength and "frequently he has invited me to feel his muscle", traits also evident in Charles Moses and Bishop Burgmann.[12]

It is unlikely that Archibald would have approached Stephens "frequently" in these muscular exchanges if he had found him unsympathetic to tests of physical strength. Stephens admired this kind of embodied force. He was in the audience to hear Professor Tucker, of Melbourne University, defend Greek and Latin because they trained the mind, but he was not convinced. He concluded that Australia wanted scholars, but that it wanted "fighters far more − fighters upon every line of human effort, fighters in every field of national progress." Australia was a society which made heavy demands upon the physical energies of its people and, with the Japanese victory over the Russian navy still fresh in the mind, Stephens hinted that the need for fighters might well increase. The wastage of physical energies through excessive mental labour was deemed a luxury Australia could not afford.[13]

Stephens worked with a different understanding of physiology from the *Vision* writers. There are, for example, many more references to particular organs and their respective functions; and for him the body was a complex physiological machine. This view of the body enabled Stephens to make statements that now seem quite extraordinary. He believed that writers could be divided into two categories: "those with bad quality brains and good quality bodies and those with good quality brains and bad quality bodies". We see Stephens imaginarily tinkering around with the internal organs of his writers, wondering what different results might have been achieved with a bigger brain, better bile or a finer liver. He found the Brontes fascinating, but wrote more excitedly about their nerves than their novels. For Stephens, their genius could be taken for granted; the real mystery was the physiology of genius. He was inclined to believe that to get a genius you wanted "a good quality blood with plenty of red blood corpuscles" from one parent and "a good quality brain and a touch of nervous disease" from the other. This fasination with the physiology of genius rather than its products is the characteristic of a culture that identified with the process of self-completion − a culture that considered itself "youthful".[14]

For the *Vision* school, energy was no longer understood solely in terms of internal organs, each individual presenting a different combination. Though energy was certainly influenced by the functioning of the body, they included more remotely caused racial and national factors. The *Vision* writers were fascinated by the historical distribution of vital epochs in the world's history and they argued that Australia would have its own chance to attain vitality. But feeble bodies and jaded nerves nevertheless remain a significant theme in *Vision's* discourse on modernity.

Though the references are inconclusive, it seems clear that an important though diverse group of male writers had come to think of Australians as physiologically different from Europeans and characteristically more energetic. What is much less clear is not so much the appeal of vitality, but the logic and sheer authority of physiological explanations of how the body was energized and how it was drained of its energies. What role might the physiological sciences have played in making nervous disorders and jaded nerves seem an inevitable consequence of modernity? This question prompts another: was there a physiology of youthful vitality and exhaustion? There are some potent legends in our culture about the death of the male; many relate to participation in two world wars, when death came as a sudden executioner. The culture of early death, its ceremonies of grief and expiation, can sometimes override other, slower deaths: the decline of energy, the often justly feared transition from splendid youth to dulled manhood.

The physiology of the mind/body relationship was a major subject of nineteenth century enquiry. Much was at stake. Many physiologists considered that their researches might explain the sources of human energy. In their efforts to conceptualize these processes, the brain and the nervous system were subjected to particularly close scrutiny. In each case it was commonly supposed that scientists would discover particular susbstances which governed the supply of mental and nervous energy. From the late eighteenth century, electricity had been advanced as a likely source. Looking back over developments in his field in 1829, Dr Pritchard noted that the discovery of electricity — "a subtle, intangible, invisible agent" — caused great excitement among physiologists, "many of whom became convinced that the vital principle was either a similar agent or was electric fluid itself". Discoveries such as these suggested that the supply of energy to the brain and the nervous system might become routine therapies. Indeed, by the end of the nineteenth century electric therapies were widely advertised as effective methods of restoring lost nervous energies.[15]

In assigning a central role to the nervous system and nervous diseases in the formation of literary genius, A.G. Stephens drew upon a physiological debate over the nature of the nervous sytem which certainly went back to the early 1800s. He also drew on half a century's speculation about the physiology of the brain. Phosphorous was said to govern mental activity. In the 1830s, an authority on the chemical composition of the brain asserted that the phosphorous content was 2% to 2.5% in the normal brain, 1% to 1.5% in idiots, and 3% to 3.5% in the over-stimulated brains of the insane.[16]

More telling was the relationship which was often said to exist between mental effort and the consumption of the brain's phosphoric content. The presence of phosphates in the urine proved that the active substance of the brain was being consumed by mental effort.

Physiologists insisted that, given certain controls, urine analysis would reveal whether an individual had engaged in mental work, physical work, or had remained at rest. In his frequently re-issued *Dictionary of Domestic Medicine and Household Surgery*, Spencer Thompson was sure enough of these findings to inform his readers that "the substance of the brain is actually consumed by the process of intense thought, the amount of consumption, probably, being in proportion to the exertion the mind is put to".[17]

Foods with a high phosphorous content, particularly fish, were valued as brain stimulants — so much so, that in the 1800s an American authority warned that the fish fad had gone too far. He dismissed claims that the great intellectual nations were also great fish eaters. The Japanese, the New Zealanders, northern Europeans and the Esquimaux were certainly great fish eaters but he doubted that any of them could "boast of much intellect". As late as 1946, medical man and essayist, W.A. Osborne, attributed the persistent fallacy that fish was a brain food to two mistakes; "that the glowing of stale fish is due to phosphorous, which it is not, and secondly, that phosphorous is a brain food", which he disputed.[18]

From the 1870s the English company, H. & T. Kirby, promoted an impressive range of phosphorous pills for those who suffered from "mental depression, induced by worry and over-work, especially brain-work". Each pill was accompanied by an elaborate account of its therapeutic power. Pil. Phosphori et Nux Vom. Fort, for example, when taken two or three times a day with food, was particularly effective in combating atomic dyspepsia, more popularly referred to as lowness of spirits, general depression and feeling "below-par". The manufacturers added that the preparations had the further advantage of being a reliable sexual stimulant.[19]

Research into the physiology of mental labour invariably proceeded on the assumption that the exhaustion that followed brain-work resulted from the consumption of what one author called "the agent of mind", that the amount consumed was measurable and that mental exhaustion was not to be confused with physical exhaustion. Brain-work was a separate category of labour with its own symptoms and specific therapies. In the 1870s, Henry Maudsley, one of the most prominent nineteenth-century English physiologists, insisted that it was only "by supposing an idea to be accompanied by a correlative change in the nerve-cells" that it was possible to explain the exhaustion produced by mental labour and "the breaking down of the brain under prolonged intellectual effort".[20]

According to Maudsley, exposure to ideas was a factor in mental breakdown, though he also retained the older view that prolonged effort explained break-down. The vulnerable nerve-cell also marked a shift away from too great a reliance upon a vital substance acting as a source of mental energy. These changes may not seem momentous, but they marked a trend. By the 1870s, students of nervous exhaustion had begun to doubt the adequacy of strictly physiological solutions to the problem of exhaustion. Though the physiologist remained a crucial figure in any attempt to explain how break-down worked, there was a growing suspicion that what seemed a remarkable increase in the incidence of nervous disorders also demanded explanation.

Before the 1870s, physiologists had acknowledged that nervous exhaustion was on the increase, but this did not cause great concern. In him monumental work on *The Principles of Medical Psychology*, translated for the Sydenham Society and published in 1847, Baron Ernst Von Feuchtersleben conceded that ". . . the nearer we approach the present time, the more manifestly mental disorders increase", but he took the subject no further. His concern was the physiology of these disorders, not the factors that caused their increase. Similarly, students of the chemical composition of the brain appeared to show very little interest whether or not the consumption of phosphorous had increased in the modern world. Their concern was to measure what took place within individuals, rather than speculate upon whether the problem was a modern one or not. From the 1870s this emphasis began to change. An American, Dr George M. Beard, perceived the change very clearly and did much to promote the idea that nervous disorders represented a new pattern of disease, inseparably linked with modernity itself. The modern manifestation of nervous diseases was no longer an incidental concern, modernity was not considered one of the leading causes of nervousness.[21]

Beard accepted the existing claim that brain-work induced exhaustion, but went further than his contemporaries in his insistence that this was a modern disease. Once confined to the individual, Beard argued, nervousness now threatened entire populations. America went through its historic transformation somewhere between 1820 and 1850, making it, Beard asserted, the first nation to become physiologically modern. Beard offered little evidence for the claim that America had entered a new era of nervous diseases. He was less interested in a strict statistical demonstration that nervous diseases had increased, than in adding his own voice to the testimony of the medical profession and the people themselves. It was they who "generally accepted" that nervous diseases had increased; Beard elaborated upon the implications of having brain-workers as a majority in the population, and he helped confirm the peculiar physiological character of this modernity.[22]

In Beard's theory, the rise of the brain-worker signalled both "the ripening maturity of mankind" and a shift in the location of disease to the brain and the nervous system. While these diseases were much commoner and more intense than ever before, they were rarely fatal. A further effect of this reformulation of brain and nervous diseases was the much wider range of conditions that were now considered nervous in origin. In effect, Beard democratized nervous disorders, making them an inevitable consequence of modernity. The shift in emphasis was important. According to the old rules, exhaustion of the brain tended to occur only after severe intellectual labour, whereas after Beard modern society itself, its pressures, excitements and manifold anxieties, caused nervous exhaustion. Being modern had become a medically recognized type of exhaustion. The term "brain-work" was a necessary invention; it overcame the confusing suggestion that only profound thought exhausted the phosphates of the brain. Brain-work did not have to involve profound or original thought; it could equally describe a range of quite routine tasks which nevertheless required a mental, rather than a muscular input.

The reception of Beard's ideas in Australia is difficult to gauge. The Sydney-based publishers, McNeill and Coffee, brought out an Australian edition of his *The New Cyclopaedia of Family Medicine*, though how it was received is obscure. We do know that James Smith, one of the most prominent and prolific men of letters in colonial Victoria, seized upon Beard's writings with great, perhaps indiscriminate, enthusiasm. In October 1881 he lectured to the Australian Health Society on "The Nervous System: Its Use and Abuse". The lecture soon appeared as a pamphlet. Smith agreed that nervous exhaustion was the disease of modern civilization and blamed increased levels of worry, noise and speed. The telegraph, railways and increased competition for business also had to share the blame for heightened nervousness, along with a sharp increase in the volume of ideas. Moreover, Smith believed that with advancing civilization, the brain grew larger and more complex, the "nervous tissues" more subtle, refined and delicate. As thought grew more intense and pervasive the higher one reached on the scale of civilization, the danger of over-taxed nerve-force intensified and the brain's "consumption of power and of material" increased. Smith's rather startling image of the growing brain consuming energies more rapidly than ever before was a faithful reflection of the prominence Beard gave to the brain in his own writings. It followed that moderns had to pay more attention to feeding the brain.[23]

Smith had first encountered Beard's writings in the *New York Tribune* early in 1881. An article on "Animal Magnetism", which was heavily indebted to Beard, soon appeared in the *Victorian Review*, the leading journal of ideas in the colony. Yet Smith's interest in physiology was well established before his exciting encounter with Beard's theories. In June 1880, Smith's "Worry as a Factor in Disease" appeared in the *Victorian Review*, trailing a long list of further reading on modern physiology. Herman Kotze's *General Principles of Physiological Psychology*, and Daniel Tuke, author of *Illustrations of the Influence of the Mind Upon the Body in Health and Disease*, were given special note. The *Review* carried other contributions on modern physiology, and expected that its readers would want to follow developments in the field, even to the point of carrying a very scholarly review article on H. Charlton Bastian's *The Brain as an Organ of Mind*.[24]

While James Smith was putting physiological explanations of modern exhaustion before Victorian audiences, Frederick Norton Manning, N.S.W. director-general of the insane, addressed the local Royal Society on the relationship between insanity and civilization. Manning argued, with an impressive array of statistics, that insanity had increased; but he also insisted that in recent years medical practitioners had noticed a great increase in "neurotic disorders". Manning was certainly convinced of this himself, and attributed the increase to that now familiar formula: "the pressure and competition, the restlessness and social upheaval of modern life". Manning wondered if the increased access to educational facilities was responsible: "Can it be that the increased amount of nervous disease and insanity is one of the penalties of this social and intellectual progress, the greater brain activity and strain, which has come in almost too hot haste?" Having posed his question, Manning cited Beard as his authority for suspecting the education system itself, along with the multiple life-choices that free societies permitted.[25]

In the midst of speculations such as these, a Sydney solicitor wrote a famous ballad in which an unnamed brain-worker in the city wondered about the life of a casual acquaintance working in a world too remote even for that intrusive modern invention, the postal system. The brain-worker was worn down by his dingy office full of ledgers, the noisy streets, the "nervous haste" that seemed to characterize the way city people moved. He could not help noticing how stunted these people seemed. He contrasted his own narrow and remorseless life with his friend's carefree existence beneath the stars. While he fancied that he would rather like to become a drover, he doubted if his old acquaintance would be at all well suited to office-work. One had to conclude that of the two the office worker was more adaptable and better able to withstand modern pressures, though it was the drover who led the more rewarding life.

For all their complexity, modern physiology and neurology seemed to confirm the suspicion that modern society drained brains and nerves of their energies. Modernity became associated with a nervous, de-vitalized population, presenting inevitable and sometimes invidious comparisons with a more robust past. The conviction that "neurotic disorders" were increasing appears to have created a growing demand for therapies that would revitalize exhausted brains and worn nerves: therapies that would prolong the effective life of the brain-working class. Kirby's pioneering phosphorous pills soon faced some sharp competition. Horsford's acid phosphate was especially recommended as a food for the "exhausted brain", though it also cured "wakefulness and sick headache", a condition that attracted increasing attention in an era of pressured brains. The headache became a sign that the brain itself had grown tired. Fellows, a leading pharmaceutical company, supplied the market with hypophosphates; and towards the end of the 1880s Fletchers' Hydrobromate syrup joined a lengthening supply of cures for exhaustion of the brain. Many of these preparations show that the confident physiological proof in the 1830s that phosphorous was the agent of the mind had become the basis of widely endorsed and mass produced therapies by the 1880s. The cure of exhaustion was becoming a major medical industry.[26]

In a similar fashion, electricity, which some physiologists had linked with nerve-force from the early years of the century, had acquired an enormous vogue in the treatment of the nervous diseases by the 1880s both within the medical profession and, more strikingly, outside it. Beard had recommended galvanism and general faradization for patients with nervous complaints. The treatment seemed to vary but it would appear that the doctor would run a mildly charged instrument from head to toe, dwelling on regions, like the spine, that seemed in need of extra attention. In January 1893 Sydney specialist, A. Jarvie Hood, reported favourably on the treatment of a neurasthenic patient with Hodgkinson's Neurotone, which had been publicized at the Third International Medical Congress in the previous year as "a novel and highly effective method for the therapeutic application of electricity". The *Australasian Medical Gazette* noted that the Neurotone had been "much noticed" by medical men. From 1894 the *Gazette* carried advertisements for what it described as the much improved Electo-Neurotone.[27]

An 1887 report on the practice of medicine and surgery in New South Wales provides striking evidence of the money to be earned from the treatment of nervous disorders by non-registered practitioners. While this was not the only form of non-registered practice, it was identified in the report as a very large sector of the sub-medical market. Brain-working males who suspected that they lacked energy were prominent among those who presented themselves as nervously exhausted people. Yet it was also clear from non-registered advertising that, of all the threats to energy in the modern world, masturbation was deemed one of the most serious. The report also noted that a number of establishments promised to restore lost "nerve force" by the therapeutic application of electricity, and certainly electrical therapies were promoted in the medical advertisements of the colonial press.[28]

If the material substance of mind was difficult to locate, there was no such difficulty in naming semen as the vital fluid in the male sexual system. Semen was confidently described as "nerve-force" in concentrated form, and the loss of its vitalizing power, particularly in youth, was said to cause lasting debility. It was commonly argued that masturbation weakened the mind; masturbation was a regular category in Norton Manning's causes of insanity, and colonial asylums received patients whose madness was attributed to masturbation. One young man in Callan Park asylum claimed that he belonged to a gang of young boys who believed that their brains would grow if they consumed semen. The practice may seem unappealing, but it followed a common enough logic. In 1893 members of Sydney's medical profession listened very attentively to a paper on Professor Brown-Sequard's recent experiments in rejuvenative science. The famous French physiologist, then in his mid-seventies, had reported a surprising increase in his capacity for laboratory work after injecting himself with testicle juice.[29]

The intensive medical interest in masturbation in the late nineteenth century had more than one cause, but among them was certainly the belief that masturbation was an extreme expression of the modern susceptibility to nervous exhaustion. One of the striking features of the modern debate about energy loss was that the symptoms of excessive brain-work were exactly the same — allowing for variations in severity from case to case — as they were for the masturbator. Brain-work became inseparably linked with the stigma of sexual disobedience or "secret vice": both produced exhaustion. Moreover, the disorders were also treated similarly: in each instance electrical therapies were commonly recommended as the best way to replace lost nerve force. The modern man faced, according to these theories, a double burden: the need to manage the expenditure of his seminal fluid, combined with the task of guarding his nervous energies in times of unprecedented nervous strain.

By 1908, Phillip Muskett, one of Australia's leading medical writers, could claim that neurasthenia or nervous exhaustion accounted for 40% of all nervous disorders treated in Australia's major hospitals. Muskett included business and professional men, journalists and teachers among the most vulnerable group; a classification that was echoed in the warnings against "brain-fag" which a leading non-registered establishment described as "the inevitable sequel to exhaustive brain-task. Scholars, thinkers in the world of Art, Letters, Music and the Sciences suffer from this affliction". For the young Frederic Eggleston these words expressed an ominous truth.[30]

In 1900, twenty-five year old Frederic suffered the first of several nervous breakdowns. His letters referred to the "old-troubles", to "hideous dreams" and to "degrading temptations". After a further breakdown in 1902, his doctor diagnosed "neurasthenia", supplied him with a nerve tonic, and informed him that he was too civilized and had to become more of a barbarian. Frederic blamed his predicament on excessive study and writing, and wondered if he would ever write again. Frederic's younger brother Charlie was even worse off. At nineteen he was working long hours as a clerk, starting work at 8.00a.m. and often not returning home until well into the evening. He too broke down and was advised to get away from cerebral activity altogether — which, then as now, meant a holiday in Queensland, the place in which to regenerate mindlessly. For a time, Charlie thought of becoming a farmer. When his condition worsened alarmingly he was sent to Kew Asylum with instructions that there would be no visitors, "the recognized cure now for nervous cases", according to Frederic. It sounds very much like the American Weir-Mitchell rest-cure, then near the height of its vogue. The treatment failed, and Charlie died in Kew Asylum at the age of twenty-two.[31]

At the time of Eggleston's first breakdown in 1900, neurasthenia was so thoroughly identified with the modern age and modern civilization — vague though the terms were — that robust health could now stand as the proud token of a better age. To be called robust and virile, suggested something more than good health; it indicated that a stand had been taken against modernity. Those who rose to the challenge of the barbarian virtues were acting therapeutically, both in their own cause, but also in the hope of keeping alive cultural energies, expressions of vitality that were fast disappearing from the modern world. J.F. Archibald, dwelling on Commemorative Schemes for Sydney, envisaged a triumphal arch for the Domain "on which should be justly symbolized the resources and the future glories of Australia, and especially its splendid breed of men".[32]

Frederic Eggleston had no taste for the barbarian style, but he was certainly attracted by the cultivated neurasthenic's acceptable compromise, a fascination with the Elizabethans. During the Great War he referred to Australians as "the New Elizabethans", claiming that they were "a reversion to an older type of Englishman before industrialism took its root in English soil". Frank Fox, the first editor of the *Lone Hand*, one of Archibald's pet projects, had earlier expressed this view, and in almost exactly the same terms, when he claimed that Australians were "a reversion to an older British type, nearer to the days of Drake and Frobisher". C.J. Dennis played with the same theme in having the Sentimental Bloke identify settings and conflicts in *Romeo and Juliet* that were not far removed from his own experience.[33]

An Elizabethan theme was also prominent in Archibald T. Strong's writings. A contemporary of Eggleston and Fox, Strong was for many years professor of English at Melbourne University, and for a period, war-time censor. In a departure from his more academic analysis of Elizabethan literature, Strong once wrote of an "Australian Elizabethan" of his acquaintance "in all essentials no modern". He lived a double life; though his body was housed in an outer suburb of a major Australian city, "his soul is ever trying for its North-West passage to the past". Strong had his Australian Elizabethan announce that Australia "was now the only place where a right Elizabethan can live with any sense of reality or self respect".

When the highly energized Randolph Bedford died in 1941, Lionel Lindsay wrote of him "as a many-sided man to whom life was a continuous adventure. I always thought of him as an Elizabethan". In the following year the *Bulletin's* "red page" maintained that in "our earthy originality and vigour we have something in common with the Elizabethans". This is not the place to pursue the theme, but the role assigned to Shakespeare and the Elizabethans by the Australian exponents of racial pride would make a fascinating study.[34]

It would appear that the Elizabethan cult attracted those who sought a cultural alternative to neurasthenic modernity. A special affinity for the pre-industrial energies of a merrier England was offered as further evidence that Australia stood outside the modern world, influenced by its fashions and susceptible to its diseases, but ultimately much too healthy in spirit to draw inspiration from what *Vision* might have called the mad, dissociated ramblings of the modernists.

By the 1880s the decay of vitality had emerged as a peculiarly modern, yet physiologically explicable problem. Nervous exhaustion was closely linked to sustained brain-work: writers and artists were said to be prominent among those susceptible to neurasthenic disorders, which sometimes led to insanity. The belief that nerve-exhausting thought was one of the harmful by-products of modernity created a countervailing hope of saving mind and body from the threat of breakdown. From within the late nineteenth-century critique of modernity, with its spectre of wasted energies, its tortured hesitancy, there emerged the hope that thought might once again become the bold, vigorous expression of a physiologically vital nationality. In the early years of the twentieth century a new and various group of Australian intellectuals mediated the transition from this physiologically bound explanation of vitality to the universalizing categories of race, climate, health. In the process, vitality became less a personal signature than a sign of racial or national character; there was a shift from personal myths of self-creation to a more collectively defined physiological vitality.

1987

Notes

1   *Vision*, No 1, May 1923.

2   *Creative Effort: An Essay in Affirmation*, London, 1924.

3   Editorial, 3 April 1920.

4   "The Two Australia's", *Fellowship*, November 1916.

5   "Novels for Men", *Bulletin*, 19 April 1923.

6   "Symptoms of Decadence: The Serious Condition of the Australian Body Politic", *The Publicist*, 1 October 1941.

7   "Colonial Culture: Its Symptoms, Causes, Prevention, and Cure", ibid., 1 Sept 1939.

8   "The Wrong Road: Australians are 'Bushed', and Don't Know Where They Are Going!", ibid., 1 April 1940.

9   For tonics and modern exhaustion see David Walker, "Mind and Body", in the 1938 volume of the Bi-centennial History, forthcoming. Stephensen's eleven, *Publicist*, 1 Sept 1937.

10   M.C. Lidwill, "Some Notes on the Diagnosis and Treatment of the Neuroses", *The Medical Journal of Australia*, I, 1923.

11   "The Butchered Brontes", *Bulletin*, 19 Dec 1896, in Leon Cantrell (ed.), *A.G. Stephens: Selected Writings*, Sydney, 1977.

12   "A Recollection of J.F. Archibald", in Cantrell, ibid. For Moses see K.S. Inglis, *This is the ABC: The Australian Broadcasting Commission 1923-1983*, Melbourne, 1983, and Peter Hempenstall, "The Bush Legend and the Red Bishop: The Autobiography of E.G. Burgmann", *Historical Studies*, XIX, 1981.

13   "Australian Education", *Bookfellow*, 3 Jan 1907 in Cantrell, ibid.

14   "Burns", *Bulletin*, 23 Oct 1897 and "The Bronte Family", *Bulletin*, 15 June 1895, in Cantrell, ibid.

15   Thomas S. Hall, *History of General Physiology*, 2 vols, Chicago, 1969, for an historical overview of theories of energy. J.C. Pritchard, *A Review of the Doctrine of a Vital Principle as Maintained by Some Writers on Physiology with Observations on the Causes of Physical and Animal Life*, London, 1829.

16   Henry McIlwain, "Chemical Contributions, Especially from the Nineteenth Century, to Knowledge of the Brain and its Functioning", in *The History and Philosophy of Knowledge of the Brain and its Functions*, (The Wellcome Historical Medical Library), London, 1957.

17   Eighth edition, London, 1859, p.168.

18   George M. Beard, *The New Cyclopaedia of Family Medicine. Our Home Physician: A Popular Guide to the Art of Preserving Health and Treating Disease*, Sydney, 1885, p.186; Osborne, "Scientific Errors in Literature and Art", in *Essays and Studies*, Melbourne, 1946, p.16.

19   H & T Kirby and Co, *Special Remedies: Phosphorous*, n.d., and Dr E.A. Kirby, *The Value of Phosphorous as a Remedy for Functional Disorders of the Nervous System, induced by Overwork etc*, n.d.

20   Maudsley, *Body and Mind: An Inquiry into their Connection and Mutual Influences, Specially in Reference to Mental Disorders*, London, 1870, p.159.

21   See John S. Haller and Robin M. Haller, *The Physician and Sexuality in Victorian America*, Urbana, 1974; Nathan G. Hale, *Freud and the Americans: The Beginnings of Psychoanalysis in the United States, 1876-1917*, New York, 1971.

22   Beard, op. cit., p.785.

23   Smith lectured on "The Nervous System: Its Use and Abuse" to the Australian Health Society, Melbourne, on 3 Oct 1881, and the pamphlet was reprinted from *Victorian Review*, Nov. 1881.

[24] "Animal Magentism", *Victorian Review*, August 1881; "Worry . . .", *VR*, June 1880; Bastian review, Edward B. Sanger, 'The Brain as an Organ of Mind', *VR*, 1881. See also Lurline Stuart, "James Smith: His Influence on the Development of Literary Culture in Colonial Melbourne", Ph.D., Monash, 1983.

[25] Manning, "Is Insanity Increasing?", *Australasian Medical Gazette*, Oct 1881.

[26] For advertisements see, for example, *Australasian Medical Gazette*, March 1884.

[27] A. Jarvie Hood, "Notes of Three Cases Treated by means of Hodgkinson's Neurotone", *Australasian Medical Gazette*, Jan 1893; medical congress, editorial, *Australasian Medical Gazette*, Oct 1892.

[28] I have developed this theme in "Continence for a Nation: Seminal Loss and National Vigour", *Labour History*, No 48, May 1985.

[29] Case cited in Stephen Garton, "Insanity in New South Wales: some Aspects of its Social History 1878-1958", Ph.D., University of New South Wales, 1984, p.196. A.F. Fieldstad, "Organo-therapeutics: A Synopsis", *Australasian Medical Gazette*, 15 Nov 1894.

[30] Philip E. Muskett, *The Attainment of Health and the Treatment of the Different Diseases by Means of Diet*, Sydney, 1908, p.459; and *Clinical Experiences of Nervous and Chronic Diseases*, n.d.

[31] Warren G. Osmond, *Frederic Eggleston: An Intellectual in Australian Politics*, Sydney, 1985, Chapter 2.

[32] On Archibald's arch see A.W. Jose, *The Romantic Nineties*, Sydney, 1933, p.74.

[33] Osmond, op. cit., p.81; Sir Frank Fox, *Australia*, London, 1927, p.14.

[34] Archibald T. Strong, "An Australian Elizabethan", in *Peradventure: A Book of Essays*, London, n.d.; Bedford's obituary, *A.B.C. Weekly*, 2 August 1941.

ROYAL PROGRESS: THE QUEEN AND HER AUSTRALIAN SUBJECTS

PETER SPEARRITT

Australian scholars have ignored the British monarchy even though a casual perusal of our newspapers and women's magazines suggests that it occupies a central place in our political culture. Some seek refuge in David Cannadine's claim that "by definition, the period since the coronation in 1953 is too recent for detailed or satisfactory historical analysis".[1] A handful of our leading historians and hordes of other social scientists have nevertheless entered the waters of post-war history, but the Sovereign rates hardly a mention.[2] The only serious attempt I have been able to find to explain the role and function of the Crown is Rex Ingamells' now forgotten volume, *Royalty and Australia*, published in 1954. Ten years later, when Donald Horne's *Lucky Country* appeared in the bookshops, republicanism got its first serious airing for many decades. Horne argued that to people under 35 "there is no basis of power or performance or reason in the monarchy". Horne's claim is doubtful because the majority of adults that he wrote about witnessed or actually participated in the 1954 royal tour – the most popular and elaborate ritual this country has ever seen. Horne predicted that it would be politically practicable to make the break from the monarchy, but that "some dramatic reason" would be needed to make it.[3]

In 1966 Geoffrey Dutton organized a symposium on the *Monarchy in Australia*, with Horne and others putting the republican position. Peter Coleman, editor of the *Bulletin*, called it all a "phoney debate", pointing out that "there is no royal oppression against which the republicans can appeal".[4] Stephen Murray-Smith, editor of the literary quarterly *Overland*, observed that the left in Australia, concerned at our increasing dependence on the U.S., were becoming almost sentimental about our British connections:

> Today there is no possibility that republicanism would be entertained by any conference of the Australian labor movement anywhere in Australia. Even the Communist Party would regard attempts to raise the issue as diversionary and irrelevant.[5]

The Dutton volume did not generate a great deal of debate, and our intellectuals quickly put our Sovereign back on the shelf. To most of them she was a myth fast on the way to becoming a cliché. Chris Cunneen's study of Governors-General and Gavin Souter's *Lion and Kangaroo* remain the only major attempts to examine vice-regal style and power in twentieth-century Australia.[6]

The events of 11 November 1975 saw renewed interest in the power of the monarchy; but everybody agreed that the Queen would not have done it, and Sir John Kerr assured us that he had not talked to her about it. A broad-based republican movement looked as if it might get off the ground, but not enough Australians were interested in maintaining their rage.[7]

To academics the Queen is a tired cliché, who just happens to get her head on many of our stamps and all of our coins. They ignore her.[8] But to many Australians she remains a mystical embodiment of family life, goodness, security, quality, position: a guarantee that democracy cannot and perhaps should not be taken to extremes. Some see in the monarchy an assurance of continuity at the apex of society. To others the Queen is protection against the monarchical and absolutist tendencies of some of our elected politicians, especially Labor men born in Balmain and educated at Fort Street Boys High School.

I pondered for some time how to dissect the role and symbolic meaning of the monarchy in Australia. Like most Australians of my age, I have grown up with the royal family. The schools I attended in Queensland, Victoria and New South Wales all had the Queen's portrait just outside the headmaster's office. In all of these schools, we pupils knew that he had the Queen on his side. And we sang her song at school assemblies.

I have one vivid memory of the 1954 royal tour — of the Queen and the Duke of Edinburgh waving from the open platform of their railway carriage — and many more memories of the 1963 tour. I spent most of my school holidays with my maternal grandmother, a stalwart of the Country Women's Association and a committed royalist. Illustrated books on royalty figured prominently in her library. My grandmother often talked of the coronation and of the 1954 tour as if they were the most important events of this century. In the semi-tropical climate of the ancestral home in Queensland all this royal paraphernalia impressed itself on my psyche. In recent years, like many of my generation, I have come to regard the Queen as an almost mythological figure of little relevance to Australian life. Writing this paper has forced me to re-examine these assumptions.

Australians had been waiting a long time for a reigning British monarch to visit them.[9] Between 1901 and 1945, we had had a number of royal visitors, of whom three were later to sit on the throne. The Duke and Duchess of Cornwall and York opened the first Federal Parliament; Prince Edward visited us in 1920 aboard H.M.S. *Renown*; another Duke and Duchess of York opened Parliament House in Canberra in 1927; and the Duke of Gloucester came out for the Victorian centenary celebrations in 1934. The New Guard wanted royalty to open the Sydney Harbour Bridge, but Lang wanted to open it himself. Despite strenuous efforts, the Sesquicentennial Committee in Sydney could not attract any member of the royal family for the celebrations. We were fobbed off with a P.G. Wodehouse character, the Earl de la Warr.

In March 1948 Chifley announced that the King and Queen had accepted his invitation to visit Australia in 1949. As Kevin Fewster has shown in his study of the tour of the Prince of Wales in 1920, the Labor party was not always well disposed towards royal tours, though Labor parliamentarians themselves were usually keen to participate.[10] In November 1948 Chifley regretfully informed an expectant public that the tour had been postponed because of the King's poor health.

One can only speculate as to what impact such a tour might have had on Chifley's fortunes in the 1949 election, but a poll in June 1953, the first time a question was asked on the monarchy, showed that 77 per cent of Australians favoured a monarch, with only 15 per cent wanting an elected President. Eighty-nine per cent of Liberal-Country party voters and 68 per cent of Labor voters favoured retaining the monarchy.[11] Soon after becoming Prime Minister, Menzies renewed the invitation, hoping to attract Their Majesties to the Commonwealth Jubilee in 1951. Their Majesties put the Festival of Britain first, so we were offered Princess Elizabeth and her recently acquired husband, the Duke of Edinburgh, in 1952.

Australians were well informed about the courtship of Corfu-born Prince Philip and Princess Elizabeth in 1946 and 1947. Journalists rushed to check on his incognito visit to Sydney in 1940 as a midshipman on the battleship *Ramillies*, and they pored over files of his visit to Australia in 1945 on the Royal Naval destroyer *Whelp*. Philip described himself to a Melbourne newspaperman as "a discredited Balkan noble". After a tour of Africa in the early months of 1947, Princess Elizabeth returned to England to become engaged to Lieutenant Philip Mountbatten, who had become naturalized and taken the family name of his uncle.[12]

The Melbourne *Age* reported that the largest radio audience in Australian history listened to their wedding at Westminster Abbey on 20 November 1947. By 9p.m. the city was deserted, and teachers the following morning received a record number of "please excuse" notes from the parents of children who had been allowed to stay up late "to hear the solemn ceremony broadcast from the Abbey". A week later newsreels of the royal wedding could be seen in all capital cities and many country towns.[13]

The press portrayed Elizabeth as a happily married woman, who by 1950 had produced both a son, Charles (1948) and a daughter Anne (1950). Princess Margaret, on the other hand, spent her life at parties, night-clubs, the races, launching ships and undertaking European trips. (Despite this adverse publicity for the Princess some Australian women formed a local branch of the Margaret Rose Society.) Australians were told that during the forthcoming tour they would enjoy the experience of "having royalty in their midst", but

> there will be no gold-panelled coaches as there are when Their Majesties pass through London on State business . . . no Tudor uniforms in gold and scarlet. These they will have been left behind in England, a land rich in traditional ceremony.
>
> Australia is a new country, her roots as yet hardly below the surface of the soil of history. . . . What little pomp and circumstance exists in our civic and corporate lives has been borrowed from the "old country", the home of our fathers. . . .
>
> For women visitors the greatest ambition is, invariably, to be presented at Court. . . . It is here that Australians feel they are one with their kinsfolk, and the Crown becomes a personal symbol in their lives. The number of Australians who have been presented at Court is legion, and helps to form a bond between the two countries.[14]

Having recovered from the shock of the King's death in February 1952, loyal Australians (my grandmother among them) prepared for the coronation. Like a number of middle-class Australians of British stock, she decided to attend. Guides to the coronation were produced by most local newspapers, and lavish British magazines, all predicting a new Elizabethan era, soon found their way on to Australian newsstands. The coronation went live on British radio and television. The sociologists Shils and Young were quick to describe it as "an act of national communion"[15]; and certainly my grandmother was well pleased with it. Her husband had accompanied her to Britain to sell the leaf of the corkwood tree to British drug companies. In doing so he met the Queensland Agent-General in London, who managed to get my grandparents into one of the coronation garden parties. I often heard accounts of this event, which was much more spectacular and exciting than anything my grandmother had ever encountered at Country Women's Association functions, when the most she could hope for was an appearance by the Governor's wife. In fact, grandmother collected so many souvenirs, books and royal pamphlets that she had to buy another two suitcases to ship it all home; and with all this material at hand, she prepared her sons, daughters and grandchildren for the royal tour of Australia that surely had to come soon.

Australians had long been inundated with hagiography about the royals. In 1953 the Herald and Weekly Times released *Australia's Royal Welcome*, to explain what the royal tour was all about, to tell us what the vice-regal couple would see here, and to present the detailed itinerary, worked out in copious detail by protocol officers at the Palace and in Canberra. The book explained, with the banal logic to be found in such publications, that "as it is impossible for most of her people to come to London to see their monarch, she has to go to visit them". The tour, Australians were assured, was being undertaken not at the Queen's suggestion but because of pressing invitations from the countries to be visited. She would be leaving behind two "tender" young children, but of course "the Queen is a devoted mother". It was she and the Duke, for example, and not the nurses, who had taught Prince Charles to print his name.[16]

Besides affirming the Queen's standing as a mother, an educator, a nurturer, and an able (if girlish) public speaker, a lot of journalistic effort went into convincing us that while the Queen had pretty divine qualities, she also faced problems similar to our own. In the last months of 1953 the *Australian Women's Weekly* ran, in six parts, "The Queen's Life Story". The fifth of these was headed, "ROYALTY HAD A HOUSING PROBLEM TOO":

> Princess Elizabeth and the Duke of Edinburgh, on returning from their honeymoon, found the housing problem was just as difficult for them as for many other young newlyweds. The King could not find any house in London suitable for the heiress to the throne and her husband. So the young couple had to be given a small suite at Buckingham Palace . . .[17]

To the hundreds of thousands of Australians who were living in cramped, overcrowded and often insanitary conditions in 1953, this story must have been heartening. These poorly housed Australians could console themselves with the thought that, once enthroned, she would have the full run of Buckingham Palace, her "real home". The Australian press deliberated over how many rooms it had, agreeing on 600, with about two hundred men and four hundred women to run it. We were told that "the number of domestic servants is dictated not by the style of living of the Royal Family, but simply by the size of the palace. . . . It is now run with the greatest economy of manpower and money." The Queen, we read, paid for everything except building maintenance, and she even had to pick up the tab for 30,000 guests each year. In case Australians thought the Queen's "salary" of £475,000 per annum excessive, the writers of *Australia's Royal Welcome* wished it known that "the people of Britain make a profit each year out of the Exchequer's financial arrangement with the Queen".[18]

Australian officials worried about whether the citizenry would know how to behave on meeting the Royals. We were assured that two world wars had "broken down many of the conventions which surrounded Royalty", and that all that the Queen and the Duke expected was "good manners".[19] But in egalitarian Australia one could not be sure that the masses knew what good manners were. As one of the Australian guidebooks pointed out,

> there are still certain rules of behaviour with which some of us may be unfamiliar. When a woman is being presented, the Queen will hold out her hand and the woman is expected to make a curtsey. . . . it is not polite to use the Royal hand as a sort of life-line to help in recovering a standing position. When the Royal Visitors are spending some time in one place, there is no need for the people to curtsey and bow every time they meet them; once is enough for the day.[20]

Eric Harrison, federal Minister in Charge of the Royal Visit, thought that his fellow citizens were not to be trusted, so he caused *The Royal Visit and You* to be published. Australians were told that the Queen did not carry around a visitors book, that she did not give autographs, that she did not accept gifts from "firms engaged in trade or commerce", and that she sat in the front pew on the right hand side of the aisle for morning services.

The parliamentarians, churchmen, aldermen, local government officers, and voluntary association officials who studied *The Royal Visit and You* were told that there were three main aspects to the Queen's life, "home life", "sport" and "public duties". Home life and family life became the dominant metaphor of the tour, in part an attempt to restore credibility after the abdication controversy of 1936, still fresh in the minds of many people. The Queen, according to the Commonwealth Government, "enshrines the simple, abiding virtues — of loving home, husband and children. At her Coronation Her Majesty rededicated herself to the service of her family of peoples".[21] Australian officialdom (and its hangers-on) were introduced, through the pages of this brochure, to the members of the royal household visiting Australia, including the Lady Pamela Mountbatten, Lady-in-Waiting to the Queen, and a host of Commanders, Wing Commanders, Lieutenants and Viscounts.

It is hard to know just how diligently the officials and citizens of places like Casino, Wollongong, Burnie and Yallourn, Bundaberg, Albany, Port Lincoln and Fremantle did their homework, but the Commonwealth was certainly preparing them for every eventuality. And hiccups did occur. The Mayor of Mackay tried to board the Royal land-rover as Their Majesties circled a children's display at the local showground. The Duke shoved him off, saying "No, you don't come".[22] Officials were told in prose and line drawings what to do when presented to Her Majesty or His Royal Highness, how to bow, how to curtsey, when to shake hands, and when to stand and sit. At a State Ball, the citizenry were told, they could "begin dancing as soon as the orchestra plays after the arrival of Her Majesty and should not wait till Her Majesty moves on to the dance floor". This was good advice, because most of the time the Queen and the Duke preferred to watch. Help was also forthcoming about what to wear at public functions. Her Majesty informed the Commonwealth Government that "no one should be put to unnecessary expense in buying clothes and accessories". Short afternoon frocks could be worn at garden parties, but hats were compulsory. At such parties the Duke would wear a top-hat and morning frock-coat, but men would be allowed to "wear the best they have, whatever it may be". But the bottom line, if one could not muster a uniform, morning dress, white tie and tails, was in all instances a lounge suit.[23]

By the time the Queen and the Duke set foot in Sydney on 3 February, Australians had been well briefed on dress and etiquette. But explicit ideological instruction was scanty. Certainly, the commemorative volumes produced to instruct us about the Royal Family and the meaning of the monarchy, like *Our Royal Guests* (1952) and *Australia's Royal Welcome* (1953), conveyed monarchical values, but they did so through a close examination of the personal and official life of the Queen, including her upbringing, her schooling, her war work, her marriage, her children, her wardrobe, and the fact that wherever she went she had to take the royal paper work with her. But in terms of the actual working of monarchy and its relevance to Australia this literature had little to offer. Rex Ingamells' *Royalty and Australia*, released in time for the beginning of the tour, filled this gap. Ingamells, from his Jindyworobak stance, saw no disjunction between his commitment to celebrating the Australian environment and his belief in the Crown which he praised as a product of "the genius of the British race" where "authority and liberty are reconciled" and their "excesses" constrained.[24] His concern about "excesses" is similar to that of W.K. Hancock, who wrote in his *Argument of Empire* a decade earlier:

> With us the monarchy is a living and popular institution. Does this mean that we are very stupid? All communities have some kind of ritual. I have read about the forms and ceremonies of American party conventions. To me they seem very queer. But ... I respect their republican symbolism. Won't they understand that the British people ... are finding their freedom by adapting the flexible institutions of the British monarchy to their own special monarchical symbolism?[25]

Ingamells, of course, was not writing for a transatlantic audience, but a distaste for the rowdiness of American presidential elections can be detected in many of the writings of Australian monarchists. Moreover, as Ingamells explained to his fellow countrymen,

> Every legislative Act that passes through our Parliaments requires the Royal assent to make it law; .... Cabinet Ministers are Ministers of the Crown; Judges are servants of the Crown; the Civil Service, the Police Force, the Defence Forces operate under the Royal authority; all State enterprises are conducted under this authority. In all these and many other ways the Crown orders and safeguards our daily life so effectively that we hardly need pause to consider the wonder of such machinery.[26]

Very few Australians have ever paused to consider the wonder of this machinery.

In the atmosphere surrounding the oft-postponed and long awaited visit of the Queen, the spectre of republicanism hardly surfaced. As *Tribune* told its readers in January 1954 under the title, "ROYAL TOUR USED FOR PROVOCATION":

> The Menzies Government, using the Royal Tour as pretext, has started a Commonwealth-wide "Red Scare" campaign. ... It is a monstrous, damnable lie to suggest that any member of the Communist Party of Australia seeks to do harm to either the Queen, her husband, or any other representative of the capitalist system. The Communist Party's attitude to royalty is well known. It is opposed to the institution of monarchy, believing, however, that the monarchy will only be done away with by the democratic will of the people. Every communist should heed the warning. The Royal Tour immediately precedes a federal election at which the traitorous Menzies Government will use very dirty tricks to stay in office.[27]

Menzies was beside himself about the Royal Visit and the political opportunities it presented him. He called his foreword to Ingamells' book "The Function of the Crown", explaining that the Crown served as "the legal nexus between all the British countries and all the British people". Menzies, as Ken Inglis has recently written, had "a conservative lawyer's delight in the mysteries of the British constitution" incarnate in the Queen.[28] In what was to be but one of many panegyrics in the coming years, Menzies, echoing the school-assembly pledge of his childhood, went on to tell Ingamells' readers that

> In the person of a monarch such as the young and lovely Elizabeth the Second the Crown is also the focus of a profound nationwide emotion. ... We love the Queen. We honour the Queen. We serve the Queen.

To Menzies her reign would be "a second Elizabethan era in British history", and Australians were lucky to be able to participate in it.

While Menzies and Ingamells were undoubtedly agreed about the genius of the British race in having invented and retained the throne, there were aspects of Ingamells' account, as there were aspects of the tour itself, that cannot have been to Menzies' liking. Ingamells urged that we leave behind us "those shreds of sycophantism which, in the past, have done so much to damage our national reputation when exhibited overseas by travelling Australians affecting shame on the score of this country's differentness from Europe in history, culture and environment". He insisted that we were "a new nation developing our own character". He called the Aborigines "the sole occupants of the continent" who had been superseded "in possession" by people of British stock. "Our Aborigines", he wrote,

> from being reviled as "the lowest form of humanity" and "more akin to beasts than men", are now, following the testimony of the world's leading anthropologists, renowned for intelligence and morality which our materialism has been slow to appreciate.[29]

When the Governor General announced in his speech that the Queen was to visit, the news was enthusiastically received on both sides of the house. E.G. Whitlam, the young member for Werriwa, who had been a member of parliament for a little less than a year, said that Australians of English ancestry would be "exhilarated" to have a monarch who was also to be called Queen of Australia. "I make that ethnic qualification", he said,

> because Queen Elizabeth the First was never Queen of Scots and was not very welcome as Queen of Ireland. The Kingdom of Australia is considerably more populous than was the Kingdom of England four centuries ago. Athens, under Pericles, is the only community known to history which rivalled the England of Elizabeth the First for literary excellence, restless inquiry and undaunted enterprise. I am confident that Australians under their first Queen Elizabeth will do their best to emulate their forebears.[30]

Whitlam, like Menzies, had a particular fascination with the British monarchy, but in fact Labor, Country and Liberal parliamentarians vied with each other in their expressions of loyalty. Robertson, the Country party member for the Riverina, enjoyed the opportunity to have a dig at those "class conscious socialists" who, thirty years ago, had been opposed to monarchy, but now, having prospered and reached places of eminence, had changed their views.[31]

Parliamentary debate about the tour centred on just where the Queen would go. Drummond, the Member for New England, complained bitterly that she would not be visiting Tamworth. Minogue, the A.L.P. member for West Sydney, bragged about the fact that the people of his electorate had seven miles of royal progress in which to take up their positions. Most Labor members were concerned to ensure that the Queen saw the full cross-section of Australian life. Cameron, the member for the Adelaide seat of Hindmarsh, alleged that the Government had "studiously avoided any possibility that the Queen will meet the people who make this country tick", the people who "work for their living", including those who lived in the slums of Hindmarsh, Brompton and West Adelaide. He went on to advocate the nationalization of General Motors Holden.[32]

Tribune also wanted the Queen to see the dark side of Australian life. "All the decorations in the world", said a front-page story, "cannot hide the slums, housing shortages, the school crisis . . . The expenditure of the wealthy on their diamond tiaras, top-hats and dress suits, and their private junketing, could well be used for this." Will all the professions of loyalty to the Queen be sincere? asked *Tribune*, which complained that the loudest loyalists were helping the "Wall Street pest" to take over the British Empire and turn our country into a "colony and a pawn for the American war plans". *Tribune* claimed that the A.L.P. and the Liberals had agreed on a truce while the Queen was here, and that Menzies wanted the workers to "hang up their gloves" for the duration of the tour. This was the nearest *Tribune* ever got to criticizing the Queen, who did not feature in any of its cartoons, including those attacking the capitalist system.[33]

All Australia appeared to welcome the 1954 royal tour. The journalists and the radio and newsreel commentators searched for new superlatives. The *Australian Worker* told members of the A.W.U. that the Labor movement was entitled to take special pride in the visit because its origins lay in Chifley's original invitation to King George VI in 1948.[34] Australians marvelled, as Ken Inglis puts it, because they could finally see "the face on the money, smiling in their own streets".[35]

On the morning of Wednesday 3 February 1954, Australians watched or listened to the progress of the S.S. *Gothic* up Sydney harbour. The following day the *Catholic Weekly* wrote,

> For years the people of Australia have waited for this day, when their sovereign ruler would come in person to receive the testimony of their tremendous affection and loyalty. ... Like a fairy-tale princess, she came on a great white ship with her prince at her side.

The *Gothic* dropped anchor in Athol Bight, and Her Majesty and His Royal Highness stepped into the Royal Barge to follow the route of Governor Arthur Phillip on their way to Farm Cove. The aim of the tour — to embrace all Australians — became immediately apparent. As the *Catholic Weekly* commented on 4 February,

> For Catholics in particular the occasion was one of joy and thanksgiving and of gratitude too. Among the first administrators of the Colony there was not a single Catholic, but yesterday a Catholic Premier was one of the four to wait on Her Majesty aboard the Gothic. Later, a Catholic Lord Mayor, with five Catholics among his 20 attendant aldermen, read the official address of welcome to Her Majesty.

The Queen and the Duke then embarked on their first royal progress on Australian soil, their motorcade starting in Macquarie Street and moving on into the city and the inner suburbs. One journalist noted that it was "in the poorer sectors that Elizabeth received her warmest, most heartfelt welcome". A B.B.C. commentator added that it was "just like in the East End of London",[36] while, according to the *Catholic Weekly* (again on 4 February),

> Along Dowling Street and Cleveland Street the royal procession passed. No elegant homes or handsome buildings here, but a proud and independent working class, enjoying their holiday to the utmost and as eager as the wealthiest conservative to do honor to their Queen.

Thousands had slept in the streets overnight, and the next night more than a million people packed the harbour foreshores to watch the royal fireworks.[37]

On her second day in Australia, the Queen opened the N.S.W. state parliament, then in Labor hands. (The politicians' wives forgot to curtsey and the politicians forgot to bow.) On her leaving Parliament House, the squashed crowds in the street greeted her with the national anthem.[38] (Crowds also burst into spontaneous singing on a number of other occasions on the tour: a reception that has not greeted the Queen or anyone else in recent years. Despite the lavish claims made for the reception meted out to President Johnson during the Vietnam War he was not greeted with a spontaneous hymn.[39]) The next evening, the Queen appeared tired at the Lord Mayor's ball, which proved a bit of a flop because most of the 2000 stood and stared quietly. The Sydney Town Hall was decorated with a huge neon crown and the letters "EIIR" picked out in lights. Neither this nor the eager young Labor Lord Mayor, Pat Hills, could keep Her Majesty more than an hour.[40] But as an up-and-coming member of the Irish Catholic right in the A.L.P., Hills determined to make the most of the visit. His Council published a lavish commemorative book, and he wrote in his foreword that the tour was "the greatest event in the lives of the people of this country".

Over the following days, the Queen and the Duke participated in an extraordinarily strenuous programme, with school children, war widows, assorted Anglican clergy, Legacy wards, hospitals, a Bondi surf carnival and, of course, the races. After this it was on to Newcastle (with an inspection of the steelworks), Lismore, Dubbo, Wollongong (where the steelworks were by-passed), and so to Wagga. Even allowing for a certain hyperbole in the newspaper accounts, the extensive still-photograph and film footage does confirm the enthusiasm shown for the royal couple, in both organized welcomes and spontaneous greetings. People lined railway-tracks to see her waving from the royal train. In Wagga one hundred thousand people — an enormous crowd for a city with a normal population of 18,000 — lined the streets for her visit. Joe Timbery, his wife and two children, Aborigines from Sydney, were imported for the day to demonstrate boomerang throwing in the "bushmen's carnival".[41] Local enthusiasts even made a film called "The Queen in Wagga".

The Queen had an equally busy time in Canberra, where she told a joint sitting of the Senate and House of Representatives that "the great institutions of parliamentary sovereignty, a democratically controlled Executive, the just and impartial administration of the law; these exist and flourish in each of the great realms which call me Queen."[42] Wearing a frock of her favourite yellow, and a tiny headhugger hat covered with sprays of wattle, Her Majesty unveiled — in an audacious display of counter imperialism — the Australian National Memorial to America, commemorating the American contribution to the war in the Pacific. British officials in Australia had opposed the Queen's participation in this ceremony.[43] That evening, at the Commonwealth banquet, Menzies told the Queen, to prolonged applause, "You may count on us. We are yours." He was supported by the leader of the opposition, Dr H.V. Evatt. At the end of the banquet, Menzies presented Her Majesty with a gift from Australia, a diamond brooch in the shape of a spray of wattle and tea-tree, reputed to have cost £25,000.[44]

In Hobart, the royal progress was greeted with polite clapping instead of the wild cheering of Sydney. On leaving the capital, the couple drove through decorated towns and hamlets, and had an overnight stop at a sheep property. They also attended a service in a Presbyterian church, reflecting the Queen's status as the Queen of Scotland. From Hobart, they flew to Melbourne, where government, business and householders vied with each other in their decorations for the 12-mile royal progress. The Queen was not at all pleased when the Sergeant-at-Arms, with Mace, escorted her into the vestibule of parliament, until the Speaker explained that under Victoria's Constitution Act the Mace was the symbol of authority for the Speaker and not the Sovereign. Further embarrassment was caused when teenagers misbehaved outside Government House, evading police and scaling the fences. At the Melbourne state banquet, Labor Premier Cain sat to the Queen's left while Menzies — who along with all the state premiers tried to steal the limelight as often as he could — sat to her right. On one occasion, Cain tried to imitate Menzies, when he referred to the Duke as "Her Majesty's Prince Charming". The Queen stayed twice as long at the City of Melbourne Royal Ball as she had in Sydney, but the Melbourne do cost £40,000 to stage and the guest list numbered 6,000. The top 1,000 guests had blue tickets, giving them access to Scotch, champagne and boars' heads. The remaining 5,000 guests had white tickets and no boars' heads. (Earlier in the day the Queen had eaten only sparingly of a cold light lunch at a meeting of women's organizations.)[45]

Melbourne provided one of the few attempts to send up the royal tour, but only the Duke was targeted. He spent 35 "uproarious minutes" at the University of Melbourne while Her Majesty attended the largest investiture of the whole tour, with 180 men and women in the line-up. Students met the Duke with a tattered piece of old carpet-runner. A 6'4" male student, dressed in a blouse, short skirt and wig, "simpered up, made an ungainly attempt at a curtsey, and presented the Duke with a bouquet of lolly walking sticks". A 10' x 15' human camera stalked the Duke to take his picture. At the end of this frolic, the President of the S.R.C. told the Duke that "with this informality we hope to convey our heartfelt pleasure at welcoming you".[46]

What did the tour represent? In every capital city the Royal couple were met by a strange mixture of obeisance to the throne and nationalistic fervour. At some ceremonies, the crowds sang both the national anthem and "Waltzing Matilda". Labor and non-labor politicians alike strove to share in the Queen's divine aura.

Why was the tour so popular? Kingsley Martin in his book, *The Crown and the Establishment* (1962), calls the first decade of Elizabeth's reign the "T.V. Monarchy", pointing out that the coronation was watched in thousands of homes or neighbour's homes on television. Australia in 1954 did not have television, and although we could listen to the radio coverage or catch highlights a week later in black and white newsreel footage, nothing could compare with seeing Her Majesty and His Royal Highness in living colour. At the time of the visit they were almost deities, although the Queen's role as Head of the Church of England was played down to encourage Catholics to declare their loyalty.

For most of the tour the Queen appeared to be distant and untouchable. The crowds were almost always kept under control, and (as far as I can discover) she was never jostled. (Police manned the barricades at all big events.) But the popular press took upon itself the role of proving that both she and the Duke were friendly, unpretentious and human — a message carried through saturation photo-journalism showing the royal couple accepting posies from little girls and pensioners. They were even depicted relaxing, though the Queen was rarely photographed without stockings, shoes, gloves, hat and handbag, except when horse-riding. At major functions the Queen's dress emphasized the spectacular and expensive range of her wardrobe, inaccessible to all but the wealthiest women. Her dress at the Wayville Oval in Adelaide was typical of her after-dark appearances:

> The Queen, whose blue crinoline gown matched the cerulean blue gleaming through the fire of the huge Andamooka opal she wore at her throat . . . was a glorious figure as she walked to the dais. . . . For her arrival she wore a stole of white mink. But when she was seated on the dais she changed it for a three-quarter-length coat of white ermine.

One hundred thousand voices singing the national anthem farewelled her into the night.[47] The huge Andamooka opal had been given to her by Thomas Playford, the Premier, on behalf of the people of South Australia.

The tour represented the acme of British monarchical symbolism in Australia. In most of its aspects it seemed a throwback to the inter-war years. The regular church services, investitures, banquets and balls were all an attempt to recreate court life in the antipodes. Both Australian and British journalists often compared the royals here with the royals at home. Some claimed that the Sydney welcome equalled the coronation in terms of patriotic fervour. Pomp and circumstance surrounded the royal couple everywhere, in part because it was what she expected and what the Queen's men had demanded, and in part because it was what Australians wanted, especially those Australians in the front line at receptions — the heads of voluntary and charitable organizations, sporting bodies, local governments and the like. Menzies orchestrated the whole, with Labor premiers and Labor lord mayors willing footmen for the royal progress. Five of the six states had Labor premiers at the time of the tour.

There can be no doubt that both the commonwealth and the state governments wanted to use the tour to support their continuance in office. The tone of "consensus" pervades all of the governmental and newspaper prose about the tour. The federal Liberal government was even prepared to admit, in one of its publications, that all was well in Queensland, even under the Labor rule of Vincent Gair, a right-wing Catholic..

> The kaleidoscopic Queensland picture was now complete. All the people, the miners, the housewives and the paint-daubed natives, the Members of Parliament, the swarms of children and the ranks of servicemen, now fell into perspective . . . the investitures, the banquets, the balls. . . . The picture is of a great State and a happy, hospitable people.[48]

Australian politicians were not the only people hoping to make political capital out of the tour. The British defence establishment used the Duke to court Australian defence connections: they were still smarting over their exclusion from the A.N.Z.U.S. treaty signed in September 1951, and feared that Australia was drifting away from a commitment to defending Commonwealth interests.[49] As well as regular inspections of the troops by both the Queen and the Duke, the latter visited Australia's atomic arsenal at Salisbury, fifteen miles north of Adelaide, and inspected the Woomera rocket range, where he declared open the Edinburgh airfield, and where (according to the Commonwealth government) "only wandering Aborigines know the whereabouts of waterholes" and "Australian and British scientists fling their test vehicles across 1250 miles of emptiness towards the north of Western Australia".[50] A year and a half before the royal tour, Britain had exploded its first atomic bomb in the Monte Bello Islands off the north-west coast of Western Australia, and just four months before the royal visit Britain had exploded further bombs at Woomera.

Aborigines figured prominently in the tour, but they were usually presented as items of anthropological interest or for their primitive art. The only Aborigine presented to the royal couple who had acquired western skills was Albert Namatjira. In Toowoomba, they saw — in the words of the Commonwealth government's Royal Visit commemorative book —

> ... the grotesque, age-old ceremonial of the corroboree performed by full-blood Aborigines who have travelled from the Northern Territory for the occasion. Twenty-two, daubed with clay, ochre and feathers in ritualistic patterns, capered and mimed to the weird cacophony of didgeridoos and music sticks. With those strange harmonies echoing in their minds, the Royal couple flew back to Brisbane.[51]

Queensland, which had the most oppressive race legislation and administration of any of the states, made a special effort to put "native culture" on display. At Townsville, the royal couple were again entertained by Aborigines, including Palm Islanders in ceremonial dress. At Cairns, a group of Torres Strait Islanders, clad in grass skirts and battle head-dress, came bare-footed onto the oval shouting battle cries and beating their war-drums. Schoolchildren then performed a "graceful maypole dance", presumably to reassure the Queen that her white subjects still clung to European culture, even in the far north.[52] Because the tour did not include the external territories, some Papua and New Guinea chiefs and representatives of mixed races were flown to Cairns to express the devotion of their people to the Queen.

At Whyalla, on her South Australian tour, the Queen saw another corroboree performed by 50 members of the Pitjantjara tribe, who had travelled from their reserve more than 300 miles away to give their "Royal Command" performance. As a supreme tribute to "Wallaba", their term for the Great White Lady, they told her the story of the sacred corroboree. One journalist wrote:

> She is the only woman ever to be told the story of an Aboriginal sacred dance, and she promised not to repeat it even to Princess Anne, Princess Margaret or her mother "The Great, Great White Lady".
> Uncivilised and wild-looking, the Pitjantjaras had daubed themselves from head to foot with red ochre and matted their hair with kangaroo blood,

The performers chanted in their own language but ended up by yelling, Yippee.[53]

It is remarkable how often Aboriginal motifs dominated displays on this royal tour, almost as if such motifs were the only genuine Australian iconography Europeans could muster, along with native flora and fauna. At one display in Adelaide the Queen witnessed more than 1,000 primary schoolgirls dressed as Aborigines, birds and animals, so as to create a picture of dawn coming to the Australian bush.[54] The Queen herself wore her wattle dress on a number of occasions.

The 1954 royal tour was the most elaborate and most publicised sequence of events Australia has ever seen. The two month tour had been planned for years, and it had also been postponed so often that when it finally did happen Her Majesty's subjects were at fever pitch. Nowhere in the press of the time can I find any hint that the claims about "nine million devoted subjects" were much exaggerated. A poll taken a month after the tour revealed that 75 per cent of the population had seen the Queen at least once. Two years later another poll indicated that 92 per cent of the population favoured royal visits and only four per cent opposed them. Some members of the Communist Party privately thought that the whole thing was a sick joke, but there does not seem to be any evidence of anyone saying so in public.

The poet David Campbell captured the fantasy of many Australians with his poem "The Australian Dream", in which the Royal Family turn up on his doorstep after 3a.m.:

> I fumbled with the lock, and on the porch
> Stood the Royal Family with a wavering torch.
>
> "We hope," the Queen said, "we do not intrude.
> The pubs were full, most of our subjects rude. . . ."
>   . . . I must admit I'd half
> Expected just this visit. With a laugh
> That put them at their ease, I bowed my head.
> "Your Majesty is most welcome here," I said.
> "My home is yours. There is a little bed
> Downstairs, a boiler-room, might suit the Duke."

The tour provided Australian officialdom — in its parliamentary, public service, military, religious and voluntary-organization forms — the chance to present Australia to the leader of the "race", and in so doing to reflect on the development of civilization in this land. The authors of the Commonwealth Government's commemorative book on the tour, first published in May 1954 and reprinted many times the same year, concluded:

Britons never conquered Australia. They were in the van of discovery, they settled it, explored it, hated it, and slowly learned to love it. Slowly it conquered them, and they became Australians, fiercely proud of their British origin. . . . Australia succumbed wholeheartedly to its young Queen. Not men, not time nor power will ever dislodge her from her conquest.[55]

A year earlier, Martin Boyd had claimed that the visit would be an opportunity to strengthen our emotional ties with Britain because

"the Queen is a living symbol of the fact that we are of one blood".[56]
And in her farewell broadcast, she herself told her Australian subjects:

> I hope that this visit has served to remind you of the wonderful heritage we
> share. I also hope that it has demonstrated that the Crown is a human link
> between all the people who owe allegiance to me, an allegiance of mutual
> love and respect and never of compulsion. And now I say goodbye. God be
> with you until next time I can visit Australia.[57]

That "next time" was heralded when, in May 1960, Menzies asked
his audience at the first Smuts Memorial Lecture:

> Are we the Queen's men and women because, as the fact is, we love and
> respect her? Or because, out of long experience, we find in the monarch
> as such a focal point, unmarred by political controversy, for our national
> tradition, consciousness and ambitions? Or perhaps, we are snobs and love
> a hierarchical society? ... We British people, not discouraged by republican
> examples, have a deep instinct for the monarchy....[58]

A couple of years later, Menzies was delighted to be able to announce
that the Queen would soon be among us again, in part to help celebrate
Canberra's jubilee. There do not seem to be any books produced for
this tour before it began, or any guides to how Australian officialdom
should behave. For the 1954 tour almost every state produced a
commemorative volume as did many cities, towns and even hamlets;
no such material accompanied or appeared after the '63 tour. This time
round, the press spoke of the Queen visiting her people rather than of
her meeting her subjects. The Australian Information Service faithfully
compiled another royal volume in which it explained that the 1954
tour had been a time of "pomp and pageantry" appropriate to a "first
meeting between a Queen and her subjects", but that this time she
came "to see rather than to be seen, to learn at first-hand what
Australians meant" when they spoke of "a nation on the march".
Then followed, in the prose for which the Information Service has
become justly famous, an account of factories that had arisen from
blueprints, rivers that had been harnessed, mountains that had been
tamed, livestock that had been made healthier, townships that were
models, and a culture that had matured. Menzies, with an eye to an
entry in a future dictionary of quotations, addressed Her Majesty at
the state reception in Canberra as "the living and lovely centre of
our enduring allegiance".[59]

The Queen's arrival in Canberra on February 18 1963 lacked the
magic of the *Gothic* steaming through Sydney Heads in 1954. Emerging
from their Qantas 707 on to a wet tarmac, the Queen and the Duke
were greeted by a be-plumed Viscount de L'Isle in vice-regal white.
The tour included every state and the Northern Territory, but it
attracted much less press coverage than the 1954 tour, though it did
receive some exposure on television, a facility now to be found in a
majority of Australian houses. Yet while television idolized the Queen,
a note of cynicism had crept into some of the press coverage,
particularly in the *Bulletin*, whose journalists kept on comparing the
visit with the 1954 extravaganza and found it wanting. The crowds in
Canberra were thin, in Adelaide quiet and subdued, and in Melbourne
rather tame. The federal Treasurer, Harold Holt, complained from the

pulpit in Wesley Church, Melbourne, that the crowds were not exuberant enough, and the Rev. Irving Benson urged everyone to get out and see the Queen. The *Bulletin's* "Batman" observed that the eager-beavers were matrons of fiftyish and over, whose "Queen-watching propensities were undiminished", but that young people were more blasé. He put it all down to television, although only ABC television gave the tour extensive coverage.[60] I myself was one of those young people, and like 40,000 other Sydneysiders I attended the "Pageant of Nationhood" at the Showground, where we all cheered when the Queen appeared in her tiara, jewels and ermine stole, spotlighted like a movie star. And certainly to our adolescent party she was more a figure of fascinating glamour than of leadership, authority or power. Moreover, this tour was actually attacked because of its cost, including the temporary airport built at Kununurra, replete with control tower, which stood for only two hours, just long enough for the Queen to fly in and fly out.[61] On the other hand, to mark the first visit by a reigning monarch to the Northern Territory, drinkers roared "You beaut, Your Majesty" as the royal progress bounded through Alice Springs.[62]

There was no organized opposition to the tour. In its 1961 prospectus the Australian Republican party had claimed it was the "only political party in Australia that publicly and unequivocally stands" for republicanism, advocating a peaceful severing of the connection with the British crown. Its platform also advocated the establishment of U.S. bases in Australia to halt the advance of Communism, the abolition of the Governor-General, and the creation of an Australian anthem.[63] But even the Republican party lay low during the 1963 tour, and the president of its Darwin branch, who had talked of a petition for "territory rights" and a hunger strike, announced that his members would refrain from demonstrations during the visit.[64]

As in 1954, *Tribune* had little to say. It interpreted the visit as an indication of the mounting crisis in the British Commonwealth and of British imperialism's weakening position in south-east Asia. One journalist complained about the "pompous and portly" Menzies hogging the television limelight, and in reference to Menzies' war record claimed that "despite Bob's fervent declarations about defending our Sovereign, it must be said that had her grandfather had to rely on Menzies, Her Majesty would now be speaking German". *Tribune* complained that workers at the General Motors Holden plant at Elizabeth had worked day and night to erect a toilet-room for the Queen — with carpet, Italian marble, dressing-table and wash-basin — for a visit that lasted 27 minutes, while the workers had struggled for years to get doors put on their own toilets.[65]

Just two weeks after the Queen departed these shores, *Oz* magazine featured her on the front cover with the heading, "royalty, chastity belts, society", and devoted two pages to sending up the tour, exaggerating the number of children and matrons who had collapsed at various events, commenting on the rudeness of Melbourne's race-going public climbing fences to get a better view, on handbags being trodden into the lawn at the Myer Music Bowl, and counting the number of small boats that capsized when the *Britannia* entered Sydney Harbour. *Oz* welcomed the suggestion that the Queen should live in Australia for a couple of months each year, claiming that the Australian Elizabethan Theatre Trust and the A.B.C. together could make royalty a "going concern".[66] All this seemed a generation away from the *Bulletin's* editorial opinion just nine years before:

> . . . as the people and their elected representatives have claimed more and more of the rights of the Crown, the bond between people and monarch have become closer and more affectionate, the interest in the Royal family more intense and universal, the symbolism of the Throne more potent, till it has come to have something of the significance of religion.[67]

In an increasingly secular society the monarchy was losing its way and the royal progress its audience. Within weeks of the Queen leaving, Menzies tried to have the main denomination in the coming decimal system called the "royal". Only 13 per cent of Australians surveyed liked the name, which was opposed by Arthur Calwell, Harold Holt, Chambers of Commerce, and the press. The "dollar" won, reflecting Australia's increasing ties with the world beyond Britain. The Queen's head would remain on the new coins, but not on the notes.[68]

The retirement of Menzies has been portrayed by most commentators on post-war Australia as the end of the British era, with Menzies the last of the Queen's men. Holt's "all the way with L.B.J.", Gorton's nationalistic stance, the spread of U.S. capital and bases, and the action of Sir John Kerr on November 11 1975, are all adduced as evidence of a gradual loosening of our ties with the throne.

In April 1977, the former Prime Minister, E.G. Whitlam, restated his "admiration" for the Queen while pointing out that her powers were extremely limited.

> The Governor General was acceptable as a de facto Head of State when it was assumed that he had no powers; he is unacceptable as Head of State when he assumes powers, or imagines that he derives inherited powers from a British monarch who is under no such delusion herself.[69]

In the space of only 23 years the rhetoric of monarchy in Australia had changed irrevocably. No one in public life any longer referred to "Her Majesty's Kingdom of Australia" or spoke of her "Australian subjects". Portraits of the Queen were confined to R.S.L. clubs, parliamentary premises, and provincial offices. "Princess Di", wife of the heir to the throne, is greeted enthusiastically whenever she visits Australia, but she is presented, and presents herself as a media star, not a future Queen.[70] Such visits are no match for the royal progress of 1954.

1986

Notes

[1]   "The Context, Performance and Meaning of Ritual: the British Monarchy and the 'Invention of Tradition', c.1820-1977", in E. Hobsbawm (ed.), *The Invention of Tradition*, Cambridge, 1984, p.155.

[2]   e.g. the various editions of A.F. Davies et al., *Australian Society* since 1965 and H. Mayer (ed.), *Australian Politics* since 1966. As far as historians are

concerned the Queen surfaces in books aimed at school children and the mass market, e.g. H. McQueen, *Social Sketches of Australia*, Melbourne, 1978; D. Watson, *The Story of Australia*, Melbourne, 1984; and M. Cannon, *Australia, Spirit of a Nation*, Melbourne, 1985. Apart from that, analysis of the monarchy is usually confined to the occasional article, some of which are cited below.

3   Melbourne, 1964, p.110.

4   Melbourne, 1966, pp.174-5.

5   Melbourne, 1966, p.168.

6   C. Cunneen, *Kings' Men: Australia's Governors-General from Hopetoun to Isaacs*, Sydney, 1983. G. Souter, *Lion and Kangaroo Australia 1901-1919: the Rise of a Nation*, Sydney, 1976, includes a provocative postscript in which Souter ponders on the fate of the monarchy.

7   J. Kerr, *Matters for Judgement*, Melbourne, 1978, p.330. On 11 November 1975, E.G. Whitlam urged the crowd at Parliament House to "Maintain your rage and your enthusiasm through the campaign for the election now to be held, and until polling day." S. Murray-Smith, *The Dictionary of Australian Quotations*, Melbourne, 1984, p.281.

8   The Queen figures prominently in a number of the accounts of how society is organized reported in R.W. Connell's *The Child's Construction of Politics*, Melbourne, 1971, but both she and the monarchy are quickly dismissed in R.W. Connell and T.H. Irving, *Class Structure in Australian History*, Melbourne, 1980. Her Majesty makes a brief appearance, at a surf carnival, in R. White, *Inventing Australia*, Sydney, 1981, and hardly rates a mention in J. Carroll (ed.), *Intruders in the Bush*, Melbourne, 1982.

9   Only one of the score or more books produced for the 1954 royal tour mentions the attempted assassination of the Duke of Edinburgh in Sydney on March 9 1868.

10   "Politics, pageantry and purpose", *Labour History*, no. 38, May 1980.

11   Herald and Weekly Times poll June 1953.

12   Herald and Weekly Times, *Our Royal Guests*, Melbourne, 1952, pp.31,33.

13   ibid., pp.33, 46.

14   ibid., p.49.

15   "The Meaning of the Coronation", *Sociological Review*, new series, I, 1953, 80.

16   Melbourne, 1953, p.1.

17   16 December 1953.

18   Melbourne, 1953, pp.3, 6.

19   ibid., p.28.

20   ibid., p.30.

21   *The Royal Visit and You*, 1953, preface.

22   Consolidated Press, *The Royal Tour of Australia and New Zealand*, Sydney, 1954, p.127 (hereafter cited as *Royal Tour*).

23   *The Royal Visit and You*, Canberra, 1953, no pagination.

24   Melbourne, 1954, p.84.

25   London, 1943, p.11.

26   *Royalty and Australia*, Melbourne, 1954, p.84.

27   13 January 1954, p.9.

28   "Ceremonies in a Capital Landscape", in S.R. Graubard (ed.), *Australia: the Daedalus Symposium*, Sydney, 1985, p.104.

29   Ingamells, op. cit., pp.92, 101.

[30] *Commonwealth Parliamentary Debates*, 12 November 1954, p.181.

[31] ibid., pp.146-7.

[32] ibid., pp.149-50.

[33] 2 February 1954, p.1.

[34] 10 February 1954.

[35] Inglis, op. cit., p.104.

[36] *Royal Tour*, op. cit., p.36.

[37] ibid., p.36.

[38] ibid., pp.39, 43.

[39] Inglis, op. cit., p.112 claims that the crowds for L.B.J.'s visit "in every city were larger than at any royal progress. ... A president was not hedged with divinity, but it was quite as wonderful for Australians to see him and they saw more of him."

[40] *Royal Tour*, op. cit., p.46.

[41] ibid., p.54.

[42] Australian News and Information Bureau, *Royal Visit*, Sydney, 1954, p.15 (hereafter cited as *Royal Visit*).

[43] *Royal Tour*, op. cit., pp.54, 57; *Sydney Morning Herald*, 2 January 1985.

[44] ibid., p.59; *Royal Visit*, op. cit., p.21.

[45] *Royal Tour*, op. cit., pp.80-92.

[46] ibid., p.102.

[47] ibid., p.151.

[48] *Royal Visit*, op. cit., p.80.

[49] T. Millar, *Australia in Peace and War*, Canberra, 1978, p.180.

[50] *Royal Visit*, op. cit., p.89.

[51] ibid., p.74.

[52] ibid., pp.75, 77.

[53] *Royal Tour*, op. cit., p.138.

[54] *Royal Visit*, op. cit., p.91.

[55] ibid., p.103.

[56] In I. Bevan (ed.), *The Sunburnt Country*, Sydney, 1953, p.241.

[57] *Royal Tour*, op. cit., p.160.

[58] Reprinted in F.K. Crowley (ed.), *Modern Australia in Documents 1939-1970*, Melbourne, 1973, p.393.

[59] Australian News and Information Bureau, *Royal Visit 1963*, Sydney, 1963, p.7. While this hardback volume ran to 103 pages, all the Herald and Weekly Times group could muster was a 64 page paperback.

[60] *Bulletin*, 2 March 1963. See also 16 March 1963.

[61] *Bulletin*, 23 March 1963.

[62] *Bulletin*, 6 April 1963.

[63] Prospectus held in Mitchell Library.

[64] *Bulletin* 6 April 1963.

[65] 20 February 1963.

[66] June 1963, p.15.

[67] 3 February 1954.

[68] *Sydney Morning Herald*, 9 April, 24-25 June, 19 September 1963.

[69] *On Australia's Constitution*, Melbourne, 1977, p.11.

[70] For an amusing and vitriolic attack on the packaging of the Princess of Wales and its implications for British Society see D. Simmonds, *Princess Di: The National Dish*, London, 1984.

All opinion polls referred to are listed in T. Beed et. al., *Australian Opinion Polls*, Sydney, 1978.

Further details on the 1954 royal tour can be gained from such exhaustive publications as F.H. Berryman, *Notes for planning the Visit of Her Majesty the Queen and His Royal Highness The Duke of Edinburgh*, Canberra, 1953, a confidential report issued to directors of the tour in each state. The Australian Archives and archives organizations in the states hold extensive records of the 1954 and subsequent royal tours. The ABC Archives hold sound and film recordings of the tours.

Acknowledgement: The author wishes to thank T. Bowden, C. Cunneen, J. Davidson, S.G. Foster, E.M. Goot, D. Everingham, B. Levy, J. Ranken, and the editors, for assistance in preparing this paper.

FESTIVALS OF NATIONHOOD:
THE INTERNATIONAL EXHIBITIONS

GRAEME DAVISON

"The world exhibitions", writes Werner Hofmann, "are the nineteenth century's official visiting cards". They announced the arrival of new members among the society of nations, gave a brief epitome of their trade and prospects, and opened the door to closer international relations. While they have an important place in the history of trade, they had an even more important cultural role for, as Hofmann remarks, "they were less concerned with what they sold than with what they represented".[1] Until the mid-twentieth century, when they were supplanted by the Olympic Games, the World Cup and the General Assembly of the United Nations, the international exhibitions were the most important of the symbolic battlegrounds on which nations demonstrated their prowess and tested the strength of their rivals.

Historians have studied many of the great international exhibitions and assessed their individual contributions to the intellectual and commercial life of the nations which sponsored them.[2] For those who approach the history of culture in the manner of customs-inspectors, they provide an excellent vantage-point for reviewing the import and export of cultural baggage. So, for example, the catalogues of paintings shown at the Melbourne Exhibition of 1888 offer students of Australian art useful evidence of the sources available to the painters of the Heidelberg School, while the programmes of the concerts conducted by the Exhibition's musical director, Frederick Cowan, are a useful index to current taste in orchestral music. But the Exhibitions were not simply collections of cultural artefacts; they were themselves a quintessential expression of the culture of the age. The immense popularity of the international exhibitions, I wish to argue, reflects certain characteristic ways of seeing, learning and celebrating, strange perhaps to our McLuhanite world, but integral to the culture of nineteenth-century industrializing societies. I propose to look at the forms and popular impact of the late nineteenth-century exhibitions, especially in Australia. The Australian exhibitions and their overseas counterparts showed, as one contemporary noted, "a strong family likeness" and the conduct of the Sydney and Melbourne shows (1870, 1879, 1880, 1888) was closely modelled upon their famous counterparts in London (1851, 1862), Paris (1854, 1867, 1878), Vienna (1873) and Philadelphia (1876) and became, in turn, the pattern for smaller colonial exhibitions such as those in Adelaide (1881, 1887), Perth (1881), Christchurch (1882), Dunedin (1889) and Hobart (1894-5).[3] Australians were never so derivative as when they attempted to express their sense of cultural identity; and the architecture, iconography and rhetoric of these local shows closely followed the conventions established at the Crystal Palace in 1851.

The conventions of the Crystal Palace, however, were themselves based upon an earlier tradition of more modest provincial exhibitions, and if we are to understand the luxuriant growth of the exhibition movement in the later nineteenth century we must begin by considering the humbler plant from which it grew. The earliest nine-teenth-century exhibitions derived from the activities of mechanics' institutes and artisans' schools of design in England's industrial north during the 1830s and '40s, and were organized for the purpose of educating working men in the contemporary state of the technical arts.[4] They were a straightforward application of the principle of learning by looking. We may be apt, as wordsmiths ourselves, to underestimate the extent to which nineteenth-century people learned about their world by observation. Despite the advance of popular education, many working people remained functionally illiterate, or at least unable to read technical literature. Moreover, the principle of learning by looking was strongly endorsed by contemporary pedagogical theory, which postulated that people learned first of all by observation of everyday objects, secondly by comparison and classification, and only finally through abstract reasoning. "The primary purpose of lessons on common objects and natural phenomena", wrote George Ricks in his textbook on *Object Lessons* was

> to cultivate the senses, to train the habits of attention, intelligent observation, and accurate comparison, and so to lead up to the higher processes of the mind — reason and judgement. . . .The object lesson is designed to assist and guide the child to discover the properties of things, and thus acquire knowledge for himself, rather than to pour information into his mind like wheat into a sack.[5]

In a typical object-lesson, on rubber for example, the child learned to describe its colour, texture and plasticity; he would heat and cool it to discover its chemical and physical properties; and he would investigate where it came from and how it was manufactured. In short, a common-place object was used to provide instruction in geometry, physics, chemistry, geography, history and political economy. Even if he was deprived of books, and never ventured outside his own parish, the village yokel could thus learn a little of his world through the commonplace objects which came into his ken. Only if we appreciate the capacity of objects to stir the curiosity and imagination of nineteenth-century people will we understand the popular appeal of the international exhibition.

It was the Victorians who perfected the science of learning by looking, and it is to them that we owe the development of its characteristic institutions: the museum, the art gallery, the diorama, the cyclorama and the *tableau vivant*. The nineteenth-century exhibition was nothing more than an extension of those principles of classification and comparison which eighteenth-century men of science had first applied to the natural universe to describe the expanding universe of man's own creation. As the contemplation of nature, and reflection upon its wonderful order and complexity, were calculated to inspire feelings of religious devotion, so did the contemplation of the man-made universe inspire feelings of pride in human achievement. Not for nothing had the exhibition movement been linked, in its origins, with Owenite and Comtean aspirations towards a new "religion of humanity".

The novelty and "greatness" of the Great Exhibition of 1851 lay not only in the number and variety of its exhibits, but in the breadth of its social appeal. A movement designed to disseminate technical knowledge among the provincial working class of Britain was transformed into a

grand exposition of the material culture of the whole world, and broad-
ened so as to appeal to all classes and sections of society. Its appeal was
not just technological but, in a sense, theological, for although the
exhibition continued to be primarily a display of material objects, these
objects were endowed with a greater than material significance.

Under industrial capitalism, Marx argued in a famous passage of
Capital, men are degraded to objects while objects are endowed with the
spiritual qualities of human beings. As men become alienated from the
products of their labour, they invest them with those qualities of beauty
and spontaneity which capitalistic production expelled from the labour
process itself. This principle, which he called the "fetishism of
commodities", reached its apotheosis in the organization of the Great
Exhibition.[6]

The Industrial Revolution gave rise to two distinctive architectures.
The first, exemplified by the factory, the asylum, the school and the
prison, was designed according to the Gradgrind principles of utility,
regularity and discipline. Its functions were to enclose, to isolate, to
segregate, and hence to control, the human beings who occupied
them. Its perfect embodiment, according to Michel Foucault, was
Bentham's Panopticon — the ingenious penitentiary in which a single
unobserved gaoler kept watch over the hundreds of prisoners incarcerated in the cells along its radial corridors.[7]

But if industrialism had created new prisons for human beings, it had
also created new palaces for the products of their labour. The Crystal
Palace reversed the panoptical principle by fixing the eyes of the multitude
upon an assemblage of glamorous commodities. The Panopticon was
designed so that everyone could be seen; the Crystal Palace was designed
so that everyone could see. With its walls of glass it created the illusion of
unlimited space and flooded its interior with white light. Contemporary
descriptions of the Great Exhibition emphasized this sense of light and
space ("a blazing arch of lucid glass"); and in his famous engravings of the
Crystal Palace, Joseph Nash accentuated the interior spaces by lengthening the perspective and dwarfing the human figures — a technique that
other exhibition artists were quick to imitate.[8]

Under the glass canopy of the Crystal Palace, even the humblest of
commodities assumed more exalted shapes. So, for example, a lump
of coal from the Duke of Devonshire's mine was presented in the
guise of a Greek temple, and a sample of zinc from the Vieille Montagne
Zinc Works cast in the ample form of Queen Victoria.[9] The more common-
place the object the more exaggerated, it seems, were the forms it assumed.
At the World's Columbian Exposition in Chicago, oranges from Los
Angeles were erected into a thirty-two foot tower surmounted by an eagle
with an orange in its beak.[10] At the Melbourne Exhibition, Swallow and
Ariell's biscuits were piled up into a colossal pyramid, and a great yellow
dodecahedron, representing the quantity of gold mined in the colony,
was suspended from the ceiling.[11] Many displays were constructed in the
form of a pyramid — a shape which conveniently suggested both bulk
and height, achievement and aspiration.

The focus of most nineteenth-century exhibitions was the machinery
hall — usually the largest and most central building in the show — where

hundreds of machines thumped and whirred to the rhythm of a great steam-engine. It was here, above all, that inanimate nature most nearly assumed the human qualities of life and movement. The climax of the opening ceremonies at the Centennial Exhibition in Philadelphia came when President Grant turned a handle to start the great 1400 horsepower Corliss steam-engine that powered the working exhibits throughout the fair. The Corliss engine, which could regulate its own speed and energy-consumption, was likened by contemporaries to "a great heart whose steady beating kept the entire exhibition alive and moving". According to the geographer, John Brickerhoff Jackson, the steady uninterrupted flow of energy produced by the Corliss engine was a fitting metaphor for the kind of flow technology and constant social mobility which were the hallmarks of the new industrializing society.[12] Yet the appeal of the great machine was not uniquely American. Many of the late nineteenth-century exhibitions, including Melbourne in 1888, made a particular feature of machinery displays and, in Melbourne at least, free motive-power in the form of compressed air was offered to overseas machinery exhibitors. The spectacle of a hall full of complex machinery, powered by a single, self-regulating source, was as inspiring to the layman's belief in industrial progress as a glimpse of the wonderful economy of nature to the religious faith of an eighteenth-century divine.

The transformation of the exhibition from a simple display of technology into a national, and quasi-religious, festival was manifest in the changing forms and confused vocabulary of its architecture. The typical provincial exhibition hall of the 1830s and '40s was modelled on a library or museum, with simple rectangular spaces divided into the various classes of exhibits, which were displayed horizontally, on tables or in display cases. The usual arrangement was to divide exhibits into a series of classes and sub-classes ascending from raw products of nature, through various manufactured goods and mechanical devices, to the "highest" forms of applied and fine art. The Great Exhibition, however, broke with this taxonomic tradition by introducing the principle of classification by nations or regions. The Crystal Palace was divided into so-called "courts" and "pavilions", a principal of organization inspired by an ideal of the exhibition as a kind of medieval tournament in which the gathered nations joined in a season of feasting and friendly jousting. Such chivalric ideals may seem to sit oddly alongside the utilitarianism and commercial ruthlessness of an industrial age. Yet, as Mark Girouard has recently shown, the code of knightly valour flourished in the Victorian age and the patron of the Crystal Palace, Prince Albert "the Good", was perhaps its most famous exemplar.[13] One of the most popular corners of the Great Exhibition was the "Medieval Court" designed by the nation's most renowned Gothic revival architect, A.W. Pugin, as a conscious evocation of those artistic and social ideals which industrialization had all but obliterated.

Most later exhibitions followed the Crystal Palace model by dividing their floor space, like a map of the world, into national encampments. The technical enthusiast who happened to be interested in a particular class of exhibits was left to follow them from one "court" to another by consulting a detailed catalogue of exhibits. At the 1876 Philadelphia

Exhibition the nations were installed, as far as possible, according to their "racial" groups: The French and the other Latin races occupied the north-east corner, the Teutonic races the south-west, Britain and the Anglo Saxons the north-west, and the Americans, the south-east. The oriental races, China and Japan, were placed on their own further to the west because, as the Director-General noted, they were situated to the west of the Americas.[14]

The most notable attempt to reconcile the taxonomic and national principles of organization was the ingenious design for the main building at the 1867 Paris Exhibition devised by the famous engineer Frederic Le Play. The ground plan of the building was a great ellipse, with a series of elliptical galleries arranged one inside the other, rather like Russian dolls. The outermost gallery displayed natural products such as wheat, coal and wood; but, as the visitor moved from the outer galleries towards the centre he ascended through the various classes of exhibits until he reached the displays of fine art which occupied the spaces around the central garden courtyard. Each nation occupied a segment of the building, so that it was possible for the visitor to tour the exhibits either by a radial route, which enabled him to trace the material progress of a nation, or by an elliptical route which displayed the current development of various nations in a particular art of manufacture.[15]

Le Play's scheme was much admired, but it had little influence upon the design of exhibition buildings elsewhere. British and Australian exhibition buildings, for example, tended increasingly toward ecclesiastical, rather than palatial, principles of design. The Crystal Palace, a strikingly modern building in most respects, was built upon a cruciform plan with a "nave", "transepts", choir and dominating organ. (Paxton's most characteristic detail — the great fanlight windows at each end of the nave and transepts — was repeated, like a leitmotiv, by many of his colonial imitators, including the architects of the Melbourne and Sydney exhibitions.)[16] It was with Fowkes's 1862 London Exhibition Building, however, that the ecclesiastical tradition became firmly established. Some of its elements, such as great domes and flanking towers, derived from classical models, such as Wren's St Paul's; but with the vistas along its arched nave, the architect, it was said, also aimed to give "something of a Gothic character to the structure".[17] Even the interior decoration of the building, which featured scriptural mottoes in Latin and English under the dome and over the main arches, was reminiscent of a nonconformist chapel. A rather ungainly building, designed in a hurry by an army engineer, the 1862 exhibition building nevertheless became the prototype for similar buildings in Sydney and Melbourne. The "Garden Palace" designed by the Colonial Architect, James Barnet, for the 1879 Sydney Exhibition was a recognizable child of its London parent.[18] Joseph Reed's design for the Melbourne Exhibition of the following year, retained a similar plan but treated the exterior in a more exuberant Italianate style. Economies by the Building Committee forced Reed to lop about a third of its projected height, yet it retained a kind of bloated grandeur. Even if it offends the architectural purist, Reed's combination of gothic and classical elements was consistent with his main aim — to create a building that was at once useful and ceremonial, secular and sacred. Contemporaries recognized this ambiguity of function in their descriptions of the building. Some called it "a great school", some a "banquet hall", some a "cathedral". But perhaps the best description was given by a journalist who called it "more a temple than a palace".[19]

The exalted architectural language of the exhibition buildings corresponded with the similarly high-flown rhetoric of the exhibitions themselves. In the opening chapter of his book *Victorian People*, Asa Briggs attempts to reach behind the ceremonial forms of the Great Exhibition of 1851 to elicit the social aspirations and anxieties of the celebrants.[20] The dominant theme of the celebrations was of thanksgiving for the national blessings of peace, prosperity and progress. "God bless my dearest Albert, and my dear Country which has shown itself so great today", wrote Queen Victoria in her journal on 1 May 1851. "One felt so grateful to the great God, whose blessing seemed to pervade the whole undertaking".[21] Yet, as Briggs notes, the mood of national rejoicing was offset by a growing sense of "conflict and frustration". The belief in prosperity and social harmony was undermined by mounting evidence of poverty and conflict. In other lands too exhibitions were often put on in troubled times. Philadelphia's Centennial Exhibition followed in the wake of a great commercial depression. On the morning of its opening the *New York Times* noted that "Industrially the nation suffers. The blow which fell upon Austria, and then upon Germany and England, has prostrated in this land also thousands of firms, closed hundreds of mills and left without employment an unprecedented proportion of our workmen".[22] Victoria's premier, Graham Berry, organized the Melbourne Exhibition of 1880 as a stimulus to recovery from the economic and political turmoil of the late 1870s, and Chicago's Columbian Exposition of 1893 was held in an atmosphere of industrial strife. That exhibition rhetoric, with its stress upon ideals of economic progress and social harmony, was so dramatically at odds with contemporary reality is not perhaps to be wondered at, for, as anthropologists would tell us, the very purpose of such rituals as the opening of the Great Exhibition was to offer a symbolic resolution of the contradictions of social life. The element of ambiguity, which we noted in exhibition architecture, and which pervaded the pomp and pageantry of the Crystal Palace, was integral, rather than merely incidental, to their purpose.

Seen in this light, the elaborate protocol of the opening ceremonies, the often-times hackneyed verse of the many exhibition odes and cantatas, the exalted rhetoric of the official speeches, and the florid imagery of commemorative paintings and medallions, may perhaps warrant more serious scrutiny than a superficial inspection would suggest.

Nearly every international exhibition began with a procession in which the officials of the host nation and visiting dignitaries advanced through the city to the site of the exhibition itself. The spectacle of the assembled nations proceeding in step towards the palace of art and industry underlined those ideals of linear progress and international concord that had inspired the exhibition movement, and confirmed the social order of the host nation. On the morning of the opening ceremony the daily newspapers published a complete list of the various officials and delegations in strict order of precedence. It was one of the few occasions on which the whole of civil society was thus arranged in order, and contemporaries seem to have been particularly concerned that everyone should be placed in his correct niche. At the opening of the Crystal Palace, Queen Victoria was pleased to see that the procession was "beautifully arranged, the prescribed order being exactly adhered to".[23] In the colonies, where social precedence was less fixed, exhibition protocol was a more contentious matter. At Melbourne's Centennial Exhibition, Chief Justice Higinbotham refused to attend the Opening Ceremony when he was relegated to a place in the procession behind the Speaker of the Parliament. There was also a rumpus over whether it should be the Anglican bishop or a trio of representative clergymen who offered the Inaugural Prayer. (Sectarianism triumphed, and the President of the Commissioners read a prayer which the *Sydney Morning Herald* described as reminiscent of "the work of a Low Church bishop".) George Belcher, a member of parliament and Vice-Consul for Denmark, attended the opening ceremony in his consular uniform but his name did not appear on the official list, an omission which he found "somewhat annoying".[24] These tea-cup storms over rank and precedence involved more than personal vanity, for in a society more attuned than our own to the functions of ritual, questions of protocol were often seen as questions of principle.

The opening ceremony itself usually followed a fixed routine of speeches, prayers and quasi-sacred music. During the course of the later nineteenth century some famous composers lent their talents to the exhibition movement. In 1862 a special exhibition overture by Meyerbeer was conducted by the composer; in 1867 Rossini presented a "Hymn to the Emperor"; and in 1876 the Philadelphians, not to be outdone, commissioned Richard Wagner to compose a "Centennial March". Less distinguished musically, but often more popular, were the choral odes and cantatas contributed by local poets and musicians. The commissioners of the 1862 London Exhibition had invited the Poet Laureate, Tennyson, to write an ode which was set to music by the Cambridge professor, Sterndale Bennett. The ideas, form and even some of the imagery of Tennyson's poem would be reproduced subsequently by many of his humbler admirers. It began on a note of thanks to the God of creation for all his past benefits, evoked the wonderful plentitude of men's present creative work, and culminated in a call to the assembled nations to practise the arts of peace and brotherhood.

> O ye, the wise who think, the wise who reign,
> From growing commerce loose her latest chain,
> And let the fair white-winged peace-maker fly
> To happy havens under all the sky,
> And mix the seasons and the golden hours,
> Till each may find his own in all men's good,
> And all men work in noble brotherhood,
> Breaking their mailed fleets and armed towers,
> And ruling by obeying Nature's powers,
> And gathering all the fruits of Peace and crown'd with all her **flowers**.[25]

In the new lands of America and Australasia, the contrast between past benefits and future aspirations naturally centred upon their recent history of conquest and settlement. So, for example, Dudley

Buck's cantata for the Centennial Exhibition of 1876 dramatized the voyage of the Pilgrim Fathers, evoking in turn the silence of the waiting land, the strife and persecution that drove the exiles from England, their tempestous passage, and their safe arrival. In her "Commemoratory Ode" for the World's Columbian Exposition of 1893, Miss Harriet Munroe scarcely alluded to the achievements of the Spanish navigator but instead apostrophized the spirit of the young republic, Columbia, whom she pictured as "a goddess rising from the misty sea" before the weary exiles of Europe.[26] Australian exhibition poets emphasized themes of material prosperity rather than political or religious liberty. R.H. ("Orion") Horne's "lyric masque", "The South Sea Sisters", written for the 1866 Melbourne Exhibition, began in the "primeval wilderness" and reviewed in turn the arrival of the first settlers, scenes of pastoral life, and the discovery of the gold fields.[27] In his long poem "Australia", composed for the Sydney Exhibition of 1879, Henry Kendall presented an almost encyclopaedic review of Australian exploration and discovery from Marco Polo to Captain Arthur Phillip.[28]

The cantatas for both the 1880 and 1888 Melbourne exhibitions were selected from the several hundred tendered as entries in a public competition. The winner in 1880 was J.W. Meaden, a local ironmonger and temperance lecturer, and his prize poem, with its dramatic contrast between the colony's dismal Past and glorious Present, sat squarely in the orthodox tradition of industrial hymnology. In the first part of the cantata Victoria, sleeping in primeval solitude, is roused by voices which foretell her speedy discovery and settlement; and soon the songs of mariners are heard as they make their way across the ocean. In the "Present", Victoria is pictured as engaged in various pursuits — pastoral, agricultural, industrial, etc. She is approached by a company of nymphs, representing the various nations of the earth. They hail her "Queen of the South" and she responds with a jubilant song of welcome:

> O welcome! Sisters gracious, and friends from every land!
> My heart warms at your coming to this bright and sunny strand.
> My banquet hall is furnished, my table richly spread,
> The grand old flag, with star gems deck'd, gleams brightly overhead.

The climax comes in a grand patriotic hymn foretelling Australia's destiny as "a greater Britain, 'neath these Southern Skies".[29]

The competition for the Centennial International Exhibition cantata drew an even larger field than in 1880. The promise of a little brief fame and a few pounds remuneration aroused poetic inspiration in the most unlikely quarters. J.H. McArthur, a farm manager at Carramut in the Western District, scribbled his entry in a single day between bursts of farm-work and gardening; but after looking it over he concluded that it wanted "a little more knocking into shape". He polished it for several days more before deciding that it wasn't up to scratch.[30] Meaden, the winner in 1880, was pipped on this occasion by the Rev. William Allen, a Congregational minister who followed much the same well-tried formula, although giving more attention to the urban virtues exemplified by the booming city of Melbourne and to the achievements of the colony's aging pioneers. Whether because of his hackneyed verse, or H.J. King's undistinguished musical score, the performance of the cantata was not reckoned a success. Judges yawned, ministers stared vacantly into space, and poor George Belcher, sweating in his consular attire, almost nodded off to sleep. By the time it was over, more than a third of the audience had left the Exhibition Buildings.[31] A few days later the Sydney *Bulletin* cruelly parodied the now-debased genre in a purported "slab from one of the unsuccessful Melbourne Exhibition cantatas". Behind the traditional "welcome to guests", it detected more sordid commercial interests:

> Brothers all with aught to sell,
> Hither come, we love you all.
> See the mighty dome arise,
> That you all may advertise.
> You of nasal twang so pure,
> Welcome with your Certain Cure.
> Bring the cannons out of date,
> And Birmingham's electroplate —
> See the mighty dome arise,
> That you all may advertise.

The conventional contrast between the dismal past and a rosy present was reversed into a satirical comparison between a "Clean Past" and a "Dirty Present":

> Farewell the crystal streams,
> Welcome the drains that stink;
> Farewell poetic dreams,
> Welcome the skating-rink.
>
> At civilisation's glance
> The gums withered, sere and dead,
> That beneath death might dance
> Rampant on typhoid bed.[32]

The *Bulletin* recognized, as many contemporaries must surely have done, that the vaunted ideals of international brotherhood and material progress stood in uneasy contrast to the self-seeking commercialism and environmental squalor of the nineteenth-century city.

The exhibition cantatas and odes had their pictorial counterpart in the symbolic murals, statues, illuminated addresses and medallions that were produced to commemorate the occasion. The exhibition movement created its own pantheon of winged deities representing the various nations, arts and industrial virtues. The medals struck for the 1851 Exhibition, for example, centred on the theme of international peace: one showed Britannia bestowing laurels on the assembled nations while another represented the arts of peace and war united under her benediction.[33] Nations were usually portrayed in idealized feminine forms — Britannia, Columbia, Germania, Australia etc. — and in attitudes suggestive of social concord and international peace, such as offering greetings, presenting gifts, bestowing laurels, and the like. These symbolic *tableaux* were often closely integrated with the architecture and rhetoric of the exhibition, and it is important, in interpreting them, to observe what was said and done at the time they were unveiled.

The paintings executed by John Mather and other painters for the dome of the Melbourne Exhibition Buildings are a fair specimen of their type, and show how the conventions of exhibition iconography could be adapted to the special circumstances of an immature and dependent industrial country. They are not remarkable for their draughtsmanship or painterly detail. The *Sydney Morning Herald* regarded them as no better than "good circus posters", and the artist himself insisted that they were not to be regarded as finished pictures but only as "outlined drawings executed in a simple way, without any touches representing light and shade".[34] On the eight interior faces of the pillars supporting the great dome were figures representing each of the principal applied arts and sciences — Agriculture, Mining, Commerce, Painting, Music, Sculpture, etc. — and in the four panels below the cornices were figures representing the Seasons. Perhaps the most interesting of the pictures, however, are the four larger *tableaux* above the main arches. The space under the great dome had been the principal focus of the ceremonies for the opening of the Exhibition, and these four pictures were orientated, in an almost liturgical way, to accentuate the themes of the Exhibition cantata and the welcoming speeches.

The main entrance to the Building was from the south, and the pictures over the northern and southern arches were concerned with themes of invitation and welcome. Over the entrance itself, on the southern arch of the dome, the assembled nations were shown responding to Victoria's invitation. The same motif appeared at the eastern entrance in the form of the motto "Victoria Welcomes all Nations". From the way in which they are depicted, we are able to discern how far each of the invited guests had themselves ascended in the scale of modern civilization. The Italian and the German both stand erect — the first, with lyre and painter's palette, representing music and the fine arts, the second, with a mallet in hand, representing industry and the applied arts. The Greek is also shown standing, with books and manuscripts, but alongside is a broken statue denoting that his native land, once the cradle of the arts, has fallen into cultural decay. A Chinaman, with pigtail and fan, sits on a tea chest; a "noble red man" squats with a peace pipe; and the unfortunate Hindoo kneels on an oriental rug, carving a piece of ivory. If they had actually attended the Exhibition, the Chinaman, the Hindoo and the "noble red man" would have been entitled to question the sincerity of Victoria's welcome. The exhibition movement was ostensibly devoted to the ideals of free trade; yet Victoria, by its high tariff and anti-Chinese legislation was doing its best, it would seem, to keep the lowly nations on their knees.

Over the northern arch, and facing the arriving guests, the figure of Peace, in a white robe, introduced Art and Science to Victoria, who stood with outstretched arms and laurel wreath ready to receive the prized immigrants. Agriculture and Commerce, who had already arrived, were also on hand to welcome the newcomers. The rapid economic progress of the colonies, and their relative backwardness in cultural matters, was often excused as a consequence of their youth.

> In a nation's history [the *Argus* claimed in 1888] intellectual and artistic culture come last. First there is the stern necessity of manual work, then the adoption of every invention that renders labour more economical and more valuable, and in

Interior of Melbourne's International Exhibition Building. Under a spangled dome, ethereal figures representing the Seasons and Arts and Sciences look down upon the dwarf-like visitors. Several features of the building, including the scriptural mottoes, were borrowed from London's 1862 Exhibition Building. The allegorical tableaux over the main arches, however, were designed expressly for the 1880 Exhibition and embodied such contemporary themes as "Victoria's welcome to the Nations" and "Peace and Plenty rewarding Happy Youth and Contented Old Age".

the end the production of a specific art and literature, and the cultivation of those things that conduce to the highest and most refined greatness of a people. . . . The slowness of artistic as compared with industrial development involves no disparagement to the colony. . . . It is the law of history and evolution. The tree must come to a certain age before it can carry the full burden of its fruit; the man must establish himself in life before he has time for mental culture; and so the nation must come to maturity before it can develop an art or literature that is distinctively its own.[35]

The idea that high culture must grow from the seed of more practical endeavours was a consoling notion to men immersed in money-making. Meanwhile the increasing prominence of the fine and performing arts in the exhibitions themselves offered reassuring evidence that the process of cultural evolution was well under way. By 1888, with the exhibition of work by Roberts and McCubbin, Victoria was perhaps beginning to show signs of developing "an art. . . that was distinctively its own". Yet the stigma of cultural inferiority was hard to shake off, as was the assumption, implicit in the exhibition *tableaux*, that art and science, when they came, would arrive like immigrants from abroad rather than spring from the land itself.

The pictures above the eastern and western arches looked back into the main exhibition hall along the "nave", and were concerned, in a broad way, with themes of progress and destiny. Over the eastern arch, Science was depicted instructing the Arts. Torchlight gives way to gaslight, the signalling-beacon to the telegraph, the hand-press to the machine printery, and the spinning-wheel to the sewing-machine. A similar composition appears in Brumidi's mural under the dome of the United States Capitol where Benjamin Franklin, Robert Fulton and Samuel Morse symbolize the inventive genius of a young nation.[36] Faith in the civilizing power of technology was perhaps the most essential article of the exhibition creed; and Australians, like Americans, were among its most ardent adherents.

The symbolism of the Exhibition was completed by the *tableau* over the western arch which depicted the figures of Peace and Plenty rewarding Labour, Happy Youth and Contented Old Age. The relationship between the generations was already a well-rehearsed theme of exhibition rhetoric. The heroes of 1851 — Stephenson, Brunel, Paxton — were men of the first industrial generation, and the Great Exhibition was conceived as a celebration of their achievements and a spur to their descendants to follow in their footsteps. By the 1880s the relationship between gold-rush pioneers and their native-born children had become, as I have argued elsewhere, a leading social question in colonial Australia.[37] Among the new paintings commissioned for the 1888 Exhibition was a *tableau* showing the heads of eight Australian pioneers surrounded by a group of cupids festooned with wreaths symbolizing the youth of Australia, while the Rev. William Allen's Cantata composed for its opening culminated in a grand chorus, "Honour the Pioneers".[38] The ideal of respect between the generations, we know, was all too seldom achieved in real life. Once again, it was precisely those relationships that contemporaries knew to be imbued with latent conflict which claimed the attention of the exhibition muralists.

None of these relationships was quite so problematical as the attitude of Labour to the values represented by the exhibitions. The Great Exhibition was conceived as a celebration of the ideal of class harmony. "Never before in this or any other country", boasted one of its promoters, "has there been so complete a fusion of classes under one roof".[39] The exhibition movement had originated, as we have seen, among the working classes of the northern industrial towns, and there is some truth in Charles Babbage's claim in 1851 that it had "advanced slowly in society from below upwards".[40] The organizers of the Great Exhibition offered popular involvement in the form of "shilling days" and concessional railway travel, and four million people from all parts of the country are estimated to have attended the show.

The promoters of exhibitions in the New World were also persuaded of their educational benefit to the working classes. "One of the greatest things to be expected from an International Exhibition in Melbourne", asserted Joseph Bosisto of eucalyptus-oil fame, "was that it would give the working classes of this colony an improved technical education. They had only to walk from one court to another in order to go, as it were, from one country to another, and see the proficiency which technical art had attained amongst other nations as compared with what was the case here".[41] Yet the growing popularity of exhibitions did not necessarily further their educational influence. It was, one suspects, for entertainment rather than instruction that most of the crowds came. Prince Bismarck, who had put up with a lot of such trade-fairs in his time, regarded them as "a necessary evil". They drew people less for "assiduous and profitable study", he concluded, than for "indiscriminate curiosity and trivial sight-seeing".[42] His opinion would certainly have been confirmed by the 1888 Melbourne exhibition, where the most popular attractions were not the technical exhibits but the sideshows such as the musical concerts and the switch-back railway. Some loyal supporters of technical education, such as the Ballarat radical Richard Vale, actually opposed the Exhibition on the ground that the working classes did not want it, that it would threaten local industries, and that, in any event, it would not teach Victorian artisans anything that they did not already know.[43]

The popular appeal of the exhibitions remains hard to assess. One of the obsessions of the exhibitioneers was a passion for statistics. The number of attendances, like the number of acres of exhibition space, the value of exhibits, the size of foreign delegations, and so on, was always carefully computed. The great European and American exhibitions strove to outdo each other in popular appeal — the six million who had attended the Crystal Palace were exceeded in turn by Paris's nine million in 1867, Philadelphia's ten million, and Paris's sixteen million in 1878. By these standards, Sydney's 1.1 million and Melbourne's 1.3 million in 1880, and 2.0 million in 1888, seem very small beer. On a population basis, however, the Australians claimed to lead the world: New South Wales and Victoria each achieved a ratio of attendances to population of over 150%, while France could boast only 43% and the United States only 22%.[44] These, of course, were rather fraudulent statistics. Comparing Philadelphia's attendances with the population of the entire United States and Melbourne's only with the colony of Victoria was hardly fair to the Americans. Yet, if we compare Melbourne's attendances with the population of all six Australian colonies, the percentages in both 1880 (59%) and 1888 (69%) still compare very favourably with contemporary overseas exhibitions. The organizers of the Philadelphia Exhibition regarded the area within about 200 miles of the city as its principal catchment.[45] Yet Melbourne secured a higher attendance ratio within its main catchment, the colony of Victoria (154.5%) than the Philadelphians did within their more densely populated one (81.6%). Even if we make due allowance for the crudity of the statistics, Australians appear to have succumbed even more readily than their American counterparts to exhibition-mania. In the ordinary course of events, nineteenth-century Australians enjoyed fewer opportunities than their contemporaries in Europe and America to become acquainted with the latest developments in technology and art, and they may therefore have put a correspondingly high value upon the kind of concentrated, all-purpose cultural binge represented by the international exhibition. Isolation also made Australians more anxious for international recognition, and in the international exhibition they may have found a stage on which they could symbolically present their accomplishments to the rest of the world.

By 1888 the railway and the telegraph had penetrated most of the Australian continent, and the progress of the Centennial Exhibition was followed even in the remotest districts. Special trains at reduced fares were run for exhibition-goers in rural Victoria. State-school pupils within 100 miles of Melbourne could make the trip for as little as two shillings return. These concessions did little, of course, to reconcile rural politicians and small town newspapermen to the big show, which they portrayed — not altogether wrongly — as a plot by Melbourne capitalists to centralize trade and power in the metropolis. They resented the way in which Melbourne's social calendar was imposed upon the countryside. The Hamilton *Spectator* thought it "a perfect farce to proclaim a holiday [for the opening of the Exhibition] in towns so far from the metropolis as this", and the Ballarat *Courier* asked why special fares were not offered so that Exhibition visitors could visit the "Golden City" as well as Ballarat people travel to Melbourne. Yet the attractions of the exhibition appear to have quickly overcome these resentments; within a week or two, more than 200 Hamiltonians had boarded the exhibition special, and more than 2500 Ballarat school-children had made the excursion to the metropolis.[46]

The journey up to Melbourne came, it seems, as a welcome relief from the tedium of rural life. Joseph Jenkins, a Welsh swagman whose thirty-years pilgrimage in the colony had never previously taken him outside the central goldfields, enjoyed an "exciting day at Melbourne", where he marvelled at the prodigious cost and size of the exhibition buildings. William Hastings, a canny South Gippsland farmer, drew a cheque for six pounds, journeyed up to Melbourne where he put up at the Bush Inn, did some business in town, and took in one of Frederick Cowan's concerts at the Exhibition. John Currie, a workaholic selector from Lardner, near Drouin, had to be "pestered" by his wife to go. "I hope he will enjoy himself better than he expects too", she wrote as he departed.[47]

An unknown, but possibly quite large, number of visitors came from the other colonies. A clothier inserted some verses, entitled "The Exodus to Melbourne" in the advertizing columns of the Sydney *Daily Telegraph*:

> They are going in dozens, our sisters and cousins
> The Great Exhibition to see
> By the train every day they are speeding away
> As happy as happy can be
> When Victorian belles see our young Sydney swells
> Dressed up in a style so immense
> They will make all their beaux dress in Summerfields clothes
> Thus showing their sound common sense.[48]

Melbourne's festivities lured tourists even from as far away as the drought-stricken back-blocks of western Queensland. By November, the dust, the heat, and the laxative effects of the bore-water had combined, so the *Town and Country Journal* reported, to persuade many of the settlers around Barcaldine to take the first available train south to the Exhibition.[49]

The International Exhibitions heralded the age of great mass events. Geoffrey Serle claims that the 300,000 who turned out for Monash's funeral in 1931 constituted Australia's largest mass event and Bill Gammage has countered with the 400,000 who greeted the Prince of Wales in Melbourne in 1920. But if "mass events" includes happenings that lasted for more than a day or so, then I contend that the Melbourne Centennial Exhibition of 1888 was probably witnessed by more Australians than any other similar event, at least in the nineteenth century. Its impact upon them, of course, is harder to gauge. More detailed research might enable us to trace the impact of new inventions shown at the Exhibition, such as the cream-separator and the Benz petrol-engine or, with more difficulty, the influence of new artistic styles. But, as I have been arguing, rather too insistently perhaps, the business of the exhibition was not simply to sell things but to symbolize, and thus to disseminate, the ruling ideals of an industrial age. "In an exhibition such as ours", a perceptive Melbourne journalist remarked in 1888, "we not only see but are seen".[50] In the end, I suspect, that pleasurable sensation of being seen by the assembled nations left a more lasting impression upon the Australians who visited the exhibition than all the ship-loads of cultural cargo sent from abroad.

The circumstances which made the international exhibitions such an important vehicle of nineteenth-century culture have dramatically changed in the twentieth. The growth of literacy has made reading a more important means of technical education than the old method of learning by looking. Air travel, cinema and television offer a more continuous, intimate and dynamic understanding of the world than the static displays at an exhibition. The paired ideals that the exhibition movement sought to promote — material and moral progress, utility and art, economic competition and international peace — may now also appear harder to reconcile and attain. The Exposition Universelle in Paris in 1900 was probably the last of the great world exhibitions. Not until the Montreal and Osaka Expos of 1967 and 1970 did the number of admissions to an exhibition exceed the 48 million who attended in Paris.[51] But if exhibitions no longer remain the greatest international festivals, they continue to hold a special attraction for new states seeking to command the world's attention. The world cities — New York, London, Tokyo — have long since retired from the lists; now it is the cities of the frontier, the Asian littoral and the sunbelt which maintain the traditions of the Crystal Palace. When planning commenced for the Australian Bicentenary the idea of an international Expo found little favour in the larger southern cities or with the Australian government. It took a unilateral bid by the parochial premier of one of Australia's least industrialized states to secure the Bicentennial Expo. But we should not be surprised by such a contradiction for, like its predecessors, the Brisbane Expo illustrates the most persistent paradox of the exhibition movement — that its promoters were usually more interested in cultivating an image of modernity than absorbing the spirit of modernity itself.

1983

Notes

1. Werner Hofmann, *Art in the Nineteenth Century*, London, 1961, p. 165.
2. John Allwood, *The Great Exhibitions*, London, 1977; John Parris and A.G.L. Shaw, "The Melbourne International Exhibition 1880-1881", *Victorian Historical Magazine*, November 1980, no. 4, pp. 237-53; Geoffrey Serle, *The Rush to be Rich*, Melbourne, 1971, pp. 285-7; Elizabeth Barrow, "The Melbourne International Exhibition: its relationship with and place in the Cultural Life of 'Marvellous Melbourne' ", B.A. Thesis, University of Melbourne, 1968; Therese Radic, "Music of the Centennial International Exhibition", *Australia 1888*, no. 7, April 1981, pp. 59-67; D.F. Burg, *Chicago's White City of 1893*, Lexington 1976.
3. *Sydney International Exhibition 1879*, Museum of Applied Arts and Sciences Commemorative Exhibition Catalogue, Sydney, 1979; Graeme Davison, "R.E.N. Twopeny and Town Life in Australia", *Historical Studies*, XVI, 1974, 292-305; Peter Mercer, "The Tasmanian International Exhibition, 1894-1895", *Tasmanian Historical Research Society Proceedings*, March 1981, pp. 17-47.
4. Toshio Kusamitsu, "Great Exhibitions before 1851", *History Workshop*, no. 9, Spring 1980, pp. 70-89; Audrey Short, "Workers under Glass in 1851", *Victorian Studies*, X, 1966, 193-202.
5. *London 1888*, p. 2.
6. *Capital*, vol. I, Book 1, ch. 4; compare Shlomo Avinieri, *The Social and Political Thought of Karl Marx*, Cambridge, 1968, pp. 117-123.
7. Michel Foucault, *Discipline and Punish*, Pelican ed., London, 1979, pp. 195-228.
8. Francis D. Klingender, *Art and the Industrial Revolution*, revised edition, New York, 1968, pp. 165, 217; on architecture of the Crystal Palace, see H.R. Hitchcock, *Early Victorian Architecture in Britain*, London, 1954, ch. 16; and compare Wolfgang Schivelbusch, *The Railway Journey*, London 1980, pp. 50-6.
9. *The Illustrated Exhibitor*, London, 1851, p. 36.
10. *The Illustrated World's Fair*, Chicago, 1893, p. 539.
11. *Argus*, 2 October 1880.
12. *American Space: The Centennial Years 1865-1876*, New York, 1972, pp. 237-9.
13. *The Return to Camelot: Chivalry and the English Gentleman*, New Haven, 1981, passim.
14. *Report of the Director-General of the International Exhibition*, Philadelphia, 1876, vol. I, p. 54.
15. Allwood, *The Great Exhibitions*, pp. 42-3 and compare Nicholaus Pevsner, *A History of Building Types*, Princeton, 1976, ch. 12.
16. See pictures in Alan Sierp, *Colonial Life in New South Wales*, Adelaide, 1974, pp. 50, 116.
17. G.F. Pardon, *A Guide to the International Exhibition*, London, 1862, p. 18.
18. *Argus*, 1 October 1880.
19. *Argus*, 2 August 1888.
20. London, 1954, ch. 2.
21. Queen Victoria's Journal 1 May 1851 as quoted in C.H. Gibbs-Smith, *The Great Exhibition of 1851*, Victoria and Albert Museum, London, 1950, p. 17.

22. *New York Times*, 11 May 1876.
23. Queen Victoria's Journal as quoted in Gibbs-Smith, *The Great Exhibition*, p. 17.
24. George Belcher Diary, 1 August 1888 (La Trobe Library).
25. Pardon, op.cit., p. 23.
26. J.D. McCabe, *The Illustrated History of the Centennial Exhibition*, Philadelphia, 1879, pp. 286-8; *Illustrated World's Fair*, Chicago, 1893, p. 365.
27. *The South Sea Sisters: a Lyric-Masque for the Opening of the International Exhibition of Australiasia*, Melbourne, 1866.
28. *Poetical Works of Henry Kendall* edited by T.T Reed, Adelaide, 1966, pp. 193-200.
29. *Argus*, 1 October 1880.
30. J.N. McArthur Diary, 4 January 1888 (La Trobe Library).
31. *Sydney Morning Herald*, 2 August 1888.
32. *Bulletin*, 18 August 1888.
33. *Illustrated Exhibitor*, pp. iv-v.
34. *Sydney Morning Herald*, 2 August 1888; *Argus*, 2 October 1880. Mather's involvement is claimed by Bernard Smith, *Australian Painting*, Melbourne, 1971, p. 65.
35. *Argus,* 2 August 1888.
36. United States Capitol Historical Society, *We the People: The Story of the United States Capitol*, Washington, 1981, pp. 74-5.
37. *The Rise and Fall of Marvellous Melbourne*, Melbourne, 1978, pp. 2-3, 130-1.
38. *Argus*, 25 January 1888; William Allen, *Inaugural Prize Poem for the Opening of the Centennial International Exhibition*, Melbourne 1888.
39. *Illustrated Exhibitor*, p. 62.
40. *The Exposition of 1851*, London 1851, p. 30.
41. *Victorian Parliamentary Debates,* vol. 54, 1887, p. 551.
42. As quoted in *Illustrated World's Fair*, October 1892, p. 362.
43. *Victorian Parliamentary Debates*, vol. 55, 1887, p. 441.
44. *Argus*, 2 August 1888.
45. *What the Centennial Is and How to See it*, Philadelphia 1876, p. 87.
46. *Hamilton Spectator*, 2, 28 August 1888; *Ballarat Courier*, 14 July, 2 August, 25, 27 October 1888. (I owe these references to Gina McWilliam and Beryl Hooley).
47. William Evans (ed.), *Diary of a Welsh Swagman 1869-1894*, Melbourne, 1975, p. 167; William Hastings Diary, 1, 23, 24 August 1888; Anne Currie Diary, 30 August 1888 (La Trobe Library).
48. *Daily Telegraph*, 2 August 1888.
49. *Town and Country Journal*, 3 November 1888, p. 899.
50. *Argus*, 4 August 1888.
51. Allwood, *The Great Exhibitions*, pp. 179-85.

Opening Ceremony of the 1880 Melbourne International Exhibition. This contemporary engraving, emphasizing the host of diminutive figures and the spacious grandeur of the building, follows the convention established by Joseph Nash's engravings of the 1851 Crystal Palace. One of the allegorical tableaux discussed in the text is shown above the arch. In the background, below George Fincham's colonial-built organ, is the massed choir and orchestra.

Under the dome in the Garden Palace. In the centre is a statue of the young Queen
Victoria by the British sculptor, Marshall Wood. The large allegorical figure on the
pillar is one of four depicting the continents of Asia, Africa, America and Europe
while the smaller panels underneath show typical Australian trades, such as miners,
shearers, etc. The Garden Palace, and the royal statue, were destroyed by fire on 22
September 1882.

The Sydney International Exhibition Building, 1879. The Garden Palace, designed by the New South Wales Colonial Architect, James Barnet, emulated the cruciform plan, dominating central dome and four flanking towers of the 1862 London Exhibition Building.

CULTURAL HISTORY: THE "HIGH" AND THE "POPULAR"

JOHN RICKARD

In embarking on the writing of a cultural history of Australia, I have been forced to consider definitions, including the distinction often made between high and popular culture. It is a distinction that, in Australia at least, has been used fairly casually and without much thought; but there is a case, I think, for historians dispensing with these two categories altogether.

Recently, I saw the London revival of the 1936 Rogers and Hart musical — now, dare one say, a classic? — *On Your Toes*. Here is satirized the great American confrontation between high and popular culture, with a young hero, born of a vaudeville family tap-dancing troupe, who goes on to become a brilliant music professor. High culture is symbolized by the Russian Ballet visiting New York — exotic, "artistic" (its stars necessarily temperamental), and foreign. One of the show's big numbers is "On Your Toes" itself, which takes the form of an "anything-you-can-do-I-can-do-better" competition between the stars of the Russian ballet, performing their *pirouettes*, *jetés* and leaps, and an energetic chorus of tap-dancing young Americans. One is reminded at times of the Marx Brothers and *A Night at the Opera*, when the chaotic and earthy comedy of Groucho and brothers is pitted against the highfaltuin world of grand opera. Except, of course, that in *On Your Toes* some kind of resolution between high and popular is effected, and the show concludes with the Russian Ballet's presentation of the jazz ballet, *Slaughter on Tenth Avenue*. Fittingly enough, the choreography for *On Your Toes* was by Balanchine, whose work has straddled both forms.

The tendency to distinguish high and popular culture, and then to agonize about having made the distinction, is itself a symptom of modern culture. If we retrace our way through the familiar territory mapped out by Raymond Williams, it may be recalled how he argued that in the nineteenth century intellectuals felt increasingly alienated from the new industrial society, and came to regard culture as something to be defended from the barbarism of the mass market.[1] Perhaps it was possible to educate or enlighten the new urban society, but such a task was a mission of the few to the many. In the twentieth century many intellectuals have had a change of heart. Rather than excommunicating the masses from the realm of culture, they have sought to re-define the concept of culture so as to include them. This essentially was what T.S. Eliot was doing, when — even while firmly defending class elitism — he nevertheless expounded the idea of culture as a way of life.[2]

The distinction between high and popular culture was born of the need felt to argue the case for studying the latter. This did not, at least for the social scientist or historian, necessarily involve any question of aesthetic judgment. But just as anthropologists sought to re-create the totality of a society, so too might other researchers feel that they could not afford to exclude from their studies the habits and values of such large sections of the community. Aesthetic evaluation has since become a matter of debate, as forms once deemed popular have acquired their own apparatus for appreciation and criticism.[3] The intellectual pursuit of popular culture has itself sometimes had the effect of promoting particular forms up some imaginary cultural ladder.

For some, like Williams, E.P. Thompson and Hoggart, "the discovery of the 'cultural'", as Richard Johnson has called it, had an obvious ideological dimension as they sought to revitalize Marxian analysis with a new emphasis on the lived experience, particularly that of the working-class.[4] They wanted to rescue the term "culture" from élitist or narrowly literary and artistic usages, and introduce it into the cultureless realm of traditional labour history.[5] Those with a taste for structuralism, much more attuned to the methodology of the anthropologists, were enchanted to be offered such virgin fields for analysis in terms of ritual and coded messages. Much of the American enthusiasm for popular culture seemed more amorphously democratic in spirit — as with Herbert Gans' introductory dictum that "all people have a right to the culture they prefer".[6] Popular culture was also seen as a field where the humanities and social sciences could fruitfully meet.

Having embarked on the study of popular culture, its devotees have hardly paused to examine the validity of the distinction. They are not even agreed if popular culture is necessarily a product of modern industrial society, and so to be distinguished from something called folk culture. C.E.W. Bigsby thinks so,[7] but others have deliberately carried the concept of popular culture back into their study of pre-industrial societies. One might note, for example, a volume of essays emanating from the Bowling Green University Popular Press, Ohio, modestly entitled *5000 Years of Popular Culture*.[8] Definitions, when offered, are sometimes all but meaningless: T.M. Kando, for example, defines popular culture as "the typical cultural and recreational activities of typical segments of society", and high culture as "the recreational, cultural and artistic activities traditionally not included in mass culture".[9]

The confusion is evident in the American *Journal of Popular Culture*. Here, often remarkably insulated from European debate about culturalism and structuralism, articles sprinkle the pages with titles having all the prettiness and substance of hundreds-and-thousands: "Dear Abby, Miss Lonelyhearts and the 18th Century", "The Spatial Behaviour Involved in Two Honeymoons", "The Changing Life of Mickey Finn: Some Notes on Chloral Hydrate Down the Ages", etc.[10] Yet every now and then, in a pause for reflection, contributors have their doubts about where the study (discipline?) is heading. "We study things, events, and people because they are *popular*, but we rarely examine them from a cultural perspective", is the alarming confession of one contributor.[11] Another laments that "Popular Culture has led us no closer to a systematic understanding of the culture of the populace than have more traditional élitist studies".[12] One article that considers definitions actually poses the question, "Should high culture be included in popular culture?" In support of the proposition, the writer plaintively observes that ballet is very popular in the Soviet Union.[13] Clearly, once one has embarked on the study of leisure activities, it is inhibiting to discover that definition prevents one from exploring the full range. Well might Richard Peterson conclude that "the popular studies movement was founded in the 1960s on the easily shaped sands of eclecticism".[14]

At the other end of the spectrum, there is some reluctance to embrace the term, "high culture". It is "so-called high culture", or "high" is defensively placed in inverted commas. Nevertheless, we in Australia have adopted the categories. If Geoffrey Serle's *From Deserts The Prophets Come*[15] was an affirmation that in Australia we had a high culture worth writing about, Peter Spearritt and David Walker's collection, *Australian Popular Culture*,[16] seemed to be making a complementary assertion. This pair seem a rather late entry in the cultural studies stakes, but it must be borne in mind that Australian historians have, until recently, been reluctant to invoke the concept of culture at all. (Even Serle preferred to use the term "the creative spirit" in his subtitle.) George Nadel was a pioneer in introducing us to *Australia's Colonial Culture* in 1957,[17] and A.A. Phillips used the term to subtitle his collection of essays, *The Australian Tradition*, in 1958.[18] An American, A.L. McLeod, gave the term a more general meaning in the 1963 volume he edited, *The Pattern of Australian Culture*;[19] and it was another American, Hartley Grattan, who said, almost wistfully, in 1974: "I want very much to define 'culture' much more broadly than is customary in Australia − I want to give it something like an anthropological range, and I also want to deal with the subject *historically.*"[20]

Perhaps the Australian reluctance to come to terms with the concept of culture needs to be understood in the context of the heightened significance that the high/popular dichotomy has for a provincial culture. This, of course, had been true for the United States as well. It is significant that in *On Your Toes* high culture is symbolized by the *Russian* Ballet, just as in *A Night at the Opera* grand opera is a cultural importation, foreign and absurd, designed to cater for the status-conscious wealthy. But for Americans at least, political and economic dependence on the old metropolitan culture had long since vanished; in the first half of the twentieth century, this was hardly true of Australia. High culture tended to be seen as English (or in a broader sense, European), while popular culture was more homegrown. This surely was the point of A.A. Phillips' identification of the cultural cringe. The "cringe direct" is invoked in terms of "the Australian reader" who, when confronted by Furphy, is compelled to ask himself "Yes, but what would a cultivated Englishman think of this?" Phillips does not expand on the "cringe inverted", but his description of "the God's-Own-Country-and-I'm-a-better-man-than-you-are Australian bore" quickly conjures up popular Australian prejudices about sport, war, climate and hygiene.[21] The argument is complicated, however, by Phillips' belief that Australia's *real* high culture was democratic or popular in temper, for Lawson and Furphy "wrote of the people, for the people, and from the people".[22] One might wonder, if this were so, why "the Australian reader" should still feel obliged to consult the "cultivated Englishman" when appraising them; or is it that the *Bulletin*, which sponsored these writers, could not — in so far as it was a "popular" journal — be authentically "high"? This is a theme also taken up by David Walker in the Introduction to *Australian Popular Culture*, when he speaks of "the popular writers of the 1890s" and ascribes the subsequent interest in that decade "a great deal to the critical distaste for the rapid emergence of the film, popular journalism and cheap reprints in the ensuing decades". He sees the 1890s as the only decade "which can be regarded with any plausibility as post-colonial yet pre-modern".[23] Later technological change meant that popular culture was less likely to be homegrown, and the fear of contamination by cheap American culture was to add a new twist to the high/popular distinction.

Having suggested the pragmatic considerations that led to high and popular culture being distinguished, and the theoretical fragility of it all, I want to look at one particular case — theatre history — in order to indicate not only the inherent difficulties in making the distinction, but the extent to which doing so pre-empts or obscures questions of cultural significance.

Opera may seem the theatrical form most obviously a candidate for the label, "high culture". In his enjoyable study of W.S. Lyster and his companies (1861-1880), *The Golden Age of Australian Opera*,[24] Harold Love refers to E.J. Hobsbawm's description of the European opera house of the nineteenth century as "the cathedral of the bourgeoisie";[25] but he amply shows the difficulties in applying that image to the Australia of the 1860s and 1870s. Lyster was playing in drama theatres, not grand opera houses; his prices of admission were considerably less; and although opera served a social function this seems to have been confined to the boxes and dress circle, whereas the theatres contained large areas of relatively cheap seating. It is one of the virtues of Love's study that he sees it as telling the story of the Australian stage "through the activities of that period's most important single entrepreneur, who, as it happened, was a specialist in grand opera"[26] — in other words this is theatre history, not opera history. One of the questions thrown up by *The Golden Age of Australian Opera* is whether the distinctions between different modes of theatre mattered less in this period than they did later on. It seems likely that, by the time of Melba and her visiting companies, opera had become much more detached from the rest of theatre: it was now, Melba herself notwithstanding, imported. In the 1860s this difference hardly existed. Virtually all theatre was then imported — yet much of it was, in another sense, local. Lyster came to Australia from Ireland via U.S.A., but his was a resident and not a visiting company.

If one considers nineteenth-century opera in Australia in the context of theatre generally, one cannot but notice that one of its essential characteristics, spectacle (it was *grand* opera after all), reflected a widespread Victorian taste. Melodrama and pantomime also catered for this taste. The new technology of theatre, with increasingly mechanized scene changes and gas lighting, helped satisfy the demand for spectacle in most dramatic mediums. The effects exploited in Lyster's production of Wallace's opera, *Lurline*, would have done any pantomime proud. They included a grotto, a waterfall, a sunset view of the Rhine with the hero entering in a skiff with sail, a storm, a scene below the waters of the Rhine, and various transformations culminating in "a shower of gold".[27] Newspaper reviews indicate the wholehearted earnestness with which such effects were enjoyed by nineteenth-century audiences.[28] In his study of the acting profession in England, Michael Baker concludes that "it is the child-like awe with which popular Victorian audiences beheld the actor on stage that is so striking".[29] This seems to have been equally, if not more, true for the colonial theatre.

To isolate Lyster's opera company as an exercise in "high culture" would not only tend to pre-empt an assessment of its popularity; it would also deflect attention from the extent to which he catered for the widespread public appetite for sensation and spectacle. Similarly, to categorize pantomime and melodrama as "popular" theatre, although understandable, is not necessarily helpful. The work of Margaret Williams, Eric Irvin and others has certainly demonstrated the development of a lively colonial tradition in pantomime and melodrama, particularly notable for the manner in which the productions were localized in setting and characters.[30] Their popularity hinged not only on the scope they (like opera) offered for stage effects, but also on their perceived relevance to a local audience.

Yet the companies that purveyed melodrama were usually presided over by actor-managers who saw themselves as leaders of their profession. Claude McKay humorously noted this in 1912:

> Comic opera players tell you about their social successes. Grand opera singers discuss their passions and their salaries. Vaudeville performers abuse the management. The heroes of romantic plays talk about things to eat. But the melodramatic actor, who is imbued with the true spirit of his profession, is loquacious on art, artistry, and interpretation.[31]

Alfred Dampier, for example, who kept a company going for many years, came to Australia in 1873 from Manchester, where he had been a member of a company that had earlier been led by Henry Irving. He made his Melbourne debut as Mephistopheles in his own adaptation of Goethe's *Faust*, and in Sydney he opened with *Hamlet*. At one time, Dampier developed the practice of playing Shakespeare on Friday nights and melodrama the rest of the week. Shakespeare might have been at the top end of the repertoire, but the lower gradations of status were not always clear. It was a common practice for actor-managers such as Dampier to adapt well-known novels such as *David Copperfield* or *Les Misérables*, and such productions would appeal at a different level from, say, *The Scout*, a piece designed to accommodate the talents of the sharp-shooting Dr Frank Carver and his Wild America Company. Of course, the novel itself still enjoyed an ambiguous cultural status; but Dampier and his fellow actor-managers always chose to emphasize their literary seriousness, even where they took liberties with plots (rather in the manner of film adaptations). It was Dampier who adapted *For The Term of His Natural Life* and *Robbery Under Arms* for the stage. According to the *Bulletin* the former was "constructed by piecing together the disjointed limbs of Marcus Clarke's famous novel", while *Robbery Under Arms* also underwent drastic surgery, Captain Starlight emerging as the undisputed hero of the piece, and earning a pardon at the end. This did not prevent Dampier presenting both plays as prestige products. Of *His Natural Life* the advertisement declared:

THE GREAT DRAMATIST ASCHYLUS AND EURIPEDES [sic] NEVER FRAMED A MORE TERRIBLE STORY OF DESTINY, FATE AND DOOM THAN THAT TOLD BY MARCUS CLARKE, AN AUSTRALIAN, IN A WORK THAT HAS ASTONISHED THE WORLD AND BEEN TRANSLATED INTO EVERY CIVILISED LANGUAGE.

And of *Robbery Under Arms'* reception, the *Bulletin* wrote: "a vast multitude rocked the cradle of Australian national drama with their feet". Bearing in mind what Phillips and Walker have said about the "popular" nature of the *Bulletin* school, Dampier's adaptations can be seen as an extension of this literary movement. To say that melodrama was a "popular" form of theatre rather begs the question. It was an accepted dramatic mode, the terms of which a Victorian audience could readily comprehend. It was a mode that could as well accommodate *Marvellous Melbourne* (a frivolous piece put together for the 1888 Exhibition) as it could *Little Em'ly* or *For the Term of His Natural Life*. Nor were Shakespeare productions exempt from its influence. In other words melodrama was "popular" but it could serve "high" purposes.[32]

In applying such categories, we risk obscuring the very nature of theatre for an actor-manager such as Dampier. Of course, he was alive to the sometimes conflicting claims of art and box-office, but this was part and parcel of the theatrical enterprise. He was both a serious actor and an entrepreneur. Theatre – like opera – in one sense *had* to be popular or it could not survive. What surely is of interest to the cultural historian is the extent to which melodrama permitted an accommodation between art and business. In one sense, Dampier, as entrepreneur, exploited the *Bulletin* ethos; in another sense, as actor and director, he was contributing to, or at least, reinforcing it.

If one looks at nineteenth-century theatre in terms of the acting profession instead of concentrating on the dramatic product (which has been the emphasis in much theatre history), one asks questions of a quite different order. In the English context, Michael Baker has argued that in the course of the nineteenth century the actor – and more significantly the actress – fought tenaciously to establish the respectability of their profession. Theatre, which in the early nineteenth century had had a raffish and disreputable reputation, slowly won its bourgeois audience. In 1895 Irving became Britain's first theatrical knight.[33] In one sense, this quest for social and moral approval reflected a sensitivity to Victorian attitudes; on the other hand, it might seem surprising that Victorian society, with its concern for moral standards and appearances, should so enthusiastically take theatre to its bosom. But the Victorian taste for moralizing was matched, as we have noted, by an appetite for spectacle. Melodrama, in satisfying both, was a suitable medium for the times.

The evidence would suggest that from its seedy beginnings, Australian theatre experienced a similar movement towards respectability. It may seem a sign of the relative openness of colonial society that the theatrical manager George Coppin — though he always cheekily put down his profession as "comedian" — should gain election to the Victorian Legislative Council in 1858. But Coppin was aware of the prejudice:

> No doubt in the minds of many there exists a great objection to anyone connected with the dramatic profession. There are some persons who entertain conscientious objections to the drama and think that an actor is not worthy of any religious or moral consideration. Why this antipathy should exist against an actor on account of his profession I can't imagine, because it is never extended to any other profession.[34]

Note his repeated use of the term, "profession". Coppin, one suspects, was accepted as something of a colonial character; women members of the "profession" were in a much more vulnerable position.

The suicide of the young actress, Marie St Denis, in 1868 illustrates how readily the press could exploit any hint of scandal. Obsessed by an unhappy love affair, she sat down on the evening of 23 October 1868, wrote several letters, and then, changing into the garb of an Ophelia, her nightgown bestrewn with jewels and flowers, took two ounces of laudanum. Her romantic desire to be beautiful in death was thwarted when the doctors summoned by her landlady fought unsuccessfully to revive her with the aid of stomach pumps, strong coffee, and exercise. Her suicide was the cause for much speculation about her character and behaviour, which was further stimulated by her physician, Dr Neild, also a critic, indiscreetly revealing intimate details of his late patient. The Victorian appetite for the morbid and sensational was well catered for. It was all very well for the *Age* to concede that the acting profession included "some most estimable members of society, of both sexes": the damage had been done.[35]

Yet it is remarkable how actresses struggled to establish their claim to respectability, and how, by the Great War, they had in large measure succeeded. Fanny Cathcart's obituary in 1880 proclaimed her "irreproachable character [which] entitled her to take a social position of the first kind ... and make the profession of acting respectable".[36] Or consider those three great artists, Stewart, Melba and Moncrieff: it is interesting that all overcame disastrous early marriages to become respected leaders of the profession. In her memoir, Stewart archly refers to her marriage as "just a mad girl's act to repent of at leisure afterwards". Repentance did not prevent her entering a life-long relationship with George Musgrove, who was also married, and by whom she had a daughter. Yet although she spoke darkly about "so many foolish accounts and fabrications of my life", Nellie Stewart survived the scandal-mongering and received much adulation — particularly, be it noted, from women theatre-goers.[37] Melba, in *Melodies and Memories*, says almost nothing about "the young Irishman, Charles Nesbitt Armstrong", and her skeletal account of the marriage appears to suggest that its failure was, if anything, due to the Queensland climate.[38] There were always to be plenty of stories about the prima donna's private life, but they did not seem to threaten the social authority that she came to command. As for Gladys Moncrieff, she mentions her wedding in her autobiography, and gives details of her dress ("the ivory georgette train edged with lace was caught by a coronet of lace and pearls"), the bridesmaids, trainbearers and page, and the big crowd at the church. Then she blandly confesses that the marriage "did not turn out to be the lifelong partnership we expected", and that it became "an episode that has its place among my memories".[39] One suspects that later on questions about the much-loved "Our Glad's" sexuality were tactfully avoided.

The case of Melba is distinguished by her having been an international star, but all three — whether their art was high or popular — illustrate a growing acceptance of theatre and the actress in particular. Whereas the death of Marie St Denis was an occasion for morbid sensationalism, Melba, Stewart and Moncrieff were able to rise above rumour and gossip, In some ways Nellie Stewart is the most striking. It was not only that her memoir made no attempt to disguise her liaison with Musgrove and the child it produced; she even went on to defend the moral standards of the theatrical community, and to offer appropriate advice to aspiring young actresses. Although she had been notable as a leggy principal boy in pantomime, her memoir played down the sexual attraction of the actress: the attraction of the actress for the average man, she claimed, "is rather a special attraction of good fellowship. The actress is independent of spirit, largely free of prejudices, she has outspoken enthusiasms, and is what is called a good fellow". In other words, the actress might be a free spirit, a bit unconventional, but she was *safe*. Stewart also made a claim which feminist historians might dispute, namely, that "as far as Australia was concerned there was no country in which the sexes met on so healthy a plane of frank comradeship."[40]

There is much more to be said about nineteenth-century attitudes to the theatre, but the point here is that its growing respectability had little to do with the demarcation between "popular" and "high": it was not a case of once "popular" theatre gaining acceptance as "high art". Perhaps vaudeville, with its more working-class and boisterous reputation, was most resistant to the rise of respectability (though one should not forget Harry Lauder's knighthood), but all branches of theatre seemed to benefit from it. When cinema captured much of the entertainment market, theatre was not left marooned on a few islands of "high culture". Most theatre in the 1920s and 1930s remained decidedly "popular" in character — that was one of the complaints intellectuals made about it — even if diminished in quantity and played increasingly to middle-class audiences. The separation from cinema served to reinforce its respectability.

It is clear, then, that the distinction between "high" and "popular" culture has little to commend it in the study of nineteenth- and twentieth-century theatre, and that any insistence on such categories only obscures important historical processes. It might be argued, perhaps, that the

high/popular dichotomy is useful in so far as it draws attention to the
apparatus for criticism and appreciation said to mark the former. But,
as already mentioned, many popular cultural forms have elevated
themselves in this manner, and this has served to draw attention, as Paul
Hinch has said, to "commonalities across all types of culture-producing
organizations, ranging from fine arts to rock music, and incorporating
the production of élite as well as popular science and religion".[41]

The greatest objection to persisting with the high/popular
categorization is that it seems, in the end, unrewarding. Certainly,
specialist historians have to define their areas of study, and it is
understandable that they should do so in terms of the selectivity of
tradition. But to isolate a subject in terms of "high" culture runs the
risk of removing it from its social context, and it also tends to distract
attention from the historical formation of the tradition being invoked.
High culture in this sense becomes something detached and self-
sustaining. For the cultural historian, in the broader sense, the
categorization seems merely superfluous once it is conceded that all
cultural forms merit study, and popular culture is acknowledged. Not
that the cultural distinctions made by a society are unimportant; the
very making of the high/popular distinction can become itself a matter
for analysis. It is no accident, surely, that the disjunction between "high"
and "popular" (why not "low"?) parallels that between upper/middle
and working-class (why not lower class?). And why was the clash
between "high" and "popular", between Russian Ballet and tap-dancing,
between grand opera and the Marx Brothers, such an American cliché
of the 1930s? In Australia, too, one suspects that cultural snobbery
reached its peak between the 1920s and 1950s. But the high/popular
dichotomy is an historical phenomenon, and it should be treated, and
explained, as such, rather than adopted as an analytical tool. For, apart
from anything else, it is such a simplistic dichotomy compared with the
complexity of cultural hierarchies. To take examples from theatre, the
cultural milieu of ballet differs markedly from that of opera, and their
audiences are different; nor is a comparison between the theatre of the
Pram Factory and the rock operas of the period much advanced by
defining both as "popular".

Perhaps it makes more sense to look at theatre in terms of "taste
cultures", to use a concept proposed by Gans. Taste culture, he says,
is "culture which results from choice"; it is only a "partial culture,
for it provides values and products for only a part of life".[42] "Taste
cultures" can then be related to the cultures of groups or classes; but
by avoiding a preliminary label of "high" or "popular", one does not
predetermine their social characterization.[43] Williams, after all, was not
simply defining culture as "a whole way of life"; "the theory of culture",
he wrote, was "the study of *relationships* between elements in a whole
way of life".[44] The problem, of course, is not so much what is meant
by "high" or "popular" culture, but what is meant by "culture".

Lurking in the background of this discussion have been the
anthropologists. When asked how I am defining "culture" in my History,
I have airily replied, "Oh, an anthropological understanding of culture".
It is no comfort to discover that the anthropologists themselves are

not agreed about definitions. Edward B. Tylor is usually credited with a founding definition in 1871: culture was "that complex whole which includes knowledge, belief, art, morals, law, custom and any other capabilities and habits acquired by man as a member of society". For Clifford Geertz, an anthropologist who, while he irritates fellow anthropologists, has some attraction for historians, it is "a system of meanings embodied in symbols which individuals use to perform various mental activities".[45] One can only hope, of course, for a nominal definition — a guide to usage — and not an essentialistic one. But it is clear that the attraction for the historian of the anthropological *type* of definition is in its sense of totality, and its emphasis on meanings embedded in social activity and relationships. The danger for the historian — though it is one many anthropologists are aware of too — is that culture, as a system, comes to be represented as something static and given. This was Thompson's point when he objected to the Eliot/Williams "whole way of life" formula, suggesting, half seriously, that it should be redefined as "a whole way of conflict". He insisted, too, that "any theory of culture must include the concept of the dialectical interaction between culture and something that is *not* culture".[46] In Australia we do well to heed the warning, given the evidence of the ideological manipulation of "the Australian way of life" in the post-war period.[47] The historian, however, does not have to be a radical to be drawn to the tensions within the cultural whole. It is these tensions, after all, which, while warning of possible fragmentation, are often the source of the culture's creativity. In this context, the emerging dichotomy between high and popular, and the debate which it has engendered, are symptoms of the culture of an industrial society at a particular stage of development.

Embarking on my impossible undertaking, I am determined that I should be writing a cultural history of Australia, not a history of Australian culture. I want to avoid the well-trodden path of the quest for national identity — or at least to be able to place it in some broader cultural context. I am interested in the process of immigration and cultural transplantation. I do not wish to avoid that which is derivative in the culture: on the contrary it seems necessary to focus on it. In this respect I think there is still some mileage in the Hartzian "fragment" thesis with its emphasis on the "old" ingredients of the "new" culture.[48] If I discard high and popular cultures as categories it is because they no longer seem relevant to this sort of analysis. Rather I would wish to treat the high/popular distinction as a developing theme within the culture, particularly in terms of the metropolitan/ provincial relationship.

1986

Notes

1. Raymond Williams, *Culture and Society 1780-1950*, Harmondsworth (Penguin), 1961 [1958].

2. T.S. Eliot, *Notes towards the Definition of Culture*, London, 1948.

3. See Roger B. Rollin, "Against Evaluation: the Role of the Critic of Popular Culture", *Journal of Popular Culture*, IX, 1975, 355/3.

4. In addition to *Culture and Society*, Williams' work includes *The Long Revolution*, Harmondsworth (Pelican), 1965 [1961], *Marxism and Literature*, Oxford, 1977, and *Culture*, London, 1981. Thompson published an extended two part review of *The Long Revolution* in *New Left Review*, nos. 9 and 10, 1961. Richard Hoggart's principal contribution is *The Use of Literacy: Aspects of Working-class Life, with Special Reference to Publications and Entertainments*, London, 1957.

5. John Clarke, Chas Critcher and Richard Johnson (eds.), *Working-Class Cultural Studies in History and Theory*, London, 1979, pp.58, 65.

6. Herbert Gans, *Popular Culture and High Culture*, New York, 1974, p.vii.

7. "The Politics of Popular Culture", in Bigsby (ed.), *Approaches to Popular Culture*, London, 1976, pp.3-4.

8. Fred E.H. Schroeder (ed.), *5000 Years of Popular Culture: Popular Culture Before Printing*, Bowling Green, 1980.

9. *Leisure and Popular Culture in Transition*, Saint Louis, 1975, pp.41-2.

10. These titles are taken from vol. XI of the *Journal*.

11. Christopher D. Geist, "Popular Culture, the *Journal* and the State of the Study: A Sequel", *Journal of Popular Culture*, XIII, 1980, 390.

12. Geoffrey Singleton, "Popular Culture or the Culture of the Populace?", *Journal of Popular Culture*, XI, 1977, 254/116.

13. Tom Kando, "Popular Culture and its Sociology: Two Controversies", *Journal of Popular Culture*, IX, 1975, 440/88.

14. "Where the Two Cultures Meet: Popular Culture", *Journal of Popular Culture*, XI, 1977, 385.

15. Melbourne, 1973.

16. Sydney, 1979.

17. Published in Cambridge, Massachusetts.

18. *The Australian Tradition: Studies in a Colonial Culture*, Melbourne, 1958.

19. Published in Ithaca, New York.

20. "Notes on Australia's Cultural History", *Meanjin*, XXXIII, 1974, 232.

21. "The Cultural Cringe", op. cit., p.112.

22. "The Democratic Theme", p.53.

23. p.5.

24. *The Golden Age of Australian Opera: W.S. Lyster and His Companies, 1861-1880*, Sydney, 1981.

25. op. cit., p.123. Hobsbawm's description comes from *The Age of Capital 1848-1875*, London, 1975, facing p.176.

26. op. cit., p.1.

27. Love, op. cit., pp.110-12.

28. Love, op. cit., p.112; see also J. Rickard, "Alfred Dampier: An Actor-Manager in the 'Land of Romance'", *Komos*, III, 1973, 44.

29. *The Rise of the Victorian Actor*, London, 1978, p.84.

30. Williams, *Australia on the Popular Stage, 1829-1929: An Historical Entertainment in Six Acts*, Melbourne, 1983; Eric Irvin, *Gentleman George — King of Melodrama: The Theatrical Life and Times of George Darrell 1841-1921*, Brisbane, 1980; Harold Love (ed.), *The Australian Stage: a Documentary History*, Sydney, 1984.

31. Harry Julius, *Theatrical Caricatures*, Sydney, 1912 (text by Claude McKay), p.109.

[32.] This material on Dampier is drawn from Rickard, loc. cit.

[33.] op. cit., p.14.

[34.] Alec Bagot, *Coppin the Great*, Melbourne, 1965, p.217.

[35.] See Mimi Colligan, "Marie St Denis: Actress and Suicide", Marilyn Lake and Farley Kelly (eds.), *Double Time: Women in Victoria — 150 Years*, Ringwood (Penguin), 1985, p.69; also *Age*, 27 October 1868.

[36.] *Argus*, 19 January 1880.

[37.] *My Life's Story*, Sydney, 1923, pp.61, 236.

[38.] London, 1925, p.7.

[39.] *Our Glad*, Sydney, 1975, p.48. (Published originally in 1971 as *My Life of Song*).

[40.] op. cit., pp.39, 146.

[41.] "Production and Distribution Roles among Cultural Organizations: On the Division of Labor Across Intellectual Disciplines", *Social Research*, XLVIII, 1978, 316.

[42.] op. cit., pp.12-13.

[43.] Gans, however (p.75), perversely retains high culture as one of his five "taste publics and cultures".

[44.] *The Long Revolution*, p.63.

[45.] Kenneth A. Rice, *Geertz and Culture*, Ann Arbor, 1980: for Tyler, see p.3; for Geertz's definition, see p.225.

[46.] loc. cit., no. 9, 33.

[47.] Richard White, "'The Australian Way of Life'", *Historical Studies*, XVIII, 1979, 528.

[48.] Louis Hartz, *The Founding of New Societies: Studies in the History of the United States, Latin America, South Africa, Canada and Australia*, New York, 1964. See also J.B. Hirst's recent article, "Keeping Colonial History Colonial: the Hartz Thesis Revisited", *Historical Studies*, XXI, 1984, 85.

POPULISM AND PRIVILEGE IN AUSTRALIAN PAINTING

TERRY SMITH

The best-known poppies in Australian painting are, of course, those which form the main subject of Will Longstaff's famous *Menin Gate at Midnight*. Painted in 1927, bought by Lord Woolavington and presented to the commonwealth government, it is enshrined in what is itself a nearly unique shrine-cum-art gallery, the Australian War Memorial in Canberra. Reference to it here takes us immediately to the central ambiguities, the awkwardness — even embarrassment — of our subject, because the ghostly flowers in this painting are, in any evident sense, neither poppies nor tall. Such a tangential denial strikes me as exactly the right approach to our subject: focusing on an apparently trivial issue can be a way of shedding light on matters of some significance, and not just accidentally. The obligation to consider the exceptional individual in Australian art (almost the last subject I would normally tackle) has enabled me to return to a topic which I had to put aside for other tasks nearly four years ago, and which I now see to be crucial both in our painting and in any estimation of its social positioning. That topic is the relations between the privileged and the popular, the constant warring across the productive sites of our culture between various kinds of élitism and populism.

What is evoked by the phrase "tall poppy"? We use it if we desire to mark an exceptional individual or an outstanding achievement. Very often, that desire is accompanied by a counter-movement, the desire to deny exceptionality, if not individuality — to cut down the tall poppy. These counter-tendencies, these movements in contrary direction, are irretrievably locked together — one never (or only boringly) occurring without the other. Between them is acted out a continual dance of necessity. It is a tango, I suggest, which seems to terrify both parties, albeit differently. Those who either feel themselves to be tall poppies, or who wish to secure the domain of their flowering, live in fear of themselves being reduced and their domain being levelled by the mob in one of its guises — ordinariness, democracy, suburbia, creeping socialism, poor standards. On the other side, there may be a self-preserving insistence on sameness, a suspicion of privilege, a fear of desertion by difference, or simply a blind blundering-on which, like some juggernaut of banality, has the incidental, scarcely intended effect of obliterating anything other. At the same time there seems to be a widespread relishing of both the appearance of "tall poppies" *and* their cutting down, as well as admiration for those who survive the decimation; so the relations between our revolving couple are not at all those of a simple two-step.

The other major connotation of the phrase goes to one of the deepest insecurities of our culture, the unequal exchange between our efforts to build culture here and the dominance of European culture in general and the cultures of England and the United States in particular. A familiar form is the ill-mix of excessive praise and surly resentment that seems to make us go abroad for both training in the arts and for initial recognition of our achievement. The "tall poppy" syndrome is connected with those constant negotiations between the international and the local that are a major cultural dynamic in Australia. International-local struggles seem as inescapable as those between the élite and the popular. I do not see these relationships as cause for impotent despair or for raging iconoclasm. On the contrary, my main point is that it is precisely in critical struggle with these contending cultural forces that the best, most relevant, most effective, and most productive Australian art has been made, and will, in all probability, continue to be made. Australian art, it seems to me, most consistently fails when its makers or its champions or its audiences persist in demanding exclusive allegiance to one or other of these contending forces, when they are insisted upon as permanent dichotomies and only one side seen as productive of good art. I am not against strategic emphasis on, say, the national when a prevailing internationalism becomes oppressive — as did New York-based form-alism in the early and mid-1970s, for example. Nor the reverse. When the likes of John Singleton (advertising), Katie Pye (fashion) and Malcolm Fraser (politics) appear as heralds of nationalism, their structural interests being quite other, it seems high time to reach for contrary values. In fact, we swing between such shifting emphases, often willy-nilly. Since there is no position outside them that we can realistically occupy, the point is to develop critical pathways through them. But this suggestion — that work of artistic value is produced in the struggle across contradictions, and that it is done best when done critically and consciously — implies a different historical mapping, a different reading of the present conjuncture, and a polemical preference within current practice. The polemical present I have recently treated elsewhere;[1] I want here to offer some speculations about the shaping of the historical map in the light of my suggestion.

Menin Gate at Midnight (plate 1) is a monumentally dull painting stamped, as it were, out of ambiguities. Amongst the prodigious outpouring of fine painting unleashed by the later years of World War I, it is exceptional both in its conventionality of form (the simple, land-sky division, the isolated edifice, the limited colour-range, the directness of detailing) and in the explicitness of its treatment of spiritual allegory. In both these respects it is more like the commemorative sculpture of the late 1920s and early 1930s in both England and Australia than the more directly-based campaign records of earlier years, such as those of Will Dyson and George Lambert. Nonetheless, it is arguably relevant to the two contraries of our topic in a particularly Australian way, especially in its straining to contain a set of ambiguities. The white "poppies" spreading across the foreground are, of course, tiny ghosts of the dead soldiers of the Australian Infantry Forces, killed during the carnage on the battlefields of Flanders, particularly in the six months from July to November 1917 during which 265,423 British and 206,000 German soldiers died in the space of seven miles between Ypres, Menin and Passchendaele. At the gates to the town of Menin large structures were built as war memorials to each section of the

Allied forces. Longstaff shows the memorial to the Australian dead and the ghosts which it guards as they marshall before it at the witching hour.

A host of associations are released by this depiction, and they help us become specific about the ambiguities of the "tall poppies" concept. These soldiers were the much-trumpeted heroic substance of Australian nationalism in the post-war period. A legendary reading evolved during the 1920s: these men sacrificed themselves for the Empire, but they did so in a way that distinguished them within it and enabled our political leaders to claim a measure of independence of voice, particularly in foreign policy. Tested in the immemorial trials of war, Australian soldiers stood up, and stood out: it was the initiation ceremony of white Australia as a nation. These soldiers also proved, with their blood, their manliness — and, by extension, the masculinity of the country itself. Was Hilda Rix Nicholas struggling with the contradictions of this when she painted out the female angel in her image of sacrifice *Have They Laid the World Away?* in 1917? Certainly the idea of achieving masculinity in its surrender to the feminine (that is, achieving spiritual "life" in the cessation of physical action) informs Raynor Hoff's astonishing sculpture *Sacrifice,* at the centre of the Anzac Memorial, Hyde Park, Sydney. But the main relevant point here is that Australian nationhood was won out of a bloody struggle occurring *elsewhere.* All our earlier nationalisms were based on either our place in global markets (especially that for wool) or on the distinctiveness of our local struggle with the land and its earlier inhabitants. Now, the "best" or the "first" Australians are those who gained us recognition abroad, whose deaths caused the nation to flower (i.e. appear) on foreign soils.

In this case, we might notice, our tallest poppies are precisely *not* exceptional individuals: they are "the people", the ranks, the masses of unskilled labourers recruited into the A.I.F. (already being transformed, by C.E.W. Bean and others, into inheritors of the ingenious, egalitarian bushmen). Not only anonymous, they are importantly absent — like all tall poppies, they have been cut down, but in numbers. Indeed, it is their cutting down that has elevated them: few surviving soldiers attest to being treated in any way commensurate with the legend developing around them. (In fact they were the focus of enormous political wrangling from all sides, from the fascist New Guard to the nascent revolutionary parties.[2]) Longstaff's painting itself does not, of course, explicitly refer to all of this ideological material. His conception wrestles with it, however. Painted in England after a long series of more obvious commissions, it signifies the national in an interesting way, for Longstaff's problem was to figure the Australian-ness of this devastated domain in a foreign place. Thus he drops his horizon line, sites the gate somewhat like a mountain in mid-distance, then unfolds some rolling plains (which are nothing like the actual place) and peoples them with the equivalent of scattered bushes. The foreignness of this place had also to be signified: thus the Streetonesque vista (by the late 1920s the dominant landscape form — indeed, the most frequent form in Australian painting *per se*) is darkened, given the opposite of the noon light favoured in the Landscape School. Finally, the painting reduces its un-Australian literary allegory by literalizing it: the ghosts of these massed soldiers appear in a way that would have been read at the time as startlingly actual. No doubt Longstaff's conception relates to the spiritualism common then, particularly the widespread hope that it was possible to communicate with the spirit of one's dead loved ones. Small wonder that when *Menin Gate At Midnight* was toured around Australia in 1928 and 1929, it attracted an audience eclipsing that which earlier saw Holman Hunt's actualization of the spiritual, *The Light of the World*. Reportedly, more than a million of a total population of six million saw this painting.[3] It became an icon, passing from the realms of art to a broader public sphere. Its character as a holy object is perpetuated in its installation in darkened, draped, roped-off rooms at the heart of the War Memorial in Canberra. One memorial wrapped around another: thus the painting itself, like the later Hall of Memory, comes to represent the spirit of those dead soldiers. Indeed, entombed within the Memorial, it *is* their spirit.

Sociologically, *Menin Gate at Midnight* is an equivalent of, say, Michelangelo's *Pietà* in the Vatican, however distant it may be aesthetically. Enshrined within this secular/sacred place, the most visible sign of its spiritual core, reproduced constantly in postcards, prints, booklets and books, it gradually enters a broader visual culture than that encompassed by art alone. As it circulates, such an image can become iconic. By similar processes, its creator can become more than an artist, more than a contributor to the history of Australian art: he becomes that social figure we will call for the moment a "cultural hero". It did not happen in the case of Longstaff, but it has in others.

There are, of course, major differences between professional artistic practices and the ways in which visual images are generated and circulated in this broader visual culture. But I do not think that the differences necessarily mark a mutual indifference between "high culture" and "popular culture". In this country perhaps more than elsewhere, there seems to be a constant although variable criss-crossing of countervailing tendencies. If one can sustain a notion of distinct "high" and "popular" cultural practices at all, it seems to me that they might be thought of as analogous to geological plates, in that their incessant, grinding mismatching creates the distinctive edge of our art. For example, painting itself has rarely been an utterly distinct practice here. From the earliest white settlement, it has taken its place amongst a variety of visual forms used by people throughout the society, while in Aboriginal societies painting seems to be an activity of symbolization carried out on a variety of surfaces, from desert sand to the person's body.

I have elsewhere proposed a general theory of what I call the "social structuring of seeing", and the social circulation of imagery within visual cultures; and I have recently attempted to relate this approach to the writing of the history of Australian art.[4] It is an approach that suggests that the main questions about the "tall poppy" group themselves under four headings: (i) achievement within Australian art; (ii) populism within Australian art; (iii) the positioning of Australian art itself within broader processes of cultural formation; and (iv) the visualization of issues of class-cultural conflict and harmony in media other than those conventionally recognized as art (cartoons, for example). Each of these is a vast subject in itself. All I can do here is concentrate on the first and offer a few brief remarks on the others.

*

What then have been the vicissitudes of individual achievement within Australian art? Certain artists have been outstanding individual talents, and have presented themselves as such. George Lambert's *Self Portrait* of 1922 (plate 2), painted the year after his triumphal return from success, both artistic and in reputation, in London and in Palestine, shows him dressed in full Edwardian splendour, echoing Van Dyck with a confidence that might eclipse even that of our more recent bearer of gladioli, Barry Humphries. In the vaults of the Art Gallery of N.S.W. is an astonishing work painted in London in 1909: at left, a plumed Royal humbly poses next to a reclining "lay figure" (a life-sized mannikin with articulated limbs) at the feet of which sits a boy watching his father, Lambert. The artist stands glancing out towards the viewer. Recalling Lambert's love of Velasquez, and that artist's sense of self-worth in the famous *Las Meninas,* we recognize this to be a picture of a studio, with the artist looking to a large mirror (us). Only such a subject would enable him to return his back so coolly on such an obviously important person. And the painting is entitled *The Shop* (plate 3). Lambert was undoubtedly a "tall poppy" — an exceptional one in many ways, for dandyism has been rare in Australia. Yet despite certain difficult moments, he seems not to have been cut down. Although he often taught, he did not found a school; he directly and deeply influenced few artists; yet even without acolytes, his flamboyance seems to have offended neither other artists nor the larger public. On the contrary, there was much appreciation of his insistence on the professional importance of art; even his outsize emu feather seems to have been popular amongst the ranks while he was painting in Palestine.[5]

Roberts, too, was conscious of his achievement, and he believed that publicly presenting himself as significant was of benefit not only to himself but to the profession as well. D.H. Souter recalls that in Sydney in the 1890s Roberts was the "sole Society Bohemian", "the successful artist with an entrée into Government House and . . . on the dining list of most people who had over a couple of thousand a year". Donning his opera cloak, he would say, "A man may be able to paint decently well and know how to comport himself in good society. Besides, you don't as a rule sell your stuff to people who rent cottages at 17/6 a week. Business, my dear boy, business".[6] Yet there is a difference between Roberts and Lambert. While very much an individual, and committed to exploring a variety of styles, Roberts also tended towards working in groups, amongst other artists: hence the camps around Box Hill, the twinned pictures of Coogee, the camps near

Mosman. This tendency shows itself in many ways: it is beautifully caught, for example, in two cigar-box lid panels by Charles Conder: *Sketch Portrait of Tom Roberts*, 1889 and *Streeton and Roberts at Heidelberg (Sunday, July 21, 1889)* (plate 4), where the individualism of the conspicuously "tall poppy" is modified in these delightful renderings of a casual communality. But if Lambert and Roberts were, in their different ways, outstanding, other artists have made equally profound contributions to Australian art without projecting themselves as "tall poppies": Sydney Ure Smith and Arthur Boyd, for example.

The constant attempts of Australian society to give formal recognition to its "tall poppies" (with knighthoods and other awards) have had some effects on Australian painting. A good example is the various proposed national portrait-galleries, to which Kings Hall, Parliament House, remains the closest approximation. Another is the Archibald Prize, which is offered for the portrait of a person "preferably distinguished in art, letters, sciences or politics".[7] Yet in the first portrait that Archibald commissioned, John Longstaff's *Henry Lawson*, 1900, the familiar contradictions appear again (plate 5). Rushed up in a few hours the day before Lawson set sail for England, penniless and bitter about his country's failure to support him, this was intended as the first of many "national" portraits, celebrations of the cultural constructiveness of outstanding individuals. The result is the straight-jacketing of an heroic victim, Lawson, in the pictorial garb of the utterly conventional bourgeois portrait.

Within modern art, a high premium is placed on originating change. Can it be said that "tall" individuals have been responsible for originating the key shifts in Australian art? Certainly this has been said of Roberts, Streeton and very much later, John Olsen. But in each case it has been said only with qualifications, and historians have mostly preferred — and I think reasonably — to attribute such historical power either to groups (the Heidelberg School), to external influences (the impact of European art styles), or to the force of major social movements (the wars, the Depression).

What of the cutting down of "tall poppies"? The most striking fact to emerge from examining a number of cases is that the hacking away is rarely done by the "general public", which is fearfully held to be philistine or at least suspicious of art. On the contrary, the hacking has notoriously been done within the institutions of the art-world, usually for reasons having to do with internecine power-struggles; the confusion arises because some have been fought in the name of "the people", or some significant section of them. Two examples come to mind. One centres on Streeton. During World War I, the desire for Nationhood discussed earlier became a crude chauvinism: artists were valued for enabling Australians to see Australia with Australian eyes. But such relevatory power depended on a single non-artistic fact: local patrimony. Thus Frederick McCubbin, in 1916, dismissed his friend, Tom Roberts, as a mere visitor to the country and elevated Withers, Davies and Streeton.[8] In the next year Lionel Lindsay celebrated Streeton's vision as based on his "native birth".[9] What was denied can be seen if we study a loving portrait by Roberts,

Smike Streeton at 24, 1891 (plate 6), and a masterpiece by Streeton the
year before, *Still Glides the Stream and Shall Forever Glide,* 1890.[10] What
was gained can be indicated by the photograph of *Streeton in Middle-age*
and by paintings such as *Land of the Golden Fleece,* 1926, perhaps the
best of the later anachronistically "natural" landscapes, which J.S.
MacDonald celebrated as expressing the vision of Australia as it should
be "with a maximum of flocks and a minimum of factories . . . . If we
so choose we can be yet the elect of the World, the last of the
pastoralists, the thoroughbred Aryans in all their nobility".[11] When,
in the early 1940s and again in the 1960s, Bernard Smith came to
attack the dominance of the Landscape School, his barbs were directed
not only at MacDonald's "pathological nationalism", but also — and
necessarily — at Streeton: "The air was heavy with the arrogance . . .
of old men, old . . . in spirit and in the handling of paint".[12]

The second example is the more recent, more tragic case of levelling
involved in the charge of "caricature" against Dobell's entry for the
1944 Archibald Prize, the *Portrait of Joshua Smith,* 1943. This charge
was brought by neither "the people", nor outstanding artists
committed to a succeeding style. It was brought by two painters
(Joseph Wolinski and Mary Edwards) whose domains of ordinariness
were threatened by this apparent "modernizing" of the practice of
portraiture on which so many artists professionally depended.[13]
Wolinski and Edwards failed to see that — like other "realists" such as
Drysdale and Badham — Dobell's war experiences, as in the *Cement
Worker* (plate 7), made for a far more radical imagery than the
anatomical exaggerations here. Dobell received some spirited defence,
of course. But in the mid-1960s, a generation later, Robert Hughes
reacted against the defence, calling Dobell a "grotesquely
overpraised . . . culture-hero" and asking, "how this painter who, on
an international stage, would be regarded as an occasionally interesting
but always minor eclectic, with his small output of uneven quality,
has come to be thought Australia's greatest artist?" Here was tall-
poppy cutting at its most grotesque — although in fairness it should
be said that Hughes was objecting to the consequences of excessive
valuation within the art-world, and seeking space for the artists he
wished to champion.[14] In fact, Hughes was contesting for the approval
of those whose superficiality of taste he despised — the Art Gallery
Society set. But the approval of this set in the 1960s was not
the same thing as the wider popularity that depends on an artist's
engagement with publicly-accessible contents; and Dobell's war
portraits were accessible in this sense then, whereas much other
of his work was not. (These relationships change constantly; their
history remains largely unwritten.) On the other hand, the approval
of that set had its importance. Wide-open to fashion as Paddington
chic may be, it is an influential distributor of taste to other audiences,
particularly when taste is given a commercial embodiment. *The
Home* in the 1920s created an audience for early modernism as surely
as did *Vogue* for a later version: if the possession of cultural artefacts
largely stops with those who can afford them, the taste-
judgments they carry do not. Furthermore, even though such

trendiness frivolously eschews the deeper values that are the basis of wide popularity, it does not in all cases prevent their dissemination in the long term.

*

I shall deal very briefly with two of the remaining topics. The first is populism in Australian art. On the whole, painting here has undoubtedly served to embody, refine and extend the sensibility and values of expensive, élite, exclusive culture. But it has also — arguably to a greater extent than elsewhere — served to embody, elaborate and reinforce certain widely-shared values. McCubbin's "pioneer pictures" from the late 1880s through the 1890s are only the most obvious examples of a constant integration of major paintings into a widely-circulating imagery of photography and black-and-white illustration.[15] The landscapes of the 1920s and 1930s, however abhorrent MacDonald's readings of them, did become an important way of visualizing deeply-rooted attachments to particular regions: a feeling for locality that cannot be dismissed as reactionary or petty. Everyday life, in all its inescapable complexities, debilitating ordinariness, yet warming relentlessness, is never far away from the concerns of even the most detached Australian artists — particularly in the use of imagery from "popular culture". The 1983 exhibition, *A Melbourne Mood,* is a clear demonstration of this; a different set of readings of similarly-rooted relationships would inform a "Sydney" equivalent. The failure of those European and American modernisms that focus on formal, "purely aesthetic" concerns to take root here is further testimony to the power of the popular.

The second topic is the position of art within the larger culture. At certain moments, one of the arts can have an important effect *qua* art-form; and in the early 1960s Australian painting became an international "cultural flagship", celebrated particularly in England for its almost primitive spontaneity. However much this may have had to do with the needs for yet another primitivizing mode within European modernism, the effect back home was to swell pride in the over-all achievement of Australian painting.[16] A more recent example is our feature-film, especially the impact of its reconstructions of late nineteenth-century landscapes. Curiously, while we are asked to identify with the national achievement of the film as such, its depictions of the landscape historicizes it in a way that makes it strange, unfamiliar. This contrasts sharply with earlier painted landscapes; film landscapes have more in common with the outback as depicted in the advertisements of the oil and mineral companies.[17]

In relation to the larger culture, certain Australian artists have become not just "culture heroes" for the fashionable, but rather cultur*al* heroes of the people: favourite sons (rarely daughters), fascinating in all they do, scarcely capable of wrong-doing — in a word, "stars". Usually, too, their public image is shaped by the iconic status of one or two of their paintings: Roberts's *Shearers,* Streeton's vista landscapes, Dobell's portraits, Lindsay's nudes, Nolan's Kelly head, Whiteley's nudes. (Lambert cannot be so readily listed.) These artists' excesses are absorbed into legend, and quite complex relations of rejection and reaching out, such as in the case of Norman Lindsay, are smothered in an uncritical embrace. Compare Lindsay's *Norman Lindsay Book no. 1*, 1912, with the image of self-isolated defeat, *Self-Portrait*, 1930 (plate 8). Similarly, compare the hedonistic self-indulgence of Whiteley's *Self Portrait in the Studio*, 1976 (plate 9), in which pleasurable looking around the painting becomes a metaphor for the pleasures of seeing as such, with the self-portrait triptych, *Art, Life and the Other Thing*, 1978. The latter dramatizes his breaking the addiction to heroin, and it was promptly awarded that year's Archibald Prize. However laudable Whiteley's personal struggle, it here becomes a part of the artist's life as a public saga, an episode in a mythic serialization, in which the climactic threat to the hero is suitably resolved in a warm glow of legitimacy.

Most cultural heroes are yea-sayers, and usually they celebrate particular Australian places. This perhaps explains the adulation reserved for Nolan rather than Tucker or Counihan, or for Olsen rather than, say, Dickerson, or for Whiteley rather than the host of socially-concerned artists contemporary with him. While the former secure the support of the "cultivated" and "the people", the latter are recognized slowly and reluctantly by both, if at all. (Patrick White is one of the few who have become cultural heroes while being systematically critical of Australian society.)

Cultural heroes are, from a perspective within the "cultivated", paradigm "tall poppies": fair game for both excessive praise and ruthless attack. Their very popularity causes suspicion in the refined breasts of the élite. In fact, it was probably this, rather than true judgment, that led me many years ago to launch an attack on the portrait of the artist in Patrick White's *The Vivisector*. While inapplicable to the artists I then knew and championed, White's portrayal was acute applied over a longer term: the romanticism that he was wrestling with there preceded the early 1970s and has succeeded them in many ways, especially in art in Sydney.[18] Yet, alongside élitist suspicions, there is also a fear of the "mob" which works to protect cultural heroes. Perhaps both factors are at work in Terence Maloon's considered dismissal of the artistic impotence of Brett Whiteley's 1983 exhibition at the N.S.W. Art Gallery; the editors of the *Sydney Morning Herald* seem to feel the need to distance themselves from Maloon's view, since it is entitled "Maloon on Whiteley on Van Gogh" (July 2, 1983). (Although rarely celebrated by Melbourne critics, Whiteley's work has not been so overtly criticized since around 1970, when it was questioned by Donald Brook and myself. I do not withdraw that judgment.)

Let me conclude these thoughts on the exchanges between the élite and the popular in our visual culture with a current example of how that exchange is coupled with that between the international and the local: Mike Parr's set of drawings *A-Artaud (Against the light) Self Portrait at Sixty-Five* 1983, (plate 10). These drawings bring out the ambiguities attaching to the individualism of the "tall poppy", because, although ostensibly a series of images of the artist's face, the orthogonal projections and the scrawling transformations imply the fragility of signifiers in relation to signifieds, and thus the impossibility of self-portraiture when the self is recognized to be a fragmented subject. All the orthodox signs of artistic self-expression are present here, but they fail to signify the specifics of self. Rather, they convey an anxiety about that failure, and thus reassert subjectivity in a more general, tentative and fragile way. The work was exhibited as part of a recent exhibition at the Melbourne University Art Gallery of five large works by five artists, some of whom exhibited in the same curator's show *Popism* at the National Gallery of Victoria last year. The Melbourne University exhibition was entitled *Tall Poppies* — a title used because the represented artists had been "selected by non-Australian curators to exhibit abroad". That this should be the criterion of choice is sickening enough. But it becomes offensive when the curator fails to take the argument further, refuses to examine critically the implications of such cultural exchanges, and, unconscious of his subscription to a fictive "internationalism", values instead these paintings' supposed deliberate rejection of the concerns of earlier Australian art, indeed their self-sufficiency "within the domain of art itself". While there is obviously a thirst for such a domain, and a more than occasional occupying of it, I think that what is important in Australian painting is not the seclusion of such a domain, but rather the constant engagement between it and its "other", the popular.

1984

Notes

[1] T. Smith, "Notes on Art Criticism Now", *Art Network*, X, 1983, pp.40-1; and "Nationalism and Culture: The 'Let's Dance' Landscape", in the supplement to *Island Magazine*, XVI, 1983, pp.26-9.

[2] See Humphrey McQueen, "Shoot the Bolshevik! Hang the Profiteer! Reconstructing Australian Capitalism 1918-21", in E.L. Wheelwright and Ken Buckley (eds.), *Essays in the Political Economy of Australian Capitalism*, vol. 2, Sydney, 1978.

[3] Humphrey McQueen, *The Black Swan of Trespass*, Sydney, 1979, p.98. The 1929 Annual Report of the Art Gallery of Western Australia estimated 105, 281 visitors (information courtesy Anne Gray).

[4] "A Science of Seeing", *Age Monthly Review*, March 1982, pp.7-8; and "Writing the History of Australian Art: Its Past, Present, and Possible Future", *The Australian Journal of Art*, III, Aug. 1983, pp. 10-29.

[5] See William Moore, *The Story of Australian Art*, II, Sydney, 1934, pp.62-4; and Judith McKay, *Lambert War Sketches*, Canberra Australian War Memorial loan exhibition, n.d. (1979-81), 9, 23.

[6] Cited R.H. Croll, *Tom Roberts, Father of Australian Landscape Painting*, Melbourne, 1936, pp.40-1.

[7] Anna Waldman, "The Archibald Prize, an Illustrated History 1921-1981", *Art and Australia*, XX, 1982, 213-36.

[8] "Some Remarks on the History of Australian Art", *The Art of Frederick McCubbin*, Melbourne, 1916, p.275.

[9] "Arthur Streeton's Place in Australian Art", *Art in Australia*, II, 1917.

[10] See T. Smith, "Teaching Art History: *Still Glides the Stream . . .*", *Creativity in Art Education*, Art Education Society of N.S.W., 1982 Conference Papers, 29-41, for an extended treatment.

[11] *Art in Australia*, 3rd series, no. XXXVII, 1931, 5.

[12] *Australian Painting*, Melbourne, 1971, pp. 195-6. See also *Place, Taste and Tradition*, Sydney, 1945, p.146, where the "Streeton" landscape is called, paraphrasing Hancock, a "national vice", and remembering that Streeton was himself a critic in Melbourne from 1929 to 1943. Presumably Croll's *Tom Roberts, Father of Australian Landscape Painting* — which he so patently was not — was an attempt to redress this unbalance.

[13] The best account is still that in Bernard Smith, *Australian Painting*, op. cit., pp.264-71.

[14] *The Art of Australia*, Harmondsworth, 1966, pp.182-3.

[15] Leigh Astbury, "Frederick McCubbin: The Spirit of the Pioneers", *Australia 1888*, no. VII, 1981, pp.26-58.

[16] Bernard Smith recognized this contradiction early: "The Myth of Isolation", Macrossan Lectures, University of Queensland, 1961, in *The Antipodean Manifesto*, Melbourne, 1976, pp.57-70.

[17] See T. Smith, "Nationalism and Culture: The 'Let's Dance' Landscape", op. cit.

[18] *Meanjin*, XXXI, 1972, 167-77. I am glad of the opportunity to withdraw this jejune, but nonetheless rather callow piece of tall-poppy chopping.

1. Will Longstaff, *Menin Gate at Midnight (the Ghosts of Menin Gate)*, 1927 (detail), oil on canvas, Australian War Memorial (9807).

2. George Lambert, *Self-Portrait*, 1922, oil on canvas, Collection Mr Tom Barr-Smith, Adelaide.

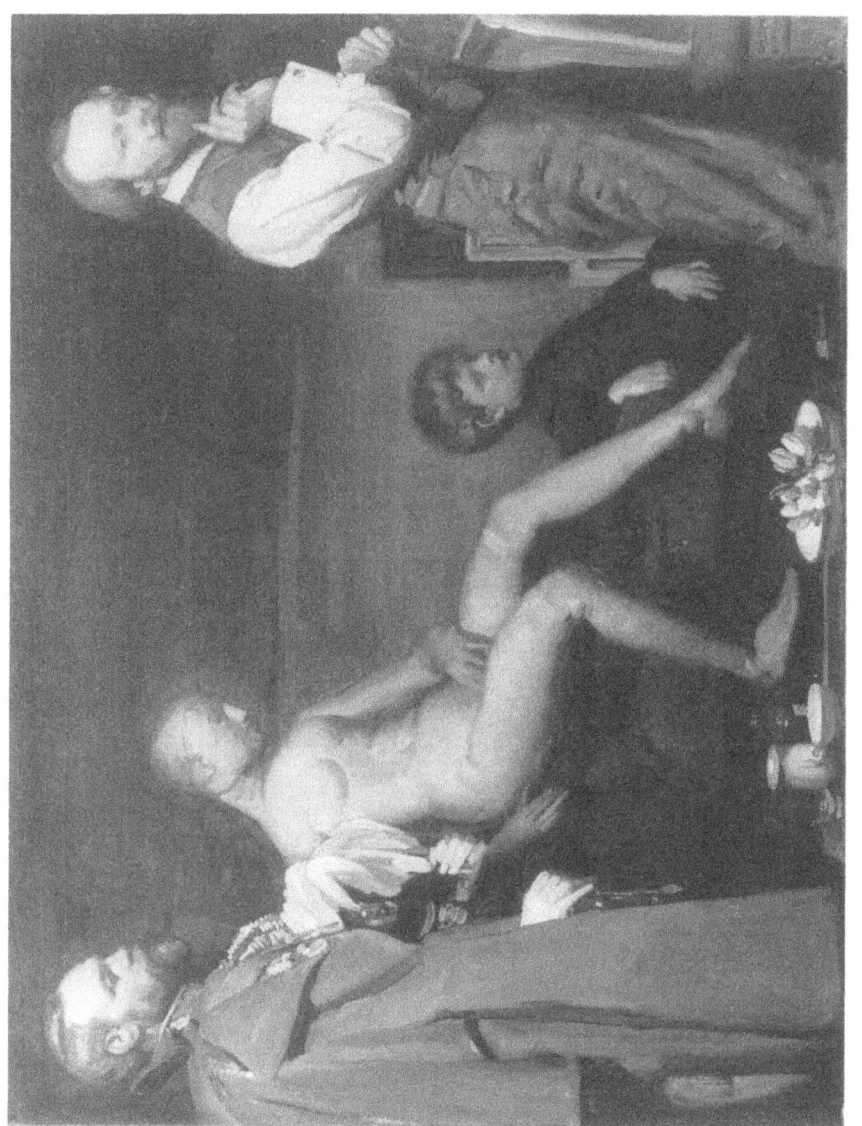

3. George Lambert, *The Shop*, 1909, oil on canvas, purchased 1961, Art Gallery of New South Wales.

4. Charles Conder, *A Winter Sunday at Heidelberg with Tom Roberts and Arthur Streeton*, 1889 (detail), oil on cardboard, Australian National Gallery, Gift of Mr and Mrs Fred Williams.

5. John Longstaff, *Henry Lawson*, 1900, oil on canvas, purchased 1901, Art Gallery of New South Wales.

6. Tom Roberts, *Arthur Streeton ("Smike" Streeton at 24)*, 1891, oil on canvas, purchased 1945, Art Gallery of New South Wales.

7. William Dobell, *Cement Worker*, 1944, oil on cardboard, Australian War Memorial (30249).

8. Norman Lindsay, *Self-Portrait*, 1930, etching, purchased 1953, Art Gallery
of New South Wales.

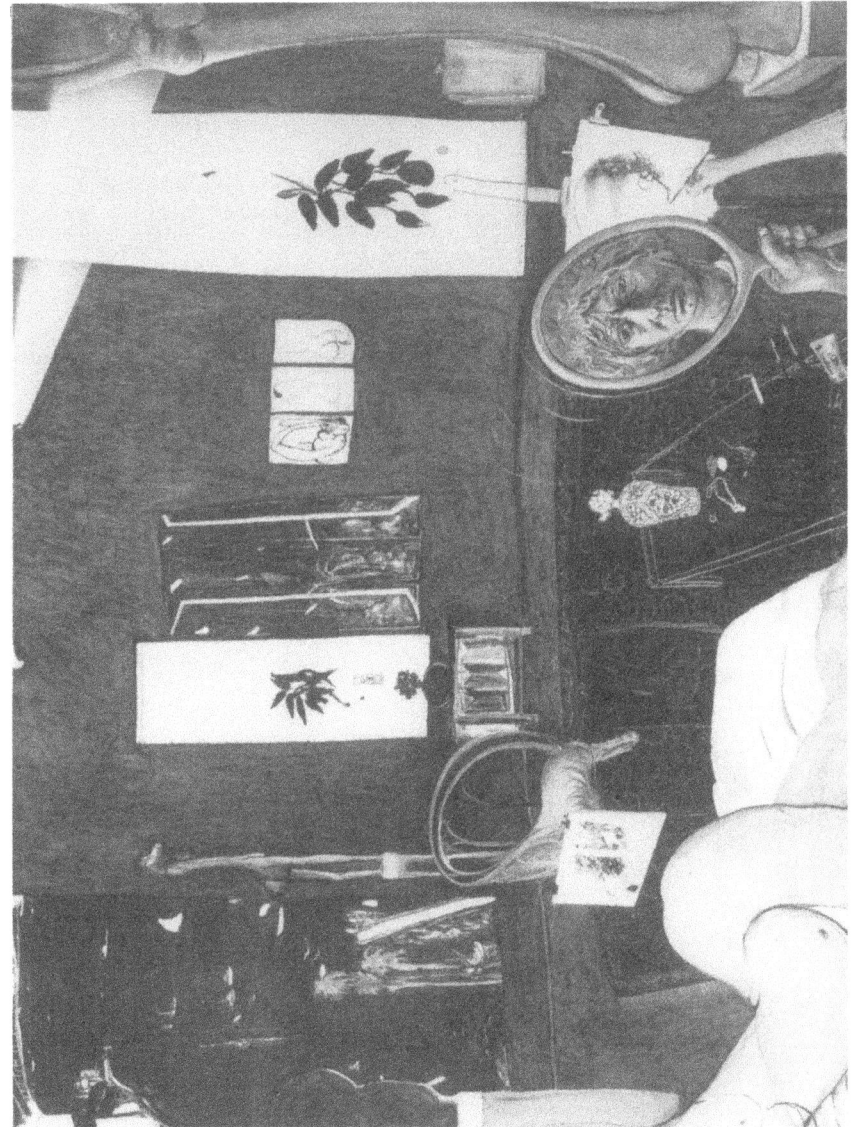

9. Brett Whiteley, *Self-Portrait in the Studio*, 1976, oil and collage on canvas, purchased 1977, Art Gallery of New South Wales.

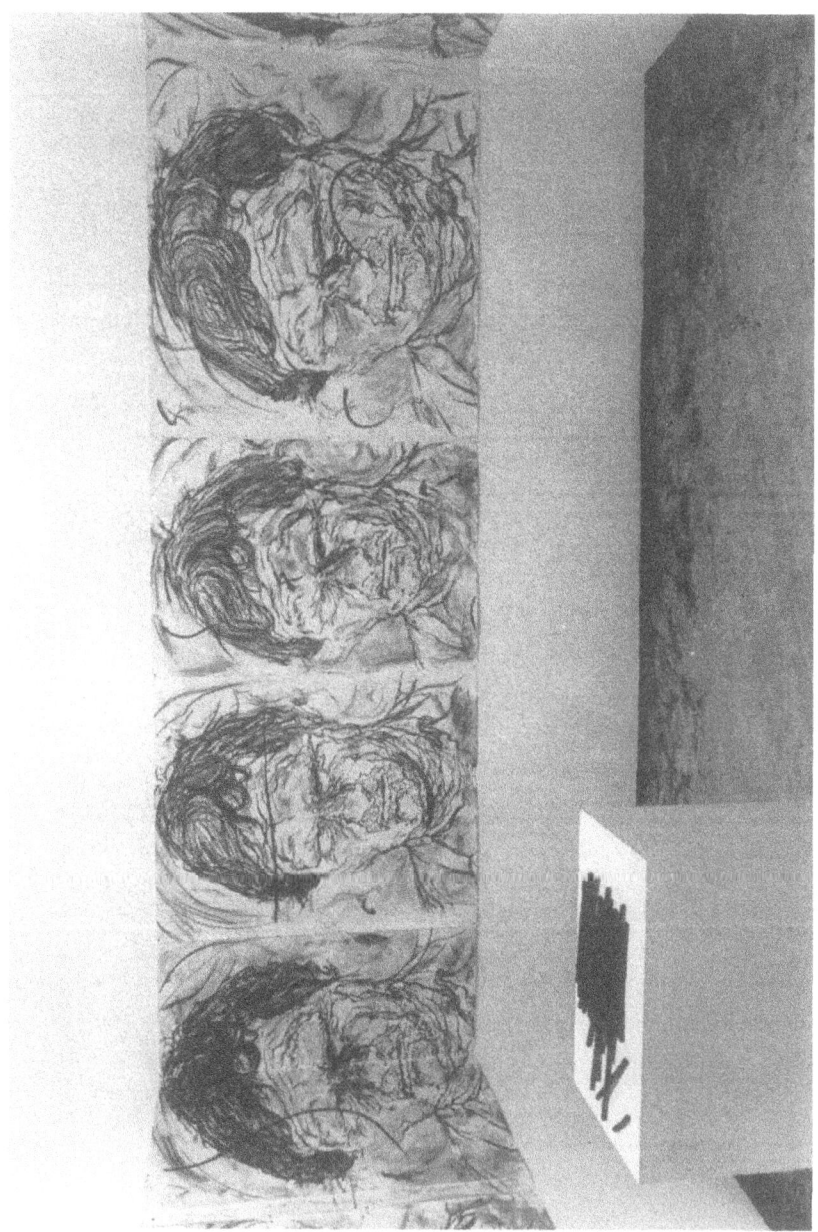

10. Mike Parr, *A-Artaud (Against the light) Self Portrait at Sixty-Five*, 1983 (detail), charcoal and paper installation, Australian National Gallery.

BODY POLITICS

ROBIN GROVE

Is milk clean, or dirty? Does it nourish and purify and soothe, bringing both innocence and strength? Or does it confer potency of a different kind, making its drinkers grown-up, spunky, tantalizing and excited? In short, does it behave like its opposite, wine? Anyone who watches TV commercials these days will know that milk has undergone a change of image, as the saying goes. Thanks to the magic of colour-film, its erotic connotations, withdrawn from view in one area, have reappeared in another, safely distant from mother's breasts. Now the boys love the girls and the girls love the boys, and they all love Big M, whose fluids are seen spurting out, being sucked, licked, wiped, spilt trickling or made to erupt, hand-held, from full-to-the-brim containers. Change of image is change of morals, and the domestic indoors of motherhood, milk's traditional domain, has given place to an "outdoors" all bounce and fun. A strange outdoors, however, since the open air as we are shown it allows virtually no distance at all. These young bodies are filmed at such short range that background disappears. Without landscape, society or time, they fill the screen, claustrophobically enclosed within their "uninhibited" gang-sensations; and the contradiction is the essence of the thing. For what we see must look like freedom, but go nowhere and do nothing. That's the safest freedom you can have. Likewise the collective romping in which the boys love the girls, girls boys, comes to focus not on their heterosexual ins and outs (those young women are quite remarkably slender-chested), but on unisex thighs instead: suggestive all right, but unripe. While as for Big M itself, its heady effects both resemble and substitute for those of alcohol, so that despite its powers of excitation the stuff is *wholesome* — an important selling-point: the drink for those who would rather not get drunk. In all, then, the ads are a splendid example of having it both ways; they let us see for ourselves that milk is unimpeachably clean yet as good as a dirty weekend.

These comparatively harmless manipulations and manoeuvres, though, do indicate how expert our reading of everyday images has become. It is simply assumed that viewers will take the point of the visual innuendos, the parallelisms and puns; and so we do. We may even go further and enjoy their absurdity as well (problem: take a milk-carton and make it exciting; time allowed, 15 seconds); this degree of consciousness is catered for too. Reading dramatized body-language in fact is second nature for most of us now. It seems a good moment therefore to ask if some of the sophistication with which we have learnt to interpret popular visuals could be directed back onto older, and long-safeguarded, cultural fields. (Which might be good for the sophistication, too.) At all events, no one is likely to be awestruck any more in the presence of the High theatre arts; the time has gone when one could think of dance — classical ballet, even — as an esoteric art-form, the preserve of a specialized few, and appropriately enough that part of our history is being reappraised right now.[1]

Of course, if government grants and public honours are what count, Australian ballet is popular these days, or at least highly regarded. A.O.s are regularly bestowed; dancers are hailed as cultural ambassadors and elevated to committee-standing; while, when it comes to money, small companies may complain that the national leviathan swallows more than its fair share, but however unjustly or justly distributed cash none the less does flow. Borovansky never won such official support. Despite all this, however, my impression is that ballet is hardly a serious topic in the circles where books, films, painting, music, are accredited subjects of debate. If anything, it attracted more attention in the old days before we had a national company and a financial commitment to it. Perhaps one reason for this was the aura of elitism and decadence that still hung round it; the combination gave off an authentic tang of the *avant-garde*. (So, in tribute to its status as a difficult art, ballet was something one did or didn't "understand") — the phrase was always being used, as though in the theatre everyone grappled with theorems of peculiar complexity, too hard for the average intellect to grasp.) But times have changed. And nowhere more evidently than in the way the young men of the Australian Ballet now dance. Compared with their predecessors of a decade or two ago, the present male dancers are a meaty lot. Where young men in tights were once the very image of the unmanly type, these dancers have become more substantial in every way. Not that they weigh more, necessarily; the point is that, whether they do or not, they look heavier, and that is how they dance. The viewer is conscious of a good deal of bone and flesh and muscle taking off, sailing, striking, rebounding from the floor. And the consequence is, the boys appear stronger. By dancing more heavily they make you realize how powerful they are and how strong they must be to do it — which embarrasses the audience less than when they were graceful (or, conversely, interests less, since the manly dancer is a more ordinary-looking creature, not so conspicuously and outrageously a work of art).

It's a very considerable change. But the usual explanation, that technique is better these days, is hardly sufficient. Leaving aside the question of why it has got better, if it has, the fact remains that the changes have taken one direction rather than another. The men dance with a lower centre of gravity, in fact. Which means that the buttocks are no longer being whisked out of sight, but believed in, and treated as a strenuous working continuation of the legs. So a whole new region of the body, between rib-cage and middle thigh, is brought into the act. You notice them turning their legs out (the classical *en dehors*) with a continuous thrust from the centre of the pelvis, exposing the inside muscles of the thigh and striving for grip and density, rather than for lightness. By contrast, male dancers in Australia twenty years ago tended to have feet and calf-muscles, but then didn't admit to anything else until your eye rose above waist-level. Basically what has altered are the dancers', and the audiences', attitudes to the male body itself. (Would Margaret Walters' study, *The Male Nude*, have been conceived or conceivable much before the last decade?)

As this example suggests, then, images of the body, right down to the buttocks, are a significant though scarcely-used resource for the history of our colonial/post-colonial selves here in Australia. The rise and fall of the felt hat, together with the social, sexual and climatic conditions it postulated, might be a further case in point; but to stay with the present subject: ballet I'd maintain is interesting not because it is Art (it may or may not be worth discussion on these terms), but because of the revelations of body it presents. For while it is true that good ballets exist, and we can be grateful that they do, you can go to the theatre and watch young people dance something quite dreadful, and still see them shaping, as they travel and pose and achieve balance and lapse out of it again, formalized images of ourselves and our aspirations, impulses, fears. The feeblemindedness of most ballets doesn't obscure these involuntary revelations. They are what bodies moving through space create. And you catch them outside performances altogether sometimes − in the unconscious style of the dancers in their daily practice-class, for instance; or in sport, or in modes of dress and habitual agilities and grossnesses, or in the gestures even of people walking in the street. But choreographies concentrate them for us; so the richer and better the choreography the dancers are given to perform, the more they will be able to reveal, whether they mean to or not.

One of the things they will show is the training they have had. To this extent, when we look at professional dancers we are seeing something of the previous generation in motion: not reading about the subject, or theorizing over how things went thirty or forty years ago, but actually receiving a portion of the physical presence of the past. Much more is transmitted to the present generation than a set of rules. The very speed and attack with which dancers move, their range of dynamism, musical responsiveness, the inflections of their bodily speech − all tell their own tale, so that in this or that dancer's way of moving we see, beyond the private style, a body re-embodying its teachers' assumptions and, summed up in those, a selection of wider social attitudes to bodily expressiveness then and now. Tradition here, as always, means continuity in the process of change. Thus the present male dancers, products of the Sixties by and large, also display themselves with more forceful confidence than their predecessors did, making the most of sheer physical prowess and its attractiveness, instead of pretending to be nobly unsexual cavaliers.

How *that* particular convention came to hold the stage is a topic in itself, for although the asexual cavalier-pose is what most of us ("instinctively") assume that men in ballet will adopt, the manner is by no means essential to the classical technique. Rather, the logic of the technique suggests possibilities of quite a different kind; not constipated deference, but movement radiating outwards from a clear central control by which gestures are proportioned and drawn into harmony with one another. It is this which is integral to the style. More spectacular developments may be added, such as dancing *en pointe*, or intricate jumps, or multiple spins, but these are intensifications, not essential. What matters is the controlling centre, for here the cross-tensions of lower-back, groin and waist are gathered, to produce in their turn the more visible features of classical ballet, such as turned-out feet and legs. From this centre the spine is poised upright and limbs are extended, stretching with unusual visibility and completeness, but not elongated so far as to pull shoulder or hip-socket awry, since a result of that sort detracts from the basic metaphor, which is that the classical dancer is master of his fate.

To this metaphoric claim the whole style bears witness. Accordingly, when the classical dancer moves or stops it is not at necessity's say-so, like the rest of us who run fast because we have to get somewhere, or fall and bend because we couldn't help it, whereas the classical dancer seems to move by his own volition entirely. Jumps and turns are set in motion, then halted just at the chosen spot. With no more legs than the rest of us, the six basic steps we are capable of (from two feet to one or the other; from right foot to left or vice versa; from two feet to two feet; and from right or left bringing both feet together again) establish a range of new freedoms, instead of signalizing, as they often do in folk-dance for example, our biological limitation and monotony. The classical dancer can even dramatize abandoned control, so complete is his mastery, for all contingency is overcome (so the illusion goes): it is overcome in fact by the body itself, the daily drudge of contingent gravity-laden lives. In ballet, this vulnerable creature itself appears to triumph over accident.

It follows therefore that the spasms, contractions and abruptnesses of Modern dance are alien to the classic style, in which effortlessly produced movement is continually reabsorbed at the centre of the body, only to issue again unabated. So muscular effort is rendered in symbolic forms instead, such as the arched foot which seems to grasp and stretch the air, or the thick plunge of the whole body into an arabesque, where the eye takes in the maximum tension of the two legs flung wide apart, while all the time the real strain of the dancing is elsewhere and deeper than these extremities an audience is likely to notice. Confidence, proportion, balance — these are not "aesthetic" values only, but the chosen manner of an autocratic style that depends on hard labour but disguises the fact, and uses contingency in secret while to all appearances holding it at bay.

Seeing classical ballet for the first time therefore most of us are likely to be struck by how upright and aerial it is. The characteristic illusion produced is of floating, skimming, flying, with ease and energy. The dancers press against and thrust off from the floor, treating it as simply the given condition on which their freedom is founded. Certainly, such aristocratic effortlessness *depends* on having something underneath, but the spectator is not asked to be concerned with this base condition of stage-level, except to notice how far the dancers soar away from it, or seem to rise and hover. Instead of its being admitted to visible importance in its own right, "the floor is your enemy" the old ballet-teachers' saying used to run — inculcating attitudes very different indeed from those of the Modern dancer who embraces the floor, seeks it, explores and (so to speak) participates in it, as if showing how possibilities of freedom emerge only if they come to terms with this underlying reality. A Modern dance performance impresses us with the importance, theatrically speaking, of the platform-stage; we are made to notice it, and to be aware of its strength, even as new images are being built on top. So the indispensable proletarian fact supporting and making possible the dance's power is visibly drawn into the dancing while we watch, whereas the images of classical ballet wish to appear self-generated and self-sustained.

Such images, created from the moving volumes of the body, bear political implications of course. Their portent is not so straightforward however as might at first be thought. Simply to dismiss the classical ballet as a luxury-product of oppressive hierarchical regimes (Louis XIV's France, Tsarist Russia) is to miss the subversive energies of its particular technique. Admittedly, ballets were used (and still are) by this or that ruling-class as exhibitions of wealth and safely-disciplined servant-power. From court masques to command performances of *The Merry Widow* the *genre* looks anything but revolutionary; and when dancers of the Australian Ballet actually went on strike, astonishment among their managers, one heard, was as great as if the entire corps had sprouted dorsal fins. Yet it cannot be altogether *safe* to train young people in an activity as powerful and free as classical dance. Whatever they make of it themselves, their audiences may reflect upon it too. For such movement shows an exercise of human powers so extensive and yet so responsible in its liberty that, if the single dancer looks like the master of his fate, exulting over conditions the rest of us obey, a whole company of dancers is like a galaxy of sovereign systems, all moving with perfect freedom yet never obstructing or colliding with each other.

That is not a view of human nature our rulers and managers happily endorse, but it is the sort of thing I think I see when watching a first-rate company at work. Certainly, the classical style belongs to a less democratic art than that of American Modern Dance. In the former, the conditions which support you (which therefore you can visibly protest against) are seldom brought to notice in their own right. But the result for ballet's autocratic mode is greater freedom rather than less. The swirling hobbling skirts of Wigmanesque dancers, or the obsessively frequent floor-contacts of the Graham style, give way to limbs bountifully and spiritedly in motion. And the better-trained the dancers, the less uniform they will look. At the opening of "Kingdom of the Shades" in *La Bayadere* a long line of dancers descends the ramp performing a single step; the result is not that they strike us as regimented; rather, each dancer individually makes her mark, then joins her peers — voluntarily, one feels. What we are being shown is collective movement which none the less allows maximum liberty to the individual as well, as though human freedom were inexhaustible. One name for this view of our condition (hardly new of course, if one thinks of *Die Zauberflöte* or Blake's *Songs of Innocence*) is Romantic pastoral.

And what happens to such a style brought into the Victorian-British colonies of Australia? What happens to the colonial imagination faced with it, come to that? Personally, I am not convinced that the best place to look for evidence is the bare documentary file of reviews and cast-lists and old programs. Even where these survive, to tell us that such-and-such a piece was performed on such a night, what we need to know is how the dancers danced it, and that knowledge it must seem can hardly be obtained.

Well, it certainly can't be obtained directly any more. Last night's performance, like all the rest, is over and done with now. Yet ballets when performed do leave some evidences behind them all the same. Like those vanished creatures who imprint their outline, their internal structure, even their soft tissues, on substances harder than themselves, these ephemeral occasions shape a public over years — until, in turn, they themselves are caught and rigidified into theatre-going tastes. In other words, styles of performance produce styles of expectation; so the Australian audience might be treated as a fossil-record of ballet as it has been danced here. Meanwhile, there are other forms of suggestive material one might use. Photographs, for example. Of course it is plain that a photograph is no performance, and may be misleading in what it actually shows.

But we are mistaken to conclude that action-photos taken while a ballet is in progress necessarily provide a more faithful record than posed studio-shots. My own impression is that the artificially arrested picture is often truer and more revealing than the unrehearsed picture taken from the wings. For after all the dancer is trained to isolate and show essentials in a single gesture, whether or not on stage; whereas the photographer snapping as the performance passes is likely to select what seem to him the spectacular moments and high points. Few would single out the extraordinary completeness of an altogether un-spectacular moment such as (1) — although you have only to compare the line Spessivtseva is holding here (tender, pensive, as though her Giselle had indeed passed beyond flesh and blood and were now memorializing the woman she used to be) with the effect of a different dancer in the role to see how much more the studio-photograph reveals. As against the action-photograph (2), the first, "posed" picture reveals just what one wants to know: namely, what Spessivtseva made of *Giselle*. Had no other record of her survived, one could be fairly sure of her greatness as a dancer from this photograph alone. (Trying to imitate her apparently artless pose is a way of ascertaining just how subtle and demanding its simplicity is.) One can guess that Spessivtseva saw the ballet as merging

(1)   (2)

together the Bride and the Wraith until each becomes transparent to the other. The series of curves passing through the figure, from neck and throat through the upper-back down without pause to the inclined angle of the foot, compose a single image in which the ghostly Giselle, who in the ballet has just at this moment risen from the grave, co-exists with the promised bride, bending as though to receive her veil. There is even a slightly heavy, "keepsake" droop to the shoulders, appropriate to a period-piece. But actually at every point the pure intentness of this dancer justifies the attention demanded from her audience.

Spessivtseva toured here in 1934; and indeed, as John Cargher points out in his valuable study of the field, right from the start in ballet Australia was hardly the uncultured outpost it has often been taken to be. Immediately before Spessivtseva, Pavlova had toured here, to tremendous applause, in 1926 and again in 1929; Spessivtseva herself, dancing with the baldly-named "Russian Ballet Company", had been followed by other Russians and other companies with such alacrity that "for five years running some part of Australia had the best ballet company in the world playing in one of its theatres'. 1936-37, 1938-39, and 1939-40 were so dominated by the Ballets Russes de Monte Carlo that even thirty years later young dancers were still cosmopolitanizing their names to make them less Anglo-Saxon. The important feature of all this however is that even the early Russian ballet companies did not come to a cultural void. On the contrary, the dance-styles of the Romantic theatre were firmly rooted in the Antipodes already. In fact the first Australian-made ballet was *The Fair Maid of Perth* (1835), which took its title, if not much else perhaps, from the novel by Sir Walter Scott. It was no isolated novelty. Those historians of dance in Australia to whom I've referred help to make it clear that ballet in this country goes far back into the 19th century, and local repertoires were closely interwoven with those of the European theatre of the time. Thus, *La Sylphide*, choreographed by Taglioni and danced by his famous daughter, had been produced in Paris in 1832. It was an immense success, and had of course almost everything Romantic ballet would show: spirits or elemental beings no man can afford to love, and for whom human love likewise will prove fatal; air-borne creatures, unattainably floating out of reach; dreams and visions; a setting — "Scotland" — gloomily picturesque; the isolated male figure; and so on. *La Sylphide* was reproduced throughout Europe, and once and for all established the new technique of rising fully onto the *pointe* or tip of the toe. By 1836, Bournonville had choreographed his own version of it for the Royal Danish company; and by 1845, surprisingly soon one might say, it was put on in Melbourne, where productions of the ballet continued to be mounted for years.

The ten-year lag is characteristic. Ballets were likely to appear in Australia a decade or so after they had first been performed in London; and often no doubt they were a good deal changed. Travestied, perhaps. Hard to say if much more than the title survived transportation to the colonies in some cases. But the ten-year gap did mean that, since popular ballets after a first production had had the chance to spread through Europe, dancers arriving in Australia were likely to have encountered the works somewhere or other at first hand back home. So we need not assume that the ballets presented here were entirely inauthentic. Anyone who has seen dancers reconstructing a piece from memory will understand how much of the Romantic ballets the visitors and emigrants from the European stage could have brought with them — fairly accurately, too. At all events, it is clear that Australian ballet is no recent thing. By 1845, *La Sylphide* in some form or other had been staged, and within the next decade half-a-dozen works almost as famous — including the greatest of them, *Giselle*. There were pieces with choreography by Taglioni; there were ballets "inspired" by Goethe, Heine, and Gautier; and a lot of unmemorable stuff as well; but by and large something like the Romantic ballet of the European theatres was being presented here.

In 1866, for example, Meyerbeer's opera *Robert le Diable* ran for a fortnight in Melbourne. It was this work, with its large-scale ballet in Act III, which yielded one of the most famous spectacles of early-19th-century theatre, as Robert, Duke of Normandy, enters the ruined chapel, and the ghosts of a whole convent-full of nuns, led by their Abbess, rise from the grave and dance an overwhelming bacchanale. Here was morbid ecstasy indeed: voluptuous forms, tempting a man to his doom while yet remaining inviolable themselves — for these apparitions are pure, not just with the purity of disembodied spirits, but doubly unseizable and doubly alluring because the ghosts of nuns. And indeed the sisterhood of dancers, bound by the mystery of their art and visibly under discipline to obey a rule laid down and known only to them, *are* nun-like, the audience can reflect. With this proviso: that "sacred" has become "secular" instead. Or maybe it is even worse as you watch what is shown on stage: for it seems that the religious life can be resurrected now only as a dance of shadows, a profane bacchanale in the ruins left by the age of Faith, whose spectral images take ideal shape in order to lure our desires to their death. The ballet, first performed in 1831, contained a powerful set of metaphors for the 19th century, if dancers and spectators were able to see what it held.

The history of Romantic ballet in Australia, however, follows much the same course as in Europe. If it began in metaphor, as a poetic theatre, in contrast to the harlequinades, the military ballets, *genre* pieces and national dances of the time, it soon found itself re-assimilated into an entertaining spectacle which put no tax on an audience's imagination. It was turned into stock numbers, stage-effects, devices. Thus the metaphoric quality of those moments when the Sylphide floated free from her earthly lover, or Giselle rose from her grave to draw Albrecht from the protection of the Cross, or Ondine discovered that, being mortal, she had gained a shadow — these were conventionalized into theatrical tricks. Whole companies of white-clad spirits were slung from wires; the shadow-dance became a highlight; dancers resolutely stiffened their satin shoes in order to dance on their toes and develop *"pointes* of steel". Romantic ballet became fairy pantomime instead. Well, that was inevitable perhaps, but it did mean that the genuine power of those early-19-century images was lost.

Still, this need not have been a bad thing altogether. A lot of Romantic ballets as I read them were curiously doom-laden. And when you think what energies and pleasures dancing bodies can express, it is evident that too-frequent recourse to sylphides, ondines and spirit-brides attenuates choreography and audience alike. So we need not be too upset that in the last quarter of the 19th century dancers of the ethereal style suffered an eclipse. They did not vanish entirely, but the spectral forms which earlier ballet had conjured onto stage turned into daintiness, while whatever imaginative life they had contained withdrew and went elsewhere.

It went into the new style of Russian dancing, I think we would have to say; and was almost instantly appropriated and transformed. Technique grew stronger, more varied: jumps, turns, extensions developed force; and from the choreography of the Petipa *regime* it is clear that the female dancer now moved with unprecedented velocity, precision, power. This was exciting, no doubt. But for all its gains, the classical ballet in late 19th-century Russia is a mass of contradictions. Coming upon photographs of the dancers with their unanimated arms and thighs, one's first impression is likely to be how materialistic this kind of theatre looks — like stage-dressing, and at high cost (3). Even the characteristic brilliance of Petipa *enchainements* can serve as sumptuous expendable display, as night after night the dancer covers the stage with turns, leaps, diagonals . . . a whole wealth of movement to be spent for the sake of the spending. Soloists perform their specialities, ballerinas are arranged to advantage, while the *corps* dances through its patterns and massed parades. These dancers may play at being empresses, pharaohs and queens, but the real power is elsewhere, employing *them* and keeping an eye on things from the Royal Box. As consumer-art therefore the ballet was expected to show off all the glamour on hand. The system called for the ballerinas to be "stars", which a number of them managed to be in court-circles and private life as well.

(3)

And yet, of course, the more the virtuoso develops her technique and moves with the stage at command, the stronger and freer are the human possibilities her dance-images will evoke. It is difficult for her to be the automaton or idol or doll late-19th-century display-ballets seem to suggest she is. The more vividly she moves, the less she will be able to look as if she is simply obeying her profession's rules; so that what begins as theatre-spectacle is liable, because of the nature of the classical technique, to develop energies of a much more challenging kind. *La Sylphide*, *Giselle* and other Romantic ballets had incorporated the paradox into myths which dramatized the destructive passion of desire: so spirits baulked of their wedding-night dance a man to death; or the Scot marries his sylphide and kills her unwittingly with the poisoned love-gift he bestows. In *Swan Lake*, for once in Petipa's career, something similar is achieved. But the effect of that ballet is virtually unique (and was the result of collaboration in any case). For the most part his great gifts as a choreographer failed to shape myths of the Romantic kind; they merely exploited the paradox of dancers at liberty in their movement (more so than anyone had ever been), yet state-employees at the service of a strictly-policed *regime*. And without wanting to be fanciful about it, I think one can see the strain of that in Russian dancers by the time our own century begins(4). Even Pavlova looks oddly thick in the shoulders, over-deliberate in torso and waist, by contrast with her sharply-pointed feet and legs. No doubt somewhat primitive photography meant she had to hold the pose, and her costume is top-heavy anyway. Nevertheless she strikes me as the perfectly finished St Petersburg product of 1907 carefully keeping herself in — not a good state for a dancer.

Australians of course neither suffered nor benefited from the conditions which helped to shape a generation and more of Russian dancers. In our case, the idea of ballet as consumer-spectacle had a more complacently middle-class air. As reported in the *Argus* in 1899, a Corn and Poppy ballet at the Princess Theatre ("a perfect feast of color") symbolized "our Land of Peace and Plenty" — almost too well perhaps. Other nationalistic exercises, such as "A Fairy-tale of Old Japan" (Melbourne, 1895), were available, in or out of disguise. And it was still the heyday of skirt-banding, so that when *Turquoisette: a Study in Blue*, "the first classical ballet entirely conceived, produced and performed in Australia", was put on in 1893 by an all-female cast (of course), at least one critic wondered whether audiences would take to the style. They did. Or at any rate it didn't take them long; in consequence when Adeline Genee with members of "The Imperial Russian Ballet" toured here in 1913 the particular excellence of the dancing was remarked upon and enjoyed. Local taste had refined enough to recognize the best in late-19th-century Empire ballet when offered it.

And that surely is what Genee represents (5). No praise is too great for the touching charm of that beautifully positioned dancer, the strong compact torseo, the plumply witty feet. All the same, one can see that she would not dream of pretending to be other than she is: a performer, that's to say, and a real warm presence in everything she does. It seems ungracious to ask for more, yet put Genee alongside dancers of the

Diaghilev troupe, and the photographs give evidence that, while she remains always herself, *they* turn into ballets.

(4) (5)

If there is such a thing as proof of genius, perhaps the proof of Nijinsky's, since we cannot see him dance, is that from role to role he becomes vitually unrecognizable, he is made so different by what he does. In 1906 (*Don Giovanni*) we see him looking like a dancer, and a good one, but nothing more; rather hefty too, with over-conscious fingers and stolid thighs. A year later, though, and he is making his first ballet with Fokine. It may be pseudo-Graeco, but a new sensuality appears. The body is visibly *feeling* the play of tensions and relaxations as the legs flex their weight against the upright pull of the hips. Nijinsky's attitude in fact, with hips tilted yet waist held level, is less natural, more of an achievement, than it seems. What spoils it still is an element of learnt-up self-impersonation: witness the passive chest and carefully folded hands. But by 1910, when Fokine's great ballets begin, self-consciousness of this kind has been left behind. One needs to study the whole collection of photos edited by Lincoln Kirstein to grasp how swift and complete and various Nijinsky's new comprehension of possibilities was. No dancer I have seen ever looked like this before (6). The arms, for example: they neither form themselves into the supported geometry of the classic style, nor hang loose, but seem as if twined around and clinging to the air itself. Out of the strong trunk of the body they've uncoiled, not to their full extent, but with a lush completeness through which the sap still flows. The head lolls like a heavy blossom; the legs, in what is almost the strangest illusion of all, are not what he's balancing upon but appear instead to branch downwards of their own accord, from the pelvis into the ground.

Strictly speaking, of course, that is illusion. Yet it is what Nijinsky creates, and we know that to intensify it he did everything he could. The costume, a net of petals, was sewn onto him and then blended into the tights and skin. Close-ups of the face show its features smothered in grease-paint: exquisitely depersonalized, as Kirstein writes, with bone and cartilage transformed into a blurred glow, certainly not human — as much insectile as floral ("ambiguous, mirthless, yet honeyed smile breathed self-containment"). What might have been sentimental, became eerie. To bring about such transformations of the body and the spectator's consciousness was the Diaghilev ballet's achievement.

So Nijinsky alone, in *Spectre de la Rose*, looks different from Nijinsky with the girl (7). He is more masculine here: the body not dreaming about itself, but pressing into the edges of the girl's own alien dream. A moment later, in another plate, their circles of consciousness have drawn apart again (8): she looks less troubled, but less enraptured too, while he is more teasingly androgynous, at once older and more remote. In *Faune* he is astonishingly different again — so powerful and yet held-in, as the insides of the legs press together, the chest swings appressively against the twist of pelvis and head, and the arms stiffen into muscular forequarters ready to attack. The whole posture is so without the tender self-possession of *Spectre de la Rose* you would hardly know the body is the same. This creature is listening, even with the back of his neck, and with every pose he re-defines the space between himself and the nearest object as his territory, and fills it with panic or curiosity or wonder.

(6) (7) (8)

It is easy to say Nijinsky is unique. Naturally he was. But whether from his genius or from his director's or choreographer's, the Diaghilev company became a place where ballets, not just dancing, occurred. I used to marvel at the costumes its soloists appeared in: how could they possibly *move*? But these dancers were committed to more than bodily feats. They were visions, imaginary creatures, pieces of art; and therefore must look as if they emanated from another world. What is more, no world is a monologue; it must contain more than one person; and under Diaghilev it did. His company survived for twenty years, while its personnel almost entirely changed. Nijinsky, Fokine, Benois, one after another moved elsewhere, yet the Diaghilev ballet went on. To have established a ballet company, then, unlike all the other organizations presenting "shows" and "starts", is another mark of Diaghilev's importance.

Certainly, it sets him apart from almost everything seen in Australia. Here, what we would get was a famous dancer or two in a repertoire judged hardy enough to withstand transportation. Pavlova was the most influential, I suppose, and it is not enough to label her a star-turn. Unlike the bejewelled favourites of the previous generation, she diffused poetic illusion: photos leave one in no doubt of that; but illusion or imaginative presence of a narrow repetitive kind. What she had to convey was spirituality; pathos, to be precise; and it tended to be the pathos of single, infinitely fragile, cherishable things: the ephemerid, the dying swan, the sylphide who melts into mist. She went mad on stage, poetically, and rose again, a spirit from the tomb. Night after night what the audience paid to see was the extinction, the dancing to death, of this marvellous, vulnerable body. And of course had she been surrounded by dancers of comparable imaginative force, some of her own beatuy would have diminshed. One slim figure lifting its breastbone to struggle unavailingly against death is a moving sight; two lonely victims, side by side, make at least one isolation too many. And besides, it was a natural corollary of Pavlova's art that the male figure, in so far as he suggested generative vitality, should be rendered almost entirely ineffectual. Worshippers, or poets, or porters were all that her men seemed called upon to be. It took Australian ballet a long time to recover from that, too.

Nevertheless, her dancing with all its shortcomings was wonderful. Those visions of her as the dragonfly, the chrysanthemum, the swan, add something to human nature. Indeed, she adds so strangely both to "human" and to "nature" that it is hard to be sure if our stress should fall on the adjective or the noun. Pavlova, so to speak, makes them equal nouns. But that achievement depended on her single unprecedented talent, and disappeared with her on her death. What was left was a conviction that ballet has to do with pathos ... which is where the de Basil Ballet Russe de Monte Carlo comes in. In the wake of Pavolva and Spessivtseva, it established the triple formula for ballet in Australia which proved profitable for forty years: namely, "the classics", plus light-hearted romps, plus tragedies on the epic scale. But the characteristic dramas of the company were the symphonic/symbolic ones, in which Man or Woman or the Young Lovers are pitted against Fate: a use of the classical technique which takes up the metaphors of freedom inherent in it, and turns them against themselves. Man is not a sovereign creature, so these symphonic ballets say; he is no longer the master of his fate, but a victim destroyed by the very forces which move him. Nijinsky had taken classicism seriously enough to see that, in order to choreograph *The Rite of Spring*, he must invent a whole anti-classical style, thick, brutal, turned-in, aghast at itself. The result was a ballet which from report, *was* tragic: that is, frightening and re-invigorating both at once. The de Basil tragedies on the other hand came cheaper. And it was de Basil's style which took up residence here. No doubt to say so is a bit unfair to Borovansky, whose energy in the cause of professional Australian ballet is quite rightly famous. He wasn't the first to create a local company, but he was the most pertinacious and magnetic; with him the triple formula swung into operation from the start. If Toumanova could make the 19th-century classics work in Sydney, Borovansky could do it in Melbourne. If *Le Beau Danube* had been a hit when the Russian dancers were light-hearted in it, then *his* dancers would be light-hearted in it till they dropped. And as for the nobly tragic ... *The Eternal Lovers*, music by Tchaikovsky of course, stayed in the repertoire for years.

Finally, however, when all is said Borovansky's far-reaching effect on Australian theatre-images of the body can be judged by the fact that his company took on a recognizable house-style. It was compact, short-rhythmed, and tended to suggest that the ballerina was electrically driven, and to save current would be switched off the moment she reached the wings. The effect was genuinely exciting at times, if pretty funny at others. I still recall with great pleasure performances Peggy Sager gave, where the speed and precision of attack seemed to come from nowhere, instantly stop dead, then strike in a different direction, like high voltage. But the most celebrated exponent of Borovansky-style was Kathleen Gorham, in whom the "feathery lightness" and "dramatic power" most critics applauded always seemed to me, I'm afraid, a product of will, and so hard-fought-for as never to open into fruitful pleasurable rhythms. So it was an odd kind of femininity Australian ballet of the Fifties conveyed: unecstatic, I think one could say, but almost anti-erotic too. Those girls danced for the *fight* of it, for bloody victory at times, and their smiles flashed at the audience were stroboscopic, like revolving lights that warn you away from a dangerous crossing. Perhaps what was wrong was their inability to stop being dancers, sweating it out, and to allow themselves, like the Diaghilev soloists, to be made imaginary beings instead.

(9)

It is a large demand. And for audiences to see it as a possibility, even, naturally takes time. More productions of merrier widows will not help. But grim or frivolous though the prospects for Australian ballet do appear at times, we have a lot to be grateful for — including the two generations full of Laurel Martyn's work, or the quite remarkable programs of the Sydney Dance Company in recent years. Indeed, it seems quite evident to me that the last two decades have produced the most wonderful bodies in motion anyone has ever seen. And not just a few acrobatic virtuosi: whole audiences from Russia, and America, and Europe, have trained young people to move as never before. Changed sexual attitudes have something to do with it; like the nakedness of Greek athletes, as Kenneth Clark points out, our dancers' new relationship to gravity and space implies the conquest of inhibitions, fears; but it involves other values and aspirations too. We are beginning to glimpse, through these symbolic liberties (9), something more of human nature's scope. Soon, what we will have are new audiences, and choreographers who will transform these extraordinary athletes into metaphors and images again.

1982

Notes

[1] In John Cargher, *Opera and Ballet in Australia* (1977); Frank Salter, *Borovansky: The Man Who Made Australian Ballet* (1980); Edward Pask, *Enter the Colonies Dancing* (1972) and *The Second Act* (1982).

SELF-LEVELLING TALL POPPIES: THE AUTHORIAL SELF IN (MALE) AUSTRALIAN LITERATURE

DIRK DEN HARTOG

> Each individual seems to feel himself pledged to put himself aside; to keep himself at least half out of count. . . . This is done with a watchful will: a sort of duel. And done with a great geniality. But the continual holding of oneself aside, out of count, makes a man go blank in his withheld self. . . . Probably this is more true of the men than of the women. (D.H. Lawrence, *Kangaroo*, 1923)

Lawrence's diagnosis of the Australian psyche has often been cited in cultural commentary, and rightly so. One familiar and very natural procedure has been to support it with comparable analyses drawn from Australian literary works.[1] One really disquieting aspect of that large slice of Australian reality that still seems to answer to the charge, however, is the extent to which significant literary works themselves appear to be implicated, the frequency with which the voice in which *they* speak seems to come from an authorial self in which much of the inner self is being withheld, or at least not allowed to come out clearly and openly. This is especially so, in a way which confirms and extends Lawrence's case, in those works written by men. Of course this should not surprise us at all if we are sitting resignedly in the structuralist conviction that literature is no more than the product of the ideologies of the general culture from which it derives. But if we still have some faith in literature as critically at odds with that culture, then the phenomenon I've noted is something worth charting and worth protesting about.

One way of approaching all this, in terms of literary and cultural history, is to think about the modification Romanticism has undergone within Australian literary culture. Romanticism contains many contradictions, but one of these in especial seems to have been particularly influential in the development of Australian literature and culture. It has also been problematically influential, as I shall argue. This has been the tension between Romanticism's democratic and aristocratic implications. Conceived in terms of Rousseauan naturalness and spontaneity, Romanticism is an essentially anti-aristocratic set of ideas. Yet is heroic conception of the individual creator — and the individual imagination — implies an aristocratic bias, in the sense of *aristoi* rather than the rule of the established social elites laying claim to the concept. Many European and American post-Romantic writers have resolved this contradiction through the figure of the noble savage, such as the Brangwens of Lawrence's *The Rainbow*, Hardy's Gabriel Oak, or Twain's Huckleberry Finn, in whom an aristocratic richness and distinctiveness of inner being coincides with a plebeian plainness of outer manner. In Australia the spiritual heroes and heroines of Patrick White's novels embody this co-presence in its most strikingly paradoxical form.

Generally, however, this resolution seems to be relatively absent in Australia. Here the democratic identification of writers has tended to be with a "levelling" egalitarianism rather than with savage but noble conceptions. A number of causal factors are probably involved here, among which are such received notions as the adversary relationship between white settlers and the land and its aboriginal inhabitants, and the experience of immigration as exile rather than promised Utopian renewal. The distinctive achievement of traditional Australian literature, too, is arguably associated with this. Yet the negative consequences has been that the expression of a democratic inclination in Australian writing has involved choosing against the ideal of a richly realised individuality — an aristocracy of *being* in a way in which the "noble savage" solution obviated.

It has been such a choice that I would see as largely responsible for that characteristically national narrative pattern Graeme Turner has elucidated in his recent reinterpretation of the myths of the battler and the anti-authoritarian larrikin as expressed in Australian literature and film. His *National Fictions*[2] takes this ostensibly radical material and shows just how fully it is linked to a stance of stoic resignation in the face of life's difficulties and society's givens, a stance which Turner sees as deeply conservative in its implications. Survival, not social transformation, is the bleak positive message of our literary and filmic tradition. Significantly for my opening comments, this is seen to lie simply in adaptation to a social norm: Turner echoes D.R. Burns's claim some years ago that ironically, in Australian fiction, "the rugged individualist triumphs by conforming, by demonstrating his ability to attain to the standards set by his society".[3] Of course such a norm, seen as collectivist mateship or manly grit, may be seen as admirable and potentially radical — as has been the Left Nationalist custom. But a different picture emerges when one stresses, as does Turner, its more narrowly Puritanical implications, when one sees the democratic bond not as a means of discovering and experiencing feelings and energies, but as based upon respect for their heroic suppression. Seen in this light, the cultural stance that prides itself upon resisting ruling class and Eurocentric hegemony itself appears as part of the hegemonic problem.

The obverse of this limited idea of heroism in Australian narrative, Turner argues, is the "fear of difference", the marked distrust or resentment of individuality. This he sees as manifesting itself in two ways, as an insistence on showing through the manipulation of plot how absurd the hopes for self-realization of strongly individuated characters are, and as a tendency towards "the eschewal of individuation in the representation of character itself."[4] In this essay I want to elaborate upon this aspect of Turner's overall argument and to point to two further ways in which this conformist impulse is present.

These are, first of all, some ways in which we can sense in the narrative voice of a number of works either explicit embarrassment about *authorial* difference, or an implicit rejection of authorial difference through the adoption of what looks like a falsely impersonal narrative voice. Secondly, there is the significance in this context of the marked ambivalence in much theatrical satire of the 1960s and 1970s directed at Australianness as "ockerism" — the reluctance to establish clearly a differentiated authorial position from the socially mainstream phenomenon that is the ostensible object of the satire. Factors of gender and class are clearly at work here and will perhaps allow us to think with a bit more exactness about the ways in which Australian culture as a whole has constrained so many Australian writers from developing a properly critical stance towards it.

What I want to do is try to shift the emphasis from seeing the "fear of difference" as an element of national narrative, to seeing it as a discernible trait of the individual writers most immediately responsible for that narrative — a shift rather alien to Turner's structuralist orientation. To do this is to focus on a peculiarly Australian phenomen: the way that so many members of a group we might define by their commitment to an ideal of individuality, hedge away from this in their writings and seem to want to hide the fullness and complexity of their own individuality behind the ventriloquist mask of a mythically national persona. My opening comments have suggested one explanation for this "being Australian" at the cost of being oneself. It now remains for me to trace the presence of this national form of *trahison des clercs* in a number of significant Australian works, and to try to analyze its effect upon them.

It seems only proper to begin here with the 1890s, and the narrative voices in which the male Bohemians of the *Bulletin* defined themselves as the spokesmen for legendary Australianism. Revisionist historians have by now thoroughly changed our understanding of what was involved in this identification. They have taught us how diverse the lived cultural reality of Australia actually was, how selective such interpretations as Ward's classic Bushman Legend thesis really were, and how projective of the ideological viewpoint from which such interpretations were made. The noble larrikin really occupies a position within Australian mythology somewhat analogous to the cowboy within the American. Richard White's particular way of standing Russel Ward on his head, in *Inventing Australia*, for instance, is to invert the established view of 1890s writers and artists as transparent mediums through whom the folk voice of Ward's "nomad tribe" spoke without distortion, or through which a hitherto unseen authentically Australian reality was reflected, and to argue for a reversed process of ventriloquistically projected Bohemian values (such as "freedom, comradeship and youthful spirits") into a Romanticized image of bush life.[5] Even if the larrikin-Bushman did have *some* basis in a lived cultural reality, as one might want still to insist, his elevation to cultural typicality and mythic nobility really tells us more about the Bohemians than the bush. Graeme Davison's well-known recent work on the Sydney Bohemians of the 1890s makes the same point, of course.[6]

But what exactly are we told of the Bohemians — or rather, how are we to interpret what we are told? Both White's and Davison's discussions of their material are naturally enough shaped and thus constrained by the particular use they make of it — i.e. the up-ending of the Ward thesis. A further question arises, however, to do with what the projective identification with the Bush idea might be seen to have entailed for the Bohemians themselves. That is, if that ideal was adopted unwittingly, as is currently accepted, as a mirror-image of the Bohemian self, as an act of self-definition against the genteel bourgeois respectability of colonial display culture, what are the full implications of this for the self that is being so defined? My suggestion is that the Bohemian identification by reflection entailed a mixture of truth and falsity: truth in that the egalitarian sympathy of the Bohemians, together with the other shared Bohemian-larrikin values, made the Bohemian adoption of the bush persona a relatively natural form of self-dramatization; and falsity in that one can't help sensing in the characteristic *Bulletin*-Bohemian stance — locked as it is in the binary opposition of the Australian versus the English, the democratic versus the genteel — a contrived self-limitation. By this, I mean the cultivated manly robustness by which the nationalists marked themselves off against the imputed effeteness of colonial Anglophilia. But also part of what I mean is the *posture* that this seems to have entailed, and the attendant implication that the adopted larrikin mirror-image can also be seen as a self-concealing mask, an expression of self that is at the same time a withholding. "They weren't troubled much with toffs/When they were pioneering" (to quote Lawson's "On the Wallaby"); the accent of manly independence can easily slide into approving self-consciousness.

An excellent example of such an authorial persona can be seen in Edward Dyson's story, "The Conquering Bush" (reprinted in the Cantrell anthology, *The 1890s*).[7] What distinguishes this tale of female mental-breakdown amidst outback isolation, and makes it typical of what I'm talking about, is the particular way the account of insanity and suicide becomes a covert affirmative of the masculinity that copes where femininity goes to pieces:

> A baby was born, and Mrs. Darton went back with her husband to their hut by the creek on the great run, to the companionship of bears, birds, possums, kangaroos, and the eternal trees. She hugged her baby to her breast, and rejoiced that the little mite would give her something to think of that would keep the awful ring of the myriad locusts out of her ears.
> Man and wife settled down to their choking existence again as before, without comment. Ned was used to the bush — he had lived in it all of his life — and though its influence was powerful upon him he knew it not. He was necessarily away from home a good deal, and when at home he was not companionable, in the sense that city dwellers know. Two bushmen will sit together by the fire for hours, smoking and mute, enjoying each other's society; "in mute discourse" two bushmen will ride for twenty miles through the most desolate or the most fruitful region. People who have lived in crowds want talk, laughter, and song. Ned loved his wife, but he neither talked, laughed, nor sang. (*The 1890s*, pp.269-70)

The tone of this implies that the bushman-husband's eerie self-sufficiency is a mark of superiority — "People who have lived in crowds want talk, laughter and song". The wife's collapse in the bush, for all its sadness, is finally all that could be expected of the person introduced to us in the story as "Mrs. Black's sentimental daughter". One can sense the author's own masculine self-image in the implicit Puritan affirmation of this.

The appeal of such a stance to a male writer is obvious, of course, given the time and place. But in its refusal to contemplate the costs entailed by such a notion of stoic self-sufficiency — as against its awareness of the consequences of "weakness" — it offends against any ideal of "fullness of being" with which we might associate a post-

Romantic sense of Art and its social role. By contrast it is Lawson's "feminine sensitiveness" (the quality Stephens reproached him for in the well-known comparison with Paterson) which, in stories like "The Drover's Wife" and "Water Them Geraniums", restrains him from seeing the ability to live a radically attenuated life as simply a virtue, and which holds him back from even the *pose* of such a conviction. But Lawson, as his peers recognized, was an odd man out within the *Bulletin* tribe of urban Bohemian nomads.

Another way of putting this is to say that 90s Bohemian nationalism failed to articulate a satisfactory alternative to colonial gentility, in that its anti-bourgeois male protest was too simply just the opposite of snobbishly "feminine" bourgeois display culture. For as Richard White argues (and to me convincingly), the Bush Bohemians ideal closely parallels the Kiplingesque ideal of manliness that served as part of the late nineteenth-century ideology of British Imperialism.[8] Some years ago the critic, Marius Bewley, affirmed the importance in nineteenth-century American literary culture of a tradition, running from Adams and Cooper to Hawthorne and Henry James, which articulated critical opposition to the falsities of plutocratic gentility without ventriloquistally adopting, as did Mark Twain, a populist and Yankee-capitalist hostility to polite culture *per se*.[9] One correlate of *Bulletin* Bohemianism and its legacy has been that accomplished exponents of this "third way" have traditionally been thin on the ground in the Australian scene, so that it is to an unpleasantly arch Tory writer such as Martin Boyd (to take a later figure) that one must look for a radical detachment from and opposition to the Victorian bourgeois ideal of energetic manliness. I quote from Boyd's family saga, *The Montforts*:

> The five earnest Riley boys seemed always to be saying reverently, "Aunt Sophie," and "Uncle Ken." They told Raoul how good his mother was. They made a virtue or a business of every pleasure. They were at their worst in the bathing place. This was a deep green pool overhung by wattle trees. Raoul's delight in bathing was purely aesthetic. He loved to swim for the sake of the easy movement, or to sit idly, lower down the river, where the clear water rippled over the clean stones, and splashed round his shoulders. He loved the light on his bare skin. But bathing for them was merely a means of keeping cool, and of learning to swim in case of shipwreck. In slightly nasal, flat-vowelled voices they vied with one another in prowess. Then Uncle Fred joined the group. He splashed into the crowded pool and bumped against Raoul. The contact was sufficiently nauseating, but when Uncle Fred jocularly told him to keep his buttocks out of the road, he felt that he could endure the society of these intolerable relatives no longer, and swam by himself up-stream. The Rileys adored their father, and called him "Pop." In fact, they exhaled a warm undiscerning affection for every one.
>
> Raoul's mere physical presence was infuriating to Fred Riley. He disliked good looks in a boy, unless they were accompanied by excessive masculinity. Raoul's skin was clear and rosy, his hair pale gold, his eyes light blue, and his nose long and pointed.
>
> Every time that his uncle looked on Raoul's face he longed to hit it, or to disfigure it in some way. It became an obsession with him. He put his hatred of Raoul's face down to his hatred of unmanliness. Fred Riley's manliness was not the antithesis of effeminacy but of boyishness. The Greeks who, in battle, would spare the life of a beautiful youth, he would have regarded not as humane nor civilized, but as weak and unpatriotic. His own sons were no more courageous, and probably less truthful, than Raoul, but

they were less fastidious, a little dirtier, and they took their pleasures sadly; therefore, he considered them fine types of British manhood.

He spent an evening urging Kenneth to send Raoul to a boarding-school. It would make a man of him. (*The Montforts*, Penguin ed., pp.180-81).

It's not an endearing passage, with its rather thin-lipped fastidiousness and an uncompromising illiberalism beside which Henry James seems promiscuously genial in his sympathies: "in slightly-nasal, flat-vowelled voices they vied with one another in prowess"; and "The Riley's adored their father, and called him 'Pop'." (This is an early Boyd novel, lacking the authorial self-awareness evident, say, in the characterization of Paul in *Lucinda Brayford*.) Yet the obverse of this *hauteur* is a clear and perceptively detailed vision of the Puritan narrowness in what is, in fact, in the Rileys, White's "Coming Man" ideal. This goes with an equally sharp sense of humanly finer alternatives, and, most importantly, an absolute sureness in maintaining this viewpoint. Offensive as it may be to us, Boyd's conviction of class-superiority helps to free him from the stridency of the mainstream conception of the masculine. Such a radical perspective was beyond *Bulletin* Bohemianism in that its own kind of robustness was itself too close to the Riley kind to permit of clear differentiation. This would seem to be true even of the aggressive anti-Puritanism of Norman Lindsay, whose paradoxically nationalist neo-Baroque credo and rage against contemporary European artistic decadence would seem to grow straight out of an earlier *Bulletin* animus against Aestheticism. Lindsay's strenuously carnal nudes always contrive to seem more athletic than erotic, as if they'd really much rather be shearing a ram or two.

In Vance Palmer, self-conscious heir to *Bulletin* nationalism, the tension is even more explicit between the nationalist self-image and the sense of personal difference attendant upon being an artist and intellectual. David Walker's stimulating study of Palmer, *Dream and Disillusion*,[10] reveals how the nationalist stance of self-conscious robustness, with its heavy reliance on terms such as "masculine" and "feminine" as touchstones of approval and disparagement, co-exists with an unease about that side of himself that was more than generically male and national. This makes it hard not to speculate about the rugged personae of earlier nationalists, and sense the impulse beyond or behind the posturing. Walker emphasizes the crucially formative effect on Palmer's world-view of his residence as a tutor on the Abbieglassie station in North Queensland; and he cites a letter to Palmer's future wife that seems to adopt the viewpoint of the station people in judgment of his own intellectual and cultural aspirations, whilst at the same time taking pride in his ability to fit into their standards:

["They look with] distrust if not contempt on all my pet vanities, my literary ambitions and my attempts at culture but treat me with respect for qualities I had forgotten — a good seat in the saddle when taking a stiff log, a discreditable knowledge of racing." (Letter in 1909; cited from Walker, p.42)

It's a well-known fact the De Tocqueville's ideas about the "levelling" effect of cultural democracy have been behind much writing on Australian culture. Documents such as this confirm one's suspicions that one motive behind a good deal of the democratic idealism of the Palmer variety has been the intellectual tall poppy's embarrassment at

its own vulnerable conspicuousness, and a consequent wish to obligingly
cut itself down to size, or at least shroud its difference within an even
self-deceiving smokescreen of egalitariansim. That such a difference can
never quite be concealed, however, would seem to be the saving virtue
of Palmer's work. In Palmer's *The Legend of the Nineties* this is
apparent in a flexibility of critical judgment that goes beyond what his
use of the masculine-feminine dichotomy might lead us to expect.
Moreover, stories such as the classic *Rainbow-Bird* show a kind of
"feminine sensitivity" that brings to mind the D.H. Lawrence whom
Palmer elsewhere critically damned. It must also be said that Palmer's
idea of masculinity can be much richer than that of the stoicism of
national mythology. Lew Calloway, for instance, the heroic male in
The Passage, is depicted in terms of a communion with Nature that at
different times recalls both Gabriel Oak and Huck Finn, rather than the
conventional legend's sense of Nature as adversary. (The sub-tropical
setting of the novel is of course relevant here.) Even an early story
from *The World of Men* such as "Father and Son" is marked by a
Conradian ambivalence about the worth of the dour emotional self-
control it seems to celebrate. (In painting a similar ambiguity also seems
to complicate Albert Tucker's excursions into Australian mythology, in
that the peculiarly dead-alive quality of these can be seen to represent a
withdrawal from the highly personal and disturbed emotionality of the
early work.)

Perhaps the most sustained expression of embarrassment at individual
difference that I know of in Australian literature, however, is George
Johnston's *My Brother Jack*. Indeed, this novel has always struck me as
a symptomatically important cultural text for this very reason. Its
representative suggestiveness in this is at one with what makes the book
unusual, for its quasi-autobiographical and confessional mode commits
it to a full disclosure of the self-disliking singularity that the more
conventional strategies of Australian narrative keep well hidden. To me,
anyway, David Meredith's narrative stands as the classic revelation of a
distinctively Australian Bohemian intellectual's insecurity about that part
of the self which cannot be reflected back by the noble larrikin image
— a dimension of self without which, nevertheless, neither Bohemianism
nor intellectuality can genuinely exist. For the obverse side of the
author-narrator's portrait of brother Jack as noble larrikin is his gratingly
relentless deprecation of what in himself differs from this traditional
ideal. Doubtless, we can see some of this self-dislike as rationally
motivated by material presented within the book, or (as Gary Kinnane
has recently argued) as influenced by Johnston's own unhappy personal
situation at the time of writing the novel.[11] Nevertheless, there does
seem to be a more general, culturally symptomatic significance in the
way in which, for instance, Johnston-Meredith interprets and evaluates,
in recall, the adolescent sitrrings of his artistic sensibility:

> Gradually, however, a secret desire began to germinate in my mind. I wanted
> to write. It began with poems, but they were very strange poems to emerge
> out of the Melbourne suburbs, because I had read *Heimskringla* and become
> obsessed by the Viking sagas and I filled whole exercise books with bad verses
> about berserk fighting men and beaked long-ships filled with corpses:

> Wildly they rolled, tightly locked on seas riven,
> Bound in war's embrace, the black ship and red:
> Corpse-ring was theirs, for the raven, unshriven,
> Had croaked in the night for the Skardaborg dead.

I kept the exercise books hidden in my mattress, in case Jack should find them. I knew that as poetry the stuff was worthless, yet the exercise books represented a privacy which I felt to be important . . . too important to survive Jack's derision.

It never occurred to me that Jack, for all his crudity and insensitivity, might have been right, and I wrong. I could not have realised then that I was beginning to fabricate a pattern which I would continue to work on for years, a pattern of evasion, where I could establish my own sense of belief and of security only in some area of the imagination that was as remote in time and place as the Norse longships, and as dissociated from the troubling present that existed all around me. Fumbling, hardly even conscious of what I was doing, I was setting out to try to side-step a world I didn't have the courage to face.

But Jack still refused to side-step anything, even the baffling nature of his own brother.

"You've got to get rid of those sonky bloody cobbers of yours," he said to me one night. "The way you lot are heading you'll end up a bunch of tonks. Why the blazes don't you get out and chase a tart or two?"

"Because I don't want to." (*My Brother Jack*, p.59)

Of course, there is *some* plausibility in this retrospective acceptance of Jack's viewpoint: the most enlightened parent might wish, say, for a more varied circle of friends for his son than the one David has just described on the previous page. Likewise the particularly gory subject of those verses tells a sad tale, in that it is chosen by a boy who has just previously confessed to the playground fiasco of having beaten up an enfeebled epileptic in desperate emulation of his brother's prowess. Yet in this self-flagellating urge to present a portrait of the artist as a young wimp, I think we have a full spelling out of that tendency towards a false denial of personal difference, a quasi-chameleon-like self-levelling, that I am arguing is the hidden premise on which traditionally-Australian larrikin-Bohemianism has been based. Only this, I think, can explain the unbalanced tough-mindedness with which David dismisses his fascination with the alien and the remote (arguably the fledgling Romanticism of any artistic sensibility) as simply evasion.

Elsewhere the novel offers a useful account of the formation of David's insecurity within the dynamics of his own lower middle-class family. The malignant Fred Riley who persecutes Boyd's Raoul is an easily despicable uncle who lacks influence within the immediate family; he is not the seductively admirable elder brother that the "typically Australian" Jack is for David. Johnston offers a perceptive sequel to these scenes in the episode where, to David's surprise and chagrin, Jack hits it off famously with the flamboyant Bohemian, Sam Burlington, David's first extra-familial "role-model":

Jack was still tensed and watchful, but I could see that he was a little bewildered too. His handshake with Sam was cordial enough. And Sam beamed at him. Sam liked to meet things full on, too. He tossed an instruction over his shoulder — "For heaven's sake, Jess, do open a window or two; the place stinks like a tart's shop!" — and then he clapped Jack on the shoulder in the friendliest possible way and said, "You just make yourself absolutely at home, Taffrail old cock, while the rest of us organise the orgy."

"His name is Jack," I said in a thick hoarse voice.

Sam's laugh snorted out. "Jack, Taffrail, Jibboom, what does it matter? he said expansively. "Does he know how to broach a niner and get the bung in, that's the point?" He waved at the nine-gallon keg of beer, which had been propped up on the sofa.

"My bloody oath he does!" said Jack enthusiastically.

Had I been a little older or a little wiser I might have known that Jack and Sam Burlington would have got on famously with each other. They were only total opposites superficially; their impulses were similar and they shared the same extravagances. (*My Brother Jack*, pp.100-101)

The approval with which Meredith-Johnston reports Burlington's seemingly rather heavy cameraderie, speaks volumes about the general cultural situation I am trying to describe. The same applies, of course, to the concluding comment of the passage I am quoting ("They were only opposites superficially", etc.) This is offered as the fruit of personal maturity, but it could more accurately be seen as the conventional ideology of Australian male bohemianism, epitomizing both its strengths and limitations. Such an ideology can seem to provide a satisfactory basis for defying the Puritan wowserishness evoked by the Jessica Wray case, or the bourgeois status-seeking of the famous satire of life in upwardly-mobile suburbia. But its capacity to undermine David's confidence in his own artistic individuality, forcing him to see himself as weak in the light of its standards, and shaping the novel's autobiographic self-understanding into a hard-boiled tale of simply "making-it", bespeaks its own kind of Puritanism. Perhaps nothing illustrates this more sadly than the way in which the adult narrator, still bearing the label of "sonk" (and crypto-"tonk") that Jack has pinned upon him in boyhood, characterizes what he sees as Jack's earthiness with a comment such as "the prospect of 'landing a sheila' would fill him with the same kind of gluttonous rapture as a second or third helping of his favourite food, which continued to be Mother's steamed jam roly-poly" (*My Brother Jack*, p.54). It's likewise significant that Burlington's studio is said to boast "a whole collection of the naughtier Norman Lindsay prints" (p.96).

An important contemporary variation on this peculiarly Australian complication in the (male) authorial sense of self can be seen in the "new wave" drama of the 1960s and 1970s, especially in the work of playwrights like Williamson, Hibberd and Oakley. This new variant appears in their ambivalence about "ockerism", which critics are (see, for instance, Peter Fitzpatrick in John Carroll (ed.), *Intruders in the Bush*, 1982, ch.10). On the one hand, the plays share a satiric sense of what they see as "ockerism" with that whole post-Humphreys ethos that brought the term into vogue. Yet at the same time the dramatic conflicts in a number of the plays echo the traditional theme of larrikin-Bohemianism — masculine vernacular earthiness versus feminine cultural pretension — in a way that continually redeems the "ockerish" object of satire into the larrikin hero of neo-nationalist comedy of manners. Robbed of stature in one way by being transported from the bush to the pub or the party, this new figure is reinvested with the strengths of wit and sardonic eloquence in, to use Russel Ward's words, "decrying affectation". I want to argue that it is in this ambivalence, this persisting in having things both ways, that the plays' culturally symptomatic significance lies. But we can best approach this large issue by looking in some detail at some of the relevant episodes in one of the by now, as it were, "classic" works in this mould, *Don's Party*.

One of the recurring interactions in this play is that between the arch-"ocker" Cooley, and Kerry, the one woman in the play with intellectual and artistic aspirations. In a sequence of exchanges, Cooley assails and finally seduces her with a display of consciously outrageous sexual crudity. Cooley is in one sense distinctly awful, and meant to be so — part of Williamson's attempt at a study of sexism. Yet given that Kerry herself is a satiric stereotype of the "liberated" woman as pretentious opportunist, Cooley's brutally debunking retorts to her modish chatter have an inevitable and surely intended audience appeal. Given her waffling hypocritically on about "organic relationships" whilst moving with Cooley towards the bedroom, we are surely meant to applaud the wit of his quip, "Organ first . . . relationship later", so that the ocker performance ceases to be simply sexist, and stands more than half-condoned as a manly puncturing of feminine cultural pretensions. Likewise the predictable selectivity informing the characterization reveals a residual sexism in the play itself, despite its diagnostic efforts. It is implicated in the same pattern of stereotypes as that by which the male characters think and act.

The same uncertainty of authorial position appears in the play's treatment of Simon, the Liberal-voting outsider at the party, whom Cooley instantly labels "the poofter with the poker up his arse". Here again, analogous to the Kerry-Cooley presentation, Williamson seems in two minds about whether he's developing his analysis of ockerishness by letting it display itself in reaction to Simon, or simply using Simon himself for a bit of good old Aussie poofter-bashing fun. The opening of the play, in which a comparison of Simon with Don is established, just *might* be seen as portending the former. In contrast to Don's amiable ineptness as a host, Simon's genuine good manners look well; and lest we be tempted to see Don's remissness here as simply a part of his boyish charm, the play underscores the point with references to his wife being on anti-depressants and by having her ask her husband to show her some affection in public during the evening. These details reveal Don's opening forgetfulness of his guests as just a surface sign of a more fundamental absence as a husband and a resolved character: something that issues later as gormless passivity in the face of the manoeuvrings of the sexually aggressive Susan. As against this, Simon, in the opening scene, has what seems like an effective social presence, and also the good grace to extricate himself from invidious comparison with Don's vagueness as host: he comments to Kath (Don's wife) that being a responsible host at his own parties has actually prevented him from enjoying himself.

Yet despite this opening impression, it's not long before Simon turns out to be no more than the wimp Cooley and the boys assume him to be. Williamson's initial notes for Simon's stage appearance stipulate a handsomeness that is "a little bit too effete and prissy". And as the other men move in for a bit of robust humiliation of him by seducing *his* wife, Simon's responses are as wetly pathetic as his wife's are bubblingly randy: in both, the reactions move smoothly to the dictates of the "ockerish" stereotype that vindicates the behavior of the sexual aggressors. Given this, the possibility that Simon might represent some alternative masculinity, or is at least someone from whom the other men have something to learn, is hopelessly blurred. Are Simon's good manners really a positive foil for Don's inadequacies, or just another side of his general daggishness? The play itself seems uncertain about this, although it's only too sure that those other signs of his non-"ockerish" sophistication, like his interest in quality films, are by definition as laughable as Kerry's artistic pretensions. "Did you get along to the film festival this year?" (p.44); "Has anyone seen *Exterminating Angel?*" (p.82): these frail little conversational gambits are ruthlessly positioned in the play so as to come across as simply awkward attempts to break uneasy silences, making the interests themselves seem stilted and unreal by implication. Which all goes towards making Simon in the end little more than living proof of the old adage that men with high cultural interests are poofters, and that both are equally contemptible.

But what then are we to make of the fact that Don and the boys not only are tertiary-educated (in the Humanities too), but pride themselves on it? In its stylized way, the play does "reflect" one kind of "new middle class" milieu. Don is a novelist *manque*, for instance, and Mal a psychologist. One of the play's most acute touches in its portrayal of these men is its rendering of the particular *kind* of intellectuality that expresses itself in the running commentary on the election, which bonds them together through the play like a higher form of "footy" gossip. Critical comment on the election-night device has concentrated on the ironic contrast between political idealism and personal squalor, or the parallel between the rise and fall of Labor's hopes (it's the 1969 election) and the fluctuation of events within the party. To me, however, its most important function is to display a recognizable form of masculine intellectual *style*. That style is at once intellectual and impeccably hard-nosed: in its gestures of ideological commitment, its inside dopester's knowingness, and its analytic toying with facts and figures. It is not really incompatible with the men's attitudes to women or high culture. It's no accident that one of the first comments to come from Mal, the most overtly predatory male after Cooley, is that he has "had a few beers with Whitlam's press secretary last Friday" (p.23). This mode neatly matches the men's wit, which is aspiringly intellectual in its range of reference and its appeal to "enlightened" attitudes, yet also limitingly *macho* in the sardonic tone in which it is forever imprisoned:

JENNY: (to Cooley) What happened to your air hostess, she was nice.
COOLEY: She had what they call a virgin cortex. No original thought had ever penetrated.

Of the men, it is Don who to me is the most interesting — or at least the most complex. Williamson depicts in him uncertainties and ambivalences that we can sense in the play itself. This is nicely brought out, for instance, in his new outer-suburban enthusiasm for "native plants" (a taste which in a 1971 text still have overtones of ideological correctness that hark back to David Meredith's gum rebellion in *My Brother Jack*). Williamson's point is made in the way Don can only introduce this new interest into conversation with his mates by at the same time sending it up. This suppressed horticulturalism, so to speak, has thus a function in the text analogous to that of the child, whose existence we are first made aware of when it awakes during the farce-like but sadly humorous conclusion of the play. Both are potent absences from the main stage-action, so that they nevertheless define the boorish squalor of what *is* present. Both indicate a gentling in Don that has in some sense taken place, but which he still has not sufficiently acknowledged to the point of socially committing himself to.

All of this would seem to tell us something important, not just about a continuity in the national literature, but beyond this, something about masculine identity within the general culture of the "new middle class" in Australia. For it reveals — and indeed enacts and exemplifies — the confused blend of newly adopted (and imported) ideas, understandings, models of behavior, and resistance to these. In the play's own way and its chosen milieu, it catches what to me seems "the *note* of the cultural present" within this class. On the one hand, the "ockerish" sexism of the men in the play has the intellectual pretension of being reinforced by the attitudes of the 60s sexual revolution. On the other, Don's "gentler side", and the play's sympathy with this and its perspective on sexism, clearly shows the impress on Williamson of a certain kind of contemporary feminism that we can associate with the "humanistic" psychology of the 1960s' counter-culture and its legacy. His ambivalence and hesitancy about this exemplifies the muddled path of assimilation such attitudes have had within "new middle class culture". We might even see this ambivalence about change and growth as deriving from the social and cultural mobility that has been such an important factor in the formation of the culture and identity of this class.

Similar significances can also be drawn from other plays in the Australian Performing Group (A.P.G.) mode, most notably those of Jack Hibberd — or, in the novel, in the work of David Ireland and — much more appealingly — Peter Mathers.[12] At the moment, however, I want to focus upon a somewhat lesser known work in the A.P.G. mode written four years after *Don's Party*: Barry Oakley's *Bedfellows*. This too celebrates the sardonic ebullience of its "ockerishly" intellectual leading male, while at the same time being a serio-comic exposure of the inadequacies which this "aggressively vernacular" habit masks. In one sense, Oakley's choosing to make the two male characters a lecturer in English and a writer is a way of heightening the gestures of masculine resentment into literary eloquence:

CAROL: Shut up and put the cat out.
PAUL: The bottles and the cat — all out. All over Australia the cats and bottles are going out. One night they'll all be put out all at the same moment and the entire continent will tremble to the cosmic thump of cats. (p.9)

The play's theatricality is largely a matter of such fanciful performances. Nevertheless, even more than in *Don's Party*, there are poignant intimations of possibilities being forfeited by the "educated ocker" synthesis, moments in which the play's awareness of what the intellectual *macho* style suppresses. And this declares it to be speaking within the discourse of the contemporary humanistic psychology that its own taste for the flamboyantly sardonic is at once madly resisting.

One important aspect of the play's working out of this conflict is that it does it in terms that restate the traditional Australian puzzlement about the relevance or irrelevance of old-world "high culture". At the beginning of Part Two, the lecturer in English, Paul, pays an avenging late-night visit to writer Bill, erstwhile friend and rival, whose adultery with his wife he has just discovered. He announces himself with a standard literary joke, comparing himself to Coleridge's "person from Porlock". He then elaborates his reference by quoting the last eight lines from Kubla Khan, pushing his meaning beyond the standard Porlock analogy in doing so, and weaving into it an allusive comparison between himself and Hamlet in a private reference to Bill's actions. In having an affair with Carol, Bill has indeed, as far as Paul is concerned, "fed . . . on honey dew" and "drunk the milk of Paradise". What the ostensibly untheatrical length of the quotation does, I think, is rupture the sardonically harsh surface of the dialogue, and create a moment in which there shines through, in Paul's feeling for his wife, a rarely expressed lyricism and Romantic wonder. The moment is poignant because rare, and rare partially because it is so incompatible with the toughly sardonic persona Paul otherwise projects in his marriage as we see it. Natural and theatrically entertaining though this persona generally is, a moment such as this shows it as limited and defensive. Oakley achieves a similar effect in the contrast of different kinds of music throughout the play, evoking the forfeited Romantic promise of Paul and Carol's marriage through the insertion into the action of Ravel's "Daphnis and Chloe" suite, which they associate with their first meetings. In thus associating emotional repression of the feminine — the key concept of counter-culturally derived psychological discourse — with an aesthetic suppression of the old-world "high-cultural", the play significantly complicates the terms of the traditional cultural debate it is invoking.

It's this last point, perhaps, that enables me to attempt some concluding comparison between the "flavour" of Bohemianism in contemporary "new middle class culture" and the traditional *Bulletin* Bohemianism that preceded it. The latter, one might say, projects at least the impression of definiteness and clarity in being able to act out *ostensibly* an identity based on the antitheses discussed above. Such a simplicity is no longer possible in the present, however, as the influence of a view of the self and of human relations derived from the counter-culture and ancillary movements such as humanistic feminism, has made the old male-oriented Bohemian-larrikinism untenable. It persists, of course, as the "educated ockers" of the A.P.G. plays testify; but it is with a guilty self-consciousness, and an awareness of alternative possibilities that makes it either defensive or conversion-prone. Hence the nervously uncertain stance of the plays: at one moment looking at "educated ockerism" from the vantage-point of a new emphasis on a feminine *gentleness* — an emphasis that cannot be dismissively equated with the traditionally genteel; yet at the next moment seeming to deny this new growth and enhanced identity by defiantly reaffirming old postures.

Nevertheless, if this uncertainty suggests something painful and problematic about the contemporary cultural situation, a tension-free attitude of progressivism would not be desirable. Williamson's latest play but one, *The Perfectionist*, is instructive here. The main action of the play traces the conversion of its chief character, the highly competitive, emotionally ungiving and sexist Stuart, "The Perfectionist", into a disciple of feminism, a new masculinity, a renegotiated marriage, etc. At first, it seems like a smooth unravelling of the tangled impulses and contrary directions of *Don's Party*: so smooth, in fact, as to be monotonously conventional. Hence my relief on reading on to find the new Stuart deliberately presented as as much of a pain as the old one, so that his only really endearing speech in the play is his confession on the last page that he is "getting fed up to the back teeth with emotional honesty and interpersonal warmth." Such a last-minute eruption of larrikin scepticism reminds us that traditional "Australian" still has something to contribute, besides obfuscation and defensiveness, to the reception and modification of imported culturally-progressive influences. For while I have been expressing hostility to larrikin-Bohemianism as a rigidly sustained attitude, I totally favour it as a strategic, deflating manoeuvre at moments when laudable sympathies or commendable attitudes become pious, too self-congratulatory.

We must hope that this national form of common-sense continues to be used, but with a tact that recognizes that its value is strategic, and its relevance thus circumstantial and momentary. There is a nice literary model of this in a recent poem by Chris Wallace-Crabbe, which seems to me (if I'm reading it properly) to exemplify, in the way it tackles the old cultural chestnut about the European and Australian, what such a gesture of larrikin *good* manners might be like. It's called "Stuff Your Classical Heritage", though despite this title, its style leans heavily on a manner of address perfected by Wallace Stevens. As I read it, the larrikin rejection of the European past which the title announces is one that urbanely *knows* itself to be temporary and strategic, a postponement of a proper, inevitable later reconciliation, in order to enjoy for the time being the Australian present:

> Gull, grevillea, galvo, Gippsland, grit —
> just singing out the chorus, bit by bit
> will get me some purchase on the primal scene.
>
> What do I say by seeing and then saying
> a ragged strip of bark rips itself off
> the slender limblike trunk of a manna gum
>
> with faintest crumbling noise?
>   Call it said,
> call it commitment to a twiggy particular
> fawn-scumbled slope or terra-cotta roof.

By naming, I seem to crush the past
like a mattress, hard down in history's
rusty cabin-trunk: stick it in the cellar.

In a way I preach the destruction of Europe,
that mental Europe which I love so much.
Cancel it. Smother it with ripe new words

or old ones triumphantly misapplied,
every solecism a seal of triumph
as light gilds a scraggy bacon-and-egg plant.

Keep Jehovah in his place with Bathurst burrs
where things are wiry, scrabbled, porous, drooped
for Oedipus romping through the undergrowth

every bit as gaudy as
those three dippingly quick rosellas
or a Violet Crumble wrapper. (*Southerly*, No.3, 1984, p.271)

All the writers I've discussed belong to a male tradition in Australian literature. Certainly, a personal compliance with a culturally-defined sense of masculinity is a crucial factor in the "syndrome" I've been outlining. It consequently comes as no great surprise to realize that women such as Katharine Prichard and Dorothy Hewett have been able to accommodate the psychological imperatives of the Romantic legacy much more confidently into their work, though the kind of reading that D.R. Burns has offered of *The Fortunes of Richard Mahoney* is cognate with the general thrust of my argument, as well as being central to his.[13] Nevertheless one can only hope that an intelligent and authentic assimilation of humanistic feminism will make a similar confidence more generally available to male writers as well. Of course, such an outcome will by no means be just a matter of individual achievement, in life or in literature. It will also be a matter of tensions resolved and a poise attained within the culture (Australian? "new middle class"?) from which individual artists and intellectuals and their works derive.

1987

Notes

[1]   See, for instance, Patrick Morgan, "Hard Work and Idle Dissipation: the Dual Australian Personality", *Meanjin*, XLI, 1982, 130-37.

[2]   Graeme Turner, *National Fictions: Literature, film and the construction of Australian narrative*, Sydney, 1986.

[3]   D.R. Burns, *The Directions of Australian Fiction, 1920-1974*, Melbourne, 1975, p.112.

[4]   *National Fictions*, p.92 ff.

[5]   Richard White, *Inventing Australia*, Sydney, 1981.

[6]   Graeme Davison, "Sydney and the Bush", in John Carroll, ed., *Intruders in the Bush*, Melbourne, 1982.

[7]   Leon Cantrell, ed., *The 1890s*, St. Lucia, Qld., 1977.

[8]   *Inventing Australia*, see esp. ch. 6.

9   Marius Bewley, *The Complex Fate*, New York, 1967.

10 David Walker, *Dream and Disillusion*, Canberra, 1976.

11 Garry Kinnane, *George Johnston: a Life*, Melbourne, 1986.

12 For a relevant critique of Ireland here see the chapter by P. Elkin in Shirley Walker (ed.), *Who is She?*, St. Lucia, Qld., 1984.

13 *The Directions of Australian Fiction, 1920-1974*. Prichard's *Coonardoo* can be seen as a critical engagement, from *within* the terms of Australian mythology, with the male ideal of Puritan-stoic self-sufficiency discussed above.

LOUISE HANSON-DYER:
THE EMERGENCE OF A PATRON

JIM DAVIDSON

Louise Hanson-Dyer's is a life that spans the period from 1884 to 1962, beginning in the Melbourne of the Land Boom and ending in Grace Kelly's Monaco. At one end of the arch stands her father, L.L. Smith, a Member of Parliament who did not scruple to physically attack his opponents in the House, Trustee of the Exhibition Buildings, friend of Tom Roberts, promoter of coal exploration and internationally-acclaimed viticulturist, theatrical entrepreneur, successful racehorse owner, and rider, pamphleteer, inventor of patent medicines, and very likely an abortionist. And, at the other, the first major recordings made by Joan Sutherland, Janet Baker, Neville Marriner and Colin Davis.

For Louise Hanson-Dyer was perhaps the last great individual patron in music. If one consults the *Oxford Companion to Music*, the article on Patronage will be found to list a number of benefactors in the section entitled "The Present Day", but these are all bequests or endowments, rather than the active exercise of patronage in the old, immediate sense. Louise Hanson-Dyer alone is mentioned in that capacity. She was probably aware of the anomaly. The only underlining to be found in one of her books of press cuttings is the following passage, from an address of the President of the [English] Board of Education (*c.* 1930): "He reminded them that the state of the arts depends on public taste, and upon patronage, in these days the democratic patronage of the public at large and of public authorities, instead of that of an aristocracy". Between public taste on one hand, and aristocracy on the other, lay an ambience which Louise would galvanize as her own. After all, as she told the French in a broadcast, the singular characteristic of Australian women was that they were adaptable.

When she settled down in Paris in 1928, having left Melbourne the year before, Louise created a salon of sorts which drew the composers Arthur Honneger, Darius Milhaud and Albert Roussel, the artists Zadkine and Prax, and, quite often, James Joyce. (Ezra Pound in fact wrote to Joyce to ask him to persuade Louise to publish the music for viols by the seventeenth-century composer John Jenkins.) There was also a supporting cast of Australians, *en passant*, whether music students, socialites, or singers such as John Brownlee.

Then, in 1933, to mark the bicentenary of the death of Francois Couperin— called le Grand — she published an edition, running to a dozen volumes, of all his works. Thus was born the Editions de l'Oiseau-Lyre — the name a marvellous congruence of musical metaphor and homage to her homeland — which became renowned for their quality. After careful preparation of new editions by musicologists, the works were printed on specially treated paper, designed to last for some hundreds of years; the best binders and designers in Paris were commissioned to work on the project. In short, even the so-called ordinary editions — for there was a deluxe one in red vellum with the bird insignia embossed in gold — were as far removed from customary notions of sheet music as possible. Launched by the President of France, the Couperin edition was to be merely the first of a series. Subsequent volumes included sonatas of Purcell and John Blow, *Trésor de Musique Byzantine, Polyphonies of the Thirteenth Century* in four volumes, and the still continuing *Polyphonies of the Fourteenth Century,* which will probably run to thirty volumes before the series is completed. Then, in 1938, recordings began — initially of Couperin and Rameau, but also of some modern music. In 1949 Louise Hanson-Dyer made what were the first long-playing records in France, and for the next ten years the white lyrebird insignia on different grounds became the way to identify her recordings immediately. Again, Couperin figured prominently; sixteen LPs of the entire harpsichord music appeared in 1955. In collaboration with people such as the brilliant English musicologist Thurston Dart and the conductor Anthony Lewis, she was the first to record complete Handel operas, the Monteverdi *Vespers*, and the stage works of Purcell — recordings that remain, years after, brilliant in their clarity. There was also some recording of works by Schönberg, Milhaud and Stravinsky.

Both the Oiseau-Lyre press and the recording company still exist. The latter is now a subdivision of Decca, while the first operates from Monaco, where it continues in association with the University of Melbourne, the main Australian beneficiary of Louise Hanson-Dyer's will. In a sense this partnership is appropriate, for Louise Hanson-Dyer's interest in baroque music first took flight in Melbourne, while her concern for music generally was of such a nature — and of such intensity — that it impelled her towards Paris, where she first located her press. Paris she saw as the intellectual capital of the world, without any notion of rejecting, or even discarding, Australia.

To some she must have seemed a somewhat wacky socialite — tall and striking, flamboyantly dressed, bustling, often humourless and self-absorbed. Politics did not interest her, except as a spectator. She was quite friendly with Evatt, and took a lofty interest in the problems confronting the Popular Front government in France in 1936. She had curiosity, a broad tolerance, and an acceptance of the varieties of human behaviour; also an engaging innocence, which enabled her to shut out from view that which she did not wish to see. A useful facility for a patron, and she was a patron of distinction, since she also possessed energy in abundance, great intelligence, a capacity for organizing and inspiring others, and a taste that was emphatic rather than absolute: a combination of high style, high standards, and brilliant opportunism. To which must be added, wealth.

What were the ingredients that went to make this brilliant career? First was her family. L.L. Smith, an entrepreneur, had a mother who was an actress. (She was also French, *née* Gengoult, which helps to explain Louise's predisposition, despite its late emergence.) L.L. Smith's house at the top of Collins Street was frequented by politicians, artists, musicians — Tommy Bent and Tom Roberts among them. For a daughter indulged by her father, flamboyance was thus but a corollary of this context. Maie Casey, who grew up next door, recalling the many parties given by the Smiths, added: "I was told that the appearance of the central figure, Louise, dressed always to surprise, had something of the shock and excitement of an Act of Nature . . ."

But family will explain only so much. Of the three children by L.L. Smith's second marriage to reach adulthood, two were intensely musical. One was not: like his father he became a doctor, and then three times Lord Mayor of Melbourne, was knighted Sir Harold Gengoult Smith, and had a royal duke as godfather to his children. As he stated, when elected Lord Mayor, he preferred things "as they are'. The other brother, Louis, was a dashing army officer, who, his widow recalled sixty years later, marched off to war like a dancer. He was killed on the Somme: he had been an accomplished violinist.

Louise's own chosen instrument was the piano. She progressed through a series of examinations, eventually, in 1905 (at the age of 21) qualifying as a Licentiate of the Associated Board (of the Royal Academy of Music & the Royal College of Music, London); she could, if she chose, teach. But, even though she was awarded the gold medal as the outstanding performer of her year, she rarely chose to play in public.

Why? It is a puzzle, for someone so naturally an exhibitionist; it may even be that her perfectionism was in part a pretext for not performing directly herself. The explanation might be that she had received some particularly devastating snub. "Louise Smith tried too hard . . ." So, I am told, thought G.W.L. Marshall-Hall, the Ormond Professor of Music, composer and powerful artistic personality; at the time when Louise was coming out he was very closely involved with the Pinschofs, Carl and Elisabeth, who as Elisabeth Wiedermann was a notable opera singer. At their home, Studley Hall in Kew, now Burke Hall, they held *soirées*, brilliant, exclusive. How did a young girl, ambitious, but the daughter of a putative abortionist, make an impression on a household that was also the Austro-Hungarian consulate, and whose leading musical light had had a symphony considered for performance by no less than the great conductor Arthur Nikisch? Patronage thus emerged, perhaps, as a kind of sublimation, a way of beating the Pinschofs at their own game.

Yet Marshall-Hall certainly would have had some impact on the young Louise, even if he did not take much notice of her directly. We know that she attended special orchestral concerts for children, and there's no doubt that she attended others: the Melbourne Town Hall is no great distance from 41 Collins Street. Here she would have first heard not only the standard repertoire, but Debussy and Ravel, life-long enthusiasms — and from the baton of a conductor held in the very highest repute by those travelling English musicians who happened to have heard him. Equally important, the great *brouhaha* over Marshall-Hall's deposition as Ormond Professor, and the intense manifestations of public support — one thinks of the flowers and placards that were flaunted at a concert in 1900 — must have made a deep impression on the sixteen year-old Louise. Music *mattered*; and nowhere else in the English-speaking world, except London, was Art locked in such a desperate struggle with the *bourgeoisie*. It was almost a colonial counterpoint to the Wilde affair. It is also possible that the demise of the Marshall-Hall Orchestra in 1912, in a rising tide of acrimony, might have suggested the desirability, if not the necessity, of working with smaller ensembles — an ideal prerequisite for an interest in Baroque music.

Interestingly enough, the second great musical influence in her life, Dr Whittaker of Newcastle-on-Tyne, attacked Sir Thomas Beecham — in an article syndicated in Australia — for equating music with opera and orchestras. "He forgets that England was a musical nation long before such things as orchestras existed, and before men had conceived the idea of opera." Whittaker was a populist, and endorsed the views of Sir Henry Hadow, who believed that "the general public is capable of appreciating the best music, and that there are few people who are not open to the right impressions, but that the deplorable taste evinced by the majority is due to the fact that they are fed upon garbage, and that they have not had a reasonable opportunity of distinguishing between good and bad". Thus he enthused about the pianola roll, and the opportunity it gave to bring first class performances into every home. All of the foregoing came to be assumed by Louise, and in part adapted by her to meet Australian conditions; in Melbourne she became involved with the Aeolian Company, which produced the rolls.

Finally, it seems that on her trip to France in 1920 — her sixth or seventh to Europe — she came across French Baroque music for the first time: a program of it was put on in Melbourne by the Alliance Francaise in 1922, under her sponsorship. On a subsequent visit she met Henry Prunières, editor of a leading French musicological journal and a scholar intent on republishing the works by Lully. Later she was to join him in that venture, for Lully s music seems to have made a profound impression on her. Part of the explanation may lie in her great interest in things visual, and in ballet: the music lent itself to *tableaux* even when not specifically written for them. But exactly why the impact was so strong is not clear. It is far more usual for *cognoscenti* to respond to the intricacies of Rameau and Couperin than to the four-square rhythms of Lully; perhaps its relative simplicity suggested that it might lend itself to productions in Melbourne.

One of the most striking things about Louise Hanson-Dyer is her slowness to emerge. She was 49 when the Couperin edition was launched in 1933, signalling her brilliant European phase; it is an age at which many people would have given up. In Melbourne, she married at 27 — relatively late — the dapper, kindly, but somewhat dull denizen of Flinders Lane, Jimmy Dyer, called in the press "the lineoleum king" He was twenty-five years older than she. It seems likely that she married partly for money, but not entirely. Her father had died the year before; it does not seem glib to imagine that she needed someone to replace him. And that, perhaps, more than a grand passion — there seem to have been no boyfriends, not even in the genteel Edwardian sense of the term. This was to come later: when in her fifties she fell in love with the scholarly J.B. Hanson, twenty-four years her junior. For the moment, there were shrinking personal horizons. At some stage early in the marriage she had a miscarriage. So by the age of 34 she had lost all prospects of having children, plus her father, her brother killed in France, and years before, her little sister Gladys, killed before the family's eyes by a boulder that rolled down a hillside at Berwick. Married as she was to an ageing man, it is not surprising that she should become more and more anxious about posterity, and ways of leaving a mark upon it. Her introduction to the Couperin edition speaks, quite explicitly, of aiming to cross time and space, it was to be a monument.

But how to reach it, given a gnawing self-doubt? Her first sphere of operations was her old school, the Presbyterian Ladies College, Melbourne. Louise Hanson-Dyer was not the least remarkable of a group of women who passed through its portals in the late nineteenth century: Henry Handel Richardson, Nettie Palmer, Dame Nellie Melba. She became Secretary of the Old Girls' Association, and in 1919-1920, President. There's no doubt that it acted as some necessary form of approval, of ratification; for the effect was immediate and liberating. She had proved that she could convene brilliant social occasions; she could now turn to the cultural matters nearest her heart.

Close to hand was the example of the Liedertafel, which her husband Jimmy had joined in 1885 as a tenor. After a period as Vice-President, he became President of the society in 1918. The Liedertafel were Germanic singing clubs; in late nineteenth century Melbourne, when the Germans comprised the largest foreign community, there had been three of them. Times were different now: during the war, in their eagerness to dissociate themselves from the enemy, the comparable body in Sydney became the Apollo Club; in Victoria, metamorphosis brought the Royal Liedertafel Society, a cumbersome royal coat-of-arms firmly surmounting the original lyre of its emblem.

The possibility of a pendant to her husband's activities in the Liedertafel meant that Louise took to the news brought by a visiting examiner of the formation of a British Music Society with alacrity. By the time a meeting had been convened at the Melbourne Town Hall on 21 August 1921, she had got herself designated Representative of the parent body. As Thomas Brentnall explained to the 37 assembled members, "the shadow of gloomy [i.e. German] music in the prewar period had passed, and British music was now coming into its own". The Society would undertake to perform it, and to establish a library of sheet music not otherwise available. Professor Laver of the University Conservatorium, Fritz Hart of the Melba, and Mr Alberto Zelman were elected Vice-Presidents: a nice balance of the musical forces of the city. Another was the election of Jimmy Dyer as Treasurer, Louise as Hon. Secretary. By the time of the first concert, held at the Dyer home in Hawthorn on 11 November 1922, Melba had agreed to become Patron. Among the other people involved was the novelist Angela Thirkell, then undergoing her purgatorial stint in Grace Street, Malvern.

Despite the location of the British Music Society firmly in the ambience of the *haute bourgeoisie*, Louise clearly intended it to be first and foremost an agency for the improvement of musical life in Melbourne. The spreading of a knowledge of British music was duly listed as the first aim in the prospectus, but it was effectively eclipsed by three others: "To encourage Australian composers./To afford facilities for Australian musicians visiting other countries./To foster the spirit of international music." The Society was not to serve merely to adumbrate patriotic sentiment. As Louise stated in her first Annual Report, in connection with the inaugural public concert, "The music was entirely British, this being considered appropriate on the occasion of the Society's first endeavour in public. That is not to say, however, that music by foreign composers will be excluded from subsequent programmes. It is as much the aim of the Society to foster the spirit of international music as it is to spread the knowledge of British music . . ."

Aware of the need for a new venue for the smaller musical evenings held by the Society, within a year Louise had traded in Torryburn (which still stands in Hawthorn Grove, Hawthorn) for Kinnoull, Heyington Place, Toorak (which unfortunately does not). From all accounts it was a large Edwardian house, red-brick and turreted, with huge rooms and a garden that ran down to the Yarra. Here she mounted lavish entertainments: chamber music evenings, or an Elizabethan night complete with appropriate table settings and herself in costume, *tableaus vivants* in the garden, or a Hebridean evening to placate the kilted Jimmy. No expense was spared: apart from careful attention to *décor*, programs were usually printed, the designers including Blamire Young.

Kinnoull was the kind of place that people wanted to visit. Louise was happy to oblige, for she had a very shrewd sense of patronage operating best through a series of concentric circles of involvement. Thus she urged the foundation members of the B.M.S. to each recruit another four; and, recognizing the importance of education in music — her library contained many books and pamphlets on the subject — she sought to cultivate Melbourne's music teachers. Before long James

Dyer was President of the L.A.B. Club (Licentiates of the Associated Board), which she entertained with customary lavishness. So inspirited by this turn of events did the Club become that by 1932 it had a membership of 700; it duly returned the compliment with a reception for the Dyers on their return visit to Australia, which included a performance of two Fritz Hart operas. But being a born proselytiser, Louise did not stop there. She gathered various head-mistresses at the Lyceum Club in 1926, to impress upon them the importance of music education; and when Lady Mayoress of Melbourne in 1932, used the office to visit various schools as guest speaker. It was in this context that her interest in recordings first surfaced: she had been aware, in France, of the gramophone being used for educational purposes; in Australia, she thought, it could prove a God-given instrument in the teaching of French.

If she understood how to propagate her ideas and activate others, she also knew how to bring people together. Her enthusiasm often had a transforming effect on those she encountered; and she was never slow to act upon the advantages given her. When Lady Mayoress to her bachelor brother, Gengoult Smith, she determined upon celebrating the birth of Lully in such a fashion that the whole city would be forced to sit up and take notice. Already she had proclaimed Byrd's "Cradle Song" a piece suitable for every Australian home, and had got 3DB to play it and the *Herald* to publish the music in its pages; and now she decided upon a production of *Le Mariage Forcé*. It was a sensible choice: one of the three collaborations between Lully and Molière (of which the best-known is *Le Bourgeois Gentilhomme*) its selection meant that the success of the venture would fall very largely upon actors and actresses, not singers — and Melbourne already had, in the Alliance Francaise (of which she had been made President of Honour for life) a widely-acclaimed troupe schooled in the production of *pièces de théâtre*. Indeed the productions of the Alliance were events in the cultural life of Melbourne in the interwar years, linking as they did the University with polite society, and enjoying the enthusiastic support of the French Consul, M. René Turc.

But the co-operation of the Alliance alone would not be enough to ensure success. To widen the social base of the venture, she linked the production to a popular charitable cause, the Berry Street Foundling Hospital. To acquaint people with the notion of what was being celebrated, she sold prints of Lully at the Lady Mayoress's flower stall. To ensure that the costuming would be both impressive and accurate, she arranged for it to be hand-sewn by voluntary workers, and, where necessary, used Jimmy's business contacts to provide such refinements as facsimile seventeenth-century shoes. The result was an unqualified success. The newspapers were exultant, exhaustively if not insightfully: after all, the production was an education for the critics, while the typesetters had difficulty in sorting out Lully from Sully. The Foundling Hospital gained some £350; and Louise the satisfaction that in her own, Australian city she had managed to carry off the first revival of the work in modern times — without the help of the musicologist Prunières, with whom she had fallen out badly. Indeed Paris did not see *Le Mariage Forcé* until eight months after Melbourne.

The preoccupation with Lully and Couperin did not mean, however, that Louise was in retreat from her times. For her, the recovery of an authentic perception of tradition was but a prelude to innovation. The introduction to the Couperin edition scorns mere antiquarianism, and makes it plain that the project was conceived to extend the range of playable music. Thus she could quite happily pronounce that "It is the art of our own day that matters". To this end she prodded the British Music Society into performing modern French music, or modern Italian: in the latter case sending out the music so that it could be performed after her return to Europe. (That concern was not a success: without Louise's galvanizing presence, there was backsliding.)

The modernist streak in her make-up was important. It explains how she came to sit for Max Ernst, purchase Picassos, and live in a dazzlingly up-to-date apartment in the best part of Paris; even more, how she was prompted to move from the publication of baroque music to recording it and further, how she rose to meet the challenge of the technological imperative by making — after an exhaustive investigative journey to America — the first LPs in France.

Scarcely less important was her Australian-ness. An observer, happening upon Melbourne in the 1920s, would have found it extraordinarily colonial, multi-cultural only in so far as it contained a number of competing cultural interests existing side by side with loose allegiances to different metropolises — the residually German Liedertafel, the Alliance Française, the British Music Society. The latter was clearly a serious matter for some, for patriotic reasons; not so for Louise, who espoused Holst, the best then going among British composers, and looked beyond. For her, Britishry was essentially a matter of establishing cultural values. That was her prime concern: as she wrote to Percival Serle, on receiving his *An Australasian Anthology*, "It is people like you upon whom we rely to keep up the artistic standards of Australia".

More particularly, Nettie Palmer was encouraged to give what must have been among the first lectures on Australian Literature in Melbourne to friends of Louise at Torryburn in 1919. Again, hearing that John Shaw Neilson had fallen upon hard times, she sought him out, invited him to Kinnoull, underwrote the publication of his second volume of verse, and, writing to Percival Serle, launched a campaign that resulted in the Bruce/Page government marginally increasing its allocation to the Commonwealth Literary Fund, though not individual pensions. She was also anxious that a song by Neilson, set to music by Whittaker, should be performed at the opening of Parliament House, Canberra. She wrote to Serle:

> I told him [Sir Earle Grafton Christmas Page] I thought it would be not only a fitting tribute to the poet, but a tribute to the literature of Australia, and that people from all parts of the world would be made acquainted with something purely Australian ... I cannot think why pure beauty should be passed by and a place given to mediocrity and so-called patriotism ... This poem has been set to music as a three-part song. What could be more appropriate than to have young Australia represented by her younger singers? Melba will be representing the old.

The relative sophistication of her Australian-ness can be appreciated when it is set beside the antics of other cultivated people of the time. The B.M.S., for example, at the farewell in 1932, presented her with a paper knife in the shape of a gum-leaf; others concerned themselves with the activities of the Wattle League. Long before Edna Everage embodied it with her gladdies, Australian consciousness was excessively floral.

It is this which helps to explain how Louise's decision to leave in 1927 did not mean repudiation: her connection with Australia, though now attenuated, was unassailable. Once established in France, she tried to interest Gallimard in publishing translations of Australian works; she herself published compositions by Margaret Sutherland and Peggy Glanville-Hicks in her Editions de l'Oiseau-Lyre, and was later to be the first to record Joan Sutherland and John Williams. At the time of her greatest triumph, the appearance of the Couperin edition, she wrote in connection with a presentation copy to the Public Library of Victoria: "Number One went to the President of the French Republic; Number Two goes to my own homeland library". Indeed, at the very moment of leaving the country, the Dyers had given £10,000 for the establishment of a permanent orchestra in Melbourne, in the hope that others would match it. The city's failure to rise to her expectations, while it disappointed, did not disillusion her: later, having been made first an Officier and then a Chevalier of the Légion d'Honneur, she was to leave the bulk of her Australian estate, valued at £241,380, to the University of Melbourne. And it is in the Melbourne General Cemetery that her ashes rest.

Louise Hanson-Dyer must be regarded as a great women — or perhaps more accurately, a great lady — in so far as she perceived and acted upon the opportunities her time presented. Although her development was slow, once she perceived its direction she pursued it relentlessly, and with gathering pace. Any initial feeling she may have had of being miffed by the Pinschofs was soon lost in the wider anti-German feeling of World War One, which no doubt she shared, having lost a brother in France. (There are stories of parties being held in Melbourne to smash up Bechsteins.) Once the war itself was over, people were predisposed to look for their classical music elsewhere. Hence Louise promoted Debussy and Ravel in Melbourne, Couperin in Paris: instinctively she knew that the German intellectual hegemony was ending, and that the symphonic tradition was at the end of its creative phase. More positively, she was inspired by the English musical renaissance, and by the populist possibilities it extended. She was interested in folk music, in folk instruments; she believed that English musical roots must be explored in order to replenish creativity. Scarcely less important was her notion of reaching out to the people: in this context the new technology, whether in the form of newspapers, pianola rolls or gramophone records, had to be used to activate musical life at all levels, both in Europe and Australia.

In fact, a good deal of her vision was beyond realization: the historical tide ran the other way. Sound technology was conscripted by popular music, with the result that the microphone, for example, divorced classical styles of singing from popular ones more decisively than had ever been the case before. Thus while the new resources made certain kinds of classical music more generally available, a liking for it had perhaps never seemed so elitist.

Her achievement was considerable all the same. If today performed music no longer begins with Bach and Handel, but includes Josquin and Jannequin, Dufay and Perotin, we owe a very great deal of this to Louise Hanson-Dyer. Anybody can go and study the great cathedrals of France, as she did when she first went to Paris; but not everyone can set about emulating their monumentality by helping to recreate the musical heritage that is their counterpart. Without being articulate about it, Louise merely took fulsome notes of architectural details as she wandered down naves and aisles; the subtle transformations came later, to the enrichment of all.

1982

Notes

Full citation of sources will be given in the biography currently being written. Quotations in this article have been drawn from Maie Casey, *An Australian Story 1837-1907* (London, 1962, p. 124) and the Percival Serle correspondence in the La Trobe Library, MS 8486. (The letter re Neilson is dated 11 February 1927, the note of thanks to Serle 13 March [1932]).

At this stage [1981] I must acknowledge grants from the Literature Board and the Music Board of the Australia Council, which enabled me to journey to Europe, and the very considerable help given by the late Miss Sibyl Hewett, Mr James Craig, Dr M.T. Radic, Mrs L.L. Smith, Mr Rodney Davidson, Mrs Marion Poynter and Madame Margarita M. Hanson, the present director of Editions de l'Oiseau-Lyre.

INDEX

Milton Keynes UK
Ingram Content Group UK Ltd.
UKHW030009201124
451403UK00008B/51